ROMANCING THE TOMES

Popular Culture, Law and Feminism

Edited by

Margaret Thornton
Professor of Law and Legal Studies
La Trobe University, Melbourne

Cavendish
Publishing
Limited

London • Sydney

First published in Great Britain 2002 by Cavendish Publishing Limited, The Glass House, Wharton Street, London WC1X 9PX, United Kingdom
Telephone: +44 (0)20 7278 8000   Facsimile: +44 (0)20 7278 8080
Email: info@cavendishpublishing.com
Website: www.cavendishpublishing.com

Cavendish Publishing (Australia) Pty Limited, 3/303 Barrenjoey Road, Newport, New South Wales 2106
Telephone: (02) 9999 2777   Facsimile: (02) 9999 3688
Email: info@cavendishpublishing.com.au

British Library Cataloguing in Publication Data

Romancing the tomes: popular culture, law and feminism
1 Sociological jurisprudence 2 Lawyers in popular culture
3 Feminist jurisprudence
I Thornton, Margaret
340.1'15

ISBN 1 85941 723 X

Printed and bound in Great Britain

ROMANCING THE TOMES

Popular Culture, Law and Feminism

Cavendish
Publishing
Limited

London • Sydney

CONTENTS

CONTRIBUTORS

Paula Baron is Associate Professor at the University of Western Australia Law School where she teaches in the areas of intellectual property and contract law. She has published in the areas of gender and the law, company law, contract and legal education. Her current research interest is in psychoanalysis and its application to both legal education and legal practice.

Sandy Cook is a Senior Lecturer in the School of Law and Legal Studies at La Trobe University. She is currently on leave working as the Executive Officer of the All Party Drugs and Crime Prevention Committee of the Parliament of Victoria. Sandy's research and teaching are in the areas of violence against women, critical criminology and women's imprisonment. She is an associate editor of *Violence Against Women*, a Sage publication, and together with Sue Davies co-edited *Harsh Punishment: International Experiences of Women's Imprisonment*. Prior to her academic life Sandy worked as a teacher in youth training centres and Fairlea Women's prison in Victoria.

MTC Cronin has had seven books of poetry published, the most recent being *Talking to Neruda's Questions* and *Bestseller* (both Vagabond Press, 2001) and *My Lover's Back: 79 Love Poems* (UQP, 2002). Her next collection is *beautiful, unfinished − PARABLE/SONG/CANTO/POEM* (Salt Publications, Cambridge, 2003). After being employed for most of the nineties in law, she has in recent years begun teaching literature and creative writing at secondary schools and universities. She is currently working on a PhD, 'Poetry and Law: Discourses of the Social Heart', and has recently received an Established Writers New Work Grant from the Australia Council for the Arts.

Susanne Davies is a Senior Lecturer in the School of Law and Legal Studies at La Trobe University. An historian by training, her teaching, research and writing interests span critical criminology, socio-legal history, sexuality studies, and feminist theory and epistemology. She is a former Director of the Women's Studies Program at La Trobe and was a founding member of the Australian Feminist Law Journal. With Sandy Cook, she co-edited *Harsh Punishment: International Experiences of Women's Imprisonment* (Northeastern University Press, Boston, 1999).

Ann Genovese holds a BA (Honours in History and Politics) and an LLB from the University of Adelaide, and a PhD from UTS. Her PhD, for which she was awarded a place on the Chancellor's List for Outstanding Doctoral Research, was a genealogy of domestic violence, and examined the intersections between legal, historical and feminist theories. She has worked as a researcher with the Law and Justice Foundation of NSW and, in 2002, she began work at UTS on a collaborative research project involving ANU, UTS and the University of Newcastle, examining the expert evidence of historians in cases involving indigenous litigants.

Judith Grbich is a General Editor of the Australian Feminist Law Journal and teaches Literature and Law, Taxation Law, and Property Law in the School of Law and Legal Studies, La Trobe University. Her works include *Thinking Through the Body of the Law*, edited with Pheng Cheah and David Fraser (New York University Press, 1996) and *Writing Against Legal Racism: Law and Literature Explorations* (Prospect, 2001), edited with Peter Hutchings.

Isabel Karpin is a Senior Lecturer in the Faculty of Law at the University of Sydney. She specialises in the areas of feminist legal theory, law and culture, and health law. She has a Masters of Law from Harvard University and a JSD from Columbia University. Her doctoral work entitled 'Embodying Justice: Legal Responses to the Transgressive Body' examined the regulation of marginalised bodies, with a particular focus on the pregnant body. She is currently involved in several major research projects in the areas of new media and regulation of emergent genetic technologies.

Rosanne Kennedy is a Lecturer in the School of Humanities at Australian National University, teaching in the areas of cultural and gender studies. She has published articles on trauma, testimony and the Stolen Generations in *Meridian* and *Aboriginal History*, and has co-edited a book with Jill Bennett on cross-cultural perspectives on trauma and memory, titled *World Memory: Personal Trajectories in Global Time* (London: Palgrave-Macmillan, forthcoming, 2002). She has also published articles on law and popular culture in *Law and Critique*, *Thinking Through the Body of The Law* (Allen and Unwin, 1996), and *Feminist Television Criticism* (OUP, 1997). She is currently working on an interdisciplinary study of the 1922 trial of Edith Thompson and its cultural legacies.

Diane Kirkby is a Reader in History at La Trobe University, Melbourne, where she teaches Australian and American history of women, work, law and welfare, and the history of food and drink. She has served as president of the Australia and New Zealand Law and History Society, and convenor of the Australian Network for Research in Women's History. She has published in the history of feminism, women's work and married women's property, and has edited two books on the history of law, *Sex Power and Justice* (OUP, 1995) and most recently with Cathy Coleborne, *Law History Colonialism: The Reach of Empire* (Manchester University Press, 2001).

Tina Loo teaches social and cultural history at Simon Fraser University in British Columbia, Canada. She is the co-author (with Carolyn Strange) of *Making Good: Law and Moral Regulation in Canada, 1867–1939*. Currently, she and Carolyn Strange are honing their hardboiled style, writing a book on Canadian true crime magazines of the 1940s.

ACKNOWLEDGMENTS

This collection arose out of a conference organised under the auspices of the Humanities Research Centre at the Australian National University, Canberra, in 2000 when the theme for the year was 'Law and the Humanities'. It is not always easy for scholars from diverse disciplines to communicate with each other, despite the prevailing rhetoric extolling interdisciplinarity. Nevertheless, as many feminist scholars were looking at similar issues of law, culture and textuality, albeit through rather different lenses, the HRC initiative offered a wonderful opportunity to embark upon a joint enterprise. I would like to express my gratitude to the HRC and its Director, Professor Ian McCalman, for their support. I am particularly grateful for the vote of confidence in feminist scholarship in a neoliberal climate that has become increasingly intolerant of the humanistic, the critical and the theoretical.

My thanks are extended to all participants at the *Romancing the Tomes* conference for contributing to what turned out to be a most delightful gathering. I would particularly like to thank Leena Messina, Programs Manager of the Humanities Research Centre, for her adept administrative skills and unfailing good humour in assisting with the organisation of the conference. My colleague, Sue Davies, is deserving of a special mention for suggesting the *Tomes* title.

I am grateful to Cavendish Publishing for agreeing to publish the collection, and I would particularly like to thank Cara Annett and Ruth Massey for their support. I would also like to thank Gail Stewart for assisting with the compilation of the collection and her serenity in the face of obdurate technology and its many gremlins. Above all, I would like to express my deep gratitude to the contributors for their imaginative and inspiring essays.

Grateful acknowledgment is made for permission to reproduce the following illustrations:

State Library of Victoria: *The Barmaid*: *The Boomerang*, 13 December, 1890

From the Rare Book Collection of the National Library of Australia: *Date Blouse*: Scoop Detective Cases, November–December 1943, Pulp Art Collection, Box 10; *Wronged Girl*: Daring Crime Cases, Vol 9(1), March 194? (date illegible), Pulp Art Collection, Box 6; *Toronto's Love Slayer*: Daring Crime Cases, April 1946, Pulp Art Collection, Box 16

PREFACE

Popular culture is usually associated with ordinary people, although the pervasiveness of the mass media, of which we are all voracious consumers, puts paid to the idea that popular culture is separate from high culture, or the culture of educated élites. Law, always backward looking, still clings to the idea that legal texts are set apart from ordinary people, thereby displaying the same disdain for popular culture. While the idea that law represents an autonomous body of knowledge has long been exposed as a myth, most comprehensively by feminist legal scholars, formal legal discourses continue to be highly resistant to social knowledges that do not fall within the conventional legal canon. The focus on the abstract principles of appellate decisions allows particularities and subjectivities to be sloughed off in the process of judicial decision making and creation of authoritative legal texts. Primary legal knowledge producers, including judges, law teachers and legal scholars, remain in denial about the significance of popular culture in creating and interpreting law. In contrast, there is no reticence about popular culture's love affair with law, nor about law's role as an ongoing source of inspiration and imagination in film, TV, fiction and other creative media.

Janus-like, the contributors to this collection direct their gaze both ways, to look at law and popular culture, although I am not suggesting anything as rigid as a stone statue between the two fields, for the boundary between them is permeable. The reading, writing and viewing practices that are invoked to make sense of social phenomena, including law and legal texts, reveal that meaning is a process involving active participants who are members of interpretative communities and who participate in the constitution of knowledge about law, about gender, and about social phenomena of all kinds.

Utilising the insights of feminist and cultural theory, the contributors present a range of imaginative rereadings of legal and cultural texts. Attention is accorded the representation of law in popular media, including film, television, newspapers, crime and popular fiction, as well as the internet. They also explore the ways in which these popular representations of law feed back into legal discourses and shape contemporary understandings of what law is, partially through judicial writings, but also through other sites where legal narratives are created, such as trial courts. The collection confounds the idea that the 'and' in 'law and popular culture' is disjunctive, for the essays show unequivocally that law and popular culture are thoroughly imbricated with each other. While the kaleidoscopic nature of law and popular culture defies capture of every instantiation in one book, highly suggestive snapshots of the intersection are possible, as the respective contributors demonstrate.

In the introductory chapter, I elaborate on the reasons why law is so resistant to popular culture. Even looking at it can induce vertigo in legal traditionalists. It is argued that the myth of legal autonomy is a central mechanism through which law seeks to maintain its authority. Popular culture has the potential to corrode this authority by challenging the rationality, objectivity and universality of law. In stressing the affective side of life – sexuality, corporeality and desire – popular culture discomforts and threatens law. Despite the pervasiveness of popular culture, the legal *dramatis personae* are themselves complicit in perpetuating the myth that law can be explained only by reference to itself. Legal education, for example, continues to rely upon appellate decisions as the primary source of law. By operating at a high level of abstraction, law endeavours to slough off the unruliness of the social and deny validity to alternative ways of seeing, including visions of justice, imagined from the perspective of feminised Others.

Part Two, *Judicial Notice,* examines how law and popular culture are imbricated through the process of judicial decision making, despite law's valiant attempts at resistance. Another well known fiction within the positivist arsenal is that judges do not make law but 'find' it by interpreting it in light of the facts of the instant case. Terry Threadgold and Isabel Karpin not only dispel this myth through their readings of case law, but show how judges rely upon meanings gleaned from their readings of popular culture to construct authoritative meanings in law. Far from law being autonomous, both authors show conclusively that the readers and writers of law, like the readers and writers of popular culture, are members of the same interpretative communities.

In exploring the reading habits of judges, Terry Threadgold examines what happens when legal training encounters popular culture. She argues that certain kinds of readings (as writings) are likely to produce certain kinds of actions, events, and behaviours in the courtroom, as in other contexts. Threadgold, drawing on Bourdieu and other theorists, argues that the legal community has created a habitus in which its fictions have become the real and the 'real' world has become a myth. She uses examples from crime and equity to show how the myths of everyday culture are imbricated in law pertaining to the body and to marriage.

Isabel Karpin also argues that judges, like the rest of us, are consumers of popular culture and are discursively embedded in ways of thinking about it, despite their disavowals. Karpin argues that the traditional image can no longer be sustained and she illustrates her thesis by reference to a number of examples. As well as a series of cases dealing with 'common sense' knowledge, which judges appear to glean mainly from the media, Karpin also considers another series explicitly dealing with the media itself in order to problematise the role of judges within the information society.

Part Three, *Testament and Textuality,* considers the role of personal testimony and other forms of evidence in constituting authoritative and probative accounts in the public domain. The artificial separation between facts and law within legal discourse has the effect of relegating the facts to the background or blanching them of emotional force in judgments, which emanate from appellate rather than trial courts. Legal testimony may also be shaped by popular culture so that the words of a testifying (woman) are no longer heard, but treated as set pieces within a prevailing narrative, as

Rosanne Kennedy and Nan Seuffert show in regard to the narratives of romance, love and sexuality. The lost facts, or narrative accounts can be brought to the fore again by new forms of writing, as Suvendrini Perera argues.

Rosanne Kennedy explores the value of trial records as a source for the study of gender, law and popular culture. Although the 19th century Scottish murder trial of Madeleine Smith is not well known today, it was a sensational event in its day – partly because the defendant was a woman, and partly because of the nature of the events surrounding the charges. Love letters written by the defendant constituted a key piece of evidence, and a lengthy portion of the trial was devoted to interpreting these documents. Not surprisingly, the private letters often defied the law's expectation of rational communication, and the various interpretations hinged upon the acceptance of ideologies of female sexuality that circulated through the popular media and fiction of the day. Drawing on semiotics, feminist and epistolary theory, Kennedy uses the trial and the letters adduced in evidence to examine the process through which meaning is constructed, in conjunction with the role of the ideologies of gender and sexuality in legal discourse. Kennedy demonstrates that popular culture is not outside law but central to it.

Nan Seuffert also looks at the representation of the affective within criminal trials, and legal discourses more generally, in the context of women who have killed men as a result of having been subjected to long periods of domestic violence. These women claim to have loved their abusive partners, but Seuffert argues that common law courts, preoccupied as they are with property and rationality, are unable to hear these claims of love. Such claims are incomprehensible, for reductive understandings of human nature are preferred to complex personhood. Seuffert argues that the prevailing themes of ownership and romantic love, which are constructed through popular culture and other discourses, not only inform common law courts, but also serve to facilitate abusive relationships.

Through an examination of Ruby Langford Ginibi's *Haunted by the Past*, Suvendrini Perera considers writing as a form of resistance to racialised punishment. Ginibi's narrative combines the testimony of the experiences of her son, Nobby, in gaol and the life stories of her family with newspaper accounts and official evaluations of Nobby's case. The chapter is concerned with the ways in which we read, receive and locate in institutional, disciplinary and generic terms certain narratives and imaginative records of Aboriginal people having trouble with the law. Perera argues that Ginibi's approach transcends the conventional genres of Anglo-Australian biographical writing. Instead, the intersecting indigenous experiences of prison, law and auto/biography produces a new genre – a testimonio.

In Part Four, *Feminist Historiographies*, Judith Grbich reads the 1990s film, *Pretty Woman*, transgressively. Rather than accepting the film as a negative depiction of the 'rescue' of Vivian from a life of prostitution, Grbich endows the modern Cinderella/Rapunzal fairytale with new meaning. She excavates the historical narratives about property, or feudalscapes, that are embedded within both the fairytales and the film. The romance involves not just the hustling and coupling of the lead characters, but the body corporate and the world of high finance. Grbich argues that *Pretty Woman* is a trope for language, a story in which the reader is the romancer. She argues that this modern iteration of the ancient feudalscapes, complete with knight in shining armour (Edward, as corporate raider) is able to maintain law's authority by enchanting the common man and woman.

Ann Genovese examines the media constructions of legal feminism, comparing 1975, International Women's Year and a high point of feminism, with 1995, the year in which Helen Garner's *The First Stone* was published. This book, based on a sexual harassment case in a university college, caused media attention to centre almost exclusively on the perceived 'generational war' between feminists. In 1975, the media also denigrated the women's movement and its leaders. Despite the antipathy, feminists were nevertheless able to use the news media strategically. Genovese thinks through some of the theoretical implications about what the media image of legal feminism means in a postmodern context, how we arrived here, and if the strategies of 25 years ago can be re-invented in order to contest the current paradox of liberalism for feminism.

While there is a tendency to equate popular culture with the technological age, particularly with the wide accessibility of TV and popular music, Diane Kirkby reminds us that the popular imagination is not constrained by chronology. She sets out to broaden the understanding of popular culture by turning her attention to pubs as a familiar site for the production of gender prior to the advent of the mass media. She problematises the body of the barmaid, a central but paradoxical figure within pub culture and contrasts the imagined wife/mother figure of the 1890s with that of the sexualised lure of the 1960s and 70s. In the former, the publican's wife occupied the ambiguous role of the 'good woman of the bar', a role supported by law, albeit that same law determined that women themselves could not be served liquor. Both the novel and the film, *Caddie*, addressed by Kirkby underscore the historical centrality – and absence – of women's presence in Australian pubs.

Part Five, *Heterosexing Cyberculture*: the internet disrupts conventional understandings of communication, the reading and writing of texts and notions of dialogic interpretative communities, of the kind discussed in previous chapters. The internet is the paradigmatic example of globalisation, as the locus, language, wealth, sex, age, race and even age of the viewer/participant are generally irrelevant. Despite the superficial appearance of equality arising from easy access and interaction with other users, the internet is not an egalitarian phenomenon, but a commodity, in respect of which there is an indubitable power imbalance between provider and user. Nor is the technology gender neutral. The essays of Baron and Davies and Cook consider the sexing of cyberspace.

In her chapter on cyberpornography, Paula Baron apprises us of an alarming statistic, which is that pornography accounts for as much as 40% of internet traffic. Not only is the preponderance of material profoundly heterosexed, the majority of consumers are male. However, Baron's essay is not a feminist plea for legal regulation, but an analysis of current debates. Because cyberculture has no respect for prevailing borders between nation states, she argues that it poses a profound challenge to the authority of the law, which, after all, is a modernist institution that is contingent on the nation state for its jurisdictional force. But this is only one of the boundaries disrupted by cyberculture. Baron considers also the way that it disrupts the boundaries between private and public, production and consumption, reality and virtuality, and entertainment and information. As an illustration of the regulatory imperative, Baron examines a recent Australian statute, which has been most trenchantly opposed by the proponents of free trade, not free speech advocates – the usual suspects. At present, Baron concludes, dominance of the profit making imperative leaves few options for feminists.

Susanne Davies and Sandy Cook consider how women in prison have become commodified objects of desire in cyberspace. Whereas popular representations of women in prison formerly tended to be confined to sensational press reports and B grade movies, they have now become a central focus of hard-core videos, pornographic literature and internet sites. *Jail Babes* is a site that offers 'consumers' the opportunity to make contact with women currently serving sentences in United States prisons. Davies and Cook examine the fantasies of love and desire that *Jail Babes* fuels for lonely men looking for romance. They show that the romantic narratives woven around incarcerated women – for a fee – contain a bleak underside. The phenomenon also reveals how the prison, with the aid of the modern technology, is a site in which highly gendered practices are produced.

The essays in Part Six, *Fictions of the Real*, look at representations of law and legality in three genres of popular fiction: true crime, crime fiction and what approximates the new genre of 'legal fiction'. The contributors hint at the ambiguities associated with law in the popular mind – its power and its proximity to crime, corporeality and trauma, as well as its seductive qualities. The popularity of crime reflects and reproduces the most common perception of the role of law circulating in Western society. A work of fiction authored by a judge is popular for a different reason altogether, but the novel in question also articulates a societal anxiety about the role of women's bodies in a masculinist space.

Carolyn Strange and Tina Loo turn their gaze to a particular genre of pulp fiction – true crime magazines – which flourished in the 1940s. Focusing on the Canadian example, they show how 'real' crimes were packaged and commodified within trashy publications for popular consumption. As well as entertaining their readers with a romantic overlay, the true crime genre adopted a didactic 'crime does not pay' stance. While the lascivious covers and titillating descriptions of women's bodies were clearly designed to appeal primarily to heterosexual men, there were morals for women to be learned too – about entering into adulterous relationships and about flaunting their beauty. Through their four examples, Strange and Loo demonstrate how true crime produced conventional iterations of gender, class, race and sexuality.

Sue Turnbull presents an analysis of the responses of Sisters in Crime, an Australian organisation of women readers of crime fiction who were asked to explain why they read crime fiction. Their responses were contradictory, signalling their appreciation of the genre in terms of its 'realism', at the same time as they argued that it offered them an escape from the 'real'. The chapter considers how these discourses of the 'real' and 'escape' articulate with larger issues to do with an aesthetic of the popular (particularly in relation to crime and its genres) and women's anxiety with regard to the representation and experience of violence. Turnbull suggests that the popularity of crime fiction is explicable in terms of its ability to satisfy a need for symbolic truth.

Margaret Thornton's chapter involves the critique of a work of fiction, *The Lawyer and the Libertine*, by Australian High Court judge, Ian Callinan. The backdrop to the novel is the nostalgic evocation of a homogeneous Anglo-Celtic and masculinist legal profession. With recourse to Baudrillard, the chapter considers how an outdated legal culture can be constructed as a representation of the 'real' world, or what Baudrillard calls the 'hyperreal'. It is suggested that the creation of an imaginary homogeneous world is a mechanism for resisting the increasing heterogeneity of the legal profession in the 'real' world. In particular, the novel reflects the prevailing anxiety about the possible 'feminisation' of the legal profession.

Margaret Thornton
July 2002

TABLE OF ABBREVIATIONS

Alt LJ	Alternative Law Journal
ABA	Australian Broadcasting Authority
ABC	Australian Broadcasting Commission
ABR	Australian Book Review
ACTV	Australian Capital Television
AGPS	Australian Government Publishing Service
AHA	Australian Hotels Association
AJA	Australian Journalists Association
ALR	Australian Law Reports
ANU	Australian National University
Aust Fem LJ	Australian Feminist Law Journal
Aust JLS	Australian Journal of Law and Society
AWBC	Australian Women's Broadcasting Co-operative
CA	Court of Appeal
Can JLS	Canadian Journal of Law and Society
CLR	Commonwealth Law Reports
DLR	Dominion Law Reports
HREOC	Human Rights and Equal Opportunity Commission
ICH	Internet Content Host
IRISS	Internet Research and Information for Social Scientists
ISP	Internet Service Provider
IWY	International Women's Year
JLS	Journal of Law and Society
KB	King's Bench
LTC	Law/Text/Culture
MLR	Modern Law Review
MULR	Melbourne University Law Review

NSWLRC	New South Wales Law Reform Commission
NYLSLR	New York Law School Law Review
OFLC	Office of Film and Literature Classification
OSW	Office of Status of Women
R	Restricted to adults 18 years and over
RC	Refused classification
ULVA Rev	United Licensed Victuallers Association Review
UNSWLJ	University of New South Wales Law Journal
UTS	University of Technology, Sydney
WASCA	Western Australia Supreme Court, Court of Appeals
WBB	Women Behind Bars
WEL	Women's Electoral Lobby
WLM	Women's Liberation Movement
X	Contains sexually explicit material; access restricted to adults 18 years and over

PART ONE

INTRODUCTION

The Law of the First Venus

I have fallen in love
With paradox
There is no history
Because of unity
The way her arms so naturally
Bind me
There is no place even
To start counting

Yet against her thrilling wall
I lean
She is unscaleable!
My arrows shoot to the stars
Yet note is taken
They reach somewhere
Just below the height
Of her lovely belly

She is the first Venus always
To be approached
By such laughable Reason
On the specious surface
Little draw
What I write
With my true love
On her willing wall

Like this
She is never finished
The big sleeping girl
The hiding doll
The twitch
Of the dreaming leg
Never actualized
Not even in death

See her coming up
Singing cups of tea today
Introducing
The line to the curve
Its sneaky self
What a beautiful Queen of Sheba!
I'm to be her toad
Her platter of fruit!

And I have fallen in love
With paradox
There is no history
Because of life
The way her arms move
So naturally to bind me
There is no place even
To begin

MTC Cronin

CHAPTER 1

LAW AND POPULAR CULTURE: ENGENDERING LEGAL VERTIGO

Margaret Thornton

AN UNACKNOWLEDGED LIAISON

This introductory chapter examines the uneasy relationship between law and popular culture. It suggests that law's resistance to popular culture emanates from a fear that it will corrode the autonomy and authority of law. Popular culture, like the feminine, has been constructed as a non-rational Other, which has been consciously confined to the margins of orthodox legal knowledge by technocratic legal methods.

Despite the pervasiveness of popular culture in contemporary society, its relationship with law, at least in a formal sense, remains tenuous and ambiguous. The academic establishment generally regards popular culture with suspicion, if not outright contempt.[1] Not only is it suspected of exercising a corrupting effect on 'Western high culture as the source of legitimate knowledge, history and truth', it is regarded as 'relatively knowledge-free'.[2] Law goes further than most disciplines of the humanities and social sciences in its resistance to all ideas and values outside its disciplinary boundary. Indeed, law itself is deemed to be the only authoritative source of law. This self-referentialism is maintained through the dominant philosophy and techniques of legal positivism, an issue to which I shall return.

Regardless of the disavowal, law is influenced by popular culture in multifarious ways of thinking about law and justice, as well as directly through the adduction of evidence, law and order policies, law reform, the role of juries, and even styles of advocacy. The role of judicial decision making as a cipher for popular culture is less apparent because of the positivistic carapace. Occasionally, however, by recourse to the arsenal of interpretive techniques at the disposal of judges, such as 'judicial notice', they may acknowledge that they are taking cognisance of what is going on in the world.[3] There is, nevertheless, an entire tantalising realm of what may be termed 'unconscious judicial notice' to be unravelled, a variation of

---

1   Chase, 1986b, pp 538–41.
2   Davis, 1999, p 281.
3   Graycar, 1995.

'constructive notice', an interpretive device by which a person or agency can be deemed to have actual notice of a particular phenomenon. Judges are not immune from the influence of popular culture, as the contributors to this volume show; they are consumers, like everyone else. Popular culture, then, contributes to the production of law.[4]

When we turn and look in the other direction to consider the influence of law on popular culture, we see that popular culture is not just influenced by law, but fascinated by it, particularly so far as the relationship between sex and crime is concerned. Audiences love the cinematic representations of trials generally with their dramatic and conflictual elements.[5] The representations of law in popular culture shape popular understandings of law and justice, and what it means to be a lawyer. These images in turn feed back into legal discourses in the hermeneutic and decision making process. Representations and 'real' life become imbricated so that it is impossible to separate them. 'Law' and 'popular culture' are therefore not in fact disjunctive, despite the best endeavours of legal traditionalists to present them as such. There is a symbiotic relationship between them, despite the fact that the impact of law on popular culture is more readily discernible than the impact of popular culture on law.

CAPTURING CULTURE

Until recently, 'culture' was understood primarily as a concept that belonged to Others. It carried overtones of the exotic, particularly in terms of language, art, dance, music, and cuisine; the norm was somehow a-cultural. Thus, it continues to be said of those of Anglo-Celtic heritage that they possess no culture, unlike Aboriginal or non-English speaking minorities. Similarly, only the latter have been deemed to have a race, only women a sex, and only gays and lesbians a sexuality.[6] The dominant sides of the dualisms claim to be able to shed the particularity of their identities and assert a monopoly over neutrality, universality and normativity. Thus, Benchmark Men, that is, those who embody a constellation of characteristics, conventionally associated with dominance, namely, whiteness, Anglocentricity, heterosexuality and able-bodiedness – the 'a-cultural' – have presented themselves in legal texts, as well as other key discourses, as de-raced, de-sexed and de-sexualised. Benchmark masculinity claims to speak from nowhere because it is everywhere. The acculturated 'other', which is permitted to speak only from its designated epistemological standpoint, is invariably represented as partial and particularised. Feminist

---

4   Cf Sherwin, 2000, p 18.
5   Bergman and Asimow, 1996, p xvii.
6   Cf Minow, 1990, p 51.

and poststructural scholarship has consistently deconstructed dualisms of this kind, together with the claims of Benchmark Men to universality.[7] Deconstruction has also challenged the meaning of culture itself. Indeed, it is now generally accepted that culture is a substratum of identity from which no member of society is immune. In the process, culture has acquired a much broader meaning within academic discourses, for it is understood to encompass all social and political institutions and practices, together with associated belief systems, rendering them the proper subject of scrutiny and critique. Nevertheless, the increasingly plural and subjective meanings of culture are highly contested, so much so that 'culture wars' has become a term of recognition regarding competing political and philosophical perspectives within the academy, a notion that corrodes the one-dimensional and homogenising concept of culture formerly associated with a minority people or group.

In the attempt to analyse and systematise, culture suggests order. Bauman describes culture as an 'anti-randomness device'.[8] He is not suggesting that it be envisaged as static but, in the struggle between order and chaos, he locates culture 'unambiguously in order's camp'.[9] The taxonomical and analytical task necessarily remains elusive, however, for culture is 'perpetually restless, unruly and rebellious'; there can be no 'hope of ever arriving at a finished and authoritative likeness of any given culture'.[10] The legal culture valiantly seeks to embrace all facets of law and meaning, including law as a cultural artefact,[11] the sociology of the legal profession,[12] the representation of law in literature,[13] and the media.[14] Law and popular culture, then, is a sub-set of contemporary legal culture, although the volatile and ephemeral character of the imagery of popular culture would seem to position it closer to chaos than order. It is the unpredictability of popular culture that makes it so threatening to law, which, in liberal societies, is order's familiar companion.

Interdisciplinary legal scholarship undertaken by legal scholars, as well as by scholars in a range of the humanities and the social sciences, has stimulated the study of legal institutions, legal discourse and representations of law as legitimate aspects of cultural studies. Utilising new theories and methods has engendered reflexive and theoretical possibilities long resisted by conventional legal methodologies. The study of law as

---

7   Eg, MacKinnon, 1989, p 120ff.
8   Bauman, 1997, p 131.
9   *Ibid*, p 131.
10 *Ibid*, p 133.
11 Eg, Kahn, 1999; Laster, 2001.
12 Eg, Weisbrot, 1990; Thornton, 1996a.
13 Eg, White, 1973; Weisberg, 1984.
14 Eg, Howe, 1998; Fineman and McCluskey, 1997.

culture goes to the heart of the postmodern critique of law as a universalising and authoritative discourse for, looking at law through the law-as-culture lens recognises the significance of micropolitical sites and new ways of seeing. The critical gaze is not restricted to the conventional hierarchical focus on legislatures and appellate courts, but includes the full range of 'non-authoritative' discourses about law, including literary texts and popular media.

Generally speaking, 'popular culture' encompasses the panoply of beliefs, practices and wisdom of ordinary people, which is handed down from generation to generation. Popular culture may be implicitly distinguished from the more intellectual, theoretical and scholarly pursuits associated with the term 'high culture'. These terms are amorphous, however, and merge haphazardly into one another. They do not lend themselves to the clear lines and neat classifications beloved of lawyers. Indeed, the pervasiveness and accessibility of popular culture, particularly the mass media that is consumed by intellectuals and the uneducated alike, puts paid to the idea that there are discrete popular and high cultures.

The concept of popular culture tends to crystallise most commonly in print media, popular music, film and television. This congruence between popular culture and *the media* has occurred to such an extraordinary degree that, metonymically, 'popular culture' has come to refer specifically to media culture, from which it has become inseparable.[15] The conflation is graphically captured by Marshall McLuhan's aphorism that 'the medium is the message'.[16] The speed at which popular culture can be globally transmitted so as to impact instantaneously on far flung communities with scant regard for tradition or locale is staggering.[17]

Ideas about law in popular culture are likely to be dependent on stereotypes or urban myths, and to be beset with contradictions. For example, surveys on the occupational standing of lawyers tend to rank them well down in professional hierarchies: they overcharge, their ethics are dubious, they engage in sophistical arguments to benefit their (rich) clients: they brazenly argue that black is white and white is black – for a fee.[18] On the other hand, lawyers are also known to devote themselves selflessly to causes, such as human rights, child sexual assault and environmental protection. As Chase establishes in his review of the portrayal of lawyers in

---

15 Friedman, 1989, p 1596.

16 Eg, McLuhan and Fiore, 1967.

17 Cf Friedman, 1989, pp 1596–97.

18 The 1999 Bulletin Morgan Poll found that 34% of Australian people (up from 8% in 1998) thought that lawyers were honest and ethical. This compared with 89% for nurses, 62% for police, 61% for judges, 13% for Members of Parliament and 3% for car salesmen.

popular culture, there is a positive and a negative formation in every case.[19] The same could be said for popular culture's treatment of any other topic: it both constitutes and reflects public opinion.

Law students invariably come to law school with preconceived views of what law is and what it means to be a lawyer. They may have encountered the reach of state regulation through, for example, family law, taxation or road rules, but are unlikely to have had little direct involvement with lawyers. Their perceptions about lawyers are more likely to have been shaped by television images or crime novels. Indeed, they may have been induced to study law because of the images of lawyering acquired from popular culture.[20] As voracious consumers of popular culture, students do not abandon this interest once they enter law school, despite the acculturation practices of legal education and the profession. Pedagogical practices, as well as law school curricula, are influenced through the mediating role of students. Denver notes how the dynamic of the law school classroom changes when films are used as a teaching tool. He observes that students are much more responsive and critical when the intellectual playing field is levelled, in contrast to the deferential stance adopted towards traditional sources of legal knowledge, such as legal philosophy.[21]

Television is the most pervasive popular culture medium. But what is the nature of the popular messages 'consumed' by law students that has the potential to influence the legal culture? In the past, television shows tended to portray lawyers as heroic individuals, usually advocates – and always male and white – such as Perry Mason and Rumpole of the Bailey. The preoccupation with justice within a conflictual and dramatic contest of 'goodies' and 'baddies' reflects, albeit in different ways, an abiding theme of the creative imagination manifested in art and literature generally. That is, if justice cannot be attained through law, how might it be imagined? However, the focus of the preponderance of contemporary TV legal drama has abandoned the heroic individual and the search for justice in favour of a more cynical view of law and the possibility of justice.[22] Rather than altruism and societal good, the contemporary genre tends to focus on promotion of the self, ambition, gratification, and 'success'. The disillusionment with law as a force for good is a manifestation of a broader dissatisfaction with institutions, which Sherwin terms 'radical disenchantment (or sceptical postmodernism)'.[23] Popular culture can capture and articulate this disillusionment in ways that formal legal discourses cannot. The focus of legal drama generally has moved away from

---

19 Chase, 1986a, p 291.
20 Rapoport, 2000.
21 Denver, 1996, p xii.
22 Menkel-Meadow, 1999; Rapoport, 2000; Chase, 1986b.
23 Sherwin, 2000, p 172.

resolving the client's predicament in just terms to the subjectivity of the anti-heroic lawyer. The sexual politics of the law firm is a popular focus, as can be seen in *LA Law*. Such shows seek to depict lawyers as real people with real emotions.[24] *Ally McBeal*, for example, is the first eponymous TV drama involving a woman lawyer.[25] The fictional Ally McBeal is a character in her own right, rather than the mere agent of a client principal, or an articulate and didactic mouthpiece for the author.[26] Nonetheless, despite the long history of the exclusion of women from the legal profession,[27] Ally McBeal is a dubious role model, since she is a caricature of a woman lawyer whose greatest dilemma would seem to be the length of her skirt.[28]

The constitution of stock roles and stereotypes, including the sexualisation of women, particularly the capable but frigid professional who needs to be 'manned' in order to attain personal fulfilment, has come to be a familiar trope of popular culture. Bergman and Asimow itemise a long list of films featuring women lawyers who are consistently portrayed in 'viciously stereotypical terms' as incompetent and unethical.[29] Such representations do nothing to ameliorate the hostility experienced by many women in law. Bergman and Asimow contrast the contemporary negative representation of women with the positive representation of a woman lawyer in the 1949 film, *Adam's Rib*. It is notable, however, that in 1949, the number of women in law was minuscule, compared with an approximate 50/50 gender split over the last 20 years. The possibility of feminisation of the legal profession authorises strategic sites of popular culture to be surreptitiously deployed in resisting the incursion.[30] Hence, an anti-feminist backlash has sought to contain the aspiration and power of women lawyers through film.[31]

The tendency to construct conservative or reactionary identities for sexed, racialised and sexualised 'others' has been a feature of the cinematic genre.[32] Creative media gives voice to what may be formally inexpressible, such as the fear engendered by the Other. Despite the trendiness of popular culture and its proximity to or conflation with state-of-the-art technology, it does not necessarily follow that its content is progressive. The media is a

---

24 Rosenberg, 1989, p 1628.
25 Having said that, the execrable Judge Judy should not be overlooked, although she plays herself – in a 'reality TV' show located in a civil claims court. For an excellent analysis and critique of the genre, see Christie, 2000.
26 This is a familiar literary device as can be seen, for example, with Raskolnikov in Dostoyevsky's *Crime and Punishment*. As Weisberg points out, many great writers have looked to law as a location for their articulate characters. See Weisberg, 1984, p 5.
27 Thornton, 1996a.
28 Cf Menkel-Meadow, 1999.
29 Bergman and Asimow, 1996, pp 90–93.
30 I have considered the slippery concept of 'feminisation' of the legal profession in Thornton, 1996a, pp 268–75. See also Chapter 14 below.
31 Lucia, 1997.
32 Denver, 1996, p xvii *et passim*.

convenient and effective site through which regressive views about women, Aboriginal people, Asians, and gays and lesbians can be articulated.[33] Talkback radio, for example, may be deployed to incite divisiveness and hatred of stigmatised minorities in the name of free speech and civil liberties. The ostensibly open 'marketplace of ideas' is manipulated by clever hosts, or 'demagogues', as Patricia Williams calls them,[34] who whip up emotion under the guise of 'infotainment'. Misogyny, racism and homophobia are grist to the mill of the radio demagogues. Their ratings may be contingent on prejudice and bigotry. The participatory and democratic appearance of the medium occludes its deeply conservative and regressive tendencies. Talkback radio is a pre-eminent reflector and moulder of public opinion, which illuminates the plural and contradictory messages of popular culture.

If the ideological messages of popular culture are suspect, what of the legal substance? Television shows, such as *Ally McBeal* and *LA Law*, present fanciful depictions of life in law firms, but they attract a huge following worldwide. Accurate portrayals, such as the American TV series, *Paper Chase*, which was located in a law school, have had to be withdrawn because of their unpopularity.[35] Similarly, the exploration and explication of legal doctrine are considered to be too dull and complex for popular media. 'Human interest' causes any consideration of legal doctrine to be relegated to the backdrop. The dramatic potential of criminal litigation is overwhelmingly preferred, in which everything is biased and distorted for dramatic effect.[36] Within the crime show genre itself, violent crimes are disproportionately over represented.

Of course, viewers do not accept that the more fanciful scenes of TV legal drama represent an accurate portrayal of legal practice for, as Corner explains, the meaning of such scenes is read poetically, rather than referentially.[37] The more forceful the degree of realism, the more likely it is that the poetic axis will be suspended.[38] Charles Rosenberg, legal adviser to *LA Law*, regards that show as being about drama, not about lawyers.[39] The genre of film filters out most of the 'real' law, because it is less cinematically interesting.[40] However, it may be hard to tell the difference when there is a deliberate blurring of boundaries, and the exaggerated and superficial

---

33 For a pointed analysis of the biased treatment of feminism in the American media, see Rhode, 1997.
34 Williams, 1997, p 23.
35 Carlson, 1985, p 104.
36 Friedman, 1989, pp 1588–89.
37 Corner, 1995, p 148.
38 *Ibid*, p 149.
39 Rosenberg, 1989. Rosenberg was replying to Gillers, 1989.
40 Rapoport, 2000.

representations of legal life become the hyperreal, that is, more real than the real, as Baudrillard suggests.[41]

It is somewhat paradoxical then, that just as women and racialised Others have become numerically significant in a profession long closed to them, legal practice is increasingly marked by cynicism and unethical conduct. Popular culture itself cannot be 'blamed' for the increasing cynicism; in any case, monocausal explanations are simplistic. The rise of neoliberalism, obsessed as it is with profit making and private good at the expense of the communal values of civil society, must play a central role. The corporate world is underpinned by lawyers who advise their clients how to circumvent regulatory regimes.[42] Lawyers have also been the anonymous force behind some of the spectacular corporate scams of recent years.[43] The intense reliance on law by questionable corporations has suggested an homology between corporate crime and law, which has proven to be grist to the dramatists' mill and which has exacerbated the popular groundswell against lawyers.

Despite the increasingly negative press accorded lawyers, students nevertheless continue to flock to law school. Focusing on punishing one bad lawyer deflects attention away from the constitution of law itself. In any case, law has successfully relied upon the technocratic approach to present itself as neutral, objective, apolitical and fair. Critical scholarship of all kinds – feminist, postcolonial, and poststructural – has been involved in deconstructing claims to neutrality, objectivity and universality, as well as a panoply of truth claims. This body of critical scholarship has exposed the partiality of law, with particular regard to its sexist, racist, and homophobic underside.

THE MYTH OF LEGAL AUTONOMY

I will now expand on how law has been able to resist popular culture through the fiction that it is autonomous. The myth of legal autonomy has been very effectively maintained through the theory and practice of legal positivism. As the word 'positivism' suggests, it refers to that which is posited, usually by virtue of the authoritative pronouncements of a legislature or judge. The proclaimed autonomy of law is a significant prop

---

41 Baudrillard, 1994b. I have expanded on Baudrillard's treatment of the real in Chapter 14 below.

42 Maureen Cain describes lawyers as 'the *par excellence* institutional inventors'. See Cain and Harrington, 1994, p 31.

43 In Australia, 'corporate cowboys' included Alan Bond, who ended up in gaol; Christopher Skase, who fled to Majorca and successfully evaded extradition, and Max Green, himself a lawyer, who embezzled more than $AU40m of his clients' money prior to his mysterious death in Vietnam.

within the positivistic arsenal designed to bolster law's authority as the pre-eminent voice of the liberal state. As Carty points out, law exercises its authority over, or acts upon, an Other, which may be called 'society'.[44] We are all subject to the rule of law, which is why so much is at stake in resisting destabilising influences.

The claim to autonomy has served a significant ideological purpose in bolstering law's power and authority. Within the process of judicial decision making, judges resort to a range of techniques and methods to reify the appearance of legal autonomy, including the legitimation of instant decisions through past decisions. By the constant privileging of technical rules, legal decisions are produced as though they were apolitical and value free.[45] The idea of the autonomy of law may be recognised as a myth but it is one that continues to have currency because it reifies law's claimed congruence with rationality and impartiality, the preconditions of justice, which is the idealised telos of law in our society.

Law is predicated upon a series of dualisms of the kind that typify Enlightenment thinking. Unsurprisingly, law is always associated with the positive and superior side.[46] Thus, law represents the normative voice of reason and authority, whereas the unruly heteroglossia associated with the social, including popular culture, represents a composite Other that needs to be restrained and disciplined by law. Hence, there is a clearly discernible ideological rationale underpinning the desire to slough off disruptive and unruly knowledges, which have the potential to dilute or diminish law's authority. HLA Hart, one of the major exponents of legal positivism, sought to draw a line between law and history, law and politics, and law and social values of all kinds, including law and morality.[47] By disqualifying non-legal knowledge, legal positivism has sought to constitute law as a closed system in which the major source of law is law. Positivism seeks to deny the subjectivity of the interpretive process, a process that necessarily disturbs the rigidity of a technocratic legal system.

The idea that law can be corralled and immunised from social influences continues to be a powerful animating myth within liberal legal culture, despite the fact that the notion of certainty within the humanities and the social sciences has received a severe battering from feminist, postmodern and poststructural theorists over the last few decades. The effect has been to put paid to the idea that universality, objectivity and neutrality are attainable, qualities, which coincidentally, happen to constitute the very essence of law's claim to truth. Although the rigidity of legal positivism has been shaken, its central tenets continue to exercise a powerful centripetal

---

44 Carty, 1990, p 7.
45 Thornton, 1998c.
46 For an analysis of the way these dualisms are mapped onto gender, see Olsen, 1990.
47 Hart, 1961, p 253n.

pull. It assumes that there are certain presuppositions underpinning the discipline of law, which should be unproblematically accepted by practising lawyers and legal scholars alike. Whereas it is deemed appropriate within the humanities to interrogate one's epistemological standpoint, particularly in a postmodern era, this is regarded as destabilising for law, where 'reflexivity ... remains ... akin to heresy'.[48] Although by no means uncontentious, the preferred approach is that law be taught primarily as a skill for practice, from a predetermined and unproblematic epistemological standpoint. The technocratic approach allows law to be presented to students as though it were value free. After all, legal practitioners are expected to represent the rape survivor one day and the rapist the next without batting an eyelid. Contextual, critical and theoretical material may be used to enhance the doctrinal or 'black letter' approach, but this material is dispensable when there are time and other constraints. The core legal education framework was developed in the 19th century to support imperialism and the free market. This curricular core has seen remarkably little change, other than to adopt a more corporatised and international flavour to serve better contemporary free market and privatising imperatives.

The overwhelming methodological focus of legal education in the English speaking common law world has been directed to the study of appellate court decisions, an approach that has served to reify the notion of the hierarchy and autonomy of law. So inured are most legal academics to accepting this as the proper substance of law that they 'experience vertigo when they open the doors and look outside the appellate courtroom'.[49] The unruly character of popular culture is so far removed from the measured tones of judicial discourse that it can only exacerbate this propensity.

Law reform may go marginally further in the way that it seeks to improve the ability of law to deliver justice, but it is likely to fall short of challenging the fundamental tenets of liberal legalism, such as the rule of law, individual rights, the separation between public and private life, and other similarly cherished principles.[50] Reformism destabilises the rigidity of existing classifications, but the basic presuppositions are left intact. Furthermore, in embarking on the path of law reform, the scholar herself affirms the legal practice paradigm:

> By taking up the project of legal reform, however, the scholar becomes a participant in legal practice and, therefore, a part of the very object that he or she set out to investigate. This collapse of the distinction between the subject

---

48 Collier, 1991, p 434.

49 Macaulay, 1989, p 1546.

50 For discussion of liberal legalism, see Kalman, 1996; Bottomley and Parker, 1997, Chapter 2; Davies, 1994, Chapters 4 and 5.

studying the law and the legal practice that is the object of study is the central weakness of contemporary legal scholarship. 'Collapse' does not happen at a moment in time, as if there were first a separation of subject and object, which suddenly disappeared. The legal scholar comes to the study of law already understanding herself as a citizen in law's republic. She is committed to 'making law work,' to improving the legal system of which she is a part.[51]

It can therefore be seen how positivism is politically imbricated with practice. All non-law is not regarded as irredeemably antipathetic, however, as law has a remarkable capacity to assimilate at least a semblance of knowledge associated with the Other in order to appear to be fair, which is an essential prerequisite to maintaining its legitimacy.[52] That which is thought to be anodyne can nevertheless be destabilising. Thus, liberal feminism, which is inclined to uphold many aspects of law's republic, nevertheless challenges the rigidity of the line of demarcation between public and private life when it begins to interrogate the pathology of domestic violence and child sexual assault, for example.

Despite the permeable nature of law's boundaries, a range of gatekeepers, including judges, as the paradigmatic legal knowers, as well as academics, lawyers, students and university administrators, all play a role in endeavouring to maintain the autonomy of law. Individual legal academics still have a modicum of freedom to challenge orthodoxy, despite increased surveillance within the corporatised academy.[53] However, the specification of designated 'priorities' in appointments and promotions, as well as scrutiny of funding and critical scholarship by the sentinels of practice, ensure that law does not stray too far in accommodating the Other. As soon as it looks as though legal education has moved beyond a modest reformist or contextual approach, it is sharply reined in. For example, the Legal Realists at Columbia in the 1920s, and Yale in the 1930s, were attacked for not teaching 'law' when they sought to develop a sociolegal approach to the study of law.[54] They challenged the idea of law as science, propounded by Langdell at Harvard in the late 19th century. The fear engendered by the Legal Realists' use of empirical social sciences and sociological jurisprudence highlights the strictness of the policing role for, as Paul Kahn suggests, the Realists remained 'firmly in the grip of legal practice'.[55] Nevertheless, the potential disorder posed by the appearance of the social sufficed to sound alarm bells.

---

51 Kahn, 1999, p 7.
52 Thompson, 1975, p 263.
53 Thornton, 2001.
54 Stevens, 1971, pp 403–548; Kalman, 1986.
55 Kahn, 1999, p 24.

In Australia, there have been similar reactions to sociolegal critiques of law, as can be seen from the examples of Macquarie and La Trobe Universities. So strongly did the proponents of the practice-oriented approach feel about the critical and theoretical approaches to law adopted by Macquarie, that a Commonwealth Committee of Review went so far as to recommend that the School either be phased out or reconstituted.[56] La Trobe developed from a Department of Legal Studies which did not teach law for practice, so that its scholars were less likely to fall victim to the problem identified by Kahn regarding the collapse of the distinction between the legal academic (the legal subject) and legal practice (the object of study). Scholars were free to bring to bear the critical insights of a range of disciplines.[57] However, the LLB programme that La Trobe subsequently structured around its sociolegal orientation was soon subject to attrition and evisceration. Feminist and cultural critiques of law were deemed to be unruly, and incompatible with the prevailing positivist pro-market paradigm.

At the broader level, critical scholars of all kinds have encountered difficulties in the academy. Feminist scholars have been warned against teaching in any area associated with 'women's issues'.[58] Some of those who have disobeyed this injunction have been denied tenure or promotion, as well as access to benefits, including research funds. The picture is not unrelievedly gloomy, however, as attested to by the plethora of books and law journal articles that do not fit the conventional paradigm, the existence of subjects which deploy critical feminist perspectives and methodologies in teaching, together with popular magazines which seriously address feminist legal issues.[59] However, the future of feminism within the law curriculum is uncertain within a neoliberal climate in which its 'use value', in terms of marketability and credentialism, is deemed to be low.

Kahn claims that law cannot be an intellectual discipline until legal scholars suspend belief in the object of their study.[60] Until they take this radical step, they are not 'studying law, they are doing it'.[61] Kahn compares the study of law with the study of Christianity, which, until the 20th century,

---

56 Pearce *et al*, 1987, Rec 44. See also Special Issue on Legal Education. Macquarie University Law School was not closed down but it was significantly restructured a decade later and 'purged' of radical elements. See Boehringer, 1999.

57 The multidisciplinary character of the department is illustrated by the fact that in 1990, 50% of the legal academics came from a range of disciplines, other than law. By 2000, the percentage had declined to 12%, even though the majority of students were legal studies students enrolled in degrees other than law.

58 Eg, Heilbrun and Resnik, 1990, p 1924.

59 For discussion of the way 'popmags' have moved into the feminist mainstream, see Hanigsberg, 1997.

60 Kahn, 1999, pp 2–3. For a percipient review of Kahn's book, see Sarat, 2000.

61 Kahn, 1999, p 27.

he argues, was a practice rather than an intellectual discipline.[62] The practice orientation has similarly militated against theory and critique in law. Furthermore, the absence of theory, together with technical functionalism, has caused law to be a derivative discipline.[63] Each time legal education appears to become more diverse, critical and theoretical, and less focused on the exigencies of (corporate) legal practice and the interests of the dominant, it has been reined back. The contemporary tendency to slough off the social in favour of practical legal skills through changed subject offerings is one manifestation of the attempt to immunise law from the seeming depredations of the social and the unsettling possibilities of reflexivity.

Popular culture, as the embodiment of non-rationality – emotion, corporeality, tactility, aestheticism and the specular – is corrosive of the authority of law. These non-rational values are also associated with the feminine, affectivity, corporeality and the Other, whereas rationality is marked as masculine within the binarisms of Western thought, which are reflective of and constitutive of legality. Fear of the effect of popular culture on law today would seem to be analogous to Plato's fear of the corrupting effect of profane poetry on philosophy in Classical Athens.[64] The integrity and authority of the privileged form of knowledge demands that which is dangerous and threatening be kept out. It is the role of technocentrism to police traditional boundaries and to occlude law's predilection in favour of benchmark masculinity. There is therefore a powerful and historic constellation of interests seeking to uphold conventional modernist incarnations of law. Despite these rearguard attempts to protect the integrity of law, the firm line of separation between law and popular culture appears to be vanishing.[65]

LAW AND IMAGINATION

The movements that seek to conceptualise law as a social science and/or humanity, as well as those that simply address law in its social context, destabilise the myth of the autonomy of law. The law and literature movement, which incorporates a number of strands, has laid the groundwork for a focus on law and popular culture. Richard Weisberg refers to the twin conceptions of literature as a source of law and literary methods, and law and literature as an analogue to law.[66] In recent years, a significant

---

62 *Ibid*, p 2.
63 Russell, 1996, p 173; Kerruish refers to the propensity of legal theory 'to pick up baubles'. See, Kerruish, 1989, p 169.
64 Plato, 1955, Book III.
65 Cf Sherwin, 2000.
66 Weisberg, 1992, p 3. Posner adopts a rather different approach towards the dualism. See Posner, 1998.

body of writing has appeared on legal narrative as a consequence of the law as literature/law in literature movements. This scholarship highlights the way new and better worlds can be imagined through popular culture, when unattainable through legal processes. Visions of justice are often contrasted with rancour and the desire for revenge, or the Nietzschean idea of ressentiment, which animates litigants.[67] These representations of the legal imaginary may then be absorbed into popular understandings of law.

Law as narratology has also emerged from the law and literature movement. Indeed, as soon as one leaves the sterility of the appellate courtroom and a technocratic hermeneusis, the social Other has to be confronted. As Sandra Berns points out, every legal case begins in polyvocality:

> It begins, that is, as stories, each story offering one possible reality, one window on events ... The stories we tell about these performances become, over time, more real than the performances themselves, and these performances in turn are always more real than the details of which they are comprised.[68]

The polyvocality of the case reveals the myth of positivism with its choice of material facts and one version of 'truth' at the end of the day, which becomes the basis of 'the law'. Storytelling manifests itself most clearly in the trial, which Friedman describes as 'narrative competition'.[69] Each side tells a story and tries to convince the judge or jury that their vision is the 'true' one. As Bauman reminds us, the 'idea of truth belongs to the rhetoric of power. It makes no sense unless in the context of opposition ...'.[70] The evidence adduced in support of a particular story embellishes the respective narratives, adding dramatic tension to the account for the jurors to piece together, discard or modify. In creative literature, accounts of the trial provide substantial scope for the interpolation of critique and commentary. Truth is thereby exposed as a variable construct within the interstices of power.

'Narrative scholarship' is also understood to constitute a particular facet of feminist legal method, which captures the experiential so as to illuminate that which has been excluded from mainstream accounts.[71] Abrams draws attention to its unsettling form, its lack of objectivity, and its self-conscious standpoint, which allows a space for the Other.[72] Stories about law can be packaged attractively and made accessible to a wide audience. Unlike the rationalising and generalising narratives of legal discourse, stories allow

---

67 Weisberg, 1984, p 5ff. See also Posner, 1998, p 49ff.
68 Berns, 1999, p 102.
69 Friedman, 1989.
70 Bauman, 1997, p 112.
71 Abrams, 1994.
72 The genre is well illustrated by, for example, Williams, 1993; Trent, 1994.

space for the affective: they remind us of human beings and their failings.[73] Stories contain a sequence of events that may be enhanced by cinematic techniques, such as flashbacks and symbols. There is likely to be some fleshing out of character, dramatic tension, a denouement and a resolution, which endows the story with a life and meaning of its own. Stories also gesture towards the inexpressible,[74] in ways not possible for a law report, as well as telling us what happens beyond law.[75] Simplistic though the packaging might be, the values associated with a progressive incarnation of law continue to be fairness, equality and justice.[76] Despite the prevailing mood of cynicism about law, the possibility of justice continues to be a powerful animating social force for good. Narrative allows the voices of victims of crime to be heard in ways not otherwise possible within the criminal justice system. The treatment of survivors of sexual assault by defence lawyers is a notorious example of the way that women have had to occupy particular subject positions laden with misogyny. Stories, films and poems can illuminate otherwise ineffable accounts. The imaginative and reflective possibilities of literature appeal to those legal scholars who feel frustrated and constrained by the technocratic imperatives of legal positivism that selectively omit key elements of the narrative.[77]

Tableaux of light and shade, good and evil, justice and injustice, are woven into dramatic and cinematic representations for effect. Justice may be contrasted with law itself, which is represented as obsessed with procedure, form and 'technicalities'. In the film *Thelma and Louise*, two women 'outlaws' do not turn to the law for justice but envision it in alternative ways.[78] Indeed, there is a dimension of popular culture that may glorify lawlessness 'in the interests of a higher justice'.[79] Popular legal culture tends to be far more concerned with what is just, than what is lawful, which is another reason why it is so subversive. Indeed, its dramatic possibilities allow ethical dilemmas to be captured with greater subtlety, economy and force than in the case of, say, a legal treatise. This does not mean that the primary role of popular culture is to be morally uplifting, any more than can be said for canonical works of literature, for its primary role, after all, is to entertain. As soon as the content becomes overly didactic, heavy-handed or intellectual, it loses its mass appeal. The majority of people are most comfortable with works that reflect traditional values or follow familiar plot lines, as is the case with romance novels.[80]

---

73 Minow, 1996, p 36; Farber and Sherry, 1996, p 43.
74 White, 1973, p 863.
75 Karpin, 1997, p 126.
76 Clawson, 1998.
77 Sandra Berns gives some graphic examples arising from sex-based cases of the 19th century. See Berns, 1999, p 107ff.
78 Spelman and Minow, 1996, p 275.
79 Friedman, 1989, p 1592.
80 Sanger, 1994, p 76.

There is no rule or principle of imagination into which popular culture can be slotted or with which it can be analogised, as is the case with legal method.[81] The struggle between the universality of law and the particularity of the social is a perennial one. To some extent, the struggle mirrors the paradox of liberalism, which simultaneously promises both freedom and equality.[82] The universal norms of law appeal to the dominant interests associated with benchmark masculinity, so as to maximise the freedom of those who have designated themselves as the Equals. However, partiality breeds *ressentiment* on the part of feminists and Others, who demand inclusion within the community of Equals. Agitation leads to at least a semblance of accommodation, which in turn, induces *ressentiment* on the part of the dominant.[83] In this way, the political pendulum swings back and forth, albeit haphazardly. The conjunction of corporatism and neoliberalism has given a boost to incarnations of legal positivism. This may be an added reason for invoking popular culture as a lever to disrupt and resist totalising discourses, as well as to compel a rethink of the exclusion of women and Others. The reflexive potential of popular culture possesses a significant discursive power.

It is unsurprising that law has sought to immunise itself from that which has been constituted as quotidian and mundane within the social script. The elitism and exclusiveness of the legal profession, particularly the judiciary and the upper echelons of corporate law firms, together with the time-honoured intersection between law and property, law and order, and law and benchmark masculinity, signals resistance to recognising the interests of women and Others. The quotidian and the mundane also necessarily include the body, sexuality and love, all of which law finds highly problematic,[84] albeit they are the very stuff of popular culture. Given the feminisation, racialisation and sexualisation of affectivity and corporeality within the social script, it is difficult to escape the metonymical association of popular culture with the feminine and the Other, which disrupt and discomfit the stern carapace of legal rationality with its masculinist hue. The cognate law and literature movement may also be portrayed as a feminising project, a way of humanising law, rather than as a 'rigorous and resistant ... source of useful knowledge'.[85]

Law, or lore as we might more properly conceptualise it, comprises much more than that which is posited. Not only does a wide lens encompass the

---

81 For a percipient critique of legal method that locates law's practices within the literary tradition, see Goodrich, 1986.

82 Brown, 1995, p 67.

83 Adapted from Nietzsche, 1969, p 127.

84 For a sustained study of the conflictual relationship between law and love, see, eg, Kahn, 2000.

85 Findlay, 1998, p 7.

ought of law, but the imaginative possibilities of what might be. We are not seeking to find 'right answers' in legal positivist vein, but understanding and a modicum of justice in an uncaring world where the citizens of civil society have being replaced by consumers in market settings. To understand better the legal culture and the power of law, no nook or cranny can escape the critical gaze. Foucault's insight regarding the nature of power, which has great relevance for law, is that we should focus on the smallest details, the capillaries, not just the institutional centres of power.[86] In addition, we need to heed Kahn's insight that we should start to look seriously at the legal imagination.[87] This will free us from the sterility of the epistemological black box on which lawyers and legal scholars have long relied as the sole repository of orthodox legal knowledge. We can no longer be bound by a blind obeisance to legal authority that typified a bygone age. Popular evocations of the disillusionment with law bear this out. Law is a dynamic social and cultural phenomenon, which cannot be explained by reference to itself alone. To escape the vacuous circularity and to persist with the task of revisioning law as an intellectual discipline, it has to be located within a wider frame, which includes the world of popular imagination, with its hope, as well as its cynicism.

---

86 Foucault, 1977, pp 136–41 *et passim.*
87 Kahn, 1999, p 135 *et passim.*

PART TWO

JUDICIAL NOTICE

Canto of Silent Men

Radio

And on the radio was a reprise which recaptured his glory
for those he could not touch
People whose feelings he could not hurt
On the radio was a song
for those who inhabit places of hardship
His voice was what was sung when they all had a sense of being separate
but in fact were blind
And there was still the sound of passion when loyalty died
When one day in a second of doubt he died
And there was still the sound of fear when his race began he ran
till every silent man had disappeared

Song of Bone

We have no more need of these lands
The sky has a very hard heart
And we want it to
There is a peculiar trust in the tyrant
Who knows how brittle bone
Was it the air that snapped our legs and broke our arms?
But looking up there is no answer
Slay the dragon knave and the fairytale may come back to our hearts
in music
We have need of the land for graves
Flowerful

MTC Cronin

LAWYERS READING LAW/LORE AS POPULAR CULTURE: CONFLICTING PARADIGMS OF REPRESENTATION

Terry Threadgold

READING/WRITING HABITS: CORPOREALITIES AND CULTURAL NETWORKS

Popular Culture is another name for the practice of media readership in modernity (I follow Gramsci on this) ... The point here is a general one – reading is not a solitary, individualist, consumptive, supplementary act of silent subjection to a series of imperial graphic impressions. On the contrary reading is a social, communal, productive act of writing, a dialogic process which is fundamental to (and may even be) popular culture.[1]

If you think of 'fields' not as terrains or machines, but as communities of discourse, groups of people defined by their willingness to talk in certain ways, the question becomes: What kind of relationships can we establish among these various ways of talking, and the communities they define? ... My initial question was: What happens if we look at the literature of the law as if it really were literature, as though it defined speakers and a world, a set of possibilities for expression and community? ...

[T]o try to see it (law) as a compositional art, as a set of activities by which minds use language to make meaning and establish relations with others.[2]

When I first begin to think seriously about the relationship between feminism, law and popular culture in order to write this chapter, I found myself asking a number of related questions, addressing a diversity of theoretical perspectives and turning to a whole range of disparate kinds of cultural representations – all in order to try to think through again, this time from somewhere else, questions I have explored at length in relation to popular culture in other contexts.[3] I want first to unpack the co-ordination in 'popular culture, feminism and law' and to question first the relation: 'law and popular culture'. Then I will turn to the question of feminism's relationship to the other two terms: law and popular culture.

---

1 Hartley, 1996, pp 47 and 51.
2 White, 1990, pp 16–17.
3 Threadgold, 1997c.

I want to argue that readings and writings, readings that are writings and writings that are readings, are central to these relationships.[4] Popular culture, when it was newly defined as an area of academic study was set up against, and located in relation to, so-called 'high culture', to which both law and literature as institutions and communities of discourse were assigned. The definition of popular culture which John Hartley is developing in the quote above is related to but different from this. He is talking about the media, or more specifically journalism and its capacity to construct readers, but he is also talking about those readers and their capacity to construct and deconstruct journalism, to rewrite or write again in reading. When he identifies this 'readership' with popular culture, he centres the media in the space of popular culture, now rethought as everyday life and imbricated in, and lived in relation to, the rhythms and schedules, the messages, fictions and representations of mediated reality:

> It is the problem, in all its social complexity, of the power and resonance of the media in our lives, articulating, albeit unevenly, their views of the world and limiting our capacity to influence and control their meanings; but equally offering the very stuff with which we can, and do, construct our own meanings, and through them (albeit equally unevenly) generate the raw materials for critique, transcendence and change.[5]

One of the problems with even very sophisticated media theory is that it often tends to forget that the media is one complex discursive formation among many that constitutes the mediated intersections between the public and private spheres of the body politic.[6] Nor does such theory always make explicit how it is that the effects of these intersecting formations can be the structuring of 'public opinion' or the making of individual selves.[7] I have argued elsewhere that these kinds of connections can only ever be theorised and understood in relation to bodies, what Vicki Kirby has called corporeography,[8] 'the body at the scene of writing', the writing of the body, by the body, the writing on the body, which is a typical embodied effect of the reading/writing practices which partially constitute the discursive formations of everyday life. Elizabeth Grosz theorises this relationship between author and text differently, using Derrida's work on the signature

---

4   Barthes, 1986.

5   Silverstone, 1994, p x.

6   Althusserian Marxism would have identified these as ideological and repressive state apparatuses respectively: education, religion, literature and the law, the police, the state for example. Althusser, 1971.

7   Colin Mercer is a notable exception, theorising the newspaper as productive of the *habitus* of the nation and thus directly connecting media influence with the dispositions, the structures and the improvisations of the *habitus* as embodied modes of everyday living. See Mercer, 1992.

8   Kirby, 1997.

to explore the ways in which texts and bodies become folded into one another:

> The third modality (of the signature) much closer to Benveniste's understanding of the paradoxical and divided position of the subject in and beyond the text, involves the necessary and irreducible trace of the one in the other, the implication of the text's outside with its inside, and of its inside with establishing its borders and thus its outside, in short its fundamentally folded, 'invaginated character ...'

> The trace of the signature, then, cannot simply be identified with the proprietary mark of the author; instead, it is an effect of the text's mode of materiality, the fact that as a product the text is an effect of a *labor*, a work on and with signs, a collaborative (even if hostile) labor of writing and reading.[9]

Grosz's deconstruction of the inside/outside binary here parallels in many ways Bourdieu's attempt to undo the opposition between subjectivism and objectivism in the theory of *habitus*:

> This system of dispositions – a present past that tends to perpetuate itself into the future by reactivation in similarly structured practices, an internal law through which the law of external necessities, irreducible to immediate constraints, is constantly exerted – is the principle of the continuity and regularity which objectivism sees in social practices without being able to account for it ... the internal dispositions – the internalization of externality – enable the external forces to exert themselves, but in accordance with the specific logics of the organisms in which they are incorporated, ie, in a durable, systematic and non-mechanical way.[10]

Judith Butler, putting these two theoretical interventions together, and focussing on a critique of Bourdieu's understanding of the linguistic *habitus*,[11] the way in which iterable speech acts 'position' subjects, speech acts which produce the things of which they speak,[12] makes the connection (via Althusser)[13] between speech acts and subjectivity that allows us to understand how it could be that popular culture becomes embedded in, folded through, and performed as *habitus* both in bodies of law as speech acts and texts and in the legal body as flesh and *habitus*:

> The performative is not merely an act used by a pregiven subject, but is one of the powerful and insidious ways in which subjects are called into social being, inaugurated into sociality by a variety of diffuse and powerful interpellations.

---

9   Grosz, 1995, pp 19–20.

10 Bourdieu, 1990, pp 54–55.

11 Bourdieu, 1991, p 18.

12 Butler, 1999, p 125: 'One need only to consider how racial or gendered slurs live and thrive in and as the flesh of the addressee, and how these slurs accumulate over time, dissimulating their history, taking on the semblance of the natural, configuring and restricting the doxa that counts as "reality".'

13 Althusser, 1971.

> In this sense the social performative is a crucial part not only of subject
> formation, but of the ongoing political contestation and reformulation of the
> subject as well. In this sense the performative is not only a ritual practice: it is
> one of the influential rituals by which subjects are formed and reformulated.[14]

The media and all of those other powerful discursive formations which
'position' the subject in this way, do so through what Bourdieu called the
'magic' of speech acts.[15] The complex processes of readership and writing
which are popular culture effect that magic by writing it on the body,
incorporating it as the very condition of being and belief. But the *habitus* is
not necessarily fixed. In receptive situations the *habitus* is always in process.
Butler argues that whenever the speech act is reformulated, made to signify
differently, its effects work back on the *habitus*, producing innovation,
creativity, improvisation and change. This is how the subject is also
'reformulated'. But as we shall see below it is much harder to reformulate
some speech acts and some subjects than others. This may turn out to be one
of the major differences between feminism's relationship to law and popular
culture and law's relationship to popular culture. Feminisms in general are
interested in reformulating speech acts and subjects and in knowing how
they are constituted while the law on the whole is not.

What is true of the media though is also true of literature and of law.
Both offer modes of reading/writing, which are formative of particular
kinds of *habitus* and are inevitably partially constituted intertextually by and
through the mediations of popular culture. This is why it is possible with
James Boyd White, to read the law as if it were literature, as a technology for
making worlds and selves. Law is a discursive community embodied and
formed in the practices of everyday life, but *qua* law habitually authorised to
magically institute what it says as performative speech acts. These by their
very generic nature as law then deny their intertextual and citational links to
the body and the everyday. In many ways this distance from the body, this
denial of the implication in the field of everyday life, is the greatest and most
dangerous fiction law constructs. It is a fiction, which denies the subject of
law, and the legal subject access to improvisation, creativity and
reformulation and that, as we will see below, produces oddly inflexible
subjectivities.

Such fictions are what Alison Young is arguing about when she explores
the 'crisis' in what she calls the 'crimino-legal complex': 'the knowledges,
discourses and practices that are deemed to fall under the rubric of
criminology, criminal justice and criminal law ... Together with the popular
discourses that are manifested in the media, cinema and advertising, in
order to convey the "sense" that crime has become (been made?) a potent

---

14 Butler, 1999, p 125.
15 Bourdieu, 1991.

sign ...'[16] It is a complex, she insists, which is as much about entertainment as it is about policing and punishment. Her argument for 'crisis' is about the confusion between and across the boundaries of these different discourses and practices, confusions which blur finally the boundaries between image and reality, simulation and the real, and which produce fictions/myths of what crime is and how it operates while constantly denying the 'crisis' produced by the inability to 'contain' crime's effects or 'to account for its meanings'.[17]

Crime as image, the way in which crime as event is imagined as the sign 'crime', transgresses these institutional, high, popular and disciplinary boundaries and circulates across them. Young is intent on demonstrating that the 'imagination' of crime within the institutions authorised to categorise and define it – criminology, criminal law, policing – the entire crimino-legal complex – is intimately and interdiscursively related to the imagining of crime in popular culture – in the media, in detective fiction, in the law's dealings with, and the media representation of, illegal immigrants and HIV/AIDS. What Young calls 'the aestheticisation of everyday life', is precisely this discursive process by which the 'real world has become a myth' made of repeated, even formulaic patterns of language and image, and lived and known only through reading/writing practices.[18] The myths thus constituted are the 'crisis' because they confuse fact and fiction, reality and signification, legal and popular reasoning and imagining.

Young's reading/writing resists the dominant narratives of the crimino-legal tradition and asks some insistent questions about criminology's 'intense and un-relenting resistance to the insistent questions of feminism'.[19] We will come back to these below when we listen to a legal subject reading/writing the work of feminists and critical legal scholars.

Young's work is important for a number of reasons. She locates the crimino-legal complex in the everyday of popular culture, showing how the criminal body and the body of criminal law/lore is produced in and by, and then becomes confused with, that space. She centres the body, the body that is always 'being constituted, brought into crisis, and reconstituted' in and through the imagining of crime. She understands that language, speech acts, forms of representation, never merely describe or represent the body but always 'structure, marginalise and divide' it and she is concerned to 'seek the unmarked emotional body of and in the crimino-legal tradition: the body that suffers under the weight of imagination as a spectacle to be consumed,

---

16   Young, 1996, p 2.
17   *Ibid*, p 3.
18   *Ibid*, p 20.
19   *Ibid*, p 23.

disciplined, repressed ... [she is concerned with] the responsive emotional body as textual, as a thing that can be read ...'[20]

Her work then enacts in many ways the theoretical positions I have drawn together above. It sits suggestively beside Remi Lenoir's interview with Andre S, a judge.[21] Asked in interview what he likes about being a judge, Andre S replies that he likes the notion of 'independence', 'everything good in the judicial institution'. Asked: 'How did that idea come to you?', he replies:

> By reading the papers a little and then I read a book ... I read that when I must have been in the first year at university, something like that, I must have read it, my grandfather had me read it, a book by a retired magistrate ... Meanwhile in the press at the time there were the debates of the magistrates union, and people talked about that ...[22]

Thus does Andre S demonstrate the way the objective world becomes *habitus* and subjects are interpellated, positioned as certain kinds of subjects while imagining themselves and the world of law in ways, which confuse the boundaries between the fictional image and the reality.

There are many other examples, which demonstrate and tease out the implications of these modes of theorising for an understanding of the relationship between law and popular culture. Michel Foucault's extraordinary representation of the discursive construction of the *habitus* (and confession) of a 19th century murderer,[23] of the way popular ballads and tales are incorporated into the criminal's 'confession' which is then made to function as the *locus* of the 'truth' of the murders committed (the real meaning must be in the text) and as a sign of criminality by the medical and legal professions is another example of the way a performative speech act, the result of the incorporation of the field in the body, 'can participate in the ongoing contestation and reformulation of the subject'.[24] Kerry Carrington's remarkable research into the *Leigh Leigh* case explores a similar crimino-legal complex in its intersections with popular culture in an Australian town.[25] So does my own work on the discursive construction of the Governor murders in Australia in 1900 and the uses of the images, narratives and imaginings of these crimes in the construction of more than a century of Australian racisms.[26]

In all three of these cases the media is a central formation in the production of selves and realities. As an institution, the media is key to

20   *Ibid*, p 18.
21   Lenoir, 1999, pp 239–54.
22   *Ibid*, p 244.
23   Foucault, 1975.
24   Butler, 1999.
25   Carrington, 1998.
26   Threadgold, 1997c.

understanding how cultural representations, high and popular, lay and expert, come to function as speech acts in the formation of the *habitus* and circulate across and through institutions, texts and bodies. Crime is in fact a global construct, which is made and remade in and through enormously complex contemporary and historical global circuits of communication.[27] So are all other legal fictions. Thus, Young's case studies of the legal and national reaction to illegal immigrants, of the generic and formulaic structures of detective fiction (now universalised through the global circulation of televisual versions), of the way nationalism and racism structure narratives of invasion and decay, pollution, corruption and colonisation around HIV/AIDS as/and immigrants, all belong to such global discursive formations. They represent hugely complex circuits of communication which are both multimodal, multigeneric and transnational.

It is then now, more than ever, important to attempt a theorisation of the imbrication of the law in the global as well as the local circuits of communication, not least because law functions within nation states in increasingly multicultural contexts which spawn mobile and transnational diasporic realities that begin to challenge the law and the legal subject which 'stays put' or is 'stuck in place'.[28] Here I want to use Appadurai to think with,[29] although I agree with Ong that his work universalises trends in cultural globalisation 'rather than deal with actually existing structures of power and situated cultural processes' and 'cries out for a sense of political economy and situated ethnography'. I want to ask with her: 'How are cultural flows and human imagination conditioned and shaped within these new relations of global inequalities?'[30] Appadurai's work is suggestive of some answers. He begins thus: 'Implicit in this book is a theory of rupture that takes media and migration as its two major and interconnected diacritics and explores their joint effect on the work of the imagination as a constitutive feature of modern subjectivity.'[31] It is the impact of new media and the way it changes the traditional field of mass media in which he is most interested:

---

27 Miller, 1998.

28 I have borrowed these two terms from Aihwa Ong. She uses them not of the law but of 'poor Americans' ... 'in rundown ethnic ghettoes', who do not have the options of mobility and transnationalism available to the new diasporas with access to global capital and population flows. Her concern is with 'the subjectivities associated with being stuck in particular US contexts'. An interesting example of an emerging supranational legal institution is the European Court of Justice within the European Union which consistently makes judgments that operate against the sovereignty of nation states. The court is produced within the very global flows of capitalism (free trade, anti-monopolism) and population (European) forms of 'flexible citizenship'. See Ong, 1999; George and Bache, 2001.

29 Appadurai, 1996.

30 Ong, 1999, p 11.

31 Appadurai, 1996, p 3.

> Electronic media are resources for experimenting with self-making in all sorts of societies, for all sorts of persons. They allow scripts for possible lives to be imbricated with the glamour of film stars and fantastic film plots and yet also to be tied to the plausibility of news shows, documentaries and other black and white forms of telemediation and printed text.[32]

He argues that because of the multiplicity of convergent forms in which new media appear, and because of the rapidity with which they become part of, and move through, daily life routines (reformulating the *habitus* as they go), new media provide the resources for 'self-imagining as an everyday social project'.[33] The conjunction of new media with migration means that both images and viewers are in constant circulation (except as Ong points out for those who are 'stuck in place') and that the imagination must become in these fluid contexts a place of contestation where people try to incorporate the global into the corporeality of the local. In his attempt to theorise how this happens, Appadurai develops a complex argument about the way the new global economy works through the disjunctive and overlapping relationships between five different dimensions of global cultural flows: ethnoscapes ('the landscape of persons who constitute the shifting world in which we live'), technoscapes ('the global configuration of technology') and financescapes ('the disposition of global capital is now a more mysterious, rapid and difficult landscape to follow than ever before'). These are further refracted by 'mediascapes and ideoscapes which are closely related landscapes of images'.[34] Mediascapes he argues are 'image-centred, narrative-bases strips of reality', which offer 'elements ... Out of which scripts can be formed of imagined lives'.[35] Ideoscapes are also 'concatenations of images' but these are often directly political and directly connected to the Enlightenment narrative which collocates 'ideas, terms and images ... including freedom, welfare, rights, sovereignty, representation and the master term democracy'.[36]

Appadurai points out that in the enlightenment master narrative from which these terms derive, a Euro-American master narrative, they were constructed in a particular context, which involved a very specific relationship between reading, representation and the public sphere (see Hartley above). Relocated in new, diasporic contexts, their internal coherence is loosened, recontextualised by different political contexts and made to mean very differently, producing often incommensurable narratives, using the same words, in different parts of the world. This makes 'communication between elites and followers' in different places

---

32 *Ibid*, pp 3–4.
33 *Ibid*, p 4.
34 *Ibid*, pp 33–35.
35 *Ibid*, p 35.
36 *Ibid*, pp 35–36.

extraordinarily difficult.[37] The difficulties, he argues, are both semantic and pragmatic and he introduces here a whole area, which needs further research, what he calls 'globally variable synaesthesia'.

He uses this phrase to encapsulate the finer pragmatic details of the difficulties of crosscultural global communication discussed above. He sees these as including the conventions by which sets of communicative genres are valued and why in different places (for example, where is the newspaper more highly valued than the cinema or vice versa?). He also discusses the 'sorts of pragmatic genre conventions governing the reading of different kinds of texts' in differently constituted public spheres.[38] He goes so far as to argue that: 'The very relationship of reading to hearing and seeing may vary in important ways that determine the morphology of these different ideoscapes as they shape themselves in different national and transnational contexts.'[39]

What Appadurai argues of the transnational and the global is also remarkably true of the current configurations within nation states where the flows of the global economy take effect by radically reconfiguring and reformulating relationships between reading, representation and the public sphere in exactly similar ways. In these contexts too we need to begin to theorise reading practices in relation to the pragmatics and semantics of habitual seeing and hearing in exactly these synaesthesic and multidimensional ways. Legal reading practices are no exception.

Bourdieu has also been thinking about these questions in relation to the social conditions of the international circulation of ideas and he has this to say:

> The fact that texts circulate without their context, that, to use my terms – they don't bring with them the field of production of which they are a product, and the fact that the recipients, who are themselves in a different field of production, re-interpret the texts in accordance with the structure of the field of reception, are facts that generate some formidable misunderstandings and that can have good or bad consequences.[40]

He goes on to insist that the conditions and ways in which texts enter a field of reception are under researched and of urgent importance in the area of international communication.[41] Once again I would suggest that these forays into the global and the international also give us new ways of thinking about the communicative tensions between different communities

---

37 A very current example as I write is the meaning of 'democratic election' and its representation in the global mediascapes in March, 2002, in the context of the elections in Zimbabwe.

38 Appadurai, 1996, p 36.

39 *Ibid*, p 37.

40 Bourdieu, 1990, p 221.

41 *Ibid*, p 222.

of practice and discourse within nation states and may help us to theorise differently constituted reading practices and their incommensurabilities. Here I will turn finally to the relationship between feminism and law and popular culture, which is in some ways anticipated above in my account of Alison Young's reading of 'crime'.

READING LEGALLY/READING CRITICALLY

Here I want to turn to Richard Posner's version of *Law and Literature*[42] and explore what happens to literature and indeed other critical legal studies readings of it when it, and they, find themselves being interpreted in terms of the structures of a field of reception which is foreign to them and which remains blissfully unaware of any such thing as global flows or even national ones. I have elsewhere characterised Posner as a naïve, untrained literary reader, one who projects his legal realist and positivist reading practices onto texts produced within the literary field as if such readings were natural, the only possible ones.[43] He seems unaware that he is 'fixed in place' within a structure of legal reading or that he is pragmatically crossing genres, disciplines, modes or institutions. His is an assimilationist reading practice, incorporating all otherness into, for him, legally comprehensible (and this means here law and economics) frameworks. There is no multi or even interdisciplinarity here, no disjunctive or overlapping flows – only more of the economy of the same. I want to explore very briefly his readings of Kafka's *The Trial* and his critique of Robin West's very different reading of the same text.[44]

The Trial has regularly been read as an allegory of what it is like to come before the law and to be denied justice, to be made subject to the law's incomprehensible processes, incomprehensible that is to someone who has not been produced as subject within the legal field. Posner is insistent that *The Trial* is not really about the law, or about the denial of justice and, although it may be 'dream-like', it is not, he argues, 'nightmarish', at least until the last chapter. He prefers to locate it with other literary writings about the alienations of 'urban modernism'. He is prepared to see that there are parallels between 'the legal process depicted in *The Trial* and the legal processes employed by Hitler's Germany, Stalin's USSR, and other totalitarian regimes in dealing with political crimes'. However, even here he confounds fact with fiction, going on to say: 'But the essential features of a totalitarian system are missing,'[45] as if a work of fiction were a documentary

---

42 Posner, 1998.
43 Threadgold, 1999b.
44 Posner, 1998, Chapters 4 and 6.
45 *Ibid*, p 137.

or a history. *The Trial*, if it has legal connotations, he says, is located very clearly with the 'dilution of adversary procedure in an inquisitorial system', that is in the context of continental and again 'foreign' legal procedures.[46] In short Posner reads the text for its limits as an account of jurisprudence, which of course it is not, and finds it wanting. When he turns to Robin West's reading of the same text, it is to take her to task for her reading of the text as an allegory of the law and economics movement. Posner argues that Kafka's fiction cannot be the place to find a critique of bourgeois values because it is not 'realistic' enough and accuses her of being a utopian dreamer, arguing that legal reform 'would have gotten little help from reading Kafka'.[47] Again of course he reads literature here as if it were meant to be law even if it is not about law.

It is interesting to note the un-self-reflective pragmatics of his own readings in the same chapter. Here, he reads from within the discourses of the law and economics movement, mapping intertextual references onto the literature he reads from within the structures of that field (my reading of his readings not his). This is exactly the method West uses, but mapping this time from the field he characterises as 'the legal academic left' and this Posner will not have.[48] There can be only one right reading. This is precisely a case of denying even the possibility of 'pragmatically different genre conventions within different public spheres' (see above). This inflexibility about possible readings from different subject positions is a mark of his realist and positivist approach to reading in general and also explains his refusal of feminist legal readings.

Posner vacillates between naïve reader (whose modes of reading are located in popular culture, in the everyday commonsenseness of knowing *how things are*) and legal reader (who knows what the law should look like as seen from within the narrow confines of the law and economics movement and knows that literature does not look like that). He does not know he vacillates because he takes reading itself for granted as he does his own legal subjectivity and *habitus* in which there is nevertheless a great deal at stake. This *habitus* is not about to allow the speech acts of literature, or of the legal left, or of feminists, to reformulate it! It fends off all comers, relegating them to the realm of the unassimilable other, the foreign. Like the illegal immigrant, they need to be deported. The readings of this *habitus* are characterised by:

* The denial of any readings that would damage the legal self, the legal body – a denial that also constitutes a denial of the other.

---

46   *Ibid*, p 140.
47   *Ibid*, p 205.
48   *Ibid*.

- A refusal to recognise the structures of any field other than the one he inhabits. This means his readings must be assimilations to the field of reception (his field, his *habitus*) and must again be failures in the recognition of otherness and difference (for example, the difference of literary theory or literary criticism).

- A metalevel reading practice which involves a pragmatics of mapping from the broad narrative structures of the text being read to the 'landscapes' of his *habitus*, mapping what he already knows (what is already incorporated as *habitus*) onto whatever he encounters, a procedure which ensures that he will encounter in fact only what looks like what he already knows.

- The absolute absence of any reference to the actual materiality of the texts he is reading – to their language – an absence which enables the metalevel of reading by never forcing it to engage with the actual processes by which the text makes its meanings. Language does exert a force on interpretation, but only if the reader is prepared to negotiate with it.

- The blurring of the boundaries between the real and fiction.

- The reformulation of whatever he finds troubling as 'foreign', what 'they do, not what "we" do'.

- The persistence in reading only canonical English literature, a practice that permits the denial of the influence of popular culture, while of course mapping its values and beliefs into the *habitus* anyway. Literature is after all always a part of those complex intertextual and discursive formations, which constitute the culture and increasingly the global.

Now I want to argue that these reading strategies are very similar to the reading strategies of judges in courtrooms, that is, that both belong discursively to the crimino-legal complex and are produced discursively within and across the intersecting discourses of that formation. Posner's reading practices are a remarkable, but in some ways absolutely predictable example of the way disciplined and rigidly closed modes of reading can and do unselfconsciously produce the invisibility and denial of otherness, alternatives and difference: and also the control and silencing of critical and feminist readings. I want to return to feminist readings here before I turn to judges in equity to make a final demonstration of the inevitable imbrication of popular culture in legal process.

The judicial reading is to be contrasted with Alison Young's careful location of her own reading practices in *Imagining Crime*. First, her readings are theorised and self-reflexive. She knows and identifies the fields and discourses she is drawing on to make them and she knows which parts of her imagination of the imagining of crime come from popular culture and which from theories and positioning within the discourses of the disciplines where she has been trained. Unlike Posner reading literature as if it were law, she knows that she is reading crime and criminology non-criminologically, from somewhere else. She uses feminist and poststructuralist strategies to read deconstructively, taking texts apart to understand how it could be, as Foucault said when he first read Borges' account of the categorisations in a Chinese Encyclopedia, that one could think *just that* and not something else.[49] She does this knowing why she does it, in order to make the texts of crime responsible for their blurred modes of production within and at the intersections of very specific fields, including popular culture, and in order to make possible undisciplined readings which will let the texts be seen, heard, understood and read very differently.[50]

She wants to understand why certain stories become the regular, normal, transparent ways of imagining crime, how the pragmatics of reading the genres of crime become habitual and why other stories are never told and other modes of reading not engaged. She has the critical, discursive and linguistic tools to do this work and she succeeds in making the genres of crime 'mean' differently but only of course for those readers who are prepared to have their subjectivities and *habitus* reformulated by her readings. That means those who are prepared to learn to read as she does. Here she comes face to face with the 'intense and unrelenting resistance'[51] within the crimino-legal complex to the questions posed by feminism, a resistance that is also played out in Posner's text.[52]

Her readings of detective fiction are particularly instructive. She begins by asking 'what can be learned about crime and the law through reading detective fictions'.[53] She makes a distinction between her own experience as a reader of such fiction, 'once a pure consumer of suspense (who experienced the visceral sensibilia of the text)', then having written about detective fiction, a reader who became a 'critic (who sought the sense of the text), making pencil notes in the margins and sticking post-its on the

---

49   Foucault, 1970, p xv.

50   Young, 1996, p 42.

51   *Ibid.*

52   Note that Posner, 1998, Chapter 10, also denies the narrativity of law or the need for different legal stories. He dismisses a whole body of feminist scholarship which has argued this need without even beginning to understand what the importance of narrative to legal analysis might be. Posner does address the issues of recent literary and cultural theory in Part Two of his book but what he has learned from reading in these areas remains limited: that interpretation is always relative and that one does not become a better reader by studying linguistics. Well, perhaps not, but the sophisticated modes of reading engaged in by Young, 1996, and other feminists, do take language and semiotics seriously, do depend for their tools and skills on the 'linguistic turn' in the human sciences and are discursively very sophisticated.

53   Young, 1996, p 80.

pages'.[54] This is of course precisely the kind of self-conscious reader that Posner is not. Many of her analytical comments on the genre of detective fiction also seem relevant here:

- Thus, the formula constitutes the general, against which the variations in detective or location constitute the particular to which the reader responds. The crimino-legal convention has always been to impose the general over the particular (thus, law is applied to the facts, or rules to the evidence).

- Criminology oscillated between, on the one hand, a desire to eliminate criminality, and, on the other, an acceptance of its inevitability and the concomitant need to manage its consequences ... In both versions, however, criminality is reduced to the observable phenomena of the psyche, the body or the environment. The scientism of the management strategies that won out deployed a positivist rationality, which produced, in detective fiction, the detective as positivist: he discovers and interprets the crime according to its observable phenomena.

- The city as sign is therefore accompanied by the figure of the detective as semiotician, able to decode the meaning of the city.

- Holmes and Dupin, for example, act like knowing seers at the centre of the social panopticon. Their deductive techniques make everything apparent; within such a *transparent* society, meaning becomes clear, ambiguity is erased.

- The detective method is precisely a *method* ... All detectives operate their method as a mode of translation, which converts the random into the connected, the circumstantial into the consequential, and the indefinite into the definite.

- The detective's work therefore is to make the crime come (in)to light ... Detective fiction's loyalty to 'science' or 'rationality' attempts to guarantee a link between naturalism and interpretivism ... In other words, what is suspended is a distinction between fiction (detective fiction) and reality (detection).

- In short the trauma of reading projects crime as meaninglessness and the detective as meaning.[55]

Without forcing the comparisons, this list of characteristics of detective fiction – of the detective constructed therein and the reading positions thus

---

54 *Ibid*, p 81.
55 *Ibid*, pp 84–91.

produced – matches very closely the positivist method of reading/detecting and bringing to light and the construction of self as 'knowing seer' that we have seen in Posner's legal readings of literature. There is also resonance with White's concept of justice as translation. What I want to suggest here is that this 'coincidence' binds Posner's reading practice, which is judicial even when he is reading literature, very firmly into the crimino-legal complex described by Young. Moreover that practice bears remarkable similarities to the reading practices of the detective in detective fiction and thus to the way both popular culture and criminology imagine and deal with crime: '... the detective story indulges a cultural will to hunt, capture and punish the criminal.' Thus is the judge folded into the texts of popular culture as they are folded into his *habitus*.

FEMINISTS READING JUDGES READING/WRITING EQUITY AS LAW/LORE

I want now to turn to the question of women, feminist readings and equity and try to explore some aspects of the 'economolegal complex' which is equity: the place of conscience, the site of judge-made law. Equity is of course precisely not part of the crimino-legal complex in that historically it has been argued to provide a necessary counter to the oppressions of the common law, to benefit women, particularly where their right to property in marriage is concerned, and in the Australian context, to prevail over the rules of common law if there is a conflict between the rules of the common law and the rules of equity.[56]

I want to ask what happens when judges read/write equity cases – or more properly – the everyday lives and narratives of subjects of equity – in ways which allow the aestheticisation of everyday life, that is the myths of popular culture and common sense, reconstituted as, and projected into, equitable categories (for example, conscionability, fiduciary duty, trust, marriage) to enter the space of judgment? I want to explore here what happens when judges read, like Posner, or the detective, at a metalevel (the general over the particular) which projects their own *habitus* onto the narratives they judge but is justified as apparently close analysis of legal language and terms. Thus justification is of course a dominant legal fiction. Then I want to ask what happens instead when a judge begins to read/write in ways that begin to let him hear what feminists and critical theorists have to offer and to understand why critical discourse analysis is not the same as the legal and judicial reading practices of detective fiction.

---

56   See Pether and Threadgold, 2000, p 137.

Marriage and *de facto* relations

Margaret Thornton has explored a number of equity cases heard by the NSW Court of Appeal in the 1990s which dealt with patriarchal property interests in marriage as status and which, she argues, have 'retarded' the modernisation of the status of marriage in equity.[57] She points, as Carole Pateman has done, to the curious form of the marriage contract, of which the distinctive feature is the sex act, what Pateman calls the 'sexual contract',[58] and she shows how the liberal doctrine of 'equality' for women 'redounds against them in cases of STD' (sexually transmitted debt). She comments: 'It is somewhat ironic that a contemporary liberal equality argument is being used to reproduce an outdated notion of Kantian passivity for women.'[59] She then shows how equality, the legal fiction of intent, and the unresolved issue of the presumption of indivisibility of husband wife against the interests of a third party, allow judges in equity to reproduce conventional marital relations as law in equity judgments. It is important to note here that equity has always defined the *'de facto* relationship' in opposition to 'marriage', which has an equitable status that the former does not share. This difference is reflected in the legislation. The *De Facto* Relations Act 1984 is sharply distinguished from the Australian Family Law Act.

Pether and Threadgold chose another group of judgments from the same court (1982–92) to explore the ideological debate among the judges of that court about the relationship between marriage, *de facto* relationships and women's rights therein.[60] Our focus was on the adjustment of interests in assets after the end of non-marital relationships and on the question of what exactly would be an 'equitable' solution to the judges in equity when such relationships break down.[61] In all of the judgments we looked at we found: '… more than the judgment purports: that is, certainly commonly repeated, discursively constituted sets of statements and attitudes which trace the ideological underpinnings of the judgment, and the *habitus* and investments of the judge.'[62] We analysed the intertextual chain of a series of judgments, which did sometimes change legal meanings to the point where in fact the rights of a *de facto* wife to share in the property accumulated in a relationship were recognised.[63] Then we turned to a 1993 decision of the NSW Court of

---

57 Thornton, 1997, p 487.

58 Pateman, 1988.

59 Thornton, 1997, pp 491–92.

60 Pether and Threadgold, 2000.

61 *Ibid*, pp 138–39.

62 *Ibid*, p 138.

63 *Seidler v Schallhofer* [1982] 2 NSWLR 80; *Baumgartner and Baumgartner* (1985) 2 NSWLR 406; (1987) 164 CLR 137.

Appeal[64] in which 'a new and complicating gendered ideological division among the judges on the court emerged'.[65]

The case concerned a mother's contribution to property registered in the name of adult sons, equity's imposition of a *resulting trust* and the operation of the *equitable presumption of advancement*. The *obiter dicta* of the majority judgment in this case contemplated extending the principle of the equitable presumption of advancement, which had previously been applied only to fathers, to mothers. This would allow the presumption by the judges that property bought by the mother in the name of the sons was intended to benefit them and therefore belonged to them equitably as well as legally. This presumption is countered by another equitable doctrine that when a person buys property in the name of another person, there is a *resulting trust* of the property in the name of the person who pays for it. The majority judgment decided that the *resulting trust* applied. The minority judgment argued that the extension of the principle of presumption of advancement to mothers should occur.

We have written about the essential subjectivity of the majority judgment which rejects the degendering of the presumption of advancement on the basis of 'judicially noticed facts', that is, facts that do not need to be proved because the judges know them to be so (the *habitus* at work), a kind of priestly divination at work, the knowing seer at the centre of the panopticon. In this majority judgment, these 'facts' are the judge's (Bryson J, Gleeson CJ in agreement) 'readings/writings' about what he thinks a 'widowed mother of modest means', now deceased, may have intended in 1958 in relation to two apparently 'able-bodied sons'. The mother was deceased before the matter came to judgment. Bryson J clearly believes that the mother may have been given gendered (inadequate) advice by her solicitor in 1958, but he also considers her class, the fact that she was of 'modest means', and that she would not therefore deliberately give away the only 'modest means' she had to 'able-bodied sons'. The pattern of modality and negation in the final lines of the judgment actively construct the judge's ambivalence and distaste about a situation where old ladies are made to give all they own to able-bodied sons: and thus the decision is made on the basis of an affidavit written by a dead women that she intended no such thing.

This judicial narrative (the familiar story of the bad sons from the mediascapes, intertextually derived from popular culture or embodied experience) is then rewritten as the law of the resulting trust. As we have pointed out,[66] the judgment protects these women from some men but 'fails altogether to change the system which potentially oppresses women as

---

64 *Brown v Brown* (1993) 31 NSWLR 582.
65 Pether and Threadgold, 2000, p 139.
66 *Ibid*.

category in cases of property relations'.[67] It does this by actually refusing to degender the presumption of advancement because in this case that would produce an outcome this judge would not like. Nevertheless there are suggestions in the judgment that overturning the gendered presumption (as demanded by liberal feminist legal reform) might not be inappropriate (*I would not decide – it did not apply*). The judge thinks it is probably inappropriate now and probably was in 1958. But this opinion is based on no evidence and no research.

Nor is the minority judgment all that it seems. President Kirby's minority argument is that presumption should be degendered. But this decision, despite its legal trappings, is equally subjective, equally nothing to do with gender equity in law, and a move which in this case supports the interests of the sons. He arrives at this point by strategically (and selectively) reading/writing precedent to argue that the liberal abstraction of 'the experience of human existence' demands a degendering of the presumption in line with the changing role of men and women in society. This is another instance of course of judicial notice but it is more systematic than this. In order to support his case about human experience he makes a number of extraordinarily gendered readings of women's histories and realities, none of which could be supported by actual sociological or historical research. All of them involve the aestheticisation of everyday life. That is, they are myths, neither researched nor evidenced, simply known, known by the body, incorporated into the *habitus* as what the judge simply knows and projects into law:

> ... the better view in the past was that where the payment was made by a mother – *who in those days had no obligation to maintain her child or children* – there was no presumption of advancement ...[68]

> The common law has never been held to be fixed in time. As times changed so did the common law. *There is no reason at this point in time where women play such an important role in the workplace* that they cannot make a gift to a child resulting in the presumption of advancement.[69]

These statements appear to have authority in precedent, but they remain judicial opinion. And again the liberal model of equality is used to redound against the interests of women in this case. Kirby P quotes Graycar and Morgan[70] for his own ends, deliberately misreading them, to support the 'removal of gender discrimination in the expression of the presumption' by

---

67 *Ibid*, p 145.

68 *Brown v Brown* (1993) 31 NSWLR, Kirby P, p 596, quoting from Powell J in *Oliveri v Oliveri* (29 March 1993, unreported), p 31, emphasis added.

69 *Ibid*, Kirby P, p 598 (quoting *Dagle v Dagle Estate* (1990) 70 DLR (4th) 201, Prince Edward Island CA (Can), emphasis added.

70 Graycar and Morgan, 1990.

arguing that in its present form it is 'discriminatory against men'.[71] This move would allow the sons in this case to have another right of appeal and this is what the judge recommends. Kirby cites feminist work here only to dismiss it by incorporating it into and thus assimilating it to the rhetorical performance of legal masculinity. As Thornton has also argued, 'legal method is accepted as neutral and authoritative' while feminist work is inevitably constructed as biased and partial.[72] Thus, Kirby's legally strategic reading can arrive at the equally strategic and self-conscious conclusion that to remove stereotypes only when they affect women would be inequitable. His is a very sophisticated legal reading/writing but it remains apparently ignorant of its imbrication in the narratives and myths of everyday life and popular culture precisely because, like Posner, it incorporates all that is other into law and denies the body at the scene of writing.[73] It rejects myths about 'able-bodied sons' only to construct others about a past in which mothers did not have to support their children and equality in the workplace is fully achieved. The point here is not whether the presumption should be degendered or not, but that there is no research done of any kind into the history of women's social and economic conditions, patterns in family ownership of assets or any other area which might help to arrive at an informed decision about the implications and consequences of acting in one way or the other. Judicial *habitus*, the judge as seer, continues to dominate the scene of writing.

Evans v Marmont

The same it seems to me cannot be said of the judges who decided *Evans v Marmont* (1997).[74] This is a case in which there is again a tightening up of legal meanings and definitions, a case, which re-asserts the differences between marriage and *de facto* relationships, precisely as Thornton foreshadowed.[75] It is the case in which the ideological differences between the judges in equity concerning marriage, *de facto* relations and women's property rights came to a head. The case revolved around the interpretation of s 20 of the *De Facto* Relationships Act 1984 (NSW) and depended on two precedents of which *Wallace v Stanford* (1995)[76] was preferred over *Dwyer v Kaljo* (1992).[77] Both precedents had offered interpretations of s 20 of the Act, but conflicting interpretations.

---

71 See Pether and Threadgold, 2000, pp 148–50.
72 Thornton, 1997.
73 Kirby, 1997.
74 *Evans v Marmont* (1997).
75 Thornton, 1997.
76 37 NSWLR 728.
77 27 NSWLR 728.

The controversy in the case itself revolved around the contributions of the female partner in a long term *de facto* relationship, which had come to an end. The consequences of the judicial disagreement concerning the meaning of the Act for other cases meant that the appeal in *Evans v Marmont* was decided before a 'specially constituted court of this court' (that is, the Equity Division). This also means that the meaning of the Act and ways of reading/writing it become central to this decision and that the judges focus apparently on the language of the Act, insisting that what they are doing is reading it in terms of the intentions of those who drafted it.

The majority judgments of Gleeson CJ and McLelland CJ read the paragraphs of s 20 of the Act as 'excluding any general right of a *de facto* partner to maintenance'.[78] Their reasons for judgment turn upon 'the language and structure of the Act – and the purpose of the legislation'.[79] It is clear, they argue, that it was not the intention of the Act to equate *de facto* relations with marriage.[80] No specific forms of language are adduced to prove this but the judges know that marriage involves matters of legal status and public commitment.[81] When they do finally perform something akin to a close reading it is only a reading of a discourse adjunct: 'we attach importance to the grammatical structure of s 20: *"having regard to"'* (my emphasis). The significance of this phrase is that it permits the judges in this case to refuse to go outside paras (a) and (b) of s 20 to which the 'having regard to' refers in deciding what is just and equitable.

These paragraphs are concerned only with the financial contributions of the partners to a *de facto* relationship.[82] By this focus, the judges can exclude any of the parallels with marriage, which in their view other judgments have improperly made. It also means that they do not need to take note of the sentence that follows the two paragraphs and allow themselves perhaps to make an equitable judgment based on the merits of the case not on the insistence of the lack of parallel with marriage. They go on to say that they also attach importance to the purpose of the legislation, 'as revealed by the history of the legislation' and that 'if the legislative intent of a statute is clear from its history, the words of the statute may be disregarded'.[83] So much for close reading. This judgment does however allow the woman's appeal, increasing her entitlement on the grounds that the couple had joint plans for retirement, which were not taken into proper account by the Master in the first case. The selective reading practices here are not unusual in legal

---

78   *Ibid*, p 4.
79   *Ibid*, p 14.
80   *Ibid*, p 14.
81   *Ibid*, p 15.
82   *Ibid*, p 4.
83   *Ibid*, p 18.

contexts but the claim to focus on language given the ability to disregard the words if one can establish the intention of a statute from history is remarkable. Meagher JA agrees with this judgment.

Mason P's minority judgment agrees with Priestley JA's and argues that 'having regard to' does not demand exclusive reference to paras (a) and (b) of s 20. The Act does not say 'only' he says. And the words 'make such an order ... as to [the court] seems just an equitable' imply very different things for this judge: that the Act 'means' that each case should be considered on its merits, that it gives judges discretion to stay abreast of community attitudes and does not require them to seek in history an intention that is not to be found.[84] Indeed he will go on to use precedent to argue that 'judges interpret law rather than reconstruct legislator's intentions'.[85] He refuses to accept that the Family Law Act is as different from s 20 as other judges have argued and insists on the right to judicial discretion as in the case of marriage under the Family Law Act.[86] He thus follows *Dwyer v Kaljo* which did work on the basis of judicial discretion to decide what extraneous factors should be taken into account in deciding what is equitable. He goes so far as to argue that Mahoney JA's reading of s 20 in the present case has 'narrow, unjust and unrealistic consequences'.[87] He relates the majority judgment here to 'the mischief of the law' in discriminating between marriage and *de facto* relations before the judgment in *Baumgartner v Baumgartner*.[88]

Clearly the ideological differences and subjectivities that are here at risk are serious ones but what seems very clear also reading this from somewhere else outside the law is that the law itself has no resources, not reading methods, not textual methods, to deal with the differences. Hence the arguments seem almost to become *ad hominem* – if couched in the typical politeness forms and formulas also typical of the pragmatics of the genre. What purports to be based in readings of the statute or of history or accommodation to the changing values of the community is in fact the subjective positioning of the judge on the issues derived from the scripts and narratives of popular culture and everyday life and incorporated as *habitus*. And when that positioning is unconscious and attached to a reading practice built on the subjective right of judges to judge, it can offer no way through this kind of difference of opinion and belief.

---

84 Mason P in *Evans v Marmont* (1997), pp 1 and 2.
85 *Ibid*, p 3.
86 *Ibid*, p 5.
87 *Ibid*, p 9.
88 (1987) 164 CLR 137.

Minority judgment: making a difference

Priestley JA's minority judgment is very important here then because it radically rewrites the genre of judgment in reading/writing the case. Priestley writes a different history of the legislation, involving some research into the context of its production (including the conflicting submissions and positions which are synthesised and to some extent resolved in it but in ways which must leave it an open and heteroglossic document). He refers to 'other rules set out in the NSW Interpretation Act which allow judges to look at certain written materials, additional to the writing in the statute itself, as an aid to understanding words with disputed meanings' and he identifies the NSW Law Reform Commission's *Report on de Facto Relationships* (LRC36) as such a text.[89] Here he is drawing on intertextuality and contextualisation to think about meanings and interpretations. He is beginning to theorise some aspects of judicial reading practices in ways, which at least make them visible.

But he also insists on contextualising the disputed phrases and sections of s 20 within the full context of the Act itself and this immediately produces different meanings. He is, for example, able to show that the argument about 'having regard to' is decontextualised in the majority judgment and that putting it back in context in LCR36 shows quite clearly that the provisions of the Family Law Act were seen as an appropriate model for dealing with *de facto* relationships when the Act was drafted.[90] He argues that those who understand 'having regard to' as meaning 'only' to, generally focus only on paragraph 7.52 of LRC36. If however one reads that paragraph along with paragraph 7.51, which immediately precedes it, one finds:

> 7.51 In our view, the most appropriate means of ensuring that a wide range of contributions is taken into account is to follow broadly the approach followed by the Family Law Act in relation to married couples. This would require the enactment of legislation empowering the court to make an order adjusting the property rights of *de facto* partners. The legislation should specify the circumstances in which such an order maybe made. The circumstances need not be identical with those specified in the Family Law Act, but should include cases where the court considers it just and equitable to make an order having regard to the contributions of the kind referred to in paragraph 7.46.

The paragraph goes on to discuss the support of almost all submissions, which were made, on this issue for drawing parallels between marriage and *de facto* relations. Paragraph 7.52 raises the issue of judicial discretion leading to uncertainty if judges adjust the property rights of *de facto* partners but in

---

89 NSW Law Reform Commission, 1983. See Priestley JA in *Evans v Marmont* (1997), pp 1–3.

90 *Ibid*, p 4.

general suggests that there are ways around this. Priestley also realises that this document, like the *De Facto* Act itself, is a compromise between conflicting opinions and 'could not represent a complete and definitive answer to questions which would be raised in individual cases when the bill became law'.[91] That is, he has come to understand the futility of looking for single intentions in what must be heteroglossic (many voiced) and semantically polysemic texts.

Perhaps even more importantly Priestley JA has learned a lot from feminist and critical work on and with language and discourse. He makes explicit in his judgment his understanding of the way popular culture and the everyday gets into the law through the lived body and its experiences and that all reading is done intertextually drawing on other texts to make sense of the one in hand: 'in every reader's mind there are an encyclopedia and a dictionary representing the result of that reader's whole experience of life and language.'[92] In conclusion he explains the differences within the court in terms borrowed from poststructuralist discourse analysis and argues for acceptance of difference on that basis:

> ... a judge cannot avoid being affected by ideas, words and the meanings of words outside the text itself. Differences of opinion in a case such as the present will result from these outside matters being blended somewhat differently in each judge's mind. I do not think there is anything in particular to be gained by a judge's dogmatically taking the position that only one view could possibly be right and any other not worth talking about.[93]

This may not be quite the language a poststructuralist feminist would use and it may be still a little too cognitive to account for the body at the scene of writing, but it has learned a lot from this kind of work and it does make a difference. He next sets about contextualising s 20 and its two controversial paragraphs with careful readings from other parts of the Act. He locates the places where the Act speaks of *de facto* relationships as being like marriage (s 3(1)), and refers to the proceedings for financial adjustment which empower the court to make an order under Part 3 of the Act 'where it is satisfied' that the applicant has made substantial contributions and where 'failure to make an order would result in serious injustice to the applicant'.[94] This is one of several carefully read and contextualised passages which he uses to demonstrate that the Act and s 20 of it can be read very differently from the ways in which it is read in the majority judgment. These all indicate that there is 'a wide range of discretionary assessment' available to judges in particular cases and that most of these involve treating partners in a *de facto*

---

91 *Ibid*, p 6.
92 *Ibid*, p 1.
93 *Ibid*, p 15.
94 *Ibid*, pp 8–9.

relationship in ways that are similar to married couples. This can be demonstrated textually in the language of the text. Priestley has then become a very different kind of critical legal reader. He theorises his readings/writings and makes them transparent and responsible as Young argued that such things must be. His is a minority judgment, but in the intertextually dialogic series of cases discussed above, minority judgments are frequently quoted as precedent. They enter into the circuit of judicial communication and they have effects and potential consequences.

The intertextual and subjective complexities of these judgments perform the tensions between stasis and change that characterise the law as social process and they offer a timely reminder that the body at the scene of writing, even if the scene is legal, is always produced and formed in the circuits of communication that formulate and reformulate both subjectivities and the aestheticisations of everyday life in increasingly complex and differentiated global and national contexts. These judgments also testify to the current state of play in the complex relations between feminism, law and popular culture: and the game must continue because it demonstrates the need for ethnography and history as well as theory and discourse analysis in order that we all understand better the contexts in which we write and in which we are written as we try to make visible and audible new discursive spaces and newly flexible and reformulable forms of legal and critical *habitus*.

CHAPTER 3

SHE'S WATCHING THE JUDGES: MEDIA FEEDBACK LOOPS AND WHAT JUDGES NOTICE

Isabel Karpin

INTRODUCTION

In 1999, the third division of the Supreme Court of Appeals in Rome overturned a 34-month sentence for rape because the woman was wearing jeans. Among other things, the court noted that it was 'common knowledge' that 'jeans cannot even be partly removed without the effective help of the person wearing them' and that it is 'impossible, if the victim is struggling with all her force'.[1] The source of this knowledge, its *commonness*, allowed the judges to conclude that the woman's story was implausible and that she must have consented to sex. Two questions immediately call to be answered in the face of the Appeals Court decision: (1) how might this view of tight jeans become common knowledge; and (2) how do the judiciary know it?

The 'jeans alibi', as it has come to be known, had an interesting run in the media. *New York Times'* fashion writer, Constance CR White, observed that 'Obviously, these judges have never slipped into a pair of ultra-baggy rapper or raver jeans'[2] at once an inadequate response to the tight jeans dilemma as well as a thrillingly implausible image of hipster justice. The press also focused on the apparently feminist response of far right MP Alessandra Mussolini, who rallied her colleagues to get into denim. Granddaughter of Benito, Alessandra featured in the popular media as a potent symbol of how times have changed and how the largely male judiciary have not. The *Sydney Morning Herald* reported that female Italian Supreme Court Judge, Simonetta Sotigu, 'slammed her male colleagues' saying: '[T]he appeals court is in the hands of men, often elderly, with old-fashioned ideas. Every day I have to do battle to change the mentality.'[3]

The fact that there was heavy media coverage of the ruling was not the only feature indicating popular and populist interest. *Time* magazine traced the impact of the case onto television screens and the ski fields: 'Television star Cristina Parodi left her Armani at home to go on air in denim, and

---

1 Tagliabue, 1999, p 2.
2 White, 1999, Sec B, p 11, col 1.
3 Block, 1999.

Italian ski great Deborah Compagnoni showed her true-blue solidarity from Vail, Colorado.'[4]

What then do we make of this move from judicial decision to popular cultural protest? *Time* observed that 'Ironically, the court's unpopular decision may do more than any legislation to change Italian attitudes toward sexual violence'.[5] The decision's lack of popularity suggests, however, that Italian attitudes toward sexual violence have already changed and are not in accord with those of the judiciary. Nevertheless, it is not until these representations are contested in the public sphere that a shift in cultural meaning is identified. The cultural authority of the judiciary, though clearly contested, is nevertheless very important in cementing popular codes of cultural meaning. Therefore the media response of collapsing judicial attitudes and 'Italian attitudes' recognises the authorising force of the judiciary in determining which representations are given legal force and take on the status of fact.

Angela McRobbie, feminist cultural theorist, argues that these kinds of representations are the result of a number of competing and opposing discourses. She uses the example of the construction 'single mother' to make her point by suggesting that it means something different for each of the following groups: 'the main political parties ... self-help groups, feminist groups, local community groups, pressure groups and campaigning organisations. There is therefore no "single" single mother.'[6]

'Tight jeans' are also a contested construction. In this case we have the competing discourses of the judiciary, the feminist MPs, the television star, the fashion writer and the media more generally all offering different accounts of what it means to be a woman wearing jeans.

In the case of the Appeals Court, jeans do not simply refer to the item of clothing but enable an extrapolative fantasy of fashion as prophylaxis and a material expression of consent by the woman wearing them. The judicial construction of the meaning of jeans differs markedly from that of the successful Italian women who registered a feminist impulse by shedding their workaday clothes for liberating, free and easy denim. Yet another account is offered by the fashion writer who invites us to consider more recent fashion practices of baggy and oversized jeans. Indeed, when one

---

4   Burke, 1999, p 41.

5   *Ibid*, p 41.

6   McRobbie, 1999, p 85. See, eg, Martha Fineman who deliberately attempts to rewrite single motherhood as radically subversive: 'Motherhood has always been and continues to be, a colonised concept – an event physically practiced and experienced by women but occupied, defined and given content by the core concepts of patriarchal ideology. The existence of single motherhood, particularly when it represents a deliberate choice in light of the availability of birth control and abortion, can be viewed as a practice of resistance to patriarchal ideology.' Fineman, 1995, p 217.

begins to explore it is surprising how often jeans are used as a means of explanation or an ironic device.

Italian critic, Umberto Eco, for instance, wrote about the significance of blue jeans in 1987. He noticed that wearing blue jeans made him aware of his 'exterior life' because he could not but be aware of himself wearing the jeans. In his words: '[N]ot only did the garment impose a demeanour on me: by focusing my attention on demeanour, it obliged me to live towards the exterior world.'[7] Earlier he says '[a] garment that squeezes the testicles makes a man think differently'.[8] While Eco concludes that fashion is women's enslavement, it is somewhat revealing to hear his first hand account. What makes Eco uncomfortable is not that his testicles are being squeezed but that while he wears jeans he is inevitably embodied. It is his incapacity to retreat to his mind that bothers him and leads him to suggest that women's enslavement by fashion results from their overt embodiment, which 'forc[es] them to neglect the exercise of thought'.[9] Is Eco here expressing something of what the judiciary understands when it says that the wearing of tight jeans renders the woman's consent inevitable? Is it because it signifies that she has no inner self and lives 'towards the exterior world?' Putting aside the fairly circumscribed political dimensions of Eco's argument what he does pick up on is at least the idea that jeans are semiotic devices. This is the kind of savvy that evades the judiciary but seems, however, reserved for advertising companies.

At the same time that the Italian rape decision was prominent in the global media an ad was running on Australian TV that began with a close shot of a woman whose face was contorted with pain. The camera pulled back to reveal a man by her side, gently soothing and encouraging her. Those of us familiar with television renditions of childbirth would recognise the narrative trope being deployed and would anticipate its likely ironic use. Sure enough as the camera pulls back for a full body shot, it reveals a woman struggling into (not out of) an incredibly tight fitting pair of jeans.

While the chances are slim that, even in this globalised media marketplace, there is any connection between what I see on television and what the Italian judiciary watches, we see again how jeans circulate meaning. Here they resonate with the Italian Court's view of them as representing the absurd but real fashion practices of women. But why take this reference to tight jeans so far? A feminist cultural analysis requires that we consider these mobile meanings in all their complexity. Further, a feminist legal cultural analysis requires that we consider the power of judicial comment as cultural authority to amplify and cement these

---

7   Eco, 1987, pp 191–95, quoted in Davies, 1994, p 239.
8   *Ibid*, p 238.
9   *Ibid*, p 239.

contestable meanings into incontestable fact. In so doing, it is necessary to look to the judge both as a consumer of meaning as well as a producer.

In this chapter, then, I play around with the judicial ambivalence toward the media as both an object of critique and a source of authority.[10] I do this by specifically examining the judge as audience.[11] This is a deliberate and strategic reversal of the maxim 'justice must be seen to be done' looking instead at the viewing practices of justice itself. What is significant here is that the viewing practices of judges tend to operate instructively, and authoritatively informing the reader not only what is but also what is known. I explore what it is the judges are doing with their popular cultural knowledges. I ask how this knowledge permeates their judgments and underwrites their understandings? How, in the manner of a feedback loop, does the judge reinforce their understanding of cultural meaning by reproducing it in their judgments as both social fact and authoritative source?

Television is a medium that must be read. We can learn the mechanics of media production, the institutional requirements of media systems, its inherent biases, what information is overrepresented, what is underrepresented and so on partly and precisely because much of television is 'the voice of entertainment'. Television is not conceived of as neutral or objective. However, judicial pronouncements, even if they are merely pronouncements about what people know from popular culture claim to be pronouncements of social fact.

---

10 Interestingly, PW Kahn describes a similar kind of confusion that exists in legal scholarship. He says 'We cannot study law if we are already committed to law', and a little later, 'That is, the source of authority for the scholar's argument is the same source that is now criticised for error.' Kahn, 1999, p 28. Kahn argues that to avoid this circularity, we need to stand outside the language and discourse of law and examine it as an object. But this creates a greater problem, in that it imagines we can cordon ourselves off from the systems in which we operate. It fails to recognise the inevitability of our implication in the systems we critique, instead identifying this entanglement as a methodological error for the scholar. In my paper, I show that judges similarly are not outside of media discourses, though they might imagine themselves to be, but are always implicated in and constituted by those discourses. Any cultural study of law then is not about standing outside legal discourse, but about identifying its implication in other discourses and the way that legal meaning as well as cultural meaning (as if they can be distinct) get made.

11 In this chapter, I examine the judge as a subset of that public which Richard Sherwin argues needs to be awakened to the techniques of television and the media. He says: 'in addition to reconsidering how legal representations are framed and disseminated by the media, we also need to give renewed thought to how such representations are being received by members of the public at large. At issue here is the public's ability to discern the various ways in which the conventions of popular meaning making distort legal issues and conflicts. For example, does the public adequately appreciate how TV formats skew political and legal matters towards exaggerated and simplistic ('stereotypical') meanings for ease of assimilation and heightened emotional impact? Is the public able to discount the artificially enhanced contentiousness of TV law talk for what it is – namely, the byproduct of ratings-driven need for drama? Sherwin, 2000, pp 251–52.

Judges, like everyone, are embedded in various interlinking discursive formations that produce, circulate and disseminate meaning – the discourses of law, science, and the media are obvious examples. In this sense judges are a complex audience like any other, their reactions to popular culture texts are not uniform, their interpretations may even radically diverge from each other but their accounts of popular culture do operate to circulate particular definitions as the truth.

It is important then, not simply to identify what judges notice but how their reading practices take account of the complex interplay of meaning systems or indeed how they fail to. Richard Sherwin argues, for instance, that not only have TV images and the visual logic of film lead to a 'flattening out' of legal meaning but that there is an 'institutional breakdown' when the judiciary 'converges on the same set of images as the mass media'.[12] The answer, however, is not to institute a false separation between law and popular culture but to equip the judge, lawyer and legal scholar to complicate and deconstruct systems of meaning making. Much of the discussion that follows shows how judges view themselves as privileged and discerning readers of the media message. It is important, then, to explore what judicial understanding there is of how these cultural knowledges are constituted, circulated and resisted.

One of the ways that judges show that that they have noticed something is through the legal concept of *taking judicial notice*, although a great deal of judicial noticing is done without resort to this rule of evidence. Judicial notice is the rule of evidence that allows a judge to take as fact something that has not been established by evidence. The classic Australian statement is Isaacs J's statement in *Holland v Jones* in 1917:

> The only guiding principle – apart from statute – as to judicial notice which emerges from the various recorded cases, appears to be that wherever a fact is so generally known that every ordinary person may be reasonably presumed to be aware of it the court 'notices' it, either *simpliciter* if it is at once satisfied of the fact without more, or after such information or investigation as it considers reliable and necessary in order to eliminate any reasonable doubt.[13]

In the later case of *Australian Communist Party v Commonwealth*, Dixon J formulated the test not in terms of 'every ordinary person' but rather in terms of the 'knowledge of educated men'[14] and in the 1998 case of *Damien John Simpson v The Queen*, Gaudron and McHugh JJ formulated the test as

---

12   *Ibid*, pp 4–5.
13   *Holland v Jones* (1917) 23 CLR 149, 153.
14   *Australian Communist Party v Commonwealth* (1951) 83 CLR 1, 96.

matters within the knowledge of 'every well-informed person in Australia'.[15]

Significantly, however, *Cross on Evidence* points out that 'neither a judge nor a juror may act on his personal knowledge of the facts'.[16] In other words a judge taking judicial notice makes use of general knowledge not personal knowledge and a juror makes use of their knowledge of everyday affairs.[17] It is worth asking whether popular culture – in particular the forms of popular culture disseminated through the globalised mass media – is a source of general knowledge? Is it where ordinary people or educated people or well informed people learn about the world?

Cultural studies examines, as Stuart Hall puts it: '... certain things about the constitutive and political nature of representation itself, about its complexities, about the effects of language, about textuality as a state of life and death.'[18] The remainder of this chapter will look at the way that the judiciary in Australia has developed a wholly inadequate jurisprudence of media knowledges and media effects.

JUDGES AND THE MAKING OF THE PUBLIC DOMAIN

In this section, I examine judicial comments on the role of the media as a putative public sphere. Part of that examination involves an analysis of the judiciary's understanding of the techniques of television and the media. The

---

15 *Damien John Simpson v The Queen* (1998) 155 ALR 571, 575. See also s 144 of the Evidence Act 1995 (Cth) which embodies in statute the rules relating to judicial notice of 'Matters of Common Knowledge'. It provides:

(1) Proof is not required about knowledge that is not reasonably open to question and is:

(a) common knowledge in the locality in which the proceedings is being held or generally; or

(b) capable of verification by reference to a document the authority of which cannot reasonably be questioned.

The section also provides a means by which a party can contest that knowledge so that they are not unfairly prejudiced.

16 Heydon, 1996, p 139.

17 *Ibid*. Note that Cross goes on to indicate the fineness of this distinction, particularly the acceptance that a judge may make use of local as opposed to personal knowledge and the view that specialist knowledge may be used, but must be disclosed in order to enable rebuttal. Perry and Melton suggest that judicial notice covers information gleaned from a variety of sources. They describe judicial notice as 'a broad doctrine which can be made to cover many types of information – indisputable truth, common knowledge, readily verifiable facts, social science authority, social fact assumptions – through a variety of mechanisms – brief of counsel, independent judicial research, judicial experience, judicial imagination – both on and off the record, explicit or implicit in opinions.' See Perry and Melton, 1983–84, p 634, n 7.

18 Hall, 1996, p 273.

purpose of this section is to begin to map out some of the ways in which the Australian High Court imagines that the media works.

The former Chief Justice of the Australian High Court, Anthony Mason, has suggested in the celebrated *ACTV* case[19] that the media offers a means by which the *citizen* can function, as citizen, in a representative and participatory democracy. This case was one of several in which the High Court identified an implied right to freedom of political communication in the Australian Constitution. The freedom was not a right to free speech as found in the American Constitution but a limited right pertaining only to political speech and found to exist not expressly but as a necessary concomitant of a functioning representative and responsible government.

At issue in the case, was the constitutionality of comprehensive provisions regulating political advertising on television and the radio. These provisions contained in Part IIID of the Political Broadcasts and Political Disclosures Act 1991 (Cth) placed a blanket prohibition on political advertisements during federal election periods. This did not, however, include policy launches, news, current affairs items or talk back radio programs. In support of his decision to strike down the legislation as unconstitutional, Mason identified the centrality of the media in equipping the actively participating citizen to participate effectively in representative government. The media enabled the citizen to criticise government decisions and actions. Mason says: 'The efficacy of representative government depends ... upon *free public discussion in the media* of the views of all interested persons, groups and bodies and on public participation in, and access to that discussion.'[20] Here the Chief Justice appears to collapse the media marketplace with the Habermasian public sphere of rational political discussion. In fact Mason's decision suggests an unmediated media, one that constitutes a free and neutral space of citizen interchange.

How else, then, might Mason have conceptualised this relationship? He could have begun by asking how the legislation worked alongside the institutions and discourses that are already operating in the public domain to produce the meaning systems at play. As noted TV and cultural theorist John Hartley asks: 'what institutions and what discourses are engaged in making the mediated representations of the public domain, what [does] the resulting picture of the public [look] like, and who speaks for – and to the public so created?'[21] Many legal scholars have, not surprisingly, criticised the decision on this basis. Anderson, for instance, argues that Mason's position puts media corporations on a par with the average citizen, 'protecting' both from the regulatory impulses of the nation state.[22]

---

19 *Australian Capital Television Pty Ltd v The Commonwealth of Australia* (1992) 177 CLR 106.
20 *Ibid*, p 139.
21 Hartley, 1992, p 2.
22 Anderson, 1998.

In the same case Justice Gerard Brennan, in dissent, argued that the regulations did not infringe the freedom of political communication (though he agreed such a freedom existed) because they impacted on non-rational discourses only. He stated: 'Television advertising is brief; its brevity tends to trivialise the subject; it cannot deal in any depth with the complex issues of government. Its appeal is therefore directed more to the emotions than to the intellect.'[23] It might be arguable, therefore, that Brennan did attempt to do as Hartley suggests and examine the kind of institutions engaged in making the representation as well as the discourses being utilised. However, he did so without recourse to any of the significant scholarship that exists on the mechanics of the advertising message. A critique of advertising based on its irrationality misses the point that the media is a zone in which meaning is made and contested whether through rational or irrational processes.[24] As Iain Ramsay says, 'Interpretation of and resistance to the secondary meanings in advertising by consumers is a political site for struggle over the management of meaning in society.'[25] So far, the judiciary has felt no compunction in attributing to the media certain effects based on what I can only suppose is some kind of judicial instinct. However, if, indeed, the judiciary is going to claim an understanding of the media it needs to have the capacity to deconstruct media content. In effect, this means it needs to be schooled in the techniques and analysis of cultural studies.

Legal scholars, too, need to begin to come to grips with the way that meaning is made and disseminated in the media age. For instance, Williams and Rosenberg argue in a similar vein to Brennan that the true effect of the legislation in the *ACTV* case would have been to further deliberative democracy not to undermine it.[26] However, while the authors are obviously right to urge an examination of the true effects of the legislation they ultimately fall into the same trap as Mason, since they and Brennan do not move beyond a simple oppositional model between good mediated speech and bad mediated speech. The idea that political communication among citizens can effectively take place only in a calm, rational and sanitised arena of debate suggests a failure to come to grips with the new mass-mediated age and the ways in which meaning is both disseminated and produced.

Interestingly, there seems to be a recognition of this in the later case of *Levy v State of Victoria*.[27] In that case although the regulation in question was found to be valid, the court held that freedom of political communication

---

23 *Australian Capital Television*, p 160. See fn 19 above.

24 A feminist analysis might also take issue with Brennan on the value of rational discourses. It is not just whether or not Brennan is right that the advertising message is irrational and inferior discourse, but also whether the distinction between rational and irrational discourse is valuable in the context of modern media forms.

25 Ramsay, 1996, p 141.

26 Rosenberg and Williams, 1997.

27 (1997) 146 ALR 248.

extended to non-rational discourse. Levy challenged the constitutional validity of Regulation 5 of the Wildlife (Game) (Hunting Season) Regulations 1994, which prohibited unlicensed persons from entering into specified duck-shooting areas. Mr Levy argued that the regulation infringed his freedom to protest against duck-shooting which he had been doing each season by collecting dead and injured birds of endangered and protected species and displaying them to the media.[28] In determining whether this constituted protected political communication Toohey J and Gummow J stated:

> It may be conceded that television coverage of actual events occurring within the permitted hunting areas during periods specified in reg 5(1) would attract public attention to those protesting duck shooting issues, even if *it would portray or stimulate appeals to emotion rather than to reason. The appeal to reason cannot be said to be or ever have been, an essential ingredient of political communication or discussion* [my emphasis].[29]

In the same case, McHugh J spoke specifically of the significance of television when he said:

> Furthermore, the constitutional implication that protects the freedom is not confined to invalidating laws that prohibit or regulate communications. In appropriate situations, the implication will invalidate laws that effectively burden communications by denying the members of the Australian community the opportunity to communicate with each other on political and government matters relating to the Commonwealth ... *That is particularly true of television which is probably the most effective medium in the modern world for communicating with large masses of people* [my emphasis].[30]

McHugh referred positively to the remarks of Mr Castan QC, who appeared for the plaintiff, that:

> The impact of television depiction of the actual perpetuation of cruelty, whether to humans or to other living creatures, has a dramatic impact that is totally different [from] saying, 'This is not a good idea'.[31]

Justice McHugh then goes on:

> Not much experience of television is needed to accept the truth of this observation. No one could fail to understand the impact of the war in Vietnam on the civilian population after seeing the picture of a terror-stricken, naked child running away from her burning village. Such an image probably had more to do with influencing United States public opinion against the war in

---

28 While the Court agreed that the protest constituted protected political communication, Levy was nevertheless unsuccessful because the regulations were viewed as appropriate and adapted to the purposes of the legislature which were to ensure the safety of all involved.

29 *Levy v State of Victoria* (1997) 189 CLR 579, p 613.

30 *Ibid*, pp 623–24.

31 *Ibid*.

Vietnam than any editorial of the the *New York Times* or *Washington Post*. It can send a more persuasive message to the public than any reasoned argument. Without the opportunity to use the medium of television, the citizen cannot make use of its unique communicative powers. Because that is so, the constitutional implication protecting freedom of communication also protects the opportunity to make use of the medium of television.[32]

Clearly then, judges are both participants in and commentators on the 'public domain'. Not the public domain of the Greek agora, or even Habermas' public sphere,[33] but a public domain of mass mediated popular pleasures and common knowledges. The judge's theorising of the way the media works by appealing to emotions, not reason, as per Toohey and Gummow, or by its pervasive and dramatic impact as per McHugh forms an essential component of any analysis of judicial cultural literacy. The judge is both audience and *de facto* cultural studies scholar. By uncovering the assumptions that inform the reading and consumption practices of judges we can identify how it is that certain ways of reading media texts are given authority and universalised as ways of knowing the world. It is important to look not just at what judges notice but also at what they do not notice and what is at stake in their noticing. For example, what articulation of gender or race or other marginalised identities are they trying to reproduce or constitute?

This is particularly important if one accepts that the contest over meaning production is vigorous. Any critique of judicial decision making then, must take account of the judiciary as a very particular kind of audience – one that is both an audience like any other but also simultaneously constituting itself as a filter (or reader) for another audience.

WATCHING THE JUDGES WATCHING …
OR LISTENING OR READING OR SURFING THE NET

David Morley has described the history of audience studies as a 'series of oscillations between perspectives which have stressed the power of the text (or message) over its audience and perspectives which have stressed the barriers "protecting" the audience from potential effects of the message'.[34] The audience that tends to be imagined in the context of these oscillations is a mass audience. How do things change when the audience is the judiciary?

One instance in which a clear division of cultural knowledges between the judicial audience and the mass audience is found in the case of *Bond*

---

32 *Ibid.*
33 Habermas, 1989.
34 Morley, 1991, p 16.

Corporation Holdings Ltd v Australian Broadcasting Corp.[35] In this case Justice Michael Kirby, then President of the Court of Appeal, said:

> Most judges occasionally listen to the radio. They are entitled to take note that the programme (PM) is a major item of the respondent's current affairs service. It has a large audience and is broadcast throughout the country. It is generally speaking, a serious and responsible programme, making an important contribution to the community's understanding of news events at home and abroad. These very features attract to its audience, people of sophistication and intellectual discernment. But there is also a mass audience of ordinary citizens many of whom (it may be inferred) listen to it on their journeys home from work or when otherwise distracted by evening chores.[36]

Kirby is providing a kind of description of judicial reception, splitting the audience into sophisticates and a mass audience. The judicial listener, while obviously included in the first group, also presumes to have a sociological understanding of the reception practices of the latter. This is borne out later in the judgment where Kirby, arguing that the jury should be allowed to determine whether a defamatory imputation against Bond Corp occurred in the context of the PM programme, says:

> In my respectful opinion this is a reason, out of the proper sense of intellectual humility and respect for the primacy of the jury, for judges to pause long and hard before they withdraw imputations from the jury. Some would consider it presumptuous for judges (many of whom lead narrow lives and some of whom may not even listen to the wireless) to assert that they know what reasonable fellow citizens will make of a broadcast.[37]

It is clear then that any examination of the judicial audience must take account of its positioning as commentator on the general audience. It is then worth exploring what accounts of the media and media effects the judiciary may have access to and their level of sophistication. LJ Shrum describes, for instance, research that has shown that television creates in viewers a real sense of the *unreal*. For example he reports that: 'heavy television viewers tend to give a higher estimate of the prevalence of crime and violence in the USA and higher estimates of the incidence of prostitution, alcoholism and drug abuse than do light viewers.'[38] But interestingly Shrum excludes the judge from this audience of viewers:

> The influence of Television is not, of course, confined to the uninformed, and being affected by television is not necessarily a sign of gullibility. I suspect that law professors notice the effects of television portrayals of lawyers in their

---

35 NSW CA 40031 of 1989, 28 June 1989 (unreported).
36 *Ibid*, p 2.
37 *Ibid*, p 13.
38 Shrum, 1998, p 261.

interactions with new students, practicing lawyers notice the effects in newly graduated lawyers and judges notice such effects in practicing lawyers.[39]

Note how judges themselves are not listed as subject to its effects but, rather, have a sarcastic disdain for those glassy eyed dupes. Shrum quotes Gerbner and Gross who illustrate this with an anecdote involving an exchange between a judge and a lawyer in a California Courtroom: 'During an overly heated cross-examination of a witness, the defense counsel jumped to his feet, shouting his objection: "your honor prosecution is badgering the witness!" The judge calmly replied that he had in fact also seen that objection raised on *Perry Mason* but unfortunately, such an objection was not included in the California Code.'[40]

This raises then the larger problematic for cultural studies of the meaning to be attributed to the text or message not simply the manner of its reception, though both are imbricated with the other. Stuart Hall's *encoding/decoding* model of communication is particularly useful here for its capacity to acknowledge the power relations between the message makers and the message receivers. He calls this the 'complex structure of dominance' at the same time as developing the argument that the way an audience decodes a message is not determined by its encoding. He does this by identifying five linked but distinctive moments – production, circulation, distribution, consumption and reproduction. No one moment fully guarantees the next moment and each moment has its own specific modality and conditions of existence. Halls describes production, for instance, as follows:

> The institutional structures of broadcasting, with their practices and networks of production, their organised relations and technical infrastructures, are required to produce a programme. Production, here, constructs the message. In one sense, then the circuit begins here. Of course, the production process is not without its 'discursive' aspect: it, too, is framed throughout by meanings and ideas: knowledge-in-use concerning the routines of production, historically defined technical skills, professional ideologies, institutional knowledge, definitions and assumptions, assumptions about the audience and so on frame the constitution of the programme through this production structure.[41]

While this process is obviously complex and according to Hall, is just one of the distinctive moments in the route from encoded to decoded message, it is instructive that the judicial accounts of the media message do not begin to unpack even this first production stage in the cases I discuss. More importantly there is no acknowledgment of the power structure and systems of dominance in meaning production. Hall points out the significance of what he calls 'dominant or preferred meanings'. He says: 'But we say

39   *Ibid*, p 267.
40   Shrum, 1998, p 267, quoting Gerbner and Gross, 1976.
41   Hall, 1999, p 509.

"dominant" because there exists a pattern of "preferred readings"; and these both have the institutional/political/ideological order imprinted in them and have themselves become institutionalised.'[42]

He then identifies three hypothetical positions from which decodings of televisual discourse may be constructed: (1) dominant-hegemonic positions (that is, where the viewer is operating inside the dominant code); (2) negotiated code (that is, where the viewer accords the privileged position to the dominant definitions of events while reserving the right to make a more negotiated application to local conditions); and (3) oppositional code (where the viewer detotalises the message in the preferred code in order to retotalise the message within some alternative framework of reference).[43] Morley argues that the value of Hall's theory is that it 'avoids sliding straight from the notion of a text as having a determinate meaning (which would necessarily impose itself in the same way on all members of the audience) to an equally absurd, and opposite position, in which it is assumed that the text is completely "open" to the reader and is merely the site upon which the reader constructs meaning'.[44] Hall's reading model, according to Morley, 'insists that readers are, of course, engaged in productive work, but under determinate conditions'.[45]

In the context of the judicial responses to media-as-information, this is particularly important. It acknowledges the audience's role in constituting the meanings attributed to the text while at the same time recognising that ownership, control and access to the media are forces that must be reckoned in any account of audience reception. I want then to turn to an examination of some cases in which judicial analysis of media effects is grossly under-theorised.

JUDICIAL CONSUMPTION PRACTICES

What about the judge? How does the judge decode the televisual or popular cultural material that appears in judicial determinations? The judge is positioned never simply as an audience for themselves but rather as an interpretive audience who can offer an authoritative decoding of the messages that speak to the ordinary folk. In the case of *Damien John Simpson v The Queen*,[46] the High Court of Australia had to decide whether a particular accused 'ought to have known' that his unlawful act was likely to cause death. In this particular case the question was whether the accused

---

42   *Ibid*, p 513.
43   *Ibid*, pp 515–17.
44   Morley, 1991, p 18.
45   *Ibid*, p 19.
46   (1998) 155 ALR 571.

ought to have known that the act of stabbing someone in the upper body might kill that person. In their judgment, Gaudron and McHugh JJ state: 'From an early age, Australian children learn from films, television, comics, books and newspapers that stabbing a person in the stomach, chest, back or neck is likely to kill that person if the knife blade is sharp and long enough and wielded with sufficient force ...'[47]

This strikes me as an example of a decoding somewhere between Hall's negotiated code and oppositional code. Here the message of popular cultural violence as entertainment is rewritten in forensic detail as an instruction in criminal homicide; 'stabbing a person in the stomach, chest, back or neck is likely to kill that person if the knife blade is sharp and long enough and wielded with sufficient force ...' and so on. In this sense, it is oppositional to the intent of the producers in that it operates as instructional information rather than entertainment. To the extent that popular culture aims to interrogate our emotions and play with our sense of reality – the suspension of disbelief etc – it takes the dominant intent of the producers to create the illusion of the real as literally 'the real'. But how should the judiciary interpret the effects of the violent scenes in movies or television shows? Should they take account of the production values, direction, cinematography, special effects and so on? Ben Crawford puts it like this:

> Everybody knows that the Russian roulette scenes in *The Deer Hunter* are a fabricated gimmick; but rather than detracting from the impact of the film, the knowledge makes those scenes doubly compelling. When we view *The Deer Hunter* or *Scarface* or *Robocop*, it is not their sanguinary world views that affect us; rather, it is the audacity of directors like Michael Cimino, Brian De Palma and Paul Verhoeven that becomes a source of delight. As violence exceeds the limits of meaning and of the body, spectatorship is gaily reduced to the jouissance of being 'grossed out to the max'.[48]

Yet, McHugh and Gaudron, acting in their role as interpretive audience for others, take an intensely literal reading of television and other popular cultural material and offer up that reading as a message consumed by the general population of Australian children. In the same case, Gaudron and McHugh JJ distinguish an ordinary person's knowledge from their own judicial knowledge, which they describe in the following terms:

> If a fact or circumstance is so well known that no reasonable person in the section or community would dispute it, a jury may safely infer that the accused knew it unless any denial by him raises a reasonable doubt about his or her knowledge.

> No doubt the category is narrower than the list of matters of which a court can take judicial notice. A judge called on to take judicial notice of a fact may have

---

47 *Ibid*, p 576.
48 Crawford, 1991, p 127.

regard to any fact or matter that is within the knowledge of 'every *well-informed* person in Australia' [my emphasis, footnotes omitted].[49]

It is important, however, to ask, not only who is a 'well-informed' person in Australia, but also how are they are informed and by what? Are they scholars of cultural studies informed in the techniques of the media? For instance, when the judges distinguish the well informed from the ordinarily informed are they suggesting different standards in terms of the sources of information or are they merely suggesting wider ranges of knowledges that accrue to the well informed? This is not a specious question since the decision itself suggests that ordinary folk ought to in fact take seriously the information they obtain from comics and the like in terms of identifying real life effects. However, the media savvy audiences of today are practised readers and interpreters of media forms. They read ironically and iconoclastically. Take, for example, a game cited by Ben Crawford in which the MTV game show 'Remote Control' asked 100 college students who they believed was the best endowed cartoon character. According to Crawford, the students voted overwhelmingly for Fred Flintstone. He goes on: 'However, of the Flintstones, the character college students would most like to see nude is Dino.'[50]

This is obviously a set up for students to play around with the genre of social science research, but it does reveal both the canniness and elusiveness of the spectator. How then can the judiciary so firmly assert what it is that the youth of Australia learn from comics, films, TV and the like? Crawford suggests that the 'ideal spectator is nothing more than a norm, which may be assumed by many but which is widely evaded through the "deviant" spectatorial strategies which I would suggest are ubiquitous among younger viewers.'[51]

If we turn, however, to the frame offered by Hall that there are dominant preferred readings that bear the imprint of the institutional and political order we can unpack the judicial reading set out above. Embedded within the commentary is the traditional disdain for popular culture by the judiciary. This disdain tends to be the most likely form of reference to popular culture sources that one comes across in surveying judgments for their mentions of popular culture. For example, an acting hearing officer presenting a decision as a delegate of the registrar of trade marks was prepared to take judicial notice of a fictional seaside town in a television show he has never watched precisely because he had never watched it:

I will not go into further discussion of evidence of the reputation of the television series or the notoriety of the fictitious place SUMMER BAY. I think

---

49 (1998) 155 ALR 571, p 575.
50 Crawford, 1991, p 124.
51 *Ibid*, p 123.

that the renown of both the series, and the mythical place containing the people whose drama-packed lives it captures, speak for themselves. It may be sufficient to observe that I have made it a habit never to watch the series *Home and Away*, yet am aware of the suppositious seaside town Summer Bay.[52]

Here we have common knowledge defined as that, which penetrates the judicial mind despite its noted intolerance for popular culture. While the hearing officer is only acting in the judicial mode, in my view the example is instructive because it suggest a kind of judicial positioning that one must take up in relation to popular culture when acting in that mode.

If popular culture is a degraded source of information for the judge then it is not surprising that in *Damien John Simpson v The Queen*,[53] the judiciary perceive the popular media as a place where the youth encounter violence in its most unmediated form. Interestingly, McHugh and Gaudron do not take up the well circulated view that television, comics, and movies desensitise people to the real effects of violence. To do so would allow the perpetrator to avoid responsibility by shifting the blame on to the media industry. They do, nevertheless endorse, by implication, the view that these forms are conduits for violent messages. This is a view that is preferred in certain moments of civil unrest but not endorsed, of course, by the media industry.[54] There was one case in the US where it was argued, in both criminal and civil proceedings, that a child committed a murder because of an addiction to television and consequent exposure to extensive televised violence. The argument was unsuccessful. The judge in the civil case, relying on the self-evidence of the absurdity of certain canonical works being caught in the civil claim, said: 'at the risk of overdeveloping the apparent, I suggest that the liability sought by the plaintiffs would place broadcasters in jeopardy for televising *Hamlet*, *Julius Caesar*, *Grimm's Fairy Tales*, more contemporary offerings such as *All Quiet on the Western Front*, and even the Holocaust, and indeed would render John Wayne a risk not acceptable to any but the boldest broadcasters.' This must be directly contrasted with the actions of President Bill Clinton in the wake of the Columbine High School shootings in 1999. He summoned high ranking leaders of the entertainment industry and other experts to the White House to discuss how violent incidents such as the school shootings in Littleton, Colorado might be prevented.[55] What this suggests is that two institutionally supported dominant readings operate in this context and neither of them can be taken to stand in for the decoding undertaken by all members of the general audience.

---

52 *Amalgamated Television Services Pty Ltd v Linda Cameron Pickard* (1999).

53 *Damien John Simpson v The Queen* (1998) 155 ALR 571.

54 *Zamora v Colombia Broadcasting System* 480 F Supp 199 (1979) USDC, Southern District of Florida, *per* Judge Hoeveler.

55 *New York Times*, 30 April 1999. And also Seelye, 1999, where Clinton is quoted as saying 'We cannot pretend that there is no impact on our culture and our children that is adverse if there is too much violence coming out of what they see and experience'.

While these examples offer up instances in which the use of popular culture tends to support normative or hegemonic political agendas, there are instances where a judge may use the media or popular culture to offer a source of relief to marginalised groups. A recent decision by Magistrate David Heilpern dealt with an Aborigine who had been arrested for using offensive language to a police officer – specifically the word 'fuck'.[56] In finding that the word 'fuck' was not in fact offensive in contemporary society, the magistrate referred to media sources to support his view. He said:

> Flipping through pay TV at any time of the evening one would be likely to encounter it once or twice. On free to air TV the word is now permitted – albeit with a warning. Of course warnings do not help those who flip from one channel to another. If your children like JJJ and listen to it in the morning, one cannot help be assailed by the word 'fuck' with regularity between mouthfuls of toast.

> Just the another night I was watching a PG movie – not M or MA or R and the word was used – twice. Clearly, those who rate our movies do not see it as very serious any longer, as the word has slowly shrunk down the ratings ladder over the last ten years.

> ...

> It is perhaps the internet that illustrate that community standards and technology have overtaken the law. If one searches the word on even a conservative search engine such as Infoseek, there are in excess of 2.5 million web pages with that word indexed. Of course that is if you are looking for it. But the real difficulty is that one cannot search other words without encountering 'fuck' without warning. For example searching 'please' will get you to 'fuckmeplease.com' ...[57]

Heilpern's own repeated use of the word fuck in his judgment both positions him as offender (alongside the accused) and as a consumer of mass mediated culture. This is in stark contrast to the earlier views of Justice Kirby, now of the High Court, who in *Bond Corporation Holdings* in 1989 made a sharp distinction between the judicial audience and the audience composed of would-be jurors. Recall his comments that 'many [judges] lead narrow lives and some of whom may not even listen to the wireless'. Heilpern's recognition of his own saturation in the media represents a new and, I would argue, positive turn. By recognising a shared mass culture, he neutralises the claim to affront created by membership of a marginalised group. But he does more, he allows for the complex meaning production of the mass mediated realm to permeate his judgment.

---

56 *Police v Shannon Thomas Dunn*, Dubbo Local Court, 27 August 1999 (unreported).
57 *Ibid*, pp 5–6.

In this paper, I began the task of exploring how judges consume popular culture. I looked at how they interpret the power of popular media forms and whether they distinguish themselves from the rest of the audience as either more media savvy or less interested in the influence of popular narratives. Through a series of examples in which judges have mapped contemporary social life through communications technologies, such as television, I draw attention to the ways in which culture and popular culture specifically is taken by the judiciary to express particular normative and hegemonic ways of knowing the world. These ways of knowing are, however, never identified as such but instead materialise in judicial pronouncement as social fact.

I have focused here on the way that the texts of popular culture circulate social meaning, not only among the general population, but also among those exemplars of elevated rationality – the judiciary. By exploring the way that popular culture permeates legal reasoning it becomes possible to tease out some of the other constitutive discourses of legal decisions. These are the discourses that exist apart from formal legal texts and precedents, the discourses in which judges were schooled through their education, and the knowledges that judges acquire as a consequence of background, identity, sex, sexuality, race and so on. Of course, all these knowledges are interlinked and contribute to determining the direction in which further knowledge acquisition occurs – the choice of TV viewing, for example.

Does the media (or the mass-mediated public domain) offer up a means by which judges can remain informed about, say, contemporary values, or know the things that are so generally known that every well informed person may be reasonably presumed to be aware of them? It is clear that the judge operates in a dynamic relation with the media, bringing to it a situated self that may be constituted through some kind of commitment to *high culture*, or rational and objective, dispassionate judging, or which may be progressive and interested in mass culture. Having ventured this far, it is important to take the next step and explore the extent to which marginalisation or disadvantage contribute to whether judges use popular culture narratives to provide crucial context in areas where they have no personal experience or background.

What is not clear is what this all means for law. While l agree with Sherwin that it is difficult to discern a line between law and popular culture, I am perhaps not as pessimistic as he is about this fact. Sherwin says for instance: 'The customary balance within the legal system among disparate forms of knowledge, discourse and power is under great strain, and is at risk of breaking down.'[58] Later he concludes by saying: 'Common sense and to an increasing extent legal discourse and knowledge are showing signs of

---

58 Sherwin, 2000, p 4.

collapsing into the same gratification-based esthetic that dominates contemporary popular culture.'[59]

But what is most clear from the study I have undertaken is that the judiciary continues to have a say and a stake in what gets counted as the real. Once a judge has absorbed a piece of cultural knowledge they make it real. To return to the case with which I began, we see that the male fantasy that women's consent to sex can be read from their clothing is elevated to new heights when given a judicial imprimatur. The judges transform this contestable knowledge into legal 'fact'. It is questionable then what is the larger problem for law: the fantasies the media portrays about the law or the judicial fantasy of themselves as discerning unembedded consumer.

---

59   *Ibid*, p 241.

PART THREE

TESTAMENT AND TEXTUALITY

Justice

After a game of blindman's-buff
and another with the kitchen scales
where we tried to weigh up
how much fun we were having
we noticed an apparition
We offered it some wine and some cake
along with an explanation of the
difference between invitation and
coercion and it took a small step ...
and was tantalized into the shape
of a woman

But everything was out of reach;
she was unable to digest food;
to hold her chin up to philosophy
and we went back inside
to have a fight about whether
to play Little Armies or Big Armies

A short time later
we were all dead

But she

She remains standing forever
where her son sometimes stood:
like Richter's Narcissus
falling out of love with his image

MTC Cronin

CHAPTER 4

LEGAL SENSATIONS: SEXUALITY, TEXTUALITY AND EVIDENCE IN A VICTORIAN MURDER TRIAL

Rosanne Kennedy

INTRODUCTION

In 1857 Madeleine Smith, the 21 year old daughter of a well to do Scottish family, was tried for murdering her lover, Emile L'Angelier. L'Angelier, a 31 year old clerk from Jersey, had died of arsenic poisoning. Shortly before his death, he told a friend that Madeleine wished to break off their illicit engagement; he had heard that she had become engaged to a man approved by her father. When Madeleine asked L'Angelier to return her letters, which revealed the intimate nature of their relationship, he threatened to give them to her father. Although her father was advised to secure the letters before the police did, he simply questioned his daughter, who denied the relationship. After the police discovered the letters, Madeleine was arrested and tried for murder, a capital offence. Due to public interest in the trial, the court was forced to issue orders that no money be taken at the door.

It was not only the facts of the case, but the law's technologies of proof – that is, the methods the prosecution used to expose Smith's transgressive sexual behaviour to a curious and voyeuristic public – that made the trial a sensation. During the trial, all 77 of Smith's love letters were read aloud, verbatim, over two days, to rapt attention in the Victorian courtroom (L'Angelier's letters to Smith were not available, since she had destroyed them to prevent her father from discovering the affair). Madeleine's letters were presented as evidence that she had the motive and the opportunity to kill L'Angelier. Since she failed to date the letters, and the postmarks were often illegible, their value as evidence was limited. Nonetheless, the letters played a key role in the trial. They provided the basic elements of character and action – young woman, lover, father, maid, secret meetings, love, sex, promises made and promises broken – which are essential for narrative. What remained for the prosecution and defence was how to plot the story – that is, what kind of story to tell with the available story elements. Without the characters, settings, and details the letters provided, there would have been little story for either the prosecution or the defence to tell.

In this essay, I argue that narrative, as it is practised in criminal jury trials, is a technology of proof. By a technology of proof, I mean that narrative, together with the presentation of material artefacts, and the use of particular discourses and epistemologies within the institutionalised context of the trial, is used to construct a particular version of past events – which may then be accepted or rejected by the jury. As Paul Gewirtz has argued, in the context of the trial, the narrative has to 'conform to certain distinctive legal rules of storytelling contained in the law of evidence and procedure'.[1] To date, however, the role narrative plays in producing the meaning of evidence has not been widely investigated. This neglect stems, I believe, from the impact of the law/fact binary, which is coded in terms of a high/low opposition. In law and literature scholarship, the process of interpreting law is associated with the high culture sphere of the appellate courts, and the process of 'finding facts' is associated with the low culture sphere of trials. As William Twining notes, 'Legal theorists ... have written a great deal about the reasoning of judges ... but have paid remarkably little attention to the argumentation of advocates, especially where it is the facts ... rather than the law which is in dispute.'[2] My aim, in this paper, is to begin to deconstruct the high/low opposition that underpins law and literature scholarship by analysing the role of narrative in the legal process of 'finding' facts in criminal trials. At the same time, I hope to contribute to the development of a more theoretical approach to narrative than now dominates in law and literature scholarship. I also hope to contribute a feminist analysis to law and cultural studies, by investigating the links between textuality, sexuality and social power in the context of a criminal trial.

The text that I analyse is the *Trial of Madeleine Smith*, which was published in the *Notable British Trials* series.[3] I have selected this trial because, although conducted nearly a century and a half ago, the role of narrative in producing the meaning of evidence is explicit. This trial demonstrates, in a particularly stark way, that trial lawyers do not simply draw from the literary stock of archetypes and figures; they also contribute to, and produce, that cultural stock.

Although legal scholars have analysed various aspects of storytelling in trials, Gewirtz is one of the few to link narrative explicitly to the process of proof. He makes two claims: first, that the process of proof, underpinned by the rules of evidence, is central to law's attempt to maintain a boundary between reason and passion, the courtroom and everyday life.[4] Secondly, he contends that in criminal trials, the struggle over boundaries is '... played out over narrative construction and reception – a struggle over what stories may be told at trial, over the way stories must be told and even listened to,

---

1   Gewirtz, 1996, p 136.
2   Twining, 1990, pp 219–20.
3   Jesse, 1927.
4   Gewirtz, 1996, p 135.

over who should be the audience for a story'.[5] Gewirtz acknowledges that, despite the law's attempt to maintain boundaries between law and life, there is always pressure to let 'ordinary life' into the trial. In this essay, I will argue that the process of proof, with its demand for evidence,[6] is the vehicle through which the passions of everyday life enter into the trial. For instance, in Madeleine's trial, accounts of illicit passion and unseemly bodily details entered into the trial through the evidence of her letters. On the basis of this analysis, I argue that the inside/outside distinction – between the trial and everyday life, legal discourse and popular discourse – is a false one. As I will show, the popular is always already inside of law, in the stories that lawyers tell about the evidence, and in the methods they use to persuade the jury.

Law and literature scholars often refer to narrative in terms of 'storytelling'. The concept of 'storytelling' emphasises the natural aspect of narrative – our unique capacity, as human beings, to make sense of and order our world by telling stories about it – rather than the interpretive or meaning-producing aspects of narrative. Scholars who recommend narrative to law do so on the grounds that narrative supposedly brings out our common humanity and encourages us to empathise with the experience of people who may differ from ourselves. As Binder and Weisberg have argued, the dominant view of law as narrative is antitheoretical and sentimental. It 'imagines law as literature, but literature that is immediately accessible, unencrypted'.[7] In their view: '[T]he task of narrative criticism is not to introduce the narrative subject into the alien and alienated discourse of the law – but to read, critique, and revise the field of narrative discourse that law already is. Attention to the narratives implied and enabled by law is a necessary part of the "Cultural Studies" of law ...'[8] In this essay, I hope to contribute to the cultural studies of law by drawing on narrative theory to show how narrative produces contingent meanings for evidence. Those contingent meanings make sense not because they necessarily provide us with a factually accurate account of what happened in the past, but because they appeal to particular ideological beliefs about morality, identity and social conduct.

This essay is informed by narrative theory, which I draw on to analyse what I call the textuality of evidence. As literary critic Peter Brooks notes, law is 'an exceptional intersection of textuality and social power'.[9] In

---

5   *Ibid*, p 136.

6   Interestingly, the root of evidence is 'e' + *videre*, which in Latin means 'to see completely'. The demand for evidence is a demand for visible proof. Thus, there is an etymological link between evidence and spectacle, which means 'an object of interest, a marvel or curiosity'.

7   Binder, 2000, p 207.

8   *Ibid*, p 209.

9   Brooks, 1996.

literary and cultural studies, textuality refers to the process of making meaning. By the textuality of evidence, I mean the way in which the meaning of evidence – including both textual evidence such as love letters and material evidence such as a fingerprint – is produced. Narrative plays a key role in this process. Narrative does not simply represent, in a neutral way, the facts that can be inferred from the evidence. Rather, it orders the facts into a storyline, and in doing so, both gives meaning to the facts, and creates a context that makes it almost irresistible for listeners to supply 'missing facts'. Thus, like Carol Clover, I use the term narrative 'to mean the textual process of plot making, not ... to refer to particular stories or plots or tale types'.[10] On this analysis, the process of proof is a semiotic process in which material and textual signs, which function as 'evidence' in the context of the trial, are interpreted.[11] When these interpretations are widely accepted as an accurate representation of 'what happened', they are called 'facts'.

This analysis of the role of narrative in the process of proof has implications for how we analyse and view evidence. In criminal trials, evidence is introduced as an impartial means of establishing disputed facts, to which the appropriate law is then applied. In textbook explanations of the process of proof, inferences are said to be drawn from the evidence, and arranged in a theory of the case.[12] A textual approach to evidence interrogates fundamental legal assumptions, such as the fact/law distinction – that is, the idea that juries find facts while the judge interprets the relevant law. A textual critic would argue firstly, that facts are the product of inference and interpretation. Even when 'found' in documentary evidence, the lawyer infers that these facts are a 'true' representation of some event or occurrence that actually happened. Secondly, a textual approach would argue that facts become meaningful by being plotted in a narrative, and that often, the logic of the narrative supports inferences that are not supported by the evidence. In this sense, narrative can be said to 'produce' facts. In Smith's trial, the prosecution and the defence told two radically opposed stories about what happened and even who the 'victim' was on the basis of the same evidence. As I will show, they used different plot structures and rhetorical devices to structure the evidence into competing stories that made sense to and moved the jury.

Madeleine was a sexually transgressive woman and, not surprisingly, her trial drew on and contributed to an extensive discourse of sexuality. The narratives the prosecution and defence constructed about the evidence produced normative ideologies of gender and class. Gender also relates to the genre of the love letter, which has historically been constructed as

---

10 Clover, 1998, p 100.
11 Carlo Ginzburg (1990) has written about the circumstantial paradigm of knowledge in semiotic terms.
12 Anderson, 1991.

feminine and private. In Madeleine's trial, the process of proof was confounded by the problem of literary genre. The court faced the problem of what facts could legitimately be inferred from love letters. Love letters have their own generic requirements of excess, fantasy, duplicity, and coyness, which do not sit easily with the law's assumptions of literalism, referentiality or intentionalism.

TEXTS AS EVIDENCE

Madeleine Smith's trial for murder took place in Glasgow in June 1857. The indictment charged her with administering arsenic with the intent to murder L'Angelier twice in February 1857, and with murdering him by arsenic on 22 March 1857.[13] The issues before the court were whether she possessed arsenic and whether she had the opportunity to poison him on the occasions cited. Since there were no eyewitnesses, the prosecution had to prove its case on the basis of circumstantial evidence. Her letters were presented as evidence that she had the motive and the opportunity to kill L'Angelier. In addition to Smith's letters, the prosecution submitted two other types of textual evidence – poison registers and L'Angelier's pocket diary. The distinctions that the judges, the Chief Advocate and the Solicitor General made between these three types of textual evidence reveal their assumptions about literary genres, the appropriate methods for interpreting them, and the possible evidential value of each.

As a means of documenting the sale of dangerous substances, the government required that anyone who bought arsenic must sign his or her name in a poison register, along with the date of the transaction. On two occasions in the six weeks preceding L'Angelier's death, Smith had bought and signed for arsenic at two apothecary shops. As a documentary record regulated by law, the poison registers were treated as *prima facie* evidence that Smith had bought arsenic on the dates noted. As *prima facie* evidence, facts are treated as 'given' rather than the product of interpretation. Since she admitted as much, there was no dispute about the meaning of the registers.

The second type of textual evidence, which raised the only significant point of law in the trial, was L'Angelier's pocket diary. In it, he noted that he had met with Madeleine for 'a few moments' on the evening of his first illness and 'passed two pleasant hour [*sic*] with M in the Drawing Room' on the evening of his second illness.[14] If the appointments recorded in the diary were accepted as establishing facts, the diary would have been damning

---

13 Jesse, 1927, p 148.
14 *Ibid*, p 407.

evidence against Madeleine – far more damning than her letters. The trial turned in Madeleine's favour when two of the three judges excluded the diary. The Solicitor General argued that the diary should be admitted on the grounds that '[t]he entries in it were made in the shape in which the book intended they should be made, that is, in the spaces ruled off and set apart for that purpose'.[15] Two judges disagreed, arguing that the factual value of the diary was dubious because it did not record appointments on a daily schedule, and was proved, on some occasions, to be inaccurate.

In addition to citing its dubious factual value, the judges gave other reasons for not allowing the diary. Their reasoning is worth quoting because it reveals gendered assumptions about writing, privacy and the protection of the law. Two of the judges argued that a man's diary should be protected from the public gaze because the author, in choosing the genre of a diary, clearly indicated that he did not intend the writing to become public. In the words of one judge, '[a] mere writing, in the way of memorandum or entry in a book, in the sole custody of the writer till his death ... [by] [i]ts very nature showed that is was not intended for communication'.[16] They also argued against admitting L'Angelier's diary on the ground that men should be able to fantasise without concern of future prosecution. As one judge pointed out: 'One could not tell how many documents might exist and be found in the repositories of a deceased person; a man might have threatened another, he might have hatred against him, and be determined to revenge himself, and what entries might he not make in a diary for this purpose?'[17] Another judge agreed, arguing that a writing not intended for communication 'might be an idle, purposeless piece of writing, or it might be a record of unfounded suspicions and malicious charges, treasured up by hostile and malignant feelings in a moody, spiteful mind'.[18]

Although the judges respected a man's right to fantasise, they did not consider the question of fantasy and desire in relation to the genre of the love letter. Instead, the prosecution lawyers treated Smith's letters as a documentary record of the affair. However, they lacked vital details, such as dates of encounters, and there were heated disputes concerning when crucial letters may have been written. This uncertainty meant that the prosecutor had to arrange the letters to construct a sequence on the basis of the story that made the most sense, in his mind, of the evidence. In a letter that the prosecution alleged referred to L'Angelier's second illness, Smith wrote: 'You did look bad Sunday night and Monday morning. I think you got sick with walking home so late – and the long want of food, so the next

---

15   *Ibid*, p 148.
16   *Ibid*, p 154.
17   *Ibid*, pp 152–53.
18   *Ibid*, p 154.

time we meet I shall make you eat a loaf of bread before you go out.'[19] The prosecution argued that this letter indicated that she had seen him on the Sunday night in question, and thus had the chance to poison him. The letter was undated, and the defence countered that it could have referred to any Sunday and Monday during the affair. Similarly, before his fatal attack, Smith had written to L'Angelier to arrange a meeting for Thursday night, but she did not realise he was out of town and would not receive the letter in time to meet her. On Saturday, she wrote another letter, asking him why he had not come and asking him to meet her that night. He received the letter too late to return to town on Saturday evening, but he did return on Sunday, the evening he was fatally poisoned. The prosecution argued, on the basis of the above two letters, that it could be inferred that Smith would have waited for L'Angelier on Sunday night, and that when he left his lodgings at 9 pm, he certainly went to visit her. (She alleged, in her sworn statement, that she had been asleep on Sunday night, and her younger sister, with whom she shared a room, testified to that effect.) On the basis of the judges' reasoning, Smith's letters, like L'Angelier's diary, should have been dismissed on the ground that they constituted an uncertain factual record, and that she did not intend them to be made public.

Today, in light of discussions of the performative construction of gendered subjectivities, a feminist reading of the letters would analyse Smith's attempt to fashion a sexual subjectivity that neither wholly conformed to nor wholly refused the gendered norms of her culture. In the letters, she constructs multiple and often conflicting subject positions. In the early stage of the correspondence, when she suggests to L'Angelier that she should stop writing because her father disapproves, she constructs herself as the obedient daughter. Later, she becomes bolder, and seems to enjoy the intrigue of arranging secret meetings. When she eventually becomes L'Angelier's lover, she takes up two conflicting positions. On the one hand, she obviously enjoys being a sexual subject and inscribing her desires in her letters. Thus, she writes of the pleasure 'of being fondeled' [sic] by her lover. Once they become lovers, however, he chastises her for giving way to his demands too easily. In response, she justifies her sexual desires in terms of her status as his 'true wife'. Thus she tells him that '[o]ur intimacy has not been *criminal*, and I am your wife before God – so it has been no sin – our loving each other'.[20] In another letter, she indicates that she refused his advances so as to avoid being reprimanded by him, while simultaneously appealing to a discourse of 'natural sexuality' to convince him to change his mind:

> Emile, you were not pleased because I would not let you love me last night. Your last visit you said 'You would not do it again till we were married.' I said

19   *Ibid*, p 378.
20   *Ibid*, p 329.

to myself at the time well, I shall not let Emile do this again. It was a punishment to myself to be deprived of your loving me, for it is a pleasure, no one can deny that ... I did feel so ashamed after you left of having allowed you to see (any name you please to insert). But as you said at the time, I was your wife.[21]

In other letters, she casts L'Angelier in the position of the pedagogue, herself adopting the position of the girl who needs to be punished. 'I am trying to break myself of all my very bad habits, it is you I have to thank for this ... I was unkind, cruel, unloving, but it shall never be repeated. No, I am now a wife, a wife in every sense of the word, and it is my duty to conduct myself as such. Yes, I shall behave now more to your mind. I am no longer a child'.[22]

Despite the court's literalist approach to Smith's letters, the letters were taken out of the context in which they were produced – the context of an illicit love affair – and were made to tell a story of which she was not the author. In the prosecution and defence narratives, the letters provided the elements of narrative. These elements in turn became the basis for telling a mythological story about Smith's fall from chastity, a story that naturalises Victorian attitudes towards female sexuality. In the following section, I show how the prosecution and defence reduce the plurality and agency of Smith's sexual self-representations to familiar archetypal stories in which the woman is figured either as a whore (that is, she seduced L'Angelier and then, when their affair became too difficult, killed him) or as a victim (that is, he seduced her, and thus, although she probably killed him, he deserved it). Before analysing the narratives in Smith's trial, I want to consider briefly the similarities between the discourse of the sensation novel and the discourse of Madeleine's trial. I do this to suggest that the analogy between law and literature is grounded not only in practises of interpretation, as Peter Brooks has argued, but also in practices of storytelling.

THE TEXTUALITY OF EVIDENCE

Smith's trial was in many ways a harbinger of the sensation novel of the 1860s. In sensation fiction, crimes do not occur in foreign countries, or among the lower classes, but in the homes of the British aristocracy. Crimes are committed by a woman rather than a man, thereby violating the separation of private and public spheres crucial to Victorian culture.[23] The sensation novel 'exploits the disparity between apparently stable families and marriages and the horrifying secrets and extremes of passion that

21 *Ibid*, p 336.
22 *Ibid*, p 325.
23 Cvetkovich, 1992, p 45.

disrupt them, in recognition (in the words of Henry James) that the "most mysterious of mysteries" are "at our own doors"'.[24] Smith's trial included all the elements of a typical sensation plot: murder by poisoning, a young female suspect from a respected family who remained unflinchingly passive throughout the trial, the revelation of a secret love affair, the failure of patriarchal authority and the titillating details of the letters. In particular, the trial exposed the extraordinary boldness of a daughter who breached the mores of the upper class household by entertaining her lover in a maid's bedroom, and in the drawing room after her parents had gone to bed – and then documented the details, sexual and otherwise, in letters to her lover. The prosecutor, James Moncrieff, introduced the case in terms of the emergent discourse of sensation fiction, commenting that: '[T]he story is strange, in its horrors almost incredible; and none can wonder that such a story should carry a thrill of horrors into every family in the land'.[25] The case was so much like a fiction that 'without clear proof, no one would believe it.'[26]

These similarities between Smith's trial and popular sensation fiction are not gratuitous, but are rooted in a common use of a discourse of circumstances. In *The Rise of the Novel*, Ian Watt suggestively observes that circumstantial discourse constitutes the grounds for a comparison between the novel and the trial.[27] He notes that the expectations of the jury, and 'those of the novel reader coincide in many ways: both want to know "all the particulars" of a given case ... [t]he jury, in fact, takes the "circumstantial view of life", which ... [is] the characteristic outlook of the novel'.[28] Watt describes the novel's imitation of reality as a set of narrative procedures premised upon the belief that 'the novel is a full and authentic report of human experience, and is therefore under an obligation to satisfy its reader with such details of the story as the individuality of the actors concerned, the particulars of the time and places of their actions, details which are presented through a more largely referential use of language than is common in other literary forms'.[29] The discursive characteristics that Watt identifies as typical of the novel – narrative, particularity, details, individuality – also characterise the discourse of Smith's trial.

24 *Ibid*, p 45.

25 Jesse, 1927, p 188.

26 *Ibid*, p 189.

27 Watt, 1957. Literary critics such as Ian Watt and Alexander Welsh (1992) have suggested similarities between circumstantial discourse in the novel and in trials. Welsh, for instance, discusses the narrative nature of circumstantial evidence. He offers readings of the discourse of circumstantial evidence in two 18th century trials to develop a theory of strong representations, which he then uses to show how circumstantial discourse functions in the novel. Whereas Welsh dismisses the discourse of the trial as 'moralising discourse', I argue that it deserves attention as a significant site where cultural meanings are produced.

28 Watt, 1957.

29 *Ibid*, p 32.

Although Watt did not pursue the comparison between circumstantial discourse in novels and legal trials, the analogy appears particularly fertile, given that the emergence of the novel was paralleled by the emergence of a modern legal discourse of circumstantial evidence.[30] In the 19th century, as circumstantial evidence became a standard mode of proof in legal trials, a number of treatises described its theoretical basis in narrative. Alexander Burrill's *A Treatise on Circumstantial Evidence*, 1868, describes the process of reconstructing a past event from fragments of evidence. Although only the perpetrator can 'fully represent' the original event in a 'narrative of the past', he notes that the event will have:

> ... left traces, more or less numerous ... The great object of all investigation is to collect these scattered remnants and vestiges of action; to examine and compare them; to adjust them to each other, by means of indications which they themselves immediately furnish, as well as by the aid of general principles for presumptive reasoning; to ascertain, as it were, their original places and positions; and, by this means, to *reconstruct* the case ... in a state of as close approximation to the form of its original occurrence as may be practicable.[31]

In this account, the productive role of the narrator in constructing the meaning of the evidence is repressed by emphasising the inherent meaning of the evidence itself. The narrator's function is simply to elicit the meaning of signs, clues and fragments, and reconstruct them in a coherent account.

Narrative was considered to be a transparent mode of representation that added nothing to the content of the evidence. For instance, Burrill renders invisible the work of narrative ('the need to reconstruct the case') by collapsing it together with the 'principles of presumptive reasoning'. His account of circumstantial evidence can be explained in terms of Hayden White's analysis of a conventional view of narrative in history: 'The form of the discourse, the narrative, adds nothing to the content of the representations; rather it is a simulacrum of the structure and processes of real events.'[32] On this view, which sees narrative and evidence (referred to

---

30 The first English treatise on evidence was published in the mid-18th century, which also saw the first regular publication of legal trials. See Shapiro, 1991.

31 Wigmore, 1988, p 298.

32 White's analysis is worth quoting in full:

> For the narrative historian, the historical method consists in investigating the documents in order to determine what is the true or most plausible story that can be told about the events of which they are evidence. A true narrative account, according to this view, is less a product of the historian's poetic talents, as the narrative accounts of imaginary events is conceived to be, than it is a necessary result of a proper application of historical 'method'. The form of the discourse, the narrative, adds nothing to the content of the representations; rather it is a simulacrum of the structure and processes of real events. And insofar as this representation resembles the events that it represents, it can be taken as a true account. The story told in the narrative is a mimesis of the story lived in some region of historical reality and insofar as it is an accurate imitation, it is to be considered a truthful account thereof. White, 1987, p 27.

by Burrill as 'remnants and vestiges of action') as independent of each other, evidence is already meaningful outside of the narrative context. As Clover observes, 'the underlying assumption of [the rules of evidence] is that an event ... can be broken down into particles of fact that pre-exist narrative and that, scrutinised singly and initially outside of story, these fact particles will, in the mind of the beholder, assemble toward their own best explanation.'[33] Narrative, as a mode of 'reconstructing the case', is simply a transparent medium that orders already meaningful evidence into a 'coherent account' of the case.

Despite law's faith that evidence will tell its own story, narrative theorists have persuasively shown that narrative cannot be regarded as a value neutral medium. Rather, narrative actively produces the meaning of evidence. As White has argued in relation to historical evidence: '[W]hat meaning ... [story elements] have depends upon the historian's decision to configure them according to the imperatives of one plot structure or mythos rather than another – an historian chooses the plot structure that he considers most appropriate for ordering events of that kind so as to make them into a comprehensible story.'[34] He adds that '[t]he important point is that most historical sequences can be emplotted in a number of different ways, so as to provide different interpretations of those events and to endow them with meanings'.[35] On this view, the narrative is not simply produced by stringing facts together; rather, narrative archetypes pre-exist any given set of facts, and the facts are plotted in accordance with a given archetype.

White has argued, controversially, that choosing a plot structure to impose on a body of facts and inferences drawn from the evidence, and thereby endowing an historical event with 'meaning of a particular kind', is essentially a literary enterprise. In his words, '*How* a given historical situation is to be configured depends on the historian's subtlety in matching up a specific plot structure with the set of historical events that he wishes to endow with a meaning of a particular kind. This is essentially a literary, that is to say fiction-making, operation'.[36] His argument, made nearly 30 years ago, heralded the literary turn in historiography. But his point, that the contents of historical narratives are as much 'invented as found' and that the forms of these narratives 'have more in common with their counterparts in literature than they have with those in science', remains persuasive.[37] As in historiography, telling stories in trials can also be regarded as a fiction-making enterprise. Advocates must plot the inferences and facts drawn from the evidence into a story about the case, and they draw their plots from

---

33 Clover, 1998, p 103.
34 White, 1978, pp 84–85.
35 *Ibid*, pp 84–85.
36 *Ibid*, p 85.
37 *Ibid*, p 82.

narrative archetypes that pre-exist a given case. Also, as I will show, advocates 'invent' – or invite the jury to invent – some of the missing facts, the gaps left in their narratives by a lack of evidence. Yet law, like historiography, has its scientific pretensions, and does not like being called a 'fiction-making enterprise'; it bears remembering that Wigmore, in his *Principles of Judicial Proof*, attempted to put the process of proof on a scientific footing.[38]

SENSATIONAL EVIDENCE

In his closing address, the prosecutor, James Moncrieff, represents his role as that of a transparent narrator, whose job is simply to 'order' the details and the inferences into a narrative. As in Burrill's account, he implies that the evidence has already told its story, but in a way that was difficult for the jury to follow:

> Gentlemen ... it is impossible that, during this long and protracted trial, in which we have laid before you so many elements ... of proof ... to a certain extent disjointed and unconnected ... you can have rightly appreciated the full bearing of those details on the proposition which this indictment contains. It is now my duty ... to draw these details together, and to present to you ... in a connected shape, the links of that chain of evidence which we have been engaged ... in constructing ...[39]

He represents his role as that of a handmaiden to the evidence – he would simply separate out the relations of cause and effect from the mass of details, and order the evidence in a linear form that could be easily assimilated by the jury. Moncreiff repeatedly uses the language of narrative to describe his practise of presenting the case. Like a 20th century narratologist, the prosecutor distinguishes between 'the story the evidence tells' and 'how the evidence was led', which parallels the well worn distinction between story and discourse. In narrative theory, the story refers to the elements or the components of the story, while the discourse refers to how the story is narrated. 'Our case,' he tells the jury, 'is that the administration with intent to poison was truly part of a design to kill; on the other hand, the facts connected with the death reflect and throw back light on the previous acts of administration.'[40] As every 19th century novel reader knew, in a well structured plot, the end gives meaning to everything that comes before it.

Both the prosecution and the defence structure their narratives around the same event: the loss of Smith's virginity. Her loss of virginity is used to

---

38 Wigmore, 1988.

39 Jesse, 1927, p 179.

40 *Ibid*, p 180.

structure the letters into a narrative of the relationship, with a 'before', an 'after', and a moral meaning. In the following passage, the prosecutor speaks as if the crime being tried is not murder, but rather, her loss of chastity:

> [T]he intercourse was again renewed, and in the course of 1856 ... it assumed a criminal aspect. From that time down to the end of the year, not once or twice, but, I have evidence to show, repeatedly, acts of improper connection took place ... I intend to read a few passages from the correspondence ... in order to show you – first, how far the prisoner had committed herself ... and, secondly, the moral and mental state to which she had reduced herself.[41]

The intercourse was criminal, and although the prosecutor does not have evidence of murder, he has evidence to show that acts of 'improper connection' took place.

Once the crime being tried is the loss of Smith's chastity – this, and not the death of a poor foreigner, is the real affront to bourgeois values – the issue becomes the question of who is responsible: Smith or L'Angelier? The narratives of the prosecution and the defence are structured as answers to this question. In the prosecutor's version of Smith's fall, she figures as the temptress who seduces L'Angelier for her own sexual pleasure, and when she tires of him, and he threatens to block her plans, poisons him for a more appropriate suitor. The prosecutor, accepting the ideology of marriage, assumes that by having sex with L'Angelier, Smith had made herself his property, and her father could not rightly hand her over to another man. Therefore, in threatening to expose her, L'Angelier only did what was proper:

> It will be necessary for you to take into your consideration that she had so completely committed herself by the end of the 1856, that she was, I will not say in L'Angelier's power (he was in her power), but she belonged to him, and could with honour belong to no one else. But her affection began to cool; another suitor appeared; she endeavoured to break off her connection with L'Angelier by coldness, and asked him to return her letters. He refused, and threatened to put them into the hands of her father; and it seemed to be said that this was taking of dishonourable threat.[42]

The prosecutor represents L'Angelier as a 'poor but honourable' man:

> Now gentlemen ... had matters not gone so far between these unfortunate persons, it might have been a dishonourable and ungenerous thing in a man in L'Angelier's position to take that line of conduct ... I must say, however that in the position in which the prisoner and L'Angelier stood, I do not see how he, as a man of honour, could allow this marriage with Mr Minnoch to take place and remain silent.[43]

---

41 *Ibid*, p 188.
42 *Ibid*.
43 *Ibid*, p 202.

In opposition to the prosecutor's tale of the seductress who controls her lover, the defence figures Madeleine as the victim of a lecherous seducer who was after not only her virtue, but also her family name and fortune. Leading the defence, Dean Inglis castigates his adversary for excessive moralising, telling the jury: 'I am going to ask you for something very different from commiseration ... I ask you for justice.'[44] Like the prosecutor, however, Inglis also resorts to literary analogies and characters to structure his argument. In opposition to the prosecutor's sensational narrative of horrors, the defence presents his story as one of 'romance and mystery': '... there are peculiarities in the present case of so singular a kind – there is such an air of romance and mystery investing it from beginning to end-there is something so touching and exceeding in the age, and the sex, and the social position of the accused ...'[45]

Although the defence, like the prosecution, tells a story of Smith's fall from chastity, Inglis places L'Angelier (rather than Madeleine) in the position of the protagonist. He plots the story as one of L'Angelier's intentional seduction of Madeleine, in which she is the innocent victim. In this version, L'Angelier got what he deserved. In the early stage of the relationship, when she had struck up a correspondence with L'Angelier, 'she no doubt yielded a great deal too easily to the pleasures of this new acquaintance, but pleasures of a comparatively innocent kind'.[46] She tried to break it off, and did for a time, but it started up again:

> Once more, in the spring of 1856, it would appear – the correspondence having in the interval been renewed, how, we do not know, but is it not unfair to suppose, rather on the importunate entreaty of the gentleman than on the suggestion of the lady who wrote such a letter as I have just read? – the correspondence was discovered by the family of Miss Smith.

When narrating the fateful event of Smith's loss of virginity, Inglis suddenly abandons the low discourse of romance, and instead resorts to Christian allegory. He describes Smith's apparently deliberate sexual acts as nothing less than the Temptation and Fall of Eve:

> But alas! the next scene is the most painful of all ... In the spring of 1856 the corrupting influence of the seducer was successful, and his victim fell ... And how corrupting that influence must have been! – how vile the arts to which he resorted for accomplishing his nefarious purpose, can never by proved so well as by the altered tone and language of the unhappy prisoner's letters. She had lost not her virtue merely, but ... her sense of decency. Gentlemen, whose fault was that – whose doing was that? Think you that, without temptation, without evil teaching, a poor girl falls into such depths of degradation? No. Influence

---

44 *Ibid*, p 233.
45 *Ibid*.
46 *Ibid*.

from without – most corrupting influence – can alone account for such a fall
...47

By casting L'Angelier as a 'seducer' with a 'nefarious purpose' who causes
'the victim' to fall, the defence attempts to exculpate Madeleine from
responsibility, thereby reinforcing the ideology that a young woman cannot
be a sexual subject: 'All past experience teaches us, that perfection, even in
depravity, is not rapidly attained ... that a gentle, loving girl passes at once
into the savage grandeur of a Medea, or the appalling wickedness of a
Borgia.'48 Inglis never suggests that Madeleine is innocent of the crime of
murder; rather, he casts her as a girl who has lost her innocence, but should
not be held responsible because she only murdered the devil himself.

The prosecution and defence did not content themselves with reading
the letters literally for evidence of murder. Rather, through their narratives,
they transform the meaning of the letters by reading them as an allegory of
Eve's temptation and expulsion from the Garden of Eden. The prosecution's
narrative implies that if Madeleine is guilty of sexual transgression, she is
probably guilty of murder. The defence grants that she is guilty of sexual
transgression, but insists that immorality does not constitute murder. Both
prosecution and defence, however, collaborate in producing an ideology that
reinforces the norms of femininity and class.

What implications does this view of the relationship between narrative
and the legal record have? White holds that narrative produces the meaning
of events, in that facts only attain a moral meaning once they are plotted in a
narrative. The prosecution's narrative reveals that narrative does not simply
give a moral meaning to events, it also 'produces' facts. In its story, Smith
and L'Angelier must have met on the relevant dates not because there was
incontrovertible evidence to support this inference, but because, according
to the rules of plot structure, which maintain that a narrative must not have
gaps, the meetings must have occurred. In other words, the relevant 'facts'
were a product of the narrative, rather than 'found' in the evidence. Thus,
narrative does not simply represent, in a neutral way, the facts that can be
inferred from the evidence, it orders the facts into a storyline, and in doing
so, it both gives meaning to the facts, and creates a context that makes it
almost irresistible for listeners to supply 'missing facts'. Luckily for Smith,
her defence lawyer was extremely persuasive in his ability to show that the
evidence did not support the prosecution's narrative. Although Smith was
shrouded in a cloud of suspicion, the jury acquitted her on the uniquely
Scottish verdict 'not proven', which indicated moral censure but carried no
legal punishment.

---

47   *Ibid*, p 237.
48   *Ibid*, p 242.

What difference did it make that the jury was all men? White, like Gewirtz, emphasises the role of the audience: 'What the historian brings to his consideration of the historical record is a notion of the types of configurations of events that can be recognised as stories by the audience for which he is writing.'[49] In other words, despite the differences in their narratives, the prosecutor and the defence attorney both shared with the male jurors certain preconceptions about female sexuality and subjectivity: an unmarried sexually active woman was either a whore or a seductress. One could speculate that the men in the jury identified more with Smith's father, who had lost the value of a virgin daughter, than with L'Angelier, a poor foreigner. In any case, they would not have been able to sympathise with Smith's own transgressive desire to be a sexual subject in a society that denied that women had sexual desires.

THE SEXUALITY OF EVIDENCE

Although it was obvious that the letters did not prove, beyond a reasonable doubt, the dates of crucial meetings, the prosecution nonetheless read all 77 letters in their entirety. To expose Smith so publicly by reading the letters in court, the law had to violate the public/private distinction that structured Victorian culture, and subject the defendant's private writings, and her intimate conduct, to a scrutinising public gaze. The context in which the letters were read was an inversion of the usual context in which love letters are read. Normally love letters are read in private, by the one to whom they are addressed; during the trial, the letters were read in public, in an open court that was crammed with spectators, in the light of day, with Smith on display for all to look at. The spectators were placed in the role of voyeurs. What Carole Vance writes about the Meese Commission hearings on pornography also applies to Smith's trial: 'The [reading of love letters], usually an individualistic ... practice, was here organized by the state ... The normal purpose in viewing ... was ostensibly absent, replaced instead by dutiful scrutiny and the pleasures of condemnation.'[50] The reading of a private letter – especially a love letter – in public could be viewed as a metaphorical rape. In her study of correspondence in the Romantic period, Mary Favret argues that when letters are '[r]ead as tempting boxes of private experience, detached from "the world", they become the repository for "private emotions", a confessional form whose "privacy, like virginity, invites violation"'.[51] This surveillance by the state – its act of making a spectacle of Smith – had the effect of publicly humiliating and shaming her. It also had the function of normalising feminine conduct, by showing how

---

49   White, 1978, p 84.

50   Vance, 1990, p 47.

51   Favret, 1993, p 20.

transgressive female sexuality would be treated. The judge's decision to allow the letters to be read could thus be regarded as an instance of the widespread expansion of surveillance/discipline that Foucault has documented.[52]

At the same time as serving the function of disciplining women, reading the letters, in all their graphic detail, had the paradoxical effect of producing 'sensation'. The sensation novel is so-named because it produces bodily effects such as nervous pleasure, excitement, anticipation and thrills in its readers.[53] The trial was a sensational event not merely because of the content of the case, but rather, because of the methods the prosecution used to expose Smith's sexual behaviour and shame her in public. It can be surmised that the act of reading the letters aloud in court – intimate letters that were meant to be read in private, by the person to whom they were addressed – eroticised the process of fact finding. Reading the letters in court produced the courtroom as a site of spectacle, and the trial as a sensational public event – thereby allowing onlookers to be voyeurs into the private and intimate sphere of the bedroom, while also allowing them to participate in condemning Smith. If the court does produce sensation, then it can be said not to be involved in boundary policing, but rather, taking perverse pleasure in parading the passions of everyday life before the public gaze. Although the letters did not provide conclusive evidence against her, the process of reading intimate letters in court undoubtedly made the trial far more sensational than it otherwise would have been. Hence, it can be argued that the sensational nature of the trial was an effect of the law's process of proof, a process legitimated by law. If this argument is persuasive, then law should not be viewed as solemnly attempting to shore itself up against the passions of the world 'outside' the courtroom. Rather, it should acknowledge that through the methods it deploys to prove its case, the law actively airs old passions and produces new ones. In the process, the law lures 'outsiders' (that is, voyeuristic spectators) into the hallowed sphere of the courtroom to participate in the drama it has produced.

CONCLUSION: SENSATIONALISING LAW

There is nothing surprising about the sexual story that the prosecution and defence told about Smith – it is a culturally familiar story about transgressive female sexuality. What is deserving of attention, however, is what this tells us about the place of popular culture in law. As I mentioned earlier, criminal trials, which often involve socially extreme or transgressive behavior, constitute the low, seamy and popular side of law. In trials, the

---

52 Foucault, 1977.
53 For a discussion of this aspect of sensation fiction, see Miller, 1988.

passions and messiness of everyday life intrude on the rationality of law. Given that the reading of the letters in court made the trial far more sensational than it otherwise would have been, I must disagree with Gewirtz's claim that the law of evidence maintains boundaries between law and the passions of everyday life. By contrast, I propose that rather than maintaining boundaries between the rationality of law and the passions of everyday life, the process of proof, in Smith's trial, demanded that the latter be given a loud and persistent voice in the courtroom. Rather than exercise restraint, the law spoke incessantly about sex, while loudly condemning premarital sex as 'acts of improper connection'. In Smith's trial, the legal process of proof did not constitute a boundary between inside and outside, between everyday life, with its uncontrolled passions, and law, with its preference for reason over emotion, and its exclusion of passion. Rather, evidence was the very site where inside and outside intersected. It was through the introduction of the love letters as evidence that the passions and contingencies of everyday life entered into the legal sphere of the court.

On the basis of my analysis of Smith's trial, I conclude that popular culture is not something that is outside of law, as the phrase 'law and popular culture' would leave us to believe. Through the narratives of trial lawyers, which use familiar literary structures, figures and archetypes, popular culture is central to law's practise of proof – at least as it is practised in criminal jury trials. Lawyers are not simply drawing from this literary stock of archetypes and figures; they are also contributing to, and producing, that cultural stock. Seen in this light, it is hardly surprising that so many novels and docudramas are based on real trials. On the basis of an analysis of criminal trials, we can begin to deconstruct not only the high/low, but also the inside/outside distinction that structures approaches to law. We do not have to look outside of law – to film, to the media – to examine links between law and popular culture. Law has its own site of popular culture – the trial.

CHAPTER 5

DOMESTIC VIOLENCE, DISCOURSES OF ROMANTIC LOVE, AND COMPLEX PERSONHOOD IN THE LAW[1]

Nan Seuffert[2]

I INTRODUCTION

Margaret Raby killed her husband after a history of abuse, which was described by the judge as 'effectively imprison[ing] ... [her] and then brainwash[ing] ... [her] physically, psychologically and sexually'.[3] Margaret Raby testified: 'I loved Keith very much with all my heart and I thought what I could give him, sir, with my love and psychiatric help, we could overcome what he did to me.'[4] She also testified, 'I thought what I could give him – my love, anything he wanted, would [stop the abuse] ... but it didn't.'[5] Later she testified, 'I loved him,' to which the prosecutor replied, '[a]nd he wasn't really a bad fellow, was he?'[6]

Olga Runjanjic and Erika Kontinnen were both subjected to severe violence by Edward Hill, who forced them into prostitution and virtually made slaves out of them.[7] When asked by the police, '[h]ow could you still love ... [Hill]?', Runjanjic replied, '[l]ove is strange, love is blind'.[8] It also came out at the trial that 'Erika said, "[s]ometimes I felt like I loved him".'[9] A psychiatrist who testified as an expert witness was asked: '[w]hy is it that she can say that she loved this man Hill who beat her to the point of requiring hospitalisation?'[10] After 11 years of often severe abuse and several attempts to leave, Gay Oakes killed her husband. At her trial the prosecutor

---

1 This chapter was originally published in a slightly different form in (1999) 23 MULR 211.

2 I would like to thank Terry Threadgold, Elisabeth Constable and Dana Takagi for great times, comments and support. Thanks to the University of California Humanities Research Institute for the space and time to work on this article. Thanks also to Wayne Rumbles for unsurpassed research assistance.

3 *R v Raby*, pp 1, 2.

4 *R v Raby*, Transcript of Proceedings, p 362.

5 *Ibid*, p 349.

6 *Ibid*, p 386.

7 Brodie, 1996, p 49.

8 *Ibid*, p 44, citing *R v Runjanjic, R v Kontinnen*, Transcript of Proceedings, p 20.

9 *Ibid*, citing *R v Kontinnen*, Transcript of Proceedings, p 432.

10 *Ibid*, p 24.

stated, 'you spent the last two days telling us what a terrible man he was and yet you say you still loved him'.[11]

The assumption that it is contradictory for women to love men who abuse them physically, psychologically and sexually[12] is sometimes used in cross examination of women who have been in abusive relationships to suggest that they are lying about the abuse,[13] or to impugn their credibility as witnesses. The (seemingly common-sense) logic is that it is contradictory for the woman to love someone who abuses her. If she says she loves him, then he must not have abused her, or she must be abnormal or crazy, or, at a minimum, her testimony must not be credible. My experience as an activist in the women's movement to end domestic violence suggests the possibility that some activists may be influenced by this logic. Sometimes activists are uncomfortable with, or embarrassed for, women who state that they love their abusers. This reaction may also be based on assumptions that loving an abuser is inconsistent with the violence, a sign of unbalance, or inconsistent with feminist conceptions of gender relations.

Domestic violence occurs at alarming levels in New Zealand[14] and in other countries. Overwhelmingly, the perpetrators are men,[15] and the victims are women. Almost 40% of all homicides in New Zealand are domestic-related,[16] and the vast majority of these are committed by men who kill their intimate female partners.[17] Women are more likely to be killed by a partner or former partner than by anyone else. Abusers often suffer no legal consequences as a result of their behaviour.[18] Some battered women do strike back, and kill their abusers, often after suffering many years of violence perpetrated by the men whom they kill.[19]

Feminists have made heroic efforts to combat the myth that women who 'stay' in abusive relationships are masochistic;[20] we know that the assumption that women are autonomous actors with the resources necessary to leave these relationships at any point is often erroneous,[21] and that, despite the often horrendous obstacles, many women do seek help and attempt to leave violent relationships repeatedly. We also know that these attempts may be thwarted by the abuser and others such as family members,

---

11   *R v Oakes*, Transcript of Proceedings, p 150.
12   Threadgold, 1997a, p 222.
13   See, eg, *R v Wang*, Transcript of Proceedings, p 73.
14   Morris, 1996, p 66.
15   Busch, 1993, p 128; Browne, 1987, p 8.
16   Norris, 1995, p 10.
17   *Ibid*, p 16.
18   Busch, 1992.
19   Callahan, 1994, pp 125–28.
20   Dobash, 1992, pp 158, 223–28.
21   Mahoney, 1991; Mahoney, 1992; Hoff, 1990.

clergy and social workers. We know that interventions that are successful in stopping the violence are rare.[22]

Feminists have also made heroic efforts spanning many centuries to attempt to ensure that the legal system listens to, and responds to, domestic violence appropriately.[23] Most recently these efforts have included the creation of women's organisations such as coalitions of shelters for battered women. Efforts have also included: public education; policy-making; judicial, legal personnel and police training; law reform; and health initiatives. Yet the quotes above tap into ongoing resistance to hearing the stories of battered women in all of their complexity. The complexity of the entanglement of the imagination with available stories is reflected in Avery Gordon's concept of complex personhood:

> Complex personhood means that all people (albeit in specific forms whose specificity is sometimes everything) remember and forget, are beset by contradiction, and recognize and misrecognize themselves and others. Complex personhood means that people suffer graciously and selfishly too, get stuck in the symptoms of their troubles, and also transform themselves.[24]

The stories of love that these women tell to make sense of their lives draw on discourses of romantic love:

> [T]he stories people tell about themselves, about their troubles, about their social worlds, and about their society's problems are entangled and weave between what is immediately available as a story and what their imaginations are reaching toward.[25]

The imagination is both shaped and constrained by the stories available; simultaneously it reaches beyond those discourses, exceeding their constraints.

Challenges to the credibility of women who love or loved abusive men are indications of the inability of society and the legal system to recognise' the complex personhood of these women. Some strands of dominant discourses of romantic love facilitate domestic violence by portraying abuse of women as an integral part of romantic love. Analysis of discourses of romantic love, and the courtroom dynamics in which the statements of love are made, facilitates our understanding of both the complex personhood of these women and the legal system's resistance to recognising this complexity.

In Part II of this article, I consider selected dominant discourses of romantic love. Kant's philosophical exposition of romantic love, Shakespeare's *Othello* and *Romeo and Juliet*, other literature, and popular

---

22 Gillespie, 1989.
23 Eg, Schneider, 1992; Crenshaw, 1991.
24 Gordon, 1997, p 4.
25 *Ibid.*

culture all shape, and are shaped by, dominant discourses of romantic love. The examples that I have chosen reflect themes represented in the women's statements of love in court. Analysis of these discourses reveals the sedimentation of these themes over time. Women who are subject to physical, sexual and emotional abuse may position themselves within the sedimented layers of constructions of romantic love in order to 'make sense' of their situations and as coping strategies.[26] Terry Threadgold's nuanced analysis illuminates the paradox of these women's assertions of agency in positioning themselves within these discourses, at the same time as the discourses work to constrain their statements within a framework that condones the violence.[27] Simultaneously, their statements may invoke a love that exceeds, or haunts, this narrow framework. These paradoxes and contradictions begin to reflect and refract complex personhood. The reductionist assumption that statements of love impugn these women's credibility because they are inconsistent with abuse by the male partner denies this complex personhood. It should be noted, however, that not all women who kill their abusers loved them, or so testify in court.[28] Indeed, dominant conceptions of romantic love, in addition to often perpetuating gender hierarchies, are also often racialised, culturally specific, heterosexual, and class specific.[29] These limitations of the dominant conceptions may preclude their adoption by many women.

Part III of this article invokes spectres of jurisdictions that haunt the common law. The common law evolved to protect private property. It addresses relationships as functions of private property. Peter Goodrich's richly textured work on women's courts of love analyses the common law's repression of jurisdiction over matters of love.[30] Goodrich's work brilliantly highlights the margins and spaces between the ubiquitous dualisms of the common law, from the two of relationships to the public-private dichotomy. His work sheds light on the void of the common law precedent into which these women's stories of love and domestic violence fall. Feminists' historicisations of domestic violence law reform and legal constructions of love complete the picture of the common law's historical jurisdictional focus on women as property circulating among men, the preservation of gender power differentials, and the continued exclusion of jurisdiction over romantic love in the current common law.[31] I argue that courtroom statements by abused women that they love or loved their abusers are

---

26   Threadgold, 1997a, p 222.
27   Threadgold, 1997b, p 76.
28   'I started not to love him': *R v Zhou*, Transcript of Proceedings, p 79. 'Even though I married him I have never loved him': *R v Wang*, Transcript of Proceedings, p 61.
29   With respect to class see, eg, Giles, 1995, pp 279–92.
30   Goodrich, 1996a; Goodrich, 1996b.
31   Eg, Siegel, 1996; Larson, 1993.

constrained within the common law's narrow recognition of relationships as functions of property. At the same time, these statements haunt the common law's narrow jurisdiction, highlighting the lack of precedents concerning love or relationships beyond, or outside of, property relations. The invocation of the spectre of love threatens the myth of closure of the common law[32] at the same time as it seems 'incredible'.

Part IV of this article considers the courtroom dynamics, within the context of the larger society, in which women make statements that they loved men who abused them. The combination of the constraints of discourses of romantic love, the lack of common law precedents of relationships and love into which these claims fall, and the paradoxical project of asserting agency in the act of constructing themselves as objects of love, results in a dynamic that occludes recognition of complex personhood and reproduces reductionist representations of love.

II ROMANTIC CONSTRUCTIONS OF LOVE

Statements of love in a courtroom evoke a sedimented history of constructions of love within which they are interpreted. This section considers selected discourses from that sedimentation in which women who kill their abusers may position themselves consistent with loving those abusers. It argues that denial of the complexity of such positioning, which may both draw on and exceed those discourses, and contradictorily require the assertion of agency to produce oneself as an object within those discourses, is a denial of the complex personhood of these women.

In her recent discussion of prohibitions on 'hate speech', Judith Butler is careful to recognise the reality of the wounds of hate speech.[33] At the same time, she emphasises that the wounding requires for its injury citation to a sedimented history of racism, sexism or homophobia.[34] These histories are part of the ability of the words to wound. The statement of love of an abusive man by a woman who has killed him is a citation to a sedimented history and social practice, as well as social construction, of love:

> [Romantic love] is one of the most compelling discourses by which any one of us is inscribed; throughout the world there are cultures in which individuals are educated in the 'narratives of romance' from such an early age that there is little hope of immunity.[35]

---

32 Goodrich, 1996b, pp 4–5, 137.

33 Butler, 1997, p 50.

34 Butler, 1990, pp 46–54, 139.

35 Stacey and Pearce, 1995, p 12.

The citation to a history of racism, sexism and homophobia in hate speech is a matter of much current philosophical and political debate. However, these women's citations to a sedimented history of romantic love constrain their assertions of agency at the same time as they are arguably not heard in the courtroom, and are not the subject of widespread debate. This section therefore analyses the sedimented history of love that these women cite, focusing on a few texts that reflect themes of love and abuse. Unravelling these narratives reveals the interweavings of the women's statements of love with sedimented tales of romance.

Shakespeare's love tragedies and comedies are powerful and both timely and timeless reflections of dominant discourses of romantic love. At the same time, they can be interpreted as challenging and reshaping those discourses. *Othello* and *Romeo and Juliet* are particularly relevant to my analysis of discourses of romantic love: *Othello* for its construction of female romantic love as constant in the face of abuse, and *Romeo and Juliet* for its tale of the tragic inevitability of sacrifice and suffering. These plays are also examples of the ways in which discourses of love are gendered, working in particular to bind women to men: 'love in Shakespeare ... [is] something that women feel for men'.[36] Loving men is the reason for women's existence and requires their complete devotion, body and soul. The orientation of women's whole identity around loving a man in heterosexual discourses of romantic love is not reciprocated by constructions of heterosexual masculine love; men retain their autonomous identity even though they are 'in love'.

As Threadgold has argued, *Othello* can be read as a play about a jealous, insecure, abusive husband and a wife who is loving and empathetic in the face of abuse.[37] Desdemona's character provides a good example of the paradoxes forced on abused women by the constraints of the dominant discourses within which they construct their love. Desdemona's love remains constant in the face of Othello's jealous insecurity, suspicion and abuse. These themes, especially an exaggerated jealousy, are reflected in many of the cases that I have quoted. For example, Oakes testified that some severe beatings were explained by her abuser in terms of exaggerated jealously triggered by trivial acts.[38]

Othello can be interpreted as consistent with patriarchal constructions of relationships, within which women are constructed as objects of desire or as property, and in which women submit to men's authority and act only as passive mirrors of men, reflecting them back at twice their size.[39] Within these patriarchal discourses, some commentators have interpreted

---

36 Gajowski, 1992, p 25.
37 Threadgold, 1997a, p 214.
38 *R v Oakes*, Transcript of Proceedings, pp 100–01, 108.
39 Woolf, 1929, pp 35–36.

Desdemona's character as passive, dumb and dazed.[40] The tendency among commentators is to deny her complex personhood in the same manner in which women who kill their abusers are denied complex personhood. This construction ignores the possibility of Desdemona's agency in choosing to construct her love as constant in the face of adversity, consistent with an idealised version of love:

> If she continues to love Othello because she denies his cruelty, her love is not an idealised love. If she continues to love him despite her admission and acceptance of that cruelty, her love is an idealised love, indeed.[41]

The ambiguities of these possible interpretations recognise an active role for Desdemona in constructing her love. Idealising it is a choice that both constructs and perpetuates patriarchal discourses of romantic love in which women endure abuse. At the same time, her exercise of agency in some sense exceeds those patriarchal constructions of love, allowing our imaginations to reach beyond the constraints of these available stories. The purity of her love and her steadfastness in it invokes a spectre of love that haunts the categories that attempt to constrain it.

The depth of Margaret Raby's conviction that her love could overcome the horrific abuse perpetrated upon her parallels Desdemona's steadfastness. Like Desdemona, she maintains her conviction under severe pressure from the prosecution:

> Is that going to be your stock, standard answer every time I ask you why you didn't tell anyone[?] that you loved him and that you thought your love would overcome all? – Yes – Is that what you are telling these members of the jury, that you put up with the behaviour that you say ... was inflicted upon you because you thought love would overcome all? – I thought it would get better – Tell me this: when did you first see a psychiatrist yourself?[42]

Rather than recognising Raby as a heroine, the prosecution labels her as psychologically unfit, a transformation enabled by discourses on women who testify against men in court, which is discussed below. Nevertheless, her testimony cannot be fully contained within a narrow psychological discourse. Raby's quiet conviction resists the attempt to consign her to madness, challenging our imaginations to reach beyond the constraints of that discourse.

Desdemona's exercise of agency also occurs within discourses that position women who construct themselves as objects of desire as whores. The definition of women as property and of male love as the possession of women constructs women who assert any form of agency as abnormal or

---

40 Gajowski, 1991, p 100.
41 Gajowski, 1992, p 77.
42 *R v Raby*, Transcript of Proceedings, p 363.

not real women. The act of agency in constructing oneself as an object of desire may therefore be interpreted as rendering the woman a whore. Desdemona's agency in constructing her love as absolute and idealised does not assist her in escaping her husband's conviction that she is guilty of adultery, nor his power, in a misogynist society, to construct her as a whore. It is with remarkable ease that he so constructs her, labelling her '[i]mpudent strumpet!' and asking in disbelief, '[w]hat, not a whore?'.[43] He even suggests that she is inhuman: 'Oh thou weed ... wouldst thou had never been born!'[44]

These themes of ownership and construction as whore, responded to with idealised love, are clear in *R v Runjanjic, R v Kontinnen,* where Hill literally made Runjanjic into a whore:

> The relationship was undoubtedly marked by Hill's dominance and Runjanjic's subservence. He put her to work as a prostitute. There was a consistent pattern of domineering and violent conduct by Hill towards Runjanjic. She was expected to attend to his every need, including quite trivial needs, and the price of disobedience was severe beating. Nevertheless it is clear that she loved Hill and was intensely loyal to him.[45]

It is the *connection* between these themes of prostitution, ownership and romantic love that is important in both *Othello* and *Runjanjic.* This connection circulates within dominant discourses and is available to women attempting to 'make sense' of the domestic violence in their lives.

Romeo and Juliet depicts another form of love, a tragic scenario in which 'the pleasure lies in the heightened value of love in the light of its loss.'[46] Juliet enacts the irrationality of a love that illogically increases even as she gives it, a reflection of gendered constructions of love, which expect infinite, bottomless giving from women. These types of tragedies also often involve a 'sexual division of suffering' in which 'the romantic heroines must suffer, if not die, for the tragic heroes to achieve their aspirations of universal transcendence'.[47] This story of infinite giving, lost love, sacrifice and suffering, is one that women who kill abusers might find particularly appropriate to their situation. Margaret Raby's conviction that the abuse in her life could be overcome by her giving 'anything he wanted' reflects this theme of infinite giving. Faced with a man they love who will not stop abusing them, little or no support from the legal system, the church, or family or friends to make him stop, and few, if any, options for 'leaving', these women often live a tragedy. Killing the man they love as the only

---

43   Honigmann, 1997, p 278.

44   *Ibid,* p 277.

45   (1992) 56 SASR 114, 115.

46   Stacey, 1995, p 17.

47   *Ibid.*

means of survival may actually heighten feelings of love and loss; the tragic inevitability of the situation, from which there was no other way out, may evoke romantic tragedies such as *Romeo and Juliet*. In these situations, as Terry Threadgold has said, the abusers 'in some sense, had to be killed',[48] their deaths were tragically inevitable. It is, however, generally taboo for women to try to usurp heroic (active) status.[49] Asserting agency by killing their abusers is inconsistent with this taboo. I will come back to this inconsistency in the next section.

In the philosophical tradition, Kant is credited with the 18th century's most rationalised expression of love.[50] He constructs woman as the object of love, man as the subject of love. Gendering Kant's theory reveals:

> [M]en are the Subjects in question, are the cultural authors as well as the cultural audience; and ... this might lead us to inquire more deeply into the nature of the feeling of life, of delight and pleasure that is the hallmark of the aesthetic. Might the disinterested aesthetic pleasure perchance be gendered?[51]

Kant's 'transcendental exposition' of aesthetic judgments structures love (sexual pleasure) as a connection to the beautiful. It is the male subject's feelings of pleasure, which determine whether the female object is beautiful; we do not ask women for their opinions of beauty.[52] Kant is at pains to make claims to universality for his ideal of the beautiful:

> [W]here any one is conscious that his delight in an object is with him independent of interest, it is inevitable that he should look on the object as one containing a ground of delight for all men. For, since the delight is not based on any inclination of the Subject ... but the Subject feels himself completely free in respect of the liking which he accords to the object, he can find as reason for his delight no personal conditions to which his own subjective self might alone be party.[53]

His claim that disinterested delight in the (male) subject is a sign of universal beauty facilitates constructions of men as the universal arbiters of love: 'Kantian aesthetics ... locate the beauty of women in the [male] subject – in the artist and the perceiver.'[54] It empowers individual men as the spokespeople for the universal aesthetic.

The power and control analysis of domestic violence[55] sheds light on the manner in which the objectification of women for male desire facilitates

---

48   Threadgold, 1997b, p 57.
49   Stacey, 1995, p 17.
50   Butler, 1989, p 62.
51   Kappeler, 1986, pp 54–57.
52   Kant, 1952, p 11.
53   *Ibid*, pp 50–51.
54   Butler, 1989, pp 73–74.
55   Pence, 1986.

abuse. One of the tactics of abuse is emotional abuse, which often includes attacks on self-esteem, including critiques of the woman's looks, or beauty, by the male abuser. Gay Oakes testified that her abuser 'had taken my self-esteem and sense of self-worth'.[56] The abusive nature of male power to construct women as beautiful, or, perhaps more importantly, as lacking in beauty, is masked by the social circulation of philosophical discourses that construct men as the arbiters of beauty and the subjects of love.

The role of the discipline and practice of psychology in pathologising women's responses to domestic violence is well documented.[57] Consistent with Kant's construction of women as objects, these discourses also often construct women as lacking agency. Some of the more recent literature, however, may be attempting to redress this problem through recognition of social constructions of gender. For example, the ambivalence of Desdemona's agency in constructing herself as an object is reflected in this statement: 'The work of becoming female is shaped by the necessity of learning how to become ... an "object of male desire", which inevitably must conflict with the task of becoming a subject in one's own right.'[58]

The contradiction of women's constructions of themselves as objects of desire, and as subjects of love, is also highlighted by discourses of love. The statements of women who have been in abusive relationships such as '[l]ove is strange, love is blind' and the ambiguity in the statement '[s]ometimes I felt like I loved him' may reflect not only these women's honesty with themselves regarding the abuse, but also an uneasiness with the ambiguity of constructing themselves as agents of love, especially in the face of abuse.

The song 'Every Breath You Take' by The Police[59] has been known among some activists in the movement to end domestic violence as 'the batterer's song'. The convergence of love and what have been identified as abusive tactics in this song is a reflection of the manner in which popular constructions of love facilitate abusive relationships. Women survivors of domestic violence sometimes describe the abuser at the beginning of the relationship as the perfectly attentive lover: 'women do not fall in love with batterers, but with individuals who often treat them with an almost exaggerated respect and attention, and can be extraordinarily appealing.'[60] One study has found that when couples in relationships where the male is violent describe the beginning of the relationship it is characterised by 'electrical connection' and 'extravagant illusions of romantic love'.[61] Others have noted that abusive relationships may begin with the man lavishing

---

56   *R v Oakes*, Transcript of Proceedings, p 137.
57   Dobash, 1992.
58   Goldner, 1990, p 349.
59   Padgham, 1983.
60   Dalton, 1997, p 336.
61   Goldner, 1990, p 360.

attention on the woman, always wanting to be with her and always wanting to know where she has been and what she has done.[62] This attention, especially in the context of social constructions and lived realities of women as caretakers, attention givers, and the ones responsible for keeping relationships going,[63] can be very seductive. However, due perhaps to the common law's lack of jurisdiction over love, or to a perceived inconsistency of these behaviours with abuse, these aspects of the relationship are rarely the focus of court cases. It can only be speculated then, that some women who testify that they love their abusers may be reflecting back to a period of extravagant romance.

This high level of attention turns abusive when it shifts from caring to control:

> The perpetrator's first goal appears to be the enslavement of his victim, and he accomplishes this goal by exercising despotic control over every aspect of the victim's life. But simple compliance rarely satisfies him; he appears to have a psychological need to justify his crimes, and for this he needs the victim's affirmation. Thus he relentlessly demands from his victim professions of respect, gratitude or even love.[64]

As abusive relationships progress, batterers may demand an accounting of all of the women's actions, sometimes literally every minute of every day.[65] Othello's irrational jealously, with no basis in fact, can operate coded as love to facilitate control:

> Every single day
> Every word you say
> Every game you play
> Every night you stay
> I'll be watching you.[66]

Read as an assertion of obsession of control, masked by discourses of romantic love, these lines from 'Every Breath You Take' have an ominous ring.

Another tactic of power and control is 'using male privilege', which includes such moves as treating women like servants or what has been called 'the possessive individualism of patriarchal romance'.[67] Gay Oakes testified that:

---

62 NCIWR, 1993, pp 29, 35.
63 Hoff, 1990, p 43.
64 Herman, 1992, p 75.
65 See, eg, *R v Oakes*, Transcript of Proceedings, pp 102–03.
66 Padgham, 1983.
67 Stacey, 1995, p 13.

... all sorts of things aggravated him, if the dishes weren't done, if the bed wasn't made, or the kids brought in dirt from the garden. I tried to keep the house spic and span. There were outbreaks of violence because I couldn't keep everything just so all the time.[68]

The lines '[o]h can't you see, you belong to me?'[69] seem perfectly consistent with this type of abuse. This song, probably written and certainly largely heard as a love song, illustrates the convergence of love and tactics of abuse perpetrated by men on women. It provides an illustration of how love can be constructed consistently with abuse in a relationship.

The major romantic scenarios of novels also deserve mention here. One theme of these relevant to my discussion is the power of transformation of romantic trajectories. This potential for transformation is often tied to other changes, such as a journey to a new and exotic place. The hopes of women who have abusive partners are sometimes tied to the ability of their love to transform the abuser into a better person or to the overcoming of barriers or obstacles in the name of love.[70] The abuser's violence may be constructed as a psychological barrier that can be overcome with love. These themes are evidenced by Margaret Raby's statement above that her partner's abuse could be overcome with her love and psychological counselling. Batterers sometimes construct their violence in these terms by making arguments that:

... just one more sacrifice, one more proof of her love, will end the violence and save the relationship. Since most women derive pride and self-esteem from their capacity to sustain relationships, the batterer is often able to entrap his victim by appealing to her most cherished values.[71]

It is social constructions of gender and of relationships that saddle women with responsibility for sustaining relationships. Women may be asked, implicitly or explicitly, to demonstrate their commitment by moving to a new geographical location, to allow a fresh start. These moves may represent hope for starting anew to the woman. Oakes testified that:

[His] letter told me ... that he was sorry for the way things had gone in Australia but he wasn't happy there and he wanted to be there in New Zealand with his family. He wanted me to come and join him in New Zealand. ... I loved him at that stage. I did want to try again. All the time we had been together he had always blamed me for what had gone wrong and by him saying he had been miserable in Australia and he was OK now in New Zealand it made me think he realised it wasn't all my fault after all.[72]

---

68 *R v Oakes*, Transcript of Proceedings, p 102.
69 Padgham, 1983.
70 Stacey, 1995, pp 15–16.
71 Herman, 1992, pp 82–83.
72 *R v Oakes*, Transcript of Proceedings, p 103.

The moves may also result in isolation from the woman's former community, helping to consolidate the power of the abuser.

My argument is not that women in violent relationships are masochists; nor am I denying that in a society structured by gender power differentials these constructions of romance and desire create, perpetuate and facilitate the subordination of women to men. In a situation of severely limited options, when women declare that they love the men who abuse them, they may be making sense of their situations in part by positioning themselves within these discourses. A prosecutor's challenge to a woman's statement that she loves or loved the man who abused her, which implies that such love must logically be inconsistent with abuse, forces the woman's statement into a narrow strand of constructions of love which pose it as inconsistent with male consolidation of power and control, through physical, psychological and sexual violence. The prosecutor's challenge, and the adoption of its logic by the legal system, feminists and activists, denies the complex personhood of these women, who may be both positioning themselves within constrained discourses and invoking spectres of love that exceed those discourses.

III THE COMMON LAW'S LACK OF LOVE

The common law presents obstacles to the invocation of love within its walls. Peter Goodrich has recently convincingly argued that among law's repressions is its inability to hear, or lack of jurisdiction over, matters of love.[73] Repression of any jurisdiction over love results in the return of love as a spectre haunting the jurisdiction of the common law.[74] Statements of love by abused women in court fall into this void of jurisdiction at the same time as they invoke the spectre of a jurisdiction over love. The spectre of the jurisdiction of love is important to the discussion of statements of love by women in court for at least two reasons. First, the possibility of legal jurisdiction over matters of love highlights the common law's void of jurisdiction and its consequent inability to deal with these women's statements. The lack of legal discourses with which to negotiate the implications of these statements leaves the statements open to interpretation, for example, as admissions of complicity, as discussed in Part IV. The judgments of the courts of love suggest other possible approaches. Second, the possibility that courts of love existed historically disrupts hegemonic conceptions of law as the absolute embodiment of 'reason' to the exclusion of 'emotion'. This disruption, combined with the particular focus of the

---

73 Goodrich, 1996b.
74 Goodrich, 1997, pp 283–84.

courts of love, opens possibilities for imagining jurisdictions capable of representing all of the complexities of personhood.

Historically, the common law has lacked jurisdictional and literary ability to hear matters of love, or emotions more generally, focusing instead on marriage and on women as functions of property. Nineteenth century legal discourses of marriage tended to preserve the dominant proprietary status of husbands while transforming the language of possession into a language of private affective relationships. These privacy discourses continue to perpetuate the law's repression of love and emotions more generally today, for example in the controversy over the federal Violence Against Women Act in the United States.[75] The common law generally lacks legal discourses and precedents of love within which to interpret women's statements that they love the men who abuse them.

It is commonplace to introduce a study of the history of the common law with brief reference to the historical plethora of courts and jurisdictions:

> In institutional terms, the profession of secular law or in England of common law, was simply one of numerous legal jurisdictions, a pluralism of laws which reflected the hierarchy and diversity of the sources of knowledge and representations of truth. The courts spiritual, the courts of conscience and of the church, courts of honour and of equity as well as of specific localities and activities, of cities and forests, of trade and matrimony, of war and of the seas all subsisted under different laws, forms of knowledge or sources of justice.[76]

These various jurisdictions were eventually all absorbed into one set of courts of the common law, a process brought to a logical conclusion with the merging of common law and equitable jurisdiction.[77] Goodrich argues that this process of unification was achieved through the repression of the 'plural epistemological frame', which characterised the earlier system of multiplicity.[78] The rhetoric of the common law developed to justify this repression through statements such as: '[The] common law is the appropriate measure of all issues tried in England and should be kept free of canon and civil law which are "but beggarly baggage, and arguments of brawling braines [sic]"'[79] and 'the common law is the absolute perfection of reason'.[80] While the first statement clearly privileges the common law over other named jurisdictions, the second statement defines the common law as 'the perfection of reason', relegating emotion to *not law*. This distinction

---

75 42 USCA s 13981 (West 1995).
76 Goodrich, 1996b, p 10.
77 Burrows *et al*, 1992, p 2.
78 Goodrich, 1996b, p 10.
79 *Ibid*, p 15, quoting Leslie, 1569, sig 97v and 120r.
80 *Ibid*, quoting Wood, 1720, pp 6–7.

between love and reason, or justice, is reflected back to the law in discourses of love. Shakespeare's point in *Othello* is that love is beyond reason.[81]

Emphasis on the common law's perfection of reason refers only through absence to the possibility of jurisdictions not focused absolutely on reason. Goodrich discusses one such possible jurisdiction, that of the courts of love, which created and applied 'an alternative law of the feminine public sphere, concerned exclusively with disputes over the art of love and relationships between lovers.'[82] This jurisdiction challenges current dominant corresponding dichotomies between reason and emotion, and between law and lifestyle, providing us with a means of interrupting the mutual exclusivity of these dichotomies.

Goodrich notes that the Courts of Love were women's courts.[83] The 12th century Court of the Countess of Champagne, for example, was composed of about 30 women who collectively 'delineated and adjudicated the distinct principles of love and marriage'.[84] The High Court of Love, established on St Valentine's Day in 1400, was to have jurisdiction over the rules of love, to hear disputes between lovers, and to hear appeals from other Courts of Love. It was organised in a non-hierarchical manner and the judges were selected by women after reciting poetry. Judgments were made collectively. The subject matter of the Courts of Love included contracts of love, remedies for amorous betrayal, deceit and slander of lovers, responsibilities of separated lovers and punishment of violence against women. Further, Goodrich argues that the courts often considered disputes between women lovers and between male lovers. What we might today call transgendered identifications may also have been common.[85]

The Courts of Love are said to have emphatically distinguished between love and marriage.[86] Also significant was their consistent acknowledgment of the role of love in law and law in love.[87] They may have dealt with relationships of love outside of marriage and unrelated to proprietary issues:

> [The] judgment is remarkable for its sensitivity to the space between the lovers: It addresses the relationship, rather than either party. There is no conventional victor, and no pronouncement of past fault; the judgment is neither punitive nor retributory; it speaks instead of future possibilities of the lovers' relationship.[88]

---

81 Gajowski, 1992, pp 53, 75.
82 Goodrich, 1996a, p 635.
83 Goodrich, 1996b, p 1.
84 Goodrich, 1996a, p 633.
85 *Ibid*, pp 633–40.
86 Walsh, 1982, pp 257–59.
87 Goodrich, 1996a, p 634.
88 Goodrich, 1996a, p 638.

Goodrich suggests that rather than rewarding a 'winner' with tangible monetary damages as a substitute for a property interest, the jurisdiction of love focused on the intangibles of emotions created through relationships.

The jurisdiction of the Courts of Love is contrasted with the jurisdiction of canon law, from which the common law of marriage developed.[89] The precedent of the Courts of Love defined love and marriage as mutually inconsistent.[90] The distinction between the two jurisdictions is apparent in this passage:

> The Christian institution of marriage was ... an essentially spiritual love ... A love invariably attached to an eternal being, a pure love ... The secular institution of marriage was to be a temporal shadow or emulation of its spiritual exemplar and was to be based upon an imitative obedience to an earthly father and conjugal hierarchy. The relationship of lovers adjudicated by women in the courts of love was, by contrast ... both spiritual and profane ... an investment of the soul inscribed ... in mundane and corporeal rules.[91]

Legal history tended to recognise love as part of canon law, incident only to the regulation of marriage and its reproductive function.[92] Relationships were often defined in terms of possession, prohibition and power; women were defined predominately as property circulating among father, husband and son, functioning primarily as adjuncts to husbands or fathers.[93] Feminists in the 19th century critiqued the common law for treating women as slaves.[94] The canon law's tradition of asceticism[95] is reflected in the common law's conscious separation of law and the domestic sphere:

> The sphere of relationships and of sexual exchanges, inside and outside of marriage, inhabit an opaque zone of cultural neglect: They exist in law only as offences or as indices of propriety.[96]

Feminists have long critiqued the law's reliance on the public-private dichotomy as justification for so-called non-intervention in the private sphere of the household that condones domestic violence.[97] The silencing of women, especially in relation to courts, was central to the foundation of the common law and its subsequent privatisation of the domestic sphere: 'Thou art none attourney at law ... nor pleadest not in courte ... Holde thou thy peace as bowldly as other speake in court.'[98] A major strand of feminist

---

89 Post, 1997, pp 284–85.
90 Goodrich, 1996b, pp 29–32.
91 *Ibid*, p 31.
92 Goodrich, 1996a, p 652.
93 Larson, 1993, p 382; Post, 1997, pp 285, 292.
94 Clark, 1991, p 197.
95 Maine, 1909, p 161.
96 Goodrich, 1996a, p 652.
97 Eg, Olsen, 1986; Thornton, 1995.
98 Goodrich, 1996a, p 652.

theory and literature responds to the silencing of women in a variety of spheres and contexts, not the least of which are legal.[99] The religious Christian strand of love reflected in canon and common law emphasises the evilness and other shortcomings of women as justification for the privileging of (platonic) relationships between men, and chastity, over romantic servitude to women. The existence of these two strands of love reflects the co-existence of these two discourses of love, courtly and Christian, throughout history.

Repression of jurisdictions alternative to the common law, with its absolute privileging of reason and the dominance of a unity of positive law, may always leave room for an analysis that suggests the return of that repressed:

> [T]he repressed returns ... the contemporary crisis of the legal form, its modern history of positivisation, irrationality and injustice are symptoms of the return of a distant and traumatic past, that of the ... exclusion or closure of law to those knowledges which were inherent in its classical designation as being also a form of justice.[100]

Goodrich's argument is that reference to the Courts of Love provides us with inspiration to imagine alternative jurisdictions beyond the common law, with its absolutist privileging of 'reason'. This inspiration might lead to rerecognition of multiple or alternative epistemological frameworks for law. In particular, the Courts of Love might suggest inspiration for jurisdictions that eschew a public-private dichotomy and that are capable of representing ambiguities and complexities in relationships that are crucial to recognition of the complex personhood of women in violent relationships.

Unearthing the genealogy of the Courts of Love sheds light on what is at stake in the law's traditional insistence that it does not enter the private realm or the 'domain into which the King's writ does not seek to run'.[101] The law's distinction between public and private realms, and the law's refusal to enter the private, can be conceived as strategies to repress a jurisdiction of love or, more simply, as repression of the 'other' within the law.[102] Highlighting the multiplicity of jurisdictions subsumed into the common law also highlights and clarifies the common law jurisdiction's preoccupation with property. The common law 'grew up' around the protection of private property and tends to view human relations, when it considers them at all, as functions of property. The limitations of this approach are foregrounded, for example, when Jane Larson's recent argument for re-recognition of the tort of seduction[103] is read through the

---

99   Seuffert, 1996a, pp 541–51.
100 Goodrich, 1996b, p 11.
101 *Balfour v Balfour* [1919] 2 KB 571, p 579.
102 Davies, 1996, pp 171, 217.
103 Larson, 1993.

lens of Goodrich's discussion of the jurisdiction of the Courts of Love. Courts' refusals to recognise emotions by awarding damages for emotional distress,[104] and the limitation of remedies in general to the award of monetary compensation, both highlight the lack of jurisdiction over emotion[105] and the use of property as the central organising concept.

Perhaps not surprisingly, Goodrich notes that legal history has effectively erased the existence of the Courts of Love; legal historians seem unanimous in their conclusion that the courts were at most an amusing literary fiction or, at worst, 'an offense to the reality of the past ... and ... an obstacle to the understanding of related literature.'[106] More importantly, courtly love as a tradition has been critiqued as concealing male domination through the illusion of the male lover serving a female, which lures women into servitude.[107] Courtly, or romantic love, and spiritual love, or Christian love, have been described as twins in the sense that both objectify women.[108] My purpose is not to take up either the question of whether the Courts of Love actually existed, or the question of whether they created and perpetuated gender power differentials. Rather, I am concerned with shedding light on, and interrupting, the inability of the courts today to hear the claims of love made by women who have killed abusive partners. The Courts of Love may also provide glimpses of possibilities of alternative jurisdiction that may kindle feminist imaginations.

It is the precedent of the canon or Christian jurisdictions that have lived on to inform the common laws related to domestic violence that feminists have challenged in the 19th and 20th centuries. Reva Siegel has written a useful and comprehensive history of the evolution, or 'preservation through transformation', of gender power differentials in the common laws related to domestic violence.[109] Siegel notes that in the 19th century common law cases a husband's ownership of property in his wife, and corresponding prerogative to chastise her, were characterised as a 'vestige of another world, an ancient legal precedent of increasingly uncertain legitimacy'.[110] It was gradually and unevenly transformed into the 'rule of love' portrayed in discourses of companionate marriage.[111] This transformation involved a reorientation from a marital regime in which 'a husband ruled and represented his wife into one predicated in significant part on the juridical individuality of its partners'.[112] Marriage was transformed into a

---

104 *Ibid*, p 404.
105 *Ibid*, pp 404–05
106 Goodrich, 1996a, p 642.
107 *Ibid*; Zizek, 1994, pp 89, 108.
108 Gajowski, 1992, p 19.
109 Siegel, 1996, p 2119.
110 *Ibid*, p 2122.
111 *Ibid*, pp 2142–61.
112 *Ibid*, p 2142.

relationship of affection characterised by cheerful and voluntary submission on the part of the wife.[113] Love featured prominently in this discourse, as Mrs Henry Ward Beecher argued:

> If all could fully realise the true difference between the service rendered by woman to authority and that poured out unceasingly, spontaneously, for love, what a difference would be found in many homes![114]

This love, which resulted in women yielding to the care and supervision of their husbands, was most closely related to altruism. Under this construction of affectionate marriage, the husband's 'impulsive' violence, if kept out of the public realm, would properly be forgiven by the altruistic wife.[115] Violence and love within these discourses are clearly consistent. Moreover, this discourse of 'love' within marriage operated as justification for courts to refuse jurisdiction over these matters.

The doctrine of marital privacy developed to rationalise the continuance of the common law prerogative under a new name.[116] Under this doctrine, courts refused to inquire into the privacy of the home on the basis that the negative effects of publicity on domestic harmony would be worse than the temporary harm inflicted by the violence.[117] The illogical assumption here is that domestic harmony is consistent with abuse of the wife by the husband. Characterisation of the wife's appropriate response as love justifies 'non-interference' on the part of the court.

The history of the jurisdiction of the Courts of Love sheds light on these constructions of domestic violence, the discourse of marital love and affection, and the protection of marital privacy. The 'love' reflected in the 19th century decisions is a specifically narrow conception employed in the service of marriage, reflecting Christian spiritual love and based on obedience. It is a mere shadow of either spiritual love, the romantic love of the Courts of Love or literary traditions of 19th century romantic love. It also retains a proprietary character.

Siegel's argument is that reforms of the common law related to domestic violence have preserved and perpetuated the privileged status of men in marriage, even while specific discourses of relationship have been transformed and women have made some gains measured in dignity and material goods.[118] The most recent of these transformations in the United States is reflected in the controversial federal Violence Against Women Act,[119] which creates a civil rights remedy for domestic violence as a form of

---

113 *Ibid*, p 2145.
114 Beecher, 1883, 246, quoted *ibid*, p 2146.
115 Siegel, 1996, pp 2150, 2155.
116 *Ibid*, pp 2150–53.
117 *Ibid*, pp 2150–61.
118 *Ibid*, p 2119.
119 42 USCA s 13981 (West 1995).

sex discrimination. Siegel argues that the controversy surrounding the Act reflects the continuing power of the 19th century privacy discourses of domestic violence, at the same time as these discourses of gender status are modernised.[120] The 1991 Conference of Chief Justices opposed the Act in part, using language that attempted to preserve a public law-private law distinction, and the relegation of domestic disputes to the impliedly inferior state family courts. Chief Justice Rehnquist based his objection, in part, on the Act's potential to involve the federal courts 'in a whole host of domestic relations disputes', which raised the spectre of contamination of the public sphere with private disputes.[121] As Siegel states:

> [A]s we examine the claim that marriage is a state-law concern, it begins to appear that federalism discourses about marriage bear strong family resemblances to common law privacy discourses about marriage, and in some instances are even direct descendants of the discourse of affective privacy.[122]

In some instances this controversy explicitly revolved around the lack of jurisdiction of these courts over love, causing Siegel to invoke the maxim that 'where love is, law need not be'.[123] Legal discourses that construct the common law as lacking jurisdiction over love continue to be powerful enough to intrude into, and shape, discussions of federal legislation.

The exclusion of love from the law related to domestic violence is also apparent today in other areas of law. The common law legal system is characterised as unable to evaluate complex human emotions; sexual disputes are seen to be 'uniquely beyond the scope of ordinary reason and judgment'.[124] A 1985 case in New York notes, '[r]elationships may take varied forms and beget complications and entanglements which defy reason'.[125] Love is irrational,[126] and therefore beyond or outside the perfect reason that is law.[127] Assumptions about the distance between law and love, and therefore the inherent silliness of legislating or codifying rules of love, underlie a recent, rare piece of humorous scholarship in the Yale Law Journal.[128]

The 19th century courts' refusal to adjudicate matters defined as belonging to the private domain on the basis of the potentially negative impact on domestic harmony is consistent with the common law's lack of jurisdiction over love, or its repression of the jurisdiction of Courts of Love.

---

120 Siegel, 1996, pp 2196–206.
121 *Ibid*, pp 2198–99, citing Rehnquist, 1992, pp 1, 3.
122 Siegel, 1996, p 2202.
123 *Ibid*, pp 2205–06.
124 Larson, 1993, p 451.
125 *Douglas R v Suzanne M*, 487 NYS 2d 244, 246 (1985).
126 Paglia, 1990, p 4.
127 Larson, 1993, p 452.
128 Rubin, 1994.

It is important to note that these 19th century cases construct the private domain at the same time as they exclude it from their jurisdiction; the jurisdiction of the Courts of Love should not be equated in a simplistic manner with a jurisdiction of what is later constructed as the private. My argument is that the repression of the jurisdiction of the Courts of Love (or even its potential), combined with the common law's limited jurisdiction over relationships as property and the development of the doctrine of marital privacy, leaves a void in the discourses and precedents of the law with respect to romantic love. When a woman states in court that she loves, or loved, an abusive partner, the court has no jurisdiction to hear her statement and no lens of precedent through which to reflect and refract this love. Her statement falls into a legal void at the same time as it invokes the spectre of jurisdiction over matters of love, which haunts the common law.

IV COURTROOM DYNAMICS: WOMEN WHO LOVE AND KILL

In this section, I hope to raise some issues, which highlight the complexities of the dynamics of the courtroom as a scene of interpretation where women who have killed abusers make statements of love. I have suggested in Part II of this chapter that women who claim to love, or to have loved, men who abuse them may be positioning themselves within one or more of a variety of discourses of romantic love which are consistent with, or may be interpreted to be consistent with, violent behaviour on the part of the man. Denial of the complexities of these discourses and of the women's acts of positioning themselves within these discourses is denial of their complex personhood. In Part III, I have suggested that a woman's statement of romantic love in a court of the common law falls into a void of precedent, at the same time as it invokes the spectre of the jurisdiction of love. In this part, I consider how the women's statements of love in the courtroom, despite their intentions, may be constructed as unreasonable. First, the assertion of agency as a speaker in court, and as a witness, is contrary to the tradition associating women with silence and with not bearing witness. Speaking in court both transforms her into something other than a woman (or a proper woman) and makes hearing her problematic. Secondly, her assertion of agency as a subject rather than an object of romantic love contradicts many discourses of love (objects of desire do not have agency).

As I have mentioned above, the jurisdiction of the common law both constructs women as silent and silences women, which is consistent with their status as objects of property. Many legal scholars have documented the numerous ways in which women are disadvantaged by and through the law. Here I provide only a few illustrative examples of the myriad forms this disadvantage takes. The 16th and 17th century roots of the common law clearly state that women are not to be attorneys or witnesses in court. Feminists' long battle to be admitted to the practice of law in the United States, Britain and other Commonwealth countries is well documented and illustrates the resistance of the law to women in courts.[129] The law of rape's traditional requirement of a second witness to corroborate the rape victim's testimony has also been the focus of feminist efforts for reform.[130] Requiring a corroborating witness both indicates that the court will not hear what the rape victim has to say and that what she has to say is not credible. It is also a reflection of the assumptions that the law makes about women's agency; the construction of women as objects is inconsistent with the assumption of agency required to testify on the witness stand. As Alison Young has argued, 'inured within legal discourse is a ... formidable conviction that a woman is both sexual and indifferent, functioning more as a signal to others than as an autonomous agent'.[131]

Traditionally, when women spoke in court their agency was transformed into psychosis, as reflected in Wigmore's statement from 1924, which was reprinted in a highly authoritative evidence treatise until well into the 1970s:

> Modern psychiatrists have amply studied the behaviour of errant young girls and women coming before the courts in all sorts of cases. Their psychic complexes are multifarious, distorted partly by inherent defects, partly by diseased derangement or abnormal instincts, partly by bad social environment, partly by temporary physical or emotional conditions. One form taken by these complexes is that of contriving false charges of sexual offences by men. The unchaste (let us call it) mentality finds incidental but direct expression in the narration of imaginary sex incidents of which the narrator is the heroine or victim. On the surface the narration is straightforward and convincing. The real victim, however, too often in such cases is the innocent man; for the respect and sympathy naturally felt by any tribunal for a wronged female helps to give easy credit to such a plausible tale.[132]

Wigmore's influential treatise inscribes the negative stereotype of women and girls who come before the courts as liars who are psychologically abnormal into the judicial process. This construction paves the way for the transformation of women's assertions of agency 'in all sorts of cases' into abnormal psychological behaviour. Women as witnesses[133] are therefore often not heard by the law, but rather are expelled from the law through construction as the law's opposite: emotional, irrational and mad. Here the law explicitly adopts literature's account of sexual relations between men

---

129 Sachs and Wilson, 1978.

130 Naffine, 1997, pp 104–11.

131 Young, 1998, p 445.

132 Wigmore, 1970, vol 3A (924a).

133 Haraway, 1997, pp 23–39 analyses the development of modern science as predicated on the exclusion of women from bearing witness, or acting as the 'modest witness' of scientific experiments.

and women. Glanville Williams, as academic interpreter of the modern English law of rape, explicitly draws on Byron in stating that men are 'masterful' and women 'welcome' their advances, despite the fact that they may be 'putting up a token resistance'.[134] Nor is this type of transformation only an historical phenomenon. As recently as 1991, Williams has argued that girls and women lie about rape.[135] For women, the act of bearing witness may be transferred into evidence of madness or other psychological abnormality. This dynamic is clearly at work in at least some of the cases in which women state that they love the abusers whom they have killed. For example, Margaret Raby's statements that she loved her abuser result in the judge concluding that she has been 'brainwashed' – her act of agency in speaking in court is thus transformed into psychosis.[136]

Both Catharine MacKinnon[137] and Judith Butler have discussed the transformation of women's assertions of agency as witnesses in a manner that undercuts their statements. This transformation occurred with the testimony of Anita Hill before the United States Senate Judiciary Committee (an all white, male body).[138] Hill's act of speaking in bearing witness is constructed as an assertion of agency; her act of speaking of sexuality is constructed as an assertion of sexual agency.[139] An assertion of sexual agency is interpreted through the lens of pornography in a manner that undercuts what she is trying to say. Her sexual agency is inconsistent with the necessity that she claim the status of a victim of sexual harassment in order to make her point: 'As Hill utters the sexualized discourse, she is sexualized by it, and that very sexualization undercuts her effort to represent sexualization itself as a kind of injury.'[140]

Hill's testimony about sexual harassment is taken as a sign of agency. By definition, within dominant discourses that construct 'good' women as passive objects or victims, that sign of agency can be misconstrued as a confession of complicity. It is the act of testimony, as a sign of agency, and the confession of complicity with the abuse, that is relevant to interpretations of women's statements of love in court. The response to the women's statements of love that challenges their credibility is consistent with the assumption that they have made a confession; she has confessed to

---

134 Naffine, 1994, p 28, citing Williams, 1983, p 238.

135 Naffine, 1997, pp 106–07, citing Williams, 1991, pp 205–07.

136 *R v Raby*, p 746.

137 MacKinnon, 1993, pp 64–68.

138 Although Butler and MacKinnon's discussions are about sexual harassment and rape, they are relevant here for two reasons. First, it is a discussion of how women's own voices as witnesses are used against them, which is relevant to the dynamic surrounding the statements of love that I am discussing. Secondly, the statements of love that I am discussing all happen in cases where sexual abuse is also a prominent factor.

139 Butler, 1997, pp 82–86.

140 *Ibid*, p 83.

complicity with the man's abuse by stating that she loves him. This construction of complicity may be resisted by women in court; Oakes resisted the suggestion that she loved her abuser.[141]

MacKinnon states that neither the law of sexual harassment nor the law of rape has found a way to challenge women's lack of sexual credibility, and suggests that the goal is for women to gain a 'voice that cannot be used against us'.[142] Butler critiques as inherently liberal what she takes to be MacKinnon's assertion that:

> [O]ne ought to be in a position to utter words in such a way that the meaning of those words coincides with the intention with which they are uttered, and that the performative dimension of that uttering works to support and further that intended meaning.[143]

Butler would disagree that this goal is possible. She states:

> [O]ne always risks meaning something other than what one thinks one utters ... [and one is always] vulnerable in a specifically linguistic sense to a social life of language that exceeds the purview of the subject who speaks ... The effort to come to terms is not one that can be resolved in anticipation but only through a concrete struggle of translation, one whose success has no guarantees.[144]

Butler seems to be suggesting that one can never be confident about conveying any particular meaning through language; testimony in court is open to interpretation through lenses ground, shaped and polished in the dominant discourses, which tend to be gender-biased against women.[145] The rules of evidence do not counter the manners in which these dominant discourses reflect, refract and perpetuate gender power differentials. Nor, of course, does the legal system provide a manner of redressing or countering the gendered aspects of the law's narrative. Butler suggests that giving meaning to assertions of love in the context of domestic violence involves a complex process of translation in the context of dominant and shifting legal and social discourses. Law's lack of precedent in the area of love, its tendency to construct women as psychologically abnormal, and its failure to redress the gender bias of dominant discourses, are all stacked against the possibility of the law reflecting the complex personhood of women who assert that they love the men who abuse them.

Desdemona's story provides an example of the difficulty of conveying complex concepts, such as love, in the context of domestic violence in the English language. The constraints within which Desdemona constructs her

---

141 Gay Oakes replied to the prosecutor's assertion that she still loved him with 'not at the end I didn't': *R v Oakes*, Transcript of Proceedings, p 150.
142 MacKinnon, 1993, p 68.
143 Butler, 1997, p 84.
144 *Ibid*, pp 87–88.
145 Seuffert, 1996b, pp 11, 13–25.

love reflect the constraints within which women who kill abusers make claims of love in the courtroom. These claims are assertions of agency open to interpretation through lenses coloured by dominant discourses, which may result in the transformation of the women's statements into evidence of madness or other psychological abnormality, or may construct their assertion of agency as an admission of complicity with the abuse perpetrated against them. Circulating with these dynamics is Desdemona's difficulty with actively constructing herself as an object of desire within discourses of romantic love, in which her act of agency risks interpretation as evidence that she is a whore, and therefore inherently 'incredible'.

V CONCLUSION

A woman's statement in court that she loves or loved the man who has abused her is unlikely to be interpreted within the discourses of love in which she may very reasonably be attempting to position herself. There are at least three obstacles to her self-positioning. First, her assertion of agency in the act of positioning herself within these discourses may be contradictory to the discourses' constructions of women as passive objects of property, or desire, and as capable of infinite giving, sacrifice and suffering. Secondly, the common law legal system has repressed its actual or potential jurisdiction over matters of love and therefore has no precedent for hearing statements of romantic love and no framework within which to interpret such statements. Paradoxically, the statements also invoke the spectre of love beyond patriarchal discourses and highlight the common law's lack of jurisdiction over romantic love. Thirdly, the very act of agency by which the woman asserts her love is, through the dynamics of the courtroom and the context in which it operates, likely to be transformed into evidence of psychosis, or perhaps misappropriated as a confession of complicity with the abuser. These obstacles circulate and interweave, denying the recognition of the complex personhood of these women who, as both agents and victims, suffer graciously and selfishly and who embody contradiction, paradox and the potential for transformation.[146] The injustice of the transformation of these assertions of agency into denials of complex personhood haunts the common law's aspirations to justice. At the same time, these statements invoke alternative epistemologies with the potential to reflect both complex personhood and plural justice.

---

146 See generally Gordon, 1997.

CHAPTER 6

HAVING TROUBLE WITH THE LAW: RACIALISED PUNISHMENT AND TESTIMONIES OF RESISTANCE

Suvendrini Perera

Prisons are a receptacle for social issues that are too hard to think about.[1]

INTRODUCTION

Against the universalist avowals of the law, its target communities produce diverse cultural forms asserting their own specific knowledges and experiences of how law works. These narratives and representations provide explanatory frameworks, critical contexts and alternative understandings of peoples' everyday 'troubles with the law'. In doing so they also insistently repose seemingly open and shut questions of the law, of the relationship between crime and punishment, and between criminality, society and prison.

In the globalised prison industrial complex, Angela Davis argues, prisons have become a means of closing down a range of social questions increasingly seen as irresolvable.[2] Prisons are our answer to the problem of homelessness; to the problem of addiction; to the problem of mental illness; to the problem of poverty; and also, especially, to the 'problem' of race. Prisons block our ability to think critically about these questions by providing a readymade answer to them.

For communities devastated by the effects of this 'answer', on the other hand, re-opening the question of the prison is a matter of life and death. Oppositional or resistant cultural forms attempt in a variety of ways to undo common sense understandings of crime and the criminalisation of particular groups, reposing the prison as a question rather than an answer and articulating challenges to the legal system and its forms of racialised punishment and criminalisation.

For Indigenous Australians, genres such as popular music or poetry play a role in raising public consciousness about racialised experiences of the law and the prison. Perhaps the most influential instance is Jack Davis's poem on the death of the 16 year old John Pat in Roebourne jail. Dedicated to 'Maisie Pat and to all mothers who have suffered similar loss', Davis's poem became a rallying point for the Black Deaths in Custody movement and raised national awareness about the scandalous ways in which Indigenous men were dying in Australia's prisons.

1 Davis, 1998c.
2 Gordon, 1998.

This essay focuses on Ruby Langford Ginibi's *Haunted by the Past*[3] as a text that presents a racialised analysis of the prison system through the narrative form of 'testimonio'.[4] Ginibi's narrative combines the testimony of her son Nobby's repeated terms in jail with the life stories of her family and newspaper accounts and official evaluations of his case. These are interwoven in turn with stories and poems of other Indigenous men in prison, young men whose names have become only too familiar in a national register of pain, injustice and death. As a form of testimonial writing, *Haunted by the Past* successfully reopens the social issues for which the prison functions as a receptacle. Simultaneously, through this narrative form Ginibi confronts us with the inadequacy of the autobiographical framework or of the individual's 'personal' story for understanding racialised experiences of imprisonment and 'trouble with the law'. *Haunted by the Past* thus also opens out questions of genre and articulates new forms of subjectivity and collectivity that serve politicised ends.

The context for this essay is the emergence of a series of questions about racialised punishment in Australia in the late 1990s. A few months after *Haunted by the Past* was published (after protracted delays for fear of legal action) in 1999, the simmering issue of Indigenous imprisonment erupted into public consciousness, triggered by the death of a 14 year old boy in the Northern Territory after he was sentenced to a mandatory term of detention for a trivial offence.[5] The case attracted international attention and raised some fundamental questions about our system of government. Although mandatory sentencing laws in the Northern Territory have been since repealed, the same period saw a rise in the number of privatised prisons, concerns over increasing levels of Indigenous incarceration and an unprecedented degree of scrutiny of the government's policy of mandatory detention of asylum seekers and refugees. The essay then is part of a more sustained effort to think critically about historical and ongoing forms of racialised punishment in Australia and the forms of resistance and dissent they have engendered.[6]

'LIVE FOR ALL OF US': THE ROLE OF COLLECTIVE STORIES

This essay is located at an intersection between the institutions and workings of the law – what Ginibi has called 'the criminal (in)justice system' – and the ways in which that system is understood, represented and

---

3   Ginibi, 1999.

4   For a description of testimonio's essential characteristics, see Beverley, 1992.

5   Perera, 2000.

6   See, eg, proceedings of the forum 'Imprison and Detain: Racialised Punishment in Australia Today' at www.transforming.cultures.uts.edu.au/imprisonforum.

contested through certain cultural forms. The title of this book, *Romancing the Tomes*, refers precisely to this intersection between popular genres – such as Romance – and the canonical tomes of the law. Questions of genre, that is, of reception, interpretation and reading, are central to my discussion. How we read, as Chandra Mohanty points out, is inescapably a political question:

> ... third world women's narratives are not in themselves evidence of decentering hegemonic histories and subjectivities. It is the way in which they are read, understood and located institutionally which is of paramount importance. After all the point is not just 'to record' one's history of struggle, or consciousness, but how they are recorded; the way we read receive, and disseminate such imaginative records.[7]

This essay focuses on understandings of Ginibi's narrative of 'trouble with the law': its reception, location in disciplinary and generic terms and its representation, dissemination and publicisation, through the key institutions that instruct and direct us how to read particular texts. Many of these points can be introduced by examining a review of *Haunted by the Past* published in the Australian Book Review (ABR). This is not a random choice of review. The publication has an institutional location and weight in Australian public life that authorises the review, and is therefore influential in how or, or indeed whether, we read the text being reviewed. In this instance the review, titled 'Writing from Behind Bars' is doubly authorised by the description of the reviewer as an 'Aboriginal writer living in Melbourne', Philip Morrissey.

My argument is not so much that this as a 'bad' review (I have admired other work on Ginibi by the same author); instead, I try to identify some of the assumptions implicit in the review and the political and narrative directions it gives to ABR readers. To cite two extracts:

> Nobby and his problems with the law ... were an important aspect of Ginibi's earlier work *Don't Take Your Love To Town*. While that book is *an Australian classic* ... *Haunted by the Past* does not have the same degree of *complexity and affective richness*: in consequence though we learn a lot about Nobby, he *remains an oddly insubstantial figure*.[8]

Elsewhere the review states:

> Underlying Ginibi's concern for Nobby is the real fear that he will end up one more Aboriginal man dying in custody, and to illustrate this possibility she provides *short biographies* of several Aboriginal men who ... don't make it out alive.[9]

Here it becomes important to distinguish between the genre of autobiography/biography under which the text is officially classified and the category to which I suggest it more properly belongs: that of the

---

7   Mohanty, 1991, p 34.
8   Morrissey, 2000 (my emphasis).
9   *Ibid* (my emphasis).

testimonial. The ABR classifies the text as 'biography', while the publishers' classification is 'Biography/Indigenous Studies'. What is at stake in these classifications?

The question may be illuminated by referring briefly to another text with which *Haunted by the Past* has certain affinities, Mumia Abú Jamal's *Live from Death Row*, a collection of prison writings by a man from the other side of the world.[10] In his introduction to *Live from Death Row*, John Edgar Wideman distinguishes Mumia Abú Jamal's writings from the highly popular Afro-American biographies and autobiographies, from Oprah to OJ Simpson to Maya Angelou, promoted in US bookstores. Wideman describes the latter as 'the countless up-from-the-depths biographies and autobiographies of black people that ... encapsulate one of the master plots Americans have found acceptable for black lives': the formula for the 'neoslave narrative'.[11] For Wideman, the neoslave narrative follows a simple movement from darkness into light, bondage into freedom, and attracts an empathetic readership precisely because it is 'about individuals, not groups crossing boundaries'.[12] Its implicit message is: 'If some overcome why don't others?', a message that downplays systemic oppression and stresses individual character and achievement. Australia's own homegrown counterpart to this individualist narrative is perhaps the battler story, a story of the resourceful, humorous character that comes through because of their fighting spirit.

According to Wideman, in the neoslave narrative:

Vicarious identification with the narrator's harrowing adventures, particularly if the tale is told in the first person 'I', permits readers to have their cake and eat it too. They experience the thrill and chill of being an outsider. In the safety of an armchair, readers can root for the crafty slave ... against an outrageously evil system ... and ignore for a charmed moment their reliance on the same system to pay for the book, the armchair.

The neoslave narratives thus serve the ambivalent function of their ancestors. The fate of one black individual is foregrounded, removed from the network of systemic relationships connecting, defining, determining, undermining all American lives. This manner of viewing black lives at best ignores, at worst reinforces an apartheid status quo ... The idea of a collective intertwined fate recedes. The mechanisms of class, race, and gender we have inherited are perpetuated, ironically, by a genre purporting to illustrate the possibility of ... transcending the conditions into which one is born.[13]

The difference Wideman identifies between the 'neoslave' Afro-American biographies and autobiographies and the writings of Mumia Abú Jamal,

10 My thanks to Charandev Singh for telling me about Mumia Abú Jamal's writings and passing on much valuable information on mandatory sentencing.
11 Wideman, 1996, p xxix.
12 *Ibid*, p xxx.
13 *Ibid*, p xxxi.

about a collective, rather than an individual, experience of prison, can be transposed in generic terms to a distinction between autobiography and testimonio. Whereas the former is a classic form of humanist narrative that tracks an individual's progress through life to the achievement of success or maturity with an emphasis on the character's inner development and emotional life, forms of testimonial writing are less interested in the interiority of the character or in the individual herself. They focus on the collective, are spiral rather than linear in movement, and draw on forms of narrative that have commonalities both with religious witness bearing and truth telling (testifying in church) as well as with evidential forms (giving testimony in a court or legal setting). Forms of prison testimonial writing have been explored in societies such as India and South America;[14] in Australia Francesca Bartlett has suggested that the form shares a number of elements with Indigenous testimonies of the effects of colonisation. The stories given as evidence to the Stolen Generations Inquiry and to the Black Deaths in Custody Royal Commission both fall into this category.[15]

Lisa Lowe describes testimonial writings as forms of narrative:

> ... that are not merely representational, disconnected from 'real' political life; neither are the[y] ... transparent records of histories of struggle. Rather these forms, life stories, oral histories, histories of community, literature – are crucial forms that connect subjects to social relations. To consider testimony and testimonial as constituting a 'genre' of cultural production ... extends the scope of what constitutes legitimate knowledges to include ... forms and practices that have been excluded form both empirical and aesthetic modes of evaluation.[16]

Haunted by the Past, located between the empirical and the purely aesthetic or literary, has most in common with these forms of witness bearing and truth telling, of testimony, rather than with more familiar works of autobiography – for example, with a text like Sally Morgan's *My Place*,[17] one of the few books by an Indigenous author to have achieved best seller status in Australia. The commercial and critical success of *My Place* in the year leading up to the bicentenary of colonisation (1988) is probably not coincidental, nor unrelated to the fact that for many non-Indigenous Australians Morgan's narrative of her own rediscovery of her 'roots' affirms the possibility of recovering the losses of colonisation.

In the passage quoted above from the ABR, Ginibi's first book, *Don't Take Your Love to Town*, also published at the time of the bicentenary, is used as an aesthetic yardstick against which to measure *Haunted by the Past*, published ten years later in a very different political climate. The review elevates *Don't*

---

14   Beverley, 1992; Panjabi, 1997.
15   Bartlett, 1999.
16   Lowe, 1997, p 356.
17   Morgan, 1987.

Take Your Love to Town to the status of an 'Australian classic', a description that removes it from a category of specifically Indigenous writing and relocates it within an – albeit reconstructed – Australian canon. In contrast with *Don't Take Your Love to Town*, *Haunted by the Past* is found wanting in the literary humanist values of 'complexity' and 'affective richness', while Nobby is found lacking as a fleshed out, rounded character: 'an oddly insubstantial figure'.

The framework of the review prevents it from pursuing a more interesting line of inquiry about why the text might be uninterested in presenting fully rounded characters as demanded by the novelistic conventions of Western autobiography. The change from the initial working title, 'Nobby's Story', to *Haunted by the Past* offers a clue, suggesting a progressive realisation that the individual auto/biographical framework may be inadequate to the narrative and political imperatives of the text. Similarly, where the review sees the stories from the Black Deaths in Custody Report as 'short biographies' provided to 'illustrate' a point, in a different critical framework, these may be understood not as mere 'illustrations', but as interweavings into the text suggesting the collective nature of the experience of prison for young black men. In this reading, the interlinked stories of black deaths in custody serve the function suggested by Wideman writing about Mumia Abú Jamal above: they lay bare the 'systemic relationships connecting, defining, determining, undermining all ... [Australian] lives', and emphasising their 'collective intertwined fate'.

This interconnectedness is underlined in a powerful and complex scene at the end of the book where Ginibi describes Nobby's wedding:

> ... as they were getting into the car, something distracted me and made me look on the top of the car. I was struck dumb! There was a circle of faces I knew very well! The spirits of John Pat, Robert Walker, Charlie Michaels, Eddie Murray, David Gundy and Daniel Yock! They were callin out to Nobby, sayin, 'On ya brother. You survived the brutal jails ... Go in peace, and live for all of us.'
>
> And then Nobby looked up and waved, and I knew he's seen them too![18]

'Live for all of us': here, instead of a successful story of an 'individual crossing boundaries', and emerging from the damage of the prison system, Ginibi makes Nobby's moment of success simultaneously mark a deep, collective and systemic, loss. The litany of familiar names carries the weight of the collective stories of those men who didn't make it, weaving them into the fabric of Nobby's happier story. The success narrative of an individual 'crossing the boundaries' of the prison system is destabilised by the simultaneous presence of other stories. What makes this moment all the more powerful is the invocation of another plane of reality, an Aboriginal belief system that has undercut rationalist understandings throughout the

18 Ginibi, 1999, pp 178–79.

text. The insistence throughout on the materiality of this belief system makes it impossible to read this closing moment as a sentimental or facile gesture.

Whereas the review perceives a qualitative difference between Ginibi's early writing in *Don't Take Your Love to Town* and her latest publication, *Haunted by the Past*, I identify a strong continuity between them in the ways both books exceed the demands of humanist autobiography.[19] The publication of *Don't Take Your Love to Town* in the bicentennial year, 1988, inevitably shaped both its production and reception. Later, Ginibi was to deplore attempts to 'gubba-ise' or whiten her work by its Anglo-Australian editor and publisher. The desire to promote the book as a text of reconciliation, and to present its narrator as a simple, all Australian type, can obscure *Don't Take Your Love to Town*'s uncompromising politics and unsparing representation of the devastating consequences of poverty and racism.

Equally, 'gubba-ising' are ongoing efforts by critics to fit the text into existing literary categories. Attempts to recruit *Don't Take Your Love to Town* into the battler genre associated with canonical Australian authors such as Banjo Patterson, Henry Lawson and Joseph Facey ignore the fact that the literary construct of the battler, a product of the nationalist 1890s, is from its inception an ideologically loaded and racially marked figure. Its consolidation as an icon of Australianness (quickly reinforced by advertising and popular culture) corresponds with the establishment of the federated white Australian state in 1901. The recurrence of this figure 100 years later in the rhetoric of Pauline Hanson's One Nation and John Howard's Liberal Party suggests the extent to which, far from being an inclusive image of the struggling people in our society, the battler remains a figure of the ethnocentric Anglo-Australian imagination.

Rather than the heroic, white, usually male, battler of 'the bush' (that other key construct of the Anglo-Australian imagination), the figure addressed by *Don't Take Your Love to Town* is the urban Aboriginal woman with her children. Rejecting the individualism of the battler genre, Ginibi's text is concerned with the collective, historically and socially produced, conditions of Aboriginal families in urban Australia. The hostile forces she contends with are not indiscriminating, apolitical 'nature' or 'the elements', but the systematically racist policies and practices of the state in housing, employment, education and, most urgently, in law and the criminal (in)justice system.

Quoting extensively from documentary sources, *Don't Take Your Love to Town* also breaks with the narrative conventions of traditional autobiography, chronicling, not the development or success of an individual self, but a complex and intermeshing, inescapably political, *collective* story

---

19 The discussion of *Don't Take Your Love to Town* in the next few paragraphs draws on a previously published essay (Perera, 1998).

that necessarily exceeds the confines of the narrowly personal. The text's inclusion of statistics and other non-literary materials on Aboriginal men in custody reinforces Ginibi's insistence on the representational nature of her story. The references to Nobby's time in prison are again connected to the stories of other young black men and their families. The collective and relational subjectivity of the narrator in *Don't Take Your Love to Town* thus also draws on a conceptual and historical understanding more adequately addressed by the genres of life writing or testimonio. As Philippa Sawyer has shown, critics attempting to read *Don't Take Your Love to Town* according to the canons of Anglo-American autobiography have, not surprisingly, sometimes found themselves out of their depth.

One might argue that in *Haunted by the Past*, Ginibi, now an established author, in many ways returns to the 'gubba-ised' materials of her first book, and reworks them in ways that make her political and narrative position more evident. Rather than falling short of her previous achievement of 'classic' Australian status, *Haunted by the Past* perhaps invites us to revisit *Don't Take Your Love to Town*, recasting the earlier text in the light of what the author now knows – or is now in a position to express through her chosen narrative form.

GENEALOGIES OF THE AUSTRALIAN PRISON

When does Nobby's story begin? With his birth ...? Or further back, with my struggles as an Aboriginal woman raising nine children mostly on my own? Or maybe Nobby's story starts even earlier than that in the 1880s, when my family went to live on Box Ridge Mission after their traditional lands were taken over by the first squatters up in the north of New South Wales. Thinking about it, I'd say Nobby's story has its roots way back ... It's part of a bigger historical picture and a longer story ... This story continues today.[20]

These are the opening lines of *Haunted by the Past*, in a chapter titled 'Beginnings'. But the 'beginning' of Nobby's story, as the passage tells us, cannot be separated from a 'bigger picture and a longer story' that starts with the removal of the Bundjulung people to Box Ridge mission. The chapter describes Ginibi's childhood on the mission:

Mrs Hiscocks was the mission manager when I was a kid. Later, she became the matron of that infamous Cootamundra Girls' Training Home where they trained the stolen children to be serviced out as slaves, which ended with a national inquiry that John Howard has never apologised for. He gets gagged on the word 'Sorry'.[21]

---

20 Ginibi, 1999, p 1.
21 *Ibid*, pp 5–6.

Ginibi immediately goes on to quote a passage from *Bringing them Home*, the official report of the HREOC's inquiry into policies and practices of child removal:

> We may go home, but we cannot relive our childhoods. We may reunite with our mothers, fathers, sisters, brothers, aunties, uncles, communities, but we cannot relive the 20, 30, 40 years that we spent without their love and care, and they cannot undo the grief and mourning they felt when we were separated from them. We can go home to ourselves as Aboriginals, but this does not erase the attacks inflicted on our hearts, minds, bodies and souls, by caretakers who thought their mission in life was to eliminate us as Aboriginals.[22]

Ginibi then continues, returning from the larger story to her own story. 'Even today people like the matron Mrs Hiscocks do not take responsibility for what they did to our Aboriginal people, as they state "they were only doing their jobs"'.[23] The passage moves between past and present, between personal and public, tracing institutional links through the movements of Miss Hiscocks from Box Ridge to Cootamundra, linking different forms of institutionalisation of Indigenous peoples, and also making extraordinarily powerful connections between collective and personal stories of home, loss and return.

The connections made here between different forms of institutionalisation can be illuminated by Angela Davis's theorising, in the US context, of a genealogy of 'racialised punishment'. As a counter to Foucault's genealogy of the prison with its obliviousness to questions of race, Davis sketches a genealogy that would:

> ... accentuate the links between confinement, punishment and race. At least four systems of incarceration could be identified: the reservation system, slavery, the mission system, and the internment camps of World War II. Within the US incarceration has thus played a pivotal role in the histories of Native Americans and people of African, Mexican and Asian descent. In all these places people were involuntarily confined and punished for no other reason than their race or ethnicity.[24]

In *Haunted by the Past*, Ginibi provides nothing less than her own racialised genealogy of the Australian prison system, showing that since colonisation the history of institutionalisation and incarceration of Indigenous peoples has taken varied forms: expulsion away from traditional country to distant camps and reserves (such as Box Ridge), as the most productive lands were claimed for sheep and cattle grazing; incarceration in detention centres or penal settlements for people deemed 'uncooperative', and the systematic forced removal of children for confinement in missions for the purposes of assimilation. And, as *Bringing them Home* shows, the removal of Aboriginal

22 *Ibid.*
23 *Ibid.*
24 Davis, 1998b, p 97.

children continues today in different forms through practices such as detention, child substitute care and creation of wards of the state.[25] Mandatory sentencing is in effect the latest mechanism in this long continuum of dislocation and dispersal of Aboriginal community and family life.[26]

In insisting on the connections between different forms of incarceration and institutionalisation, *Haunted by the Past* provides its own alternative genealogy of the Australian prison system. Going even further, Ginibi's book positions itself as a direct intervention in, as well as a 'talking back' to, the (in)justice system. This occurs on a number of levels in the text. At one level Ginibi constantly comments on and contextualises the legal judgments against her son and other Aboriginal men, pointing out the lie of a 'justice system' based on the paramount injustice of colonisation, as well as the role of the police in implementing and maintaining that system. Here, the text outlines ground more systematically mapped by Chris Cunneen in his book *Conflict, Politics and Crime*, revealing the structural and institutional links between the 'processes of colonisation and criminalisation, and in particular the role of the police in that process'.[27] At another level, Ginibi continually points to the levels of documented corruption in the NSW police force, challenging the authority of the police and judges as custodians of law and order.[28]

At a further level, Ginibi repeatedly engages in an (unequal) dialogue with the law in its various forms. As author, she points out the punitive consequences of talking back to the law, identifying the excisions that had to be made to the book for fear of legal action. She writes of her inability to 'include all the facts as I know them or write about all the people that have died. I have had to cut back on some details I think you all should know. That's the white fella's law for you, aye?'[29] In addition to exposing the gaps left by 'white fella's law', the text narrates two even more direct attempts by Ginibi to intervene in the (in)justice system. The first occurs when she confronts the sergeant at Annandale police station with her writing:

> I told the sergeant who I was and I said I was writing the story of my son's life, about the years he had given to the prison system. I told him ... that I'd been researching Aboriginal deaths in custody. I told him it was a big shame on Australia that the killing times are still with us. The police sergeant said it was procedure ... The police sergeant couldn't give a damn. I could see that it annoyed him to even try to explain to me (a black woman) what was happening to my son.[30]

---

25   Buti, 1996, p 23.
26   Perera, 2000.
27   Cunneen, 2001, p 3.
28   Ginibi, 1999, pp 24, 65, 68.
29   *Ibid*, p 78.
30   *Ibid*, p 152.

The disjunction here is between Ginibi as the author who researches, records and analyses, and Ginibi as the police sergeant sees her, 'a black woman', unworthy even of a response to a query about her son – let alone with any power to question his actions. This disjunction between public and private roles is one that plays out over and over again in the responses to Ginibi's writing.

A more extended exchange along the same lines is detailed in the last part of the book when Ginibi is recognised by a judge after Nobby once again gets into trouble with the law: 'The judge recognised me sitting there and said "I've read your books Mrs Langford, I admire your writing." I was so disgusted ... that I stood up and said "You couldn't have been listening very much to what I've been writing about, Your Honour".'[31]

Ginibi then writes a letter to the judge, again explaining Nobby's history and attaching copies of her books to add weight to her words. Although permission was withheld to publish the judge's response in *Haunted by the Past*, Ginibi summarises it for her readers and proceeds to argue back with the judge through several pages of the book:

> I really wanted to include the judge's reply to my letter in this book, but he wouldn't give permission ... I was very offended by some of the things he said. He didn't mean to offend me but some of his remarks and the language he used did. He addressed me by my first name in a paternalistic way as if he was a personal friend, which he is not. And every time he referred to Aboriginal people, which was on numerous occasions, he always used a small 'a'... He returned, by postpak, my three books which I had sent to his chambers to edu-ma-cate him.[32]

The judge's rejection of Ginibi's books graphically represents his repudiation of any dialogue between them and a refusal to be 'edu-ma-cated' by Indigenous understandings of the law.[33] It does not, however, represent the end of Ginibi's attempts to confront and intervene in the justice system. *Haunted by the Past* itself constitutes Ginibi's defiant response to the judge, embodying her determination to continue talking back to the law.

TAKING IT POLITICALLY

Ginibi's determination to pursue her attempts to edu-ma-cate the judge can be read as 'personal' since they begin with her response as Nobby's mother to an exchange at his trial. But they are also more than that – part of 'a bigger

---

31 *Ibid*, pp 164–65.

32 *Ibid*, p 169.

33 The Koori Kriol word 'edu-ma-cate' has a particular significance in Ginibi's work, underscoring the distinctiveness of the Indigenous knowledge being imparted. For further discussion of the point, see Perera, 1998.

historical picture and a longer story', just as her indignation at being addressed condescendingly by her first name is linked to the judge's use of the insulting small 'a' to refer to Aboriginal people. *Haunted by the Past* represents Ginibi's determination to make her family story visible as *a public story* and to make her role as Nobby's mother count as *a public role*, entitling her to speak with a weight of authority beyond that of the individual. Unlike the autobiographical form with its emphasis on the subjective and 'personal', the testimonial claims *representational* status; its narrative aims are explicitly social and political.

The reception and dissemination of *Haunted by the Past* reveal a degree of reluctance to acknowledge these wider, specifically political, claims of Ginibi's story, or to read it as anything more than the tale of a single family. Significantly, this reluctance is couched in terms of a 'natural' scepticism aroused by the author's gendered positionality. In the ABR, Ginibi is described as 'an indulgent mother' whose maternal affection leads her to overlook the possibility of her son's responsibility for his own actions – and by extension, the responsibility of the other men discussed in the book. This view is reinforced, perhaps even more damagingly, on the back cover of *Haunted by the Past* by the publisher's blurb referring to Ginibi's 'bias of mother love'. In both cases positioning Ginibi as a mother immediately depoliticises her analysis and undercuts the authority of her parallel roles as writer, researcher and social critic. The title of the review, 'Writing from Behind Bars', takes on an added layer of meaning in this context, suggestive of a partiality in the author's vision, obscured by its own bars of love.

The reviewer writes:

> As I understand it 53% of the Aboriginal men whose deaths were investigated by the Royal Commission were being held for crimes of violence against women. The values which sustain prisoners' rights to safe and humane treatment in custody are equally applicable to victims of crime; *deaths in custody and criminal acts are separate issues which need to be understood on their own terms.* They meet in *Haunted by the Past* because Ginibi insists on *personalising* and to some extent *romanticising* stories of individual men rather than sustaining a *political analysis* of the impact of racism and colonialism on Aboriginal life.[34]

The two operative words in this quotation are 'personal' and 'political', posed here as mutually exclusive categories. Ginibi is seen as 'personalising' the prisoners' stories at the expense of a 'political analysis'. A more accurate description might be that the text reconfigures the boundaries between personal and political, showing them as entwined and inextricable. Rewriting the 1970s feminist adage, Ginibi reveals not only that the personal is political, but also that the political is personal. Ginibi's positionality in the text is irreducible to a singular role – 'mother', 'Indigenous social critic',

---

34 Morrissey, 2000, p 20 (my emphasis).

'autobiographer', 'writer'; her attempts to edu-ma-cate the judge, for example, flow from the multiple positions she occupies as an Indigenous woman, as Nobby's mother, and a nationally famous Koori writer and edu-ma-cator.

The review's reference to a narrative of 'victims' rights' and the charge of 'personalising and to some extent romanticising stories of individual men' reveals how a rhetoric of 'crime', 'individual responsibility' and 'victimhood' can work to obscure and depoliticise questions of the *criminalisation* of racialised populations. 'Crime', as Davis indispensably points out, 'is ... one of the masquerades behind which "race" with all its menacing ideological complexity, mobilises old public fears and creates new ones'.[35] The mobilisation of a narrative of victims' rights once again shuts down the argument with the 'obvious' answer that the proper place for the criminal is the prison. The logic of the review seems to be one that renders a focus on gender and a focus on race mutually exclusive – Ginibi's focus on racialised incarceration of Aboriginal men is seen as dismissing, or by implication, perhaps even condoning, the men's sexual violence against women. But is the re-inscription of black men as sexual predators a productive way to address questions of sexual violence, most of it directed at black women, in a society? Whereas factors of gender and race need to be thought *together* in their complex historical configurations, in the review, prison appears to function once more as the receptacle for the social ills of a racist and sexist system.

The assertion in the review that 'deaths in custody and criminal acts are separate issues which need to be understood on their own terms' suggests that the 'criminal act' exists in isolation. Yet 'crime', as Cunneen argues, must be understood as a 'social artifact [that] needs to be continually deconstructed'.[36] 'Crime' and 'the criminal act' are also determined by factors such as policing:

> There is little doubt that policing shapes the measuring of crime, and police decisionmaking can significantly impact on what we 'know' as offenders and offences. In the specific case of Indigenous people in Australia we can expect an even greater shaping of offending levels through police practices, given their contemporary role in Indigenous communities and their historic role in colonial policy.[37]

Cunneen's analysis suggests that 'deaths in custody and criminal acts' are emphatically not 'separate issues', but intimately and structurally connected through the historical relationship between the police and Indigenous peoples. Simplified understandings of crime as a self-evident category, what

---

35 Davis, 1998a, p 67.

36 Cunneen, 2001, p 45.

37 *Ibid*, p 45.

we 'know', ignore factors like the overpolicing of Indigenous people in contemporary Australia,[38] as well as continuing histories of colonisation, racism and criminalisation.

It is precisely the circulation of historically generated, racialised fears of black men that Ginibi attempts to circumvent in her narrative. Although her love and support for her son are unconditional – these are the values of the 'survival culture' that are stressed throughout her writing – her attitude is not simply one of 'indulgence' or biased 'mother love', for example when she deplores Nobby's uncritical belief in mateship or discusses his transaction with a sex worker. A mother intent on romanticising the narrative may have glossed over the latter incident. Instead, it is described in painful detail. Neither can Ginibi's comments about the Kings Cross police in this episode be dismissed as maternal gullibility or blame shifting; ample evidence has emerged in recent years about the corruption of NSW police, and in particular the complicity between the Kings Cross police and the sex industry.

Ginibi's account seems less blindly romanticising than an attempt to *humanise* Nobby in his experiences of the prison system:

> Pauline ... went out to see him but came back runnin back in tears, cryin, 'Quick, Mum! Come and talk to im! He's kickin and swearin at em ...'
>
> I hurried out to the station wagon, starting to cry myself, and pleading, 'Come on son, please behave' ... Looking at him made my heart bleed as he was handcuffed with only a smock and a pair of jockettes on ... I screamed out, 'Where's his clothes? He's a human being y'know!' Nobby was spittin and kickin at the police as they manhandled him out of the station wagon. His eyes were wild like a terrified, lost animal.[39]

This clear-eyed, precise description reads less as 'bias', 'indulgence' or sentimentality, but as a moment of empathy for a young man terrorised by the law.

READING POSITIONS: THE GOOD, THE BAD, THE 'GENERAL'

The 'Writing from Behind Bars' review suggests that the success of *Don't Take Your Love to Town* may have promoted certain assumptions about Ginibi's audience that lead *Haunted by the Past* to be targeted towards 'university courses in Indigenous studies' rather than to the 'less committed general reader'. In some ways this immediately renders my reading suspect, since I do indeed sometimes teach Indigenous writing to students at my

---

38 *Ibid*, pp 84–85.
39 Ginibi, 1999, p 152.

university. The invocation here of a familiar spectre, the 'general reader', however, returns us to implicit assumptions about reception and reading, of *how* we read, who reads, and most important, *who can be validated as a reader*. As much as the 'universal story', the 'general reader' is a figment of the humanist imagination, one which works coercively to delegitimise forms of reading and writing that challenge normative assumptions.

My critique of 'Writing from Behind Bars' has been directed primarily at its underwriting assumptions about writing, literature, autobiography, readership, location and address, assumptions that foreclose a non-humanist, non-common sense reading of the text, and elevate the 'less committed general reader' at the expense, presumably, of a reader with explicit political investments in the text. But what might be at stake for a non-general, even 'committed', reader – me, for instance, as a non-Indigenous, non-Anglo, Australian woman – in producing a counter-reading of Ginibi's text as testimonial?

In the months since the publication of *Haunted by the Past*, combined State, Territory and Federal Government actions on Indigenous and refugee issues have made for a massive boom in the incarceration industry. Even as Northern Territory and Western Australian jails bulge as a result of mandatory sentencing, isolated camps have been constructed for the mandatory detention of asylum seekers to Australia, mostly of Muslim and Middle Eastern background, who have been subjected to ongoing demonisation by government and tabloid media. Detention camps and private prisons are both operated by a US-based multinational, Australasian Corrections Management (ACM) and testify to the exponential increase in the privatised prison industry in recent times. On the day this essay was first delivered at the Australian National University in April 2000, the coroner found that the operator's negligence had contributed to the deaths of five men at Port Philip private prison, a direct intimation of some of the consequences of that increase.

This, of course, is matter for a different essay.[40] What I began mapping above, however, is an environment where the intimate connections between 'confinement, punishment and race' identified by Davis are becoming increasingly evident. These are connections that Ginibi's text tries to open out in productive ways – not least in the connections it makes between the racism experienced by migrant and Indigenous Australians through its inclusion of a letter written to Ginibi by one of Nobby's fellow inmates, a migrant from Malta.[41] *Haunted by the Past* as testimonial then, is an enabling form of writing – and reading. It allows a space for articulating new sites, subjectivities and solidarities of struggle against the forms of racialised punishment produced and reproduced by the law. Lowe's remarks about the

---

40   Perera, 2002, forthcoming.
41   Ginibi, 1999, p 72.

role of testimonial writing are important to cite here. Reading texts as testimonials, Lowe argues, can:

> ... displace the categorizing drive of disciplinary formations that would delimit the transgressive force of articulations within regulative epistemological or evaluative boundaries ... While specifying the difference between forms, this understanding of cultural production troubles both the strictly empirical foundations of social science and the universalising tendencies of aesthetic discourse. In this mode we can read testimony ... as a complex mediating genre that selects, conveys and connects 'facts' in particular ways without reducing social contradiction or compartmentalising the individual as a site of resolution. Likewise we can read literary texts like the novel not merely as the aesthetic framing of a 'private' transcendence, but as a form that may narrate the dissolution or impossibility of the private domain in the context of the material conditions of work, geography, gender and race. In this sense cultural forms of many kinds are important media in the formation of oppositional narratives and crucial to the imagination and rearticulation of new forms of subjectivity, collectivity and practice.[42]

Locating *Haunted by the Past* within the testimonial genre of cultural production makes the text available to oppositional and resistant readings and enables the formation and articulation of new subject and speaking positions. Through the medium of life stories, the text connects subjects to social relations and 'personal' stories to collective histories, making visible the systemic and insitutionalised ways in which the law and the prison implicate and impinge on particular racialised groups.

'I haven't discovered fiction yet', Ruby Langford Ginibi is fond of declaring; 'I'm too busy writing the truth'. *Haunted by the Past* is a text that speaks back to the 'disciplinary and categorizing drives' of both law and literature, and in doing so produces new critical and interpretive positions. This essay has discussed how we may read testimonial and evidential forms of cultural production and the effects and potentialities of our reading. As 'complex mediating genres' testimonial writings clear new spaces and create unexpected sites for readers at different institutional and disciplinary locations. To end with just one instance, recently, law students at one university in Sydney adopted Ginibi as their 'patron'. This imaginative and transgressive act both remakes the role of academic 'patron' and suggests productive possibilities for troubling the study and practice of law. I like to think of Ginibi as a robust, passionate and troublesome presence as the students repair to their law books: the image for me supplies a whole new understanding to the phrase *Romancing the Tomes*.

---

42 Lowe, 1997, pp 356–57.

PART FOUR

FEMINIST HISTORIOGRAPHIES

Little Daffodils of Spring

for Michelle A Taylor

The killing is warm
and separates us,
keeps us going.
We run to the dead
as we never would
to the living.
There is a secret about this
badly kept
because we know the way
life unworks itself.
Yellow leaves the field for the eye.
What is cruel finds history
where it may shelter,
find new legs,
and again learn to walk.
And there you are
among the little daffodils of Spring
sharing whatever is in your hands
with all who can
with some part of themselves
love what grows.
You know that judgement
bends itself back to the judge.
That justice
is what the smallest flower knows.

MTC Cronin

LANGUAGE AS THE 'PRETTY WOMAN' OF LAW: PROPERTIES OF LONGING AND DESIRE IN LEGAL INTERPRETATION AND POPULAR CULTURE

Judith Grbich

INTRODUCTION

Questions of law's authority are usually approached by enquiries into legal documents, such as legislation and judicial judgments. Within modern jurisprudential traditions these questions of law's authority are usually debated and discussed by a focus upon texts already having authoritative legal status, and upon readers and interpreters credentialled already in law. Unacknowledged within these practices is the contingency of law's authority upon interpretive conventions used by the common man and woman in their engagements with numerous forms of popular culture – novels, newspapers, films and television. In a Western culture it is the common man and woman's enjoyments of these popular forms of culture, which maintain the interpretive conventions upon which the legal professional draws for producing certainty about the meaning of legal texts. The forms of enjoyment of popular culture provide a resource for lawyers in their practice of the legal hermeneutics of finding authoritative meanings to all the language-based texts of legal practice. The 1990s film *Pretty Woman* provides one form of popular culture in which questions of law's authority and its contingency upon the pleasures and desires of the common man and woman can be pursued.

Pretty Woman opens with several women and a magician. We are watching some women watching a magician and also watching his trick of the appearance and disappearance of coins. He has three coins in his hand and finds another behind a woman's ear – as we look towards his gesturing the three other coins have disappeared. We are asked to ponder his phrase 'a penny from the ear, how much for the rest'? Or was it a penny from the air? Is it 'the ear' or 'the air', it is hard to hear the difference, and our image of the performance does not seem to assist. Image and text coincide in meaning if we see him taking the coin from her ear, but perhaps he took it from out of thin air? How the viewer decides upon what is heard will influence what one sees, and what one sees will influence how one decides upon which word was spoken. Sound and 'sight' oscillate as the viewer tries to make some sense from the wider narrative itself, from the magician's whole performance. As the magician continues his party tricks, his performance of the sensory qualities of speech opens onto a metanarrative of the dilemmas of modern banking, and the picturing of the magical sequences by which hearing of words can transform the meanings which written language presents to the eye. The strolling magician – who reappears throughout the film – tells us that 'no matter what they say, it is all about money', and 'imagine ladies that you are a savings and loan officer. You have it all and we have nothing'. With these words of the magician the viewer of the movie is drawn into the tale of the romance – the longing that impels a quest for an unknown, a longing for a consummation, which always remains out of reach despite having found the girl in the end.

As the magical performance within the film continues it is 'we who have nothing' in one sense who are brought into the magical sequencing of the human senses – of how coins can appear and then disappear and leave us wondering how much are worth the ones we cannot see in our hands. How much is the money we cannot see worth? When some of these coins have been transformed into paper money or other forms of incorporeal property, what are the practices of recognition whereby practices of writing, human aspiration and a code of entitlement bring to cognition a new thing of value? What are these sensory contexts of human longing[1] and desire by which a pictured absence – a posited negative – can confirm an incorporeal presence, a thing of value and not simply 'words on parchment'? How are one's desires, and images of young women in movies, used as forms of pleasure upon which law's authority remains contingent?

My paper is at heart a historiography of the idea of property in general,[2] of the narrative of feudal tenurial relations which passes for a code for property in general, and the enplotment of that ideoscape of entitlement felt as citizenship in western modernity. Tales of feudal tenurial relations have passed as a code for property in general at least since the time of Blackstone's treatment of the rights of things,[3] and his narrative of the carving out of the private rights of dominion over a thing from something previously held in common. Even in Blackstone's narrative in 1766 of the coming into being of modern tenures in real property law, the tale of ancient tenures is barely disguised as a code or plot of a mythical nature. At the centre of his tale is writing, the writing of conveyances, and the possibility of the displacement of the rights of sons by the process of enculturation. Modernity for Blackstone is the right of fathers to devise their property to persons other than the eldest son. Modernity is when the son's right of primogeniture – to his entitlement as eldest son – can be overlaid and overridden by a father's desire to do otherwise. Blackstone places writing,

---

1   See Stewart, 1993.

2   On other approaches to this question see: Gray and Gray, 1998, pp 15–51; Schroeder, 1998; Threadgold, 1999a; Watson, 2000.

3   Blackstone, 1979.

paradoxically, as the performance by which property things first pass into civil society, and yet he questions this very practice, and thereby sets in train that practice of wondering upon the marvel of writing and the engagement of the reader within the conventions of imagining *how* 'things' become.[4] These are conventions of fairytale, or 'wondertale', characters and plots, which repeat that magical sequencing of the senses which is reading. Reading is the sound of speech and the sighting of poetical meanings of words which produce in the mind of the reader of texts or the viewer of films an insight of worthfulness or pleasure as the reader's imagination takes on a quest from the literal to the figural and possibly back again.[5]

Blackstone's musings on the questions which frame his narrative of the coming into being of civil property are worth repeating here, as they bring together my themes of legal authority, recognition of entitlement, narrative, writing, and pleasure:

> There is nothing which so generally strikes the imagination, and engages the affections of mankind, as the right of property; or that sole and despotic dominion which one man claims and exercises over the external things of the world ... And yet there are very few, that will give themselves the trouble to consider the original and foundation of this right. Pleased as we are with the possession, we seem afraid to look back to the means by which it was acquired ... not caring to reflect that (accurately and strictly speaking) there is no foundation in nature or in natural law, why a set of words upon parchment should convey the dominion of land; why the son should have a right to exclude his fellow creatures from a determinate spot of ground, because his father had done so before him ...[6]

In my study of the sensory forms of recognising and constituting legal authority the 'pretty woman' of law is language itself, a commonly held medium for conveying the ground of culture, and the reader is her romancer. The reader carves out for oneself a meaning of one's own, as if sight, sound and feeling were the tools of a sculptor or the eating of an apple from the tree of wisdom. Language's qualities of enchantment attract the viewer of her figurations – to dwell within and create with her those images of self and satisfaction through which each reader comes into an inheritance of one kind or another. While legal interpretation can appear to fix meanings and legislate which name shall stand for a thing, this juridical quest for certainty is too dependent upon the sensory qualities of reading itself – the emotions and desires of humankind, ever to make the meaning of words

---

4   Foucault provides one historiography of these conventions: Foucault, 1970. Legal historiographies, of how things become, are different, see: Duncanson and Tomlins, 1982; Goodrich and Hachamovitch, 1991, pp 159–81; Grbich, 1993; Grbich, 2001; Duncanson, 2000.

5   On images, law and practices of representation, I am indebted to: Mitchell, 1994; Young, 1996; Douzinas, Goodrich, and Hachamovitch, 1994; Young, 1997; Douzinas, 1999.

6   Blackstone, 1979, p 2.

come to a closure. In the sensory structuring of reading itself law's romance with language remains forever unrequited.

The film *Pretty Woman* is usually interpreted as yet one more example of the western fairytale in which a poor but beautiful young woman is rescued from a life of struggle and tedium by a prince who is captivated by her beauty. The characters of Vivian and Edward in *Pretty Woman* are usually interpreted as variations of Cinderella and Prince Charming, or Rapunzal locked in the tower and the rescuing Knight. Vivian is working as a prostitute in Hollywood where she is rescued by Edward, a rich and powerful corporate raider. Interpretations from film studies and cultural studies usually emphasise the destructive effects for women in the western cultural pursuit of the retelling of these narratives[7] – destructive ideals of youthful embodiment which regulate women's sense of self worth, and the ideals of female passivity which remain out of reach and out of mind for most women.[8] But these interpretations also focus on the enduring pleasures the young girl in the fairytale narrative of romance holds for women, and perhaps the being of a Prince for whom all things in life seem possible.

ROMANCING THE BODY CORPORATE

Pretty Woman can be read differently. This is the romance of Edward with the body corporate. It can be understood as a romancing of old technologies, and also a quest for finding what is intrinsically valuable about new technologies, about those new financial practices, which appear as things,[9] as commodities known collectively as paper money, 'commercial paper'. This romancing and questing structure can be understood as establishing again the cultural groundings for new technologies – the making of new 'financial derivatives' and the newer still electronic means of disposing of their benefits of ownership.

Edward wants the body corporate for himself. Morse made it; it is Morse's baby, his daughter. Edward desires to take it over and use it for himself, to the exclusion of Morse. In the romance of the body corporate Edward repeats the codes of the romance tale but disturbs the sequence of hero as rescuer of the feminised body.[10] Morse is father of the body corporate, having created the paper entity. He is also at the beginning of the narrative a father at risk of losing his right to exclude others from the use of her body and the things of her body. We are told he has spent 40 years of his

---

7   See Smith, 1997; Caputi, 1991.

8   Critical approaches to these questions include Lapsley and Westlake, 1992; Cooks, Orbe, and Bruess, 1993.

9   Grbich, 1997.

10 On analysis of the folktale, see Propp, 1968; Propp, 1984.

life making this company, it is a shipbuilding company, and it manufactures ships. Grandson David also tells us that 'grandfather believes that the man who has created a company should control its destiny'. At the beginning of the tale Morse is in control of the company, but it appears that his company is in need of capital and a corporate restructure is being planned as a way of gaining the capital needed for maintaining the manufacture of ships. Morse may lose his majority shareholding position and his control of the Board of Directors. Negotiations begin for the marriage of Edward and the company.

Edward at first appears to be the villain of the tale, he wants to stop Morse's control and use of his offspring's body – he intends to stop Morse's company making ships. When Vivian asks Edward what he does, what is his occupation, he says, 'I buy companies'. He says, he 'borrows money from banks, and investors to buy companies'. 'Not an easy thing to do,' he assures Vivian. Once he buys the company, he says, he breaks them up into pieces, and sells the pieces, 'the parts are worth more than the whole'. In the case of Morse's company he wants the prime industrial property, the real estate at the port of Long Beach, the site of the shipyards in Los Angeles. During the negotiations between Edward and the Morse family at the restaurant, Morse speaks as though Edward were courting a daughter, 'we find it hard to figure out what your real intentions are'. There is a hint that Edward's intentions are not honourable. It appears that Morse needs to consider a suitor because the company assets are mortgaged to the bank, and the company's capital for carrying on the manufacture of ships has diminished. He needs Edward's capital. It appears that if Edward borrows money from a bank, he can buy more shares and as he owns 10 million of the Morse company shares already, his takeover of the Morse company can proceed without the consent of the present Board or present owners of the shares. Edward has simply to buy more minority shares and proceed with his hostile takeover plan.

Morse believes during the restaurant negotiations that he can retain control of the company. The price of shares has been set high enough to prevent Edward gaining a majority. He would have to pay too much to buy up sufficient shares held by minority shareholders. But the share price is contingent on a contract with the state Defence Department to purchase ships, a contract requiring approval by a Senate Appropriations Committee. It appears that Edward believes he can keep the contract buried or stalled at the Committee stage and prevent the share price being held up by the expectation of shareholders that this lucrative contract with the state will proceed. While the contract remains buried in Committee proceedings the share price will fall. During the restaurant negotiations Morse's grandson narrates the times of old, 'when men built ships the size of cities, and men like my grandfather made this country'. These were the 'olden times' when the making of things was the making of the country. Edward's villainous nature comes to light when he discloses that he can have the state approval of the shipbuilding contract delayed indefinitely. Members of the Appropriations Committee are 'in his pocket'. Morse fights back by raising the price for the shares of minority shareholders, thereby hoping to defeat Edward's attempt to buy more shares. We are told that Morse will finance these purchases by 'throwing in with the employees', and borrowing from the Plymouth Bank. Edward's lawyer, Phil, has a plan to use their influence at the bank to prevent Morse obtaining a loan from the bank. It is a coincidence that Edward's villainous nature flounders as he approaches Plymouth, a name for a place of new life for the pilgrim fathers, in American history and folklore? Plymouth is the landing place in Massachusetts of the pilgrim's flight from persecution under the old European order of things.

After telling Vivian that 'I won't let myself become emotionally involved in business' and her reportage of a similar way of doing the prostitution business, Edward observes that 'you and I are such similar creatures ... we both screw people for money'. As he reveals to her a remnant of emotion for a lost father and himself as a lost soul, he seems to find empathy for Morse about to lose a child, the corporate child. He complains to his lawyer still planning the hostile takeover, that 'we don't build anything, we don't make anything'. Phil the lawyer explains in return that 'we make money Edward. We worked for a year on this deal; it is what you said you wanted. Morse's jugular is exposed; it is time for the kill. Let's finish this, call the bank.' It becomes clear that Edward never calls the Plymouth bank to stop Morse's loan. Vivian becomes the medium through which Edward experiences an emotional level to this life – to her he expresses anger towards a philandering father and the loss of his inheritance, and confesses his first corporate takeover was that of his father's company; his motivation was revenge. As Edward's sensibilities towards Vivian develop, as he comes to see her as a person with qualities in addition to sexual services, as she becomes his object of pursuit – for her intrinsic qualities rather than simply sexual services, he emerges as the hero of the romancing of the corporate body tale. His marriage with Morse's corporate child proceeds. Edward agrees to reform his asset stripping habits and build big ships with Morse.

But what he longed to seize is now no longer determinative of his sense of quietude, satisfaction or achievement. His longing remains, and shifts to that other unattainable union – a meeting of spirits with a Vivian who trades only in the use of her body. Left undecided is whether Edward's use of promissory notes, his use of bank notes, has been sufficient to qualify as a new kind of 'making the country great' again. The intrinsic value of his underwriting of the company's new things is undecided. The old technology of manufacturing things is revealed as simply the making of 'destroyers', of warships, things that destroy.

THE CINDERELLA CODE AND THE PERSONS AND THINGS OF PROPERTY LAW

In property law theory – that curious contemporary practice of deploying the terminology of feudal office holding and its supplementation by the recognition and naming of new kinds of freeholding persons and things – landed or real property is divided from personal property. This categorisation preserves a distinction between things belonging to the king – real, landed or royal property, and things capable of ownership of a freeman, which was not necessarily held by the king – personal property. Within property law theory, Roman Law conceptions of citizenship, of personhood as free or enslaved, and of *patria potestas* – the power of the father, remain encoded as learnt practices for recognising when a new kind of human practice can be named as creative and its fruits claimed for oneself. Contemporary property law textbooks narrate an imagined landscape of feudal persons and their estates,[11] peopled in the mind of the legal reader by the freeman and the unfree man, their families and households, their obligations and various incidents of tenure holding or servitude. While the characters of the unfree have been largely absent in 20th century property law textbooks,[12] and legal judgments, their presence and obligations remain within the classificatory structure of property law's terminology for confirming the presence of any new kind of financial property, practice or effect. Writing and its figural dimensions stand in to perform the scripts for these phantom characters. Or is it the reader who animates the 'plain' words of 'ordinary' language? The actions of finding, gathering, making and using conjure memories of Roman woods, fields, vineyards, wild animals, slaves and the poetical forms for representing their rightful ownership and use. While poetical terms for these actions repeat the feudal order of a freeman's holding of tenure and the uses of his estate, this feudal landscape of the legal imagination is embedded within the Roman Law narratives of Justinian and his scripts for the characters of fathers and freemen – the conditions of their rights over things naturally under their control and other things which might be brought under their control:

> When a man makes a new object out of materials belonging to another, the question arises to which of them, by natural reason, does this new object belong? to the man who made it, or to the owner of the materials? ... If the new object can be reduced to the materials of which it was made, it belongs to the owner of the materials, if not, it belongs to the person who made it ...[13]

---

11 Anne Bottomley has written on the tradition of real property texts and the theme of landscape; see Bottomley, 1996, pp 109–24.

12 They are returning to academic texts in contemporary critiques of the Australian native title practices; see Grattan and McNamara, 1999.

13 Justinian, 1913, pp 39–40.

In the feudal order of things an unfree man belonged to his lord, did that mean the offspring of his making were also the things belonging to the feudal lord? Recognising that an offspring was made by the actions of 'a person who was not unfree' encapsulates the limits of both the feudal order and contemporary property law, but its focal point or image is as near or far as one imagines the actions of finding, gathering, making and using. These are actions of the imagination for picturing the person who is not unfree, pictures interwoven with narratives of daughters and absent fathers in European fairytales, and sons and godly fathers in biblical tales.

The poetical structuring of persons and things and the aesthetics of actions, which animate them, are sufficiently alike in contemporary property law and in the romantic wondertale of the Europeans for each to stand in for the concept of property in general. In each there is a struggle by a hero to find and take for himself the offspring of an absent father.

The focal point of desire

In *Pretty Woman*, the romancing of the body corporate does not stop at the marriage of Edward with Morse's grown up corporate child, Edward's desires are displaced and our questions about the intrinsic worth of Edward's business practices in making the country great again remain unresolved. It appears that the hostile takeover and revenge strategies have been only personal tactics for dealing with his own emotional confusion at the loss of his father at the time of his parents' divorce. Edward's willingness to accept the regard of Morse as if he were a father seems to permit Edward some compensation and he emerges with new sensibilities, which he directs towards Vivian. His desires are displaced to the takeover of her body for his sexual gratification; he wants to buy her sexual services for a longer term. His desires now lead him to another land of commerce, back to Hollywood Boulevard. But it is now a land of commerce in which Vivian will no longer deal on the same terms. His desires have led him also to the land of her dreams where she is Cinderella wanting a knight to rescue her – from herself. It is in the giving up of his desires to pay for the use of her body and entering into the fantasy of her body being in need of rescue that the romance moves through the Cinderella fairytale to become one of the viewer's engagement with the romancing of language and writing.

There is an ambiguity about the representation of Vivian's body. In the land of commerce inhabited by Edward and Vivian the hooker, money paid for her services suggests that things of substance can be substituted for an equivalent value of money. Vivian trades in the use of her body, she owns it and she gets to say 'when ... where ... how much'. Property can be known, its value estimated and exchanged at a price known to the holder and representing the similar price the buyer puts upon the satisfaction of his desires. Money can represent the proprietary thing and what one is willing to pay for it. Or can it? Where the proprietary thing has a physical substance, such as land, or gold, or Vivian's body, then perhaps this is the case. But can an estimate of desire be a substitute for a non-physical thing, such as incorporeal property, such as writing the words of money on paper? How can words be a substitute for an estimate of one's desire? How and where can desire replace words? When Edward desires Vivian more, for longer than the six day deal, he is willing to pay more. But the narrative of *Pretty Woman* takes Edward, and the viewer, to the door of Vivian's dreams, the fairytale world of the Cinderella tale.

At this point there is an ambiguity for the viewer. Where is the place of the viewer, commerce land or fairytale land? Are we still in the land of commerce where money can buy things, anything, or have we been transported to some more noble place – the land of chivalry, of higher morality, of domesticity, private life, and marriage. Does Vivian's body mean Edward's desire for a new takeover – to use her for himself, or does her body mean Edward's desire is for her as his wife and himself as husband; and can we tell the difference? How do we interpret Edward's actions in securing the consummation of his desires for this daughter of Hollywood?

At this point I want to turn to the story in legal histories of tenure in law books, stories that provide another account of daughters and the meanings which attach to the price to be paid for their hand in marriage. These legal histories that picture daughters of absent fathers provide a negative logic to the father's identity as a free man, and the suitor's actions provide us with the clues to interpret those forms of entitlement – linked in fiction to tenurial relations, and in practice to the narrative form for transforming written words into monetary things.

FEUDALSCAPES: THE IMAGINARY LAND OF TENURE AND ESTATES IN HISTORIOGRAPHIES OF LAND LAW

In property law theory, the division of real property and personal property follows historical lines of categorisation. The terms and theory of real property remains within 13th century English terminology for specifying which kinds of property passed on the death of a feudal lord to his son. 'Real' property included the kinds of corporeal and incorporeal hereditaments that passed with the inheritance of office or status of Lord under a system of primogeniture. The heir of a lord took up occupation of the immovable incidents of being Son, of filiation, of entitlement.

Contemporary practices of diverse propertisations of relations in modernity remain within these imagined worlds or 'feudalscapes' –

imaginary worlds,[14] in which a reader with juridical conventions for picturing the work of making things with words and writing can recognise privileged forms of being,[15] of citizenship, and of entitlements. Appadurai has coined some phrases[16] for exploring various disjunctions in contemporary global economies between economy, culture and politics, explorations based upon the theorisation of the politics of global commoditisation as involving language, interpretation and themes of landscape. His purpose is, in his words, to:

> ... use terms with the common suffix scape to indicate first of all that these are not objectively given relations which look the same from every angle of vision, but rather that they are deeply perspectival constructs, inflected very much by the historical, linguistic and political situatedness of different sorts of actors ... these landscapes thus, are the building blocks of what, extending Benedict Anderson, I would like to call 'imagined worlds', that is, the multiple worlds which are constituted by the historically situated imaginations of persons and groups spread around the globe.[17]

Using Appadurai's insights, 'feudalscapes' are part of an aesthetic of how things of writing can confirm the presence of a legal character or person, and how this character can be recognised as capable of performing wondrous feats of financial capabilities, which far outwit and outweigh the efforts of any human being.

As the pre-Norman system of many lords changed to one in which the land was assumed to be occupied under notions of tenure, the Crown became both the one lord or sovereign and the one titleholder to land. This narrative of the coming into being of the historical coincidence and reality of sovereignty and legal ownership of real things is repeated in 20th century property law textbooks. Land was occupied as Knight service or as service free of military obligation, provided the duties of occupation were commuted by a money payment to the King. Tenure was the service, which the Knight owed, and the service incumbent upon the tenement or land while it was in the Knight's hands.[18] Where the Knight could not perform the service the Crown could enforce the duty owed against the land. The land owed its 'fruits' to the Crown, almost as if it were a person. The term tenure means the power of the lord to deal in both the land and the fruits of the land, his interests in the uses of the land. As the services owed by the Knight came to be commuted by a money payment other categories of tenure became blended into the category of freeholding of land. Land

---

14 Anderson, 1983.

15 On the anxiety of representation involved in recognition of being legal, see Rush, 1997.

16 Appadurai, 1990. These terms are: ethnoscapes, mediascapes, technoscapes, financescapes, ideoscapes.

17 *Ibid*, p 296.

18 Pollock and Maitland, 1968, vol I, pp 232–40.

tenures became either freehold tenements for the life of the holder or for a term of years, each with both services owed by the holder and fruits owed by the land.[19] Where the services owed by the holder were certain or finite, and the fruits of the land measurable in certain quantities both kind of tenements were thought of as 'free' or limited. The holders' liberties were known.

In these narratives of times past, not all inhabitants of feudal Britain lived as freeholders of land, some lived under conditions of villeinage or unfree tenure. In Pollock and Maitland's *History of English Law*, their status as villeins was one of entitlement of occupation to the land of a sublord who held from the overlord – an entitlement by descent and the performance of uncertain and unlimited duties to the sublord. Pollock in 1882 cites a passage from Bracton on 'the legal theory of villenage which prevailed in his day':

> The tenement changes not the condition of a free man any more than a slave. For a free man may hold in mere villenage, doing whatever service thereto belongs, and shall not the less be free, since he does this in regard of the villenage and not in regard of his person ... Mere villenage is a tenure rendering uncertain and unlimited services, where it cannot be known at eventide what service hath to be done in the morning – that is, where the tenant is bound to do whatever is commanded him.[20]

Pollock continues his extract from Bracton:

> Again: 'Another kind of tenement is villenage, whereof some is mere and other privileged. Mere villenage is that which is so held that the tenant in villenage, whether free or bound, shall do of villein service whatever is commanded him, and may not know at nightfall what he must do on the morrow, and shall ever be held to uncertain dues; and he may be taxed at the will of the lord for more or for less ... yet so that if he be a free man he doth this in the name of villenage and not in the name of personal service ... but if he be a villein [by blood] he shall do all these things in regard as well of the villenage as of his person.'[21]

In Pollock and Maitland's *History*, some men held tenure subject to more certain duties, such as three days' labour for the sublord per week, the ploughing and planting of so many acres of wheat to be given to the sublord.[22] The customary duties to the sublord both evidenced their entitlements of occupation and their unfree status. To the extent some entitlements of tenure were 'by copy of court roll', by 'copyholding' came to be viewed as by the authority of the lord's manor courts and unfree tenements were difficult to distinguish at a later age from free tenements. In

---

19 Pollock and Maitland, 1968, vol II, pp 106–17.
20 Pollock, 1901, p 333.
21 *Ibid.*
22 Pollock and Maitland, 1968, vol I, p 376.

this historiography of Pollock and Maitland of the coming of modern English property law, at the time of the King's courts admitting jurisdiction, 'the term "unfree tenement" becomes the pivot of a whole system of remedies'.[23]

In the history books of Pollock and Maitland, the dividing line between the incidents of holding tenure coincident with free status and the incidents of holding coincident with the unfree was blurred, and consequently the jurisdiction of the King's courts was blurred, at least in the history writing. It appears that it had become blurred by the Lords treating the holding of some use of the land as transferable, such as a leasehold for a certain number of years. Were the monies paid by the leaseholder for the uses of the land a sign of unfree service, or of freeholding? How could the wheat paid by an unfree villein to his Lord for the occupation of land as an unfree villein be distinguished from the monies of equivalent value paid by another possibly free villein for similar benefits of occupation? In this history narrative at stake was a 13th century distinction for determining the jurisdiction of the Kings' courts.

Pollock and Maitland's *History* speaks of the difficulties of reading the 'process of commutation'. How does one read the meaning of villeinage when dues can be paid in money or in produce?

> We may see the process of commutation in all its various stages, from the stage in which the lord is beginning to take a penny or a halfpenny instead of each 'work' that in that particular year he does not happen to want, through the stage in which he habitually takes each year the same sum in respect of the same number of works but has expressly reserved to himself the power of exacting the works in kind, to the ultimate stage in which there is a distinct understanding that the tenant is to pay rent instead of doing work.[24]

And also at stake in the telling of this blurred line dividing the free status and the unfree, was a picturescape for plotting the beginnings of the commercialisation of the benefits of landholding. Writing in the 19th century this picturing, of feudal office holding and status in the 13th century, created a prehistory for monetary forms of property yet to be thought.

The mark of the unfree man

One method of detecting or distinguishing the free villein from the unfree was the presence, in his incidents of holding, of the right to dispose at his will of the fruits of his body. Pollock argued in 1882 that:

---

23 *Ibid*, p 358.
24 Pollock and Maitland, 1968, vol I, p 366.

The only difference in the services was that the merchetum on marrying a daughter, being an incident of personal servitude (as a fine paid to the lord for depriving him of a slave), was not demandable from the free man holding in villeinage.[25]

The benefits of the uses of the unfree man's body – his sons and daughters – were subject to the control of the lord. His daughter could be married out of the manorial jurisdiction only by paying a fine to the lord. His daughter was, in effect, the property of the lord in similar manner to the wheat of her father's labour, or the new calves of her father's husbandry. She was part of the stock on the tenement. The unfree man must pay the *merchetum* before his daughter could be removed from the tenement, and used by a husband. In the history book of Pollock and Maitland, the merchet was a base payment or mark of personal unfreedom.[26] Pollock and Maitland argue that a man who did not have the power to control the giving of his daughter in marriage, the man who did not own and control the fruits of his reproductive labour was an unfree man. Being able to treat one's daughter as if she were a produced and disposable thing of a fatherly maker was not determinative of the status of a freeman, but not being able to treat one's daughter as a made thing was determinative of an unfree man.

Whether we regard the theory of real property law produced by Pollock and Maitland as faithful accounts of 'land law', as 'theory' faithful to a history written in the 1880s, or whether we read them as postmodern historiographies written for the coming into being of a new legal life for monetary property, their jurisprudence did record the place of the daughter or young girl in the legal imagination of western law. Having to pay another for leave to give one's daughter in marriage was the mark of personal unfreedom. Payments made for the right to take and hold the future uses of the things of the tenement – whether the field and its wheat, the cows and their calves, or the serfs of the tenement and their offspring, had an indeterminate meaning or effect, a meaning for the future only if one knew the civil and legal origin of that for which payment was proffered. But these same civil and legal origins of things were being transformed by the making of payments for rights to future use. And rights to future use – the character of the *chose in action* – were taking up a place as hero in the scripts of a feudal order, in the feudalscapes of property law textbooks. Here were the future heroes of commercial life, without a narrative, unless Pollock and Maitland could create one for them. Through daughters, fathers can dream of any alliance with other men and make this happen, if he has the gift of her in marriage;[27] and if a juridical community can recognise the characters in the

---

25   Pollock, 1901, p 334; see also Pollock, 1887, pp 202–14.

26   Pollock and Maitland, 1968, vol I, pp 372–73.

27   Levi-Strauss pursues these questions of women, exchange, language, alliance and communication in Levi-Strauss, 1969, pp 478–97.

paper work of this dream, which underwrites the adventures and conquests of corporate and financial capital.

READING THE IDEOSCAPE OF ENTITLEMENT: RESCUING VIVIAN AND EDWARD

The fairytale narrative within Vivian's dream for herself in *Pretty Woman*, with its code of the maiden trapped in the tower by a wicked Queen and the Knight on the white horse with colours flying, provides a picturing of the textbook theories of property law, and the characters of its feudalscapes. The Cinderella or Rapunzal code and the rescuing Prince or Knight repeats the system of signification of property law theory, that feudalscape of tenurial relations which passes for the idea of property in general. In the fairytale an 'ideoscape'[28] of feudal land and office, of *res* and *persona* – the thing and the mask of persona, form the structure of the character's spheres of action. Each daughter's marriage is not within her leave. Cinderella or Rapunzal is the focal point in how the Knight's actions can be meaningful. We do not know whether she is the daughter of a freeman who can decide for himself whom she will marry, or whether she is a daughter of an unfree man who can be married only on payment to the feudal lord for the loss of a manorial subject. In the fairy tale narrative of the Cinderella or Rapunzal genre father is always missing. She cannot be married until a complex event occurs, a quest is completed, or a series of barriers are surmounted. These events, quests or barriers are sufficiently complicated for their completion to be possible only by a heroic character. The meaning of the hero's actions provide one part of a larger narrative of a father, perhaps an earthly father with qualities of being free, or perhaps a spiritual father towards whom longing remains coded by a life long quest.

As Edward enters Vivian's dream world and its feudalscape of the maiden locked in the attic and the rescuing Knight, the viewer is transported to fairyland. There is an ambiguity to Edward's actions as he is drawn from corporate world into the feudalscape. The images and signs of what Edward's money means are displaced from the funds he contributed to saving Morse's company to the outlay of an apartment and living expenses for a 'paid woman', or at least the offer of these moneys. Edward is willing to pay for Vivian's sexual services on a long term basis.

---

28 Appadurai has coined this term and notes that, '"ideoscapes" are also concatenations of images ... composed of elements of the Enlightenment world-view, which consists of a concatenation of ideas, terms and images, including "freedom", "welfare", "rights", "sovereignty", "representation" and the master-term "democracy"'. See Appadurai, 1990, p 299.

Edward's desires for Vivian and how he will achieve his object are doubly coded.[29] While still in corporate land he believes that money will buy her body and her sexual services. In Vivian's feudalscape this means that she is the daughter of an unfree man, the ideoscape of property law theory is confirmed as inhabited by the personae of Lords and others who serve as things for Lords. Vivian rejects Edward's offer to be a 'paid woman' and holds out for her dream. As Edward is drawn into her dream and the sequence of patterns of action available in the fairytale narrative, he changes the path of his quest. Whereas in the corporate world, payment always joined Edward with the object of his desires, it is now his own efforts as rescuing hero that is required. He must charge on the White Horse with colours flying, find the trapped maiden and climb the tower despite the dangers of the quest. Monetary performance is replaced with a performance by him of the character in her dreams.

But does this performance by Edward of the quest struggle mean that Vivian is a daughter for whom payment must be made? Is she the sign of an unfree man, a daughter of the unfree? Do we read Edward's performance as Knight as the struggle of payment, the return to the feudalscape of tenurial relations? Or do we read Edward's actions from the land of private life in modernity – the 'real time' of the present towards which Edward and Vivian appear to be moving, to the point of recognition that a non-commercial love is possible. In this mythical land of private life, it is his desire that has brought him to the recognition that she is intrinsically valued, a person to be loved for herself.

The ambiguity of Edward's actions lies in his performance of both the scenario of private life with its corporate world, and that of fairyland and its rescuing Knights. Are we in the present or the past? As the viewer struggles to contain both readings, Vivian's body stands as the ground upon which the viewer makes sense of each scenario. What does Vivian's body mean? And how does the movie viewer's desire to recognise the meaning of the film structure which reading of Edward's actions emerges? Has Edward rescued Vivian from her attic and completed the heroic quest that scripts the life of monetary persons within the juridical mind of corporate lives? Or has Vivian rescued Edward from his failing to make things of value from his life as a corporate raider? Has an intrinsic value of the writing of Edward's commercial paper or his performance of this character been established? As Edward completes the climb to the top of the stairs outside the windows of Vivian's apartment, he asks her what happens next to the characters in her childhood dream: 'So what happened after he climbed up the tower and rescued her?' Vivian says that 'she rescued him right back'.

---

29 See Bal, 1996.

But right back where? Back to the reality of that somatoscope of the Europeans where a reader's feelings and emotions for the characters of feudal actors in financial scripts enliven a global commodification of cultures? Or has he exchanged a reality for the dreamworld of the feudalscape, a reality of the present in which there are scenarios of private life outside a corporate world in which people stand in as things for persons in feudalscapes of monetary exchanges? Or has he exchanged this for the land of her dreams, the times past where rescues of maidens can only confirm an order of heroes transformed into things or things acting as if they could become heroes?

In each of these endings to my wondertale of language as the 'pretty woman' of law, the legal character of the 'writer' or 'maker' is confirmed as having made words on paper into something of intrinsic monetary value. The writer or maker is a well known character of banking and finance law. He is also a character through whom the interpretive conventions by which words refer to things of monetary value, or are things of monetary value, have entered the cultural repertoire of transformation narratives. The writer makes paper money; he makes 'commercial paper'. His written signs on paper, alphabetical signs arranged as words become things of monetary value. His materials partly belong to himself and partly belong to another; the writer in the legal imagination of the feudalscape uses words on paper of his own, the poetical forms of a reader for picturing finding, gathering, making and using these words, and the emotions of a viewer of movies, and life, for making sense of the actions of persons. These feelings of longing and desire can re-present an ancient narrative as one of new insight and its hero as the subject of the human will. In feelings of longing the human subject emerges as that hero of the struggle to be human destined during life never to survive the Fall from Grace.

But Justinian's Institutes have already laid down that a new object made partly by the materials belonging to one shall be rightfully owned by him who has contributed to both the labour of making and part of the materials.[30] Recognition of a new idea remains within the scenarios of Roman life. While these poetical forms for the work of the juridical imagination are bound by pictures of Roman life and scenarios of citizenship and servitude, they retain their capacity to enchant by their re-enactment within the enjoyments of popular culture. Each reader's pleasures taken in the figurations of speech, her sounds and sights, draw the eyes towards the place of next time, and compel the soul to long for home.

---

30 Justinian, 1913.

CHAPTER 8

MADONNA AND/OR WHORE?: FEMINISM(S) AND PUBLIC SPHERE(S)[1]

Ann Genovese

... as subject for history, woman always occurs simultaneously in several places.[2]

PUBLIC SPHERE(S)

Feminisms' relationship with, and in, the public sphere has always been difficult, because the public sphere is constituted upon the bedrock of traditional liberal theory and practice. The result for those who wish to reconcile the contradictions between woman as a subject 'different' from the individual championed by liberalism, yet still logically entitled to the equality that liberalism bequeathed, is a status Joan Scott describes as 'feminism's incurable paradoxical condition'.[3] This 'incurable paradoxical condition' is exacerbated by the location of men and women into the categories of 'public' and 'private' spheres. Western, liberal law is a key arbiter of the divide between the two. It wields great power in determining how, and when, women can be conceived of as equal citizens within the foundations of liberal theory, and when they must remain in the private. It is for this reason that legal feminists have always, in particular, been held in the grip of the 'paradoxical condition', and sought theoretical and practical ways of dealing with it.[4]

Yet the 'public' is a divided sphere. The fact that there exists a broader web of technologies of definition and control, beyond the state or law *per se*,

---

1 This paper was written in April 2000 during a short fellowship at the Humanities Research Centre, Australian National University, when I was fortunate enough to take part in their 'Law and the Humanities' program. I would like to thank and acknowledge the support of my colleagues at, and fellow visitors to, the HRC who assisted with the writing of this paper, in particular, Dr John Docker.

2 Cixous, 1976, p 252.

3 Scott, 1997, p 698.

4 For example, Margaret Thornton, in reflecting upon law's role in constituting the idea of a public/private divide has argued that as a dichotomy, it is a well-nurtured 'myth'. She argues that the 'temporally permeable nature of the "dichotomy" enables it to operate as an ideological device: "private" being effectively invoked if the state espouses non-intervention; "public" to the contrary': Thornton, 1995, p 11. This ideology leaves unchallenged the male/female split entrenched in liberal theory, and dominant since Rousseau's *Emile*, which has resulted in real difficulty and hostility for women as they attempt to claim a distinct, yet equal, subjectivity in a public sphere delineated by state and law, while using the public sphere to get it done.

from which simple categorisations of social order escape, must also be acknowledged.[5] From this perspective, I want to view the 'public' as a multiple site of contest for women. The Fourth Estate, or mass media, plays an important role in the 'civilised scenario' constructed by liberalism because rational debate about the state of the public sphere, staged in the public consciousness, is an integral part of democracy.[6]

Where feminism is concerned, viewing the media as an inextricable element of the liberal public seems to raise different questions from those raised in relation to the law.[7] The very fact that the media offers the material conditions for the development and transmission of conflicting, as well as new, opinions and ideas has arguably allowed women a space within the public to critique the public. As Catherine Lumby puts it, the media has been a 'Trojan horse' for women, and 'Suddenly, the barbarians weren't simply at the gates – they were inside, redecorating the castle in garish new colours'.[8]

She goes on to raise a good question. She argues that feminists have, despite considerable exertions on trying to theorise how women and gender politics have shaped the mass media, 'spent very little time looking at how the mass media has shaped and influenced feminism'.[9] In short, feminism's relationship with and in the media is involved in a different kind of paradox. It is one that seems to have resulted from the fact that despite rubbing up against each other these last 20 years, and although both have changed as a result, that the 'old-style' feminist position, inherently critical of a masculinist public, has been slow to take up the possibilities that are the artefact of the new, mediated media/feminist relationship. I see the value in this argument, but I am left wondering what happens to those who are still, necessarily, in the grip of the 'incurable paradox', no matter how ready they are to speak and hear of a different way forward? And what of the legal issues they are still attempting to have heard, modified, or contested?

I want to think through the relationships that exist between feminism, the media and the law, and to raise some questions about the relationships of all three to an overarching idea of 'the public'. As an historian, I would like to revisit how Australian feminists 25 years ago were handling these very questions, specifically by revisiting International Women's Year, 1975,

---

5   See Fraser, 1995, pp 175–95, where she advocates a re-reckoning of the public sphere as a multiple and shifting entity.

6   Lumby, 1997, p xi.

7   Lumby argues, in relation to feminisms' relationship to the media as part of the public sphere, that for a start, an understanding of the 'the media' as 'an amorphous lump' is unhelpful. Such a definition ignores the fact that 'the medium is the message', and that it is not 'a stable platform for pushing political or moral values of any single persuasion'. *Ibid*, p xxiii.

8   *Ibid*, p xii.

9   *Ibid*, p xxii.

when feminism declared itself, and also was declared, in the public eye in a particularly prominent way. I will aim to stage a conversation between this moment, and one 20 years later, in 1995, to try and understand why the uneasy alliances forged in the 1970s between feminism and the public sphere to secure particular legal rights and recourses for women seemed dissipated, demoralised, or defunct within public debate staged in the media.

1995: FROM SEXUAL HARASSMENT TO SEX

In 1995, I became enraged, and confused, because Helen Garner published a book about sexual harassment, which wasn't about sexual harassment at all. In 1992 two young women were allegedly sexually harassed at a Melbourne University college party by the College Master, and used the legal channels open to them to find some semblance of public justice. In Garner's account, *The First Stone*,[10] the case was transformed into a tale of 'priggish and pitiless' young feminists, who should have been able to deal with being felt up by a bloke at a party in a sassier, and less formal way. The young women in Garner's story were not the victims but the persecutors: ruining the career of a senior academic over a trifle, refusing to tell Garner their stories (although she had publicly declared that her sympathies lay with the Master), colluding with the dark, cabal-like forces of 'organised', moralising academic feminism. These women were emblematic of 'what had gone wrong' with feminism (which, by inference, one assumes that Garner herself had, and was still getting, absolutely right).

This was the bit that enraged me. The press lovingly fed the story, or aspects of it, most days in March, April and May 1995, and the resultant debate seemed pandemic. The nature of this debate, to characterise it crudely, was about feminism off the rails, and the 'generational war' being waged within feminism itself. Many feminists beside myself, of all ages, felt sufficiently galled and censured to enter into the debate publicly. They tried to explain in and to the press how they felt about where feminism had arrived at, 25 years after the halcyon days of the '70s had passed.[11] One correspondent summed this up neatly:

---

10 Matthew Ricketson has discussed the implications of Helen Garner describing *The First Stone* as 'reportage', as part of New Journalism, and the impact that the form of the story had on the subsequent public debate: Ricketson, 1997, pp 79–100.

11 Ann Summers was instrumental in fixing the parameters of the discourse around the feminist malaise. She wrote in the *Sydney Morning Herald* on 4 April 1995 of 'the failure of feminisms to instill in young women today a sense of their own strength and power, and the ability to fend off unwelcome advances be they from peers or professors'. As editor of *Good Weekend* she also provoked the response from feminists of all ages by posing the direct question of why weren't younger women today voicing their concerns, and published some of the responses in the 13 May 1995 edition.

It is not a struggle that is very visible in a collective sense ... It is a struggle in which the victories are often in individual offices or on factory floors. Armed with avenues to redress inequality and discrimination ... younger women are now out there using them and making them work. In other words, the battle in many areas has moved on ... we are now implementing the peace.[12]

The problem was that the 'peace' was actually difficult to identify in the public, media-mediated discourse, of the *First Stone* event. Jenna Mead (who had personally been vivisected and fictionalised in Garner's version of events), wrote in 1997:

As the *Ormond* case and *The First Stone* appeared in the media, the complex issues they raised of sexual harassment, legal obligation and redress, the legitimacy of women's access to equity, the responsibilities of fiduciary care – to name only a few – were reduced to the language of melodrama and scandal.[13]

In short, the press was hot for this story. In Mead's reckoning, the scandal had two aspects. The first was caused by the complainants in pursuing a legal remedy for what they 'alleged' was sexual harassment, and as a consequence, 'destroying a man's career'.[14] The second was about feminism: that young women were so vengeful that they would resort to the law rather than give the Master a swift kick and get on with it, and that young women were refusing to talk to Garner, and were thus written into Garner's narrative as pitted personally against her, and her way of seeing. Mead argues:

... [t]his code too is ancient: we all know when to recognise a 'catfight' among women ... this code works, ultimately, for men. It is a code that teaches young women their place in the ancient hierarchy that has men exercising power and women practicing submission.[15]

These two scandals, somewhere along the line, became conflated, and in the process sexual harassment all but disappeared,[16] and became both sex crime and intrasex crime (with young, allegedly very sexy, women as the

---

12 *Good Weekend*, 13 May 1995, p 22.

13 Mead, 1997, p 12.

14 As columnist Bettina Arndt, for example, argued, if men could be hit with sexual harassment complaints, the workplace would be threatened forever, and as Mead notes, 'the fear [this] evoked was an ancient one – not the failure of justice but – the triumph of a woman's sexuality over a man's power'. *Ibid*, p 13.

15 *Ibid*.

16 Discussion of sexual harassment in the terms I am suggesting was not completely absent. Note particularly Paul Gray in *Sun Herald*, 1 April 1995, and Adele Horin in the *Sydney Morning Herald*, 12 August 1995. Questions about where the legal discourse of sexual harassment had gone were also raised by academics and commentators after the event, most notably by collaborators to Mead's 1997 edited collection of essays on *The First Stone*. See in particular Morgan, 1997, pp 101–15, and Curthoys, 1997, pp 189–212.

protagonists).[17] And sex sells. It was this process that confused me. Somewhere in the midst of the harangue about this case, this text, and this media event, the worthy rights discourse that had emerged from the engagement of feminists with the law, and with reform more generally, had disappeared from the media. Or perhaps sexual harassment legislation, and feminist legal discourse, had been a Pyrrhic success, didn't need to be promoted as a right, and was no longer newsworthy *in that way*. Or, preferably, perhaps it was only effaced in the palimpsest of other competing struggles to control the discourse of what feminism should mean, both in the media, and in the other strands of a differentiated public.

If it is not already obvious, I will declare myself now. Feminism for me is visible yet differentiated, and certainly not over. I am a feminist of my generation who is concerned with how to make liberalism, and the paradox it presents to women through the law, contested, but also workable. I also care desperately that the struggles with law and government, which feminists have waged to place sexual harassment onto a public agenda, no matter how fraught, are still debated within that public agenda in a way that does not disguise the reality of the physical and legal harm women continue to suffer.

It is for these reasons, despite my confusion over where sexual harassment was on the screen of popular consciousness in 1995 that I am trying to understand the preconditions of the contemporary moment. I wish now, therefore, to re-visit International Women's Year (IWY) 1975 when public discussion of feminism, feminism's role in the public, and feminism's relationship to the media were well and truly on the agenda, and were then, as well as now, highly contested issues for debate and disapprobation.

IWY '75: BUMS, BREASTS AND BITCHES

From its earliest moments, the 1970s wave of Australian feminisms, as Sara Dowse has suggested, were dancing a 'fandango with the state'.[18] Although many of the participants of early Women's Liberation Movement (WLM) groups were drawn from those involved in both New Left and Libertarian circles, and the state was seen as part of an oppressive patriarchal machinery, there was a parallel recognition of and need for reform within,

---

17 Jenna Mead argues: 'If an offence is reported as a sex crime, it's a relatively easy matter to impute motive and culpability to the women because that's what the discourse of sex crime is set up to achieve' – Mead 1997, p 17.

18 Dowse, 1983, pp 205–26.

and of, the state.[19] This recognition crystallised in the Women's Electoral Lobby (WEL), which emerged out of two WLM groups in Melbourne in 1972.[20] WEL was all about social, state-directed protest and the movement toward reform, on a large and effective scale. For many, WEL was provocative. Yet there were crossovers between Women's Liberation and WEL, for despite the reform/revolution distinction, in practice many women belonged to both groups, and saw their different focus as part of the same project for contemporary feminism at that time.[21]

From the very beginning, WEL used the press as a means of trying to get their agendas recognised. Marilyn Lake notes that '[t]he mainstream media seemed to embrace WEL ... reassured that some feminists, at least, looked familiar and sounded reasonable, not posing a threat to the family or men's sexual prerogatives'.[22] Before the 1972 Federal election campaign, WEL published through the national and local media a 'form guide' of candidates' attitudes and sympathies to 'women's issues' (like abortion).[23] The campaign was a success: numbers within WEL increased rapidly, and the exertion of political pressure on major parties had a direct result. As Ann Curthoys notes, the Whitlam Labor Government was elected in 1972 'for all sorts of reasons, but it was clear that, once in power, it needed to take on board the demands WEL had made during the campaign'.[24]

One of the most significant initiatives taken by the new Government in response to the WEL's reformist stance was the appointment of a prime ministerial advisor to assist on women's issues. The media immediately became fascinated with the appointment process, which was quickly labelled the 'hunt for the PM's supergirl', or the 'supergirl contest'. Stories appeared about the 'finalists', and a cartoon showed them as beauty queen

---

19 Reform based campaigns were successfully used in the cases of abortion law reform (in NSW, at least) and equal pay: tactics like the petition and lobbying were recognised as important processes of engagement. In fact, the enthusiasm and euphoria of the early success put many Women's Liberation women on a steep learning curve. The establishment of Elsie, Australia's first feminist refuge, provides a good example. What began as an exercise in disrupting the state to achieve a desired goal (the squatting of Elsie to realise a gap in state protection of abused women) became an exercise for the Elsie collective to learn very quickly the benefits of funding – both how to get it and how it could be maximised. See for example, Elsie Women's Refuge Collective, 1978; Elsie Women's Refuge Collective, 1975.

20 Mercer, 1975, pp 395–404.

21 Alliances over a number of projects in the early 1970s were, however, uneasy. Marilyn Lake argues that: '[W]omen's Liberationists barely concealed their scorn with WEL's desire to engage in conventional politics, while members of WEL professed impatience with the radicals' preoccupation with theory and self-knowledge.' See Lake, 1999, p 239. For contemporary accounts of this issues see: Richter, 1975, pp 35–39; Radford, 1975, pp 158–61.

22 Lake, 1999, p 238.

23 The form guide had been derived from a Ms-style questionnaire, supplemented with information from interviews with the candidates: Mercer, 1975, pp 396–97.

24 Curthoys, 1993, p 27. See also Sawer, 1993, pp 1–21.

contestants with sashes proclaiming '$10,000' (the senior advisor's salary on offer, until then unheard of for a woman). To some extent, the short listed appointees parodied their own media treatment, and seemed to attempt to harness it, turning up to a press conference in yellow 'supergirl' t-shirts, and issuing a joint press statement, pledging their sisterhood and support for whoever got the job, to head off any press-generated possibility of an internal squabble.[25]

There was good reason for this. Despite the sentiment of collectivity to which 1970s feminism aspired, and the uneasy alliances between WLM and WEL, there was tension in the grassroots of the movement about the entire concept of one to represent the many. After Elizabeth Reid was announced as the successful candidate in 1973, the editorial collective of the feminist publication MeJane, for example, argued: 'No woman chosen by men to advise upon us will be acceptable to us. We believe that it is not your right to choose for us our spokeswoman, any more than it is any woman's right to act as the single spokeswoman for the rest of us.'[26] The 'mainstream' publications also scrutinised Reid, and by association, the women's movement more generally, albeit in a fetishised as opposed to a theoretical fashion.[27] From a cultural perspective, it could be argued that Reid was treated like a libertine, and a policy version of a Page Three girl. The *Daily Mirror* banner headline when she was appointed read 'PM's Supergirl says: "Legalise Pot, Abortion".' The *Herald* in August of that same year excited its readers by exhorting:

> Would the sisterhood stand still for a moment and stop wobbling under their t-shirts? I have been talking to the M stroke S who represents your interests in the capital ... Miz Liz – in flared jeans, tank top and no bra – was speaking in her office in the new prime ministerial suite in Parliament House.[28]

The media therefore began to interact with the kind of feminism that was interested in reform, by producing a single public face, a commodity, embodying and sexualising what they perceived to be the 'legitimate' movement at the same time. The 'other' kind of feminism, the 'radical' kind that eschewed any liberal state engagement (and by extrapolation any potentially corrupting or co-optive engagement with other aspects of the pubic sphere) was given different treatment. Feminists of this persuasion were labelled drug addicts, zealous lesbian separatists, filthy in their personal habits, and generally ratbags,[29] and not able to be sexualised in any

---

25 Sawer and Groves, 1994, p 4.

26 26 March, 1973, quoted by Sawer and Groves, 1994, p 7. The collective also pointed out that all the candidates for the position were white, well educated and heterosexual.

27 Sawer and Groves, 1994, note at p 5 that the responses of the media to Reid 'ranged from trivialisation and distortions of her ideas to highly personal attacks.'

28 *Ibid*, p 6.

29 See, for example, *The Glebe*, 15 October 1975; Melbourne Women's Liberation Newsletter, January, July 1973.

conventional way. Sale-ability for this face of feminism was its potential to create trouble, to disrupt, to caterwaul with the libertine, yet embraceable, image of more engaging feminisms.[30]

1975, which was declared by the United Nations as International Women's Year (IWY), and the start of the Decade of Women, created a framework for these tensions within feminism to be relayed to the public. Reid and her co-workers viewed IWY as a valuable vehicle for changing public attitudes towards women's role,[31] and under its banner, they convinced the Government to provide substantial funds for various feminist initiatives.[32] The process for identifying suitable projects was administered by a specially appointed National Advisory Committee, comprised of women both within and outside the bureaucracy, convened by Reid.[33] It was the symbolic and actual authority Reid and the OSW possessed in administration of the grants program, however, that caused pre-existing tensions over who could, or should, represent the women's movement to blister. The irreverent publication *Liberaction* from Tasmania, for example, had on its March 1975 cover a cartoon depicting 'SuperFem', fronting up to Prime Minister Gough Whitlam begging 'Please Sir, can I have some more?'.[34] The sentiments from Tasmania were echoed on the mainland. In Sydney, in January 1975, 200 women met at the Balmain Town Hall to publicly protest the IWY grants decisions. The main thrust of the criticisms (voiced by other 'prominent' WLM members, like Ann Summers) was that several WLM projects had been ignored in favour of non-feminist ('reformist') proposals.[35]

---

30 The antagonism many in the grass roots of the movement felt towards 'the stars' the media created (like Germaine Greer) is well articulated by Brown, 1978.

31 Despite public and internal feminist opprobrium, and despite the fact that she was in a precarious position, relying on the goodwill of a controversial Prime Minister, since 1973 Reid had gone about systematically figuring out what her agenda should be. She attempted to try and identify what Australian women wanted as women to improve the fairness and the decency of their lives, and at the same time to develop strategies of using the state to 'bring women to the threshold' (through challenging bureaucratic structures, and women's presence within the bureaucracy, with some success). For a general discussion of what was achieved by Reid and the fledgling Office of the Status of Women, see Eisenstein, 1996, pp 15–27.

32 Lake, 1999, p 258. Somewhat predictably, this was reported with provocative disbelief by the press, *The Age* headline, for example, running: '$2 million for the Sheilas: Surprisingly It's No Joke'.

33 Lake, 1999, p 258; Eisenstein, 1996, p 25. Successful grant recipients included projects like the 'Coming Out Show' on ABC Radio, the Working Women's Centre, and the Women's Film Fund, with interim support for refuges until the appropriate department could take up their financial support on a permanent basis.

34 *Liberaction*, March 1975. The editorial, by Kay Daniels, was a highly critical examination of the representative function of Reid's position, its contribution to a 'fragmented' WLM, and its role in fuelling a public relations obsessed ALP.

35 Shirley Castley, a member of the National Advisory Committee, attended in lieu of Reid, and recorded: 'Basically, the meeting was an excuse for [WLM] to go to the national press and TV to criticise IWY – the reasons for them wishing to criticise IWY are simply that they themselves had not been funded.' Castley, 1975, quoted in Lake, 1999, p 258.

To a certain degree, the public-distrustful WLM feminists had some success. Marilyn Lake argues that in the public eye, IWY, although administered by the more palatable reformists, 'came to symbolise excess ... [and was] cited as evidence that taxpayer's funds were being wasted on extremist and/or trivial causes'.[36] The coverage of 'Women and Politics Conference' held in September 1975 in Canberra, as part of IWY, cemented this reputation. Reid perceived the conference as a way for diverse groups of women to both develop political skills, and to publicise the ways in which women were already politically active.[37] Yet the diversity of women to whom she was appealing (women drawn from the Country Women's Association to Women's Liberation), although many were committed to collectivity as a political aspiration, were, ironically, too critical of Reid's *de facto* relationship with the state to allow this conversation to take place unimpeded.

The opening of the conference, when the 700 invited delegates descended upon Parliament House in Canberra, was an unmitigated public relations disaster. Reid herself viewed the event like this:

> Aboriginal women demonstrated outside, criticising inadequate representation of their concerns in the programme. Labor women stood behind the Prime Minister during his opening speech with placards denouncing the decisions recently taken by him on East Timor. His speech was interrupted when the Aboriginal women proceeded into the hall, chanting and singing. Women from the women's movement wearing men's suit [invitations had stated appropriate dress was lounge suits] mingled in the audience with farm women, factory workers, church women ... The statue of King George V in King's Hall was draped with a placard reading 'Women and Revolution, not Women and Bureaucracy' and 'lesbians are lovely' and similar slogans were written in lipstick on the mirrors of the men's toilets. The press, accustomed to sensationalising every aspect of my work, and my beliefs, had a heyday.[38]

Although it could be argued that the attendant media attention on the Conference was damaging to pro-reformists' agenda of changing the attitude of the public through the public sphere,[39] it is quite remarkable that any debate about feminism was actually carried out in the public eye at all. The movement may have been getting bad press, with the forces of unruly,

---

36 *Ibid*, p 259.

37 Eisenstein, 1996, p 26.

38 Lake, 1999, p 259.

39 Eisenstein, 1996, has argued at p 27 that the conference was 'the occasion of Reids' downfall, as it produced a virtual media blitz against her ... The [Conference], with its attendant extravagances, provided the already unfriendly media with a field day. By midweek of the conference, Whitlam's advisers had convinced him that his commitment to women's issues and to Reid was going to be an electoral disaster.' (By the end of 1975, her position had been moved from the office of Prime Minister and Cabinet, and ended her public role, precipitating her public resignation months before the Government itself was dismissed.)

virago-like dissent dominating IWY, but it was still public relations. 1975 therefore marked the moment when the media began to take feminism (if not the issues it attempted to raise) on board as news.

The other important effect of the Women and Politics Conference in 1975 was the extent to which debate was had inside the conference itself about what feminisms' relationship should be not only to the state, but also to the media. The lessons learned *from* the 1975 'event' began to effect feminism contemporaneously at the event. The response to 'the media question' was a debate about publicity versus representation. Women's Liberationist Biff Ward, for example, in the 'Politics of Feminism' session noted that short of a 'girlcott', feminists had to put up with the media, but to fight head-on the sexist ways in which feminists were represented. She maintained that:

> [W]e can't get good publicity, because we threaten the system, threaten the power and the forces of the conservative mass media ... they try to contain you, to blunt the radicalism ... it is inevitable that ... [the press] will trivialise and try to put down anything they are afraid of, and they are afraid of women's liberation.[40]

For other speakers, particularly those on the Media discussion panel, representation and the need to set agendas were part of the same problem. The speakers were journalists, or involved in formalised relationships with the state, and advocated more mediated relationships. Evan Williams, then Whitlam's press secretary, argued that news was assessed according to moral values, and that feminism, the more outrageous and affronting it publicly showed itself to be, was good copy. As a result, feminism, in general, and especially during the Conference itself, was shaped in the press in the image of the most strident feminist activist: '... she's unfeminine ... she's probably morally lax, she's shrill, she's intolerant, slovenly, noisy and of course she hates men.'[41] To control the image was to control the message, and Williams urged those present to play by the rules, in order to mediate the inherent nature of most journalists and editors to sensationalise what was serious (a response that was met with some scorn by the female journalists present).[42]

Speakers on this panel were also patently aware of the paradoxical ways in which the media felt the need to sexualise feminism to make it palatable, more often than not by embodying spokeswomen differently to the broader movement itself. For example, speaker Adele Koh was conscious that the press reduced women attempting to engage with the state to pre-existing

---

40 Ward, 1975, p 157. Similar sentiments were made by Kennedy, 1975, pp 228–35.

41 Williams, 1975, p 225.

42 Fell, 1975. Fell records that some feminist journalists who were present staged a 'sit in' at the *Canberra Times* office to force an improvement in the way that the Conference was represented.

codes, as 'beauty queens, entertainers, and sports stars'.[43] Her introduction to the nature of women's place in the Australian state she described as:

[T]aking the shape of a girl's bum. It was apparently a bottom of such amazing qualities that its movement held sway over the whole of the nation. It could make or break politicians, and it exercised more influence and power than political parties, and parliament itself. I need hardly say that I am referring to Ms Ainslie Gotto and her famous wiggle.[44]

Koh saw this archaic code as continuing, with the media's ambivalent relationship to Liz Reid, both making her a 'star', and trivialising her agendas at the same time, as she railed against the normative public character of women.[45]

By 1975 then, the relationship between the media, feminism and the public sphere was ambivalently sexualised. Margaret Thornton has argued that 'the association of the feminine with the erotic signals the possibility of corruption of the public sphere values of rationality, objectivity, and universality'.[46] As part of a public sphere coming to terms with feminisms prepared to take on the state, the media in 1975 certainly played a part in promoting fear of this corruption. It both lusted after and condemned the women's movement for its ideas, identities, and appearances. Feminism was both a good sort, and a harridan, but she was always a whore. For those feminists who wanted to shift the traditional barriers while not entirely dismantling them, the 1975 experience had given many lessons in how to approach the issue of agenda setting when the next round began.

FEMINISMS, PROFESSIONS, AND THE MADONNA AGENDA

An effect of the attention given to feminisms in IWY, as well as the attention given to the role and responsibility of the media by feminists at the Women and Politics Conference, was a move toward the politicisation of journalism

---

43 Koh, 1975, p 221.

44 *Ibid*, p 220. Ainslie Gotto was Prime Minister John Gorton's (1968–71) private secretary. Her appointment was controversial, because she was young, attractive, forthright and did not rise through the usual bureaucratic ranks.

45 Koh argued: 'You all saw [Reid] on "Monday Conference" last night. And I think you will agree with me that she conducts herself in a very dignified way ... she resists every temptation to show off her boobs, or to emasculate male reporters on the spot. She deals with questions in a direct, serious, and amiable fashion. Yet what invariably appears the next day? The kind of awed and banal description which includes facetious and inane statements such as: "Ms Reid, despite her championing of women's causes, has not lost her femininity, and in fact wears make-up"': Koh, 1975, p 221.

46 Thornton, 1996a, p 7.

as a profession.[47] Just as women interested in transforming the state joined the state to achieve change, women working within the media began to organise industry based activism to take control of the feminism/media relationship. This was directed both toward improving the representation of women by the media, and improving the presence of women in the media to challenge the process of agenda setting.[48] These initiatives ranged from the writing of 'Guidelines for the media' directed at the Australian Broadcasting Control Board to counter sexist portrayals of women, to campaigns conducted by the Media Women's Action Group to achieve proper representation in the Australian Journalists' Association (AJA).[49] A related focus was allowing women journalists appropriate scope to get stories out that dealt with feminist issues, as opposed to feminism.[50] A significant aspect of this agenda was the challenge to broadcast programs made by women for women, to spread the causes for concern of divergent but organised feminist groups to those women who were for whatever reason unable, or unwilling, to become practically involved.

The 'Coming Out Show', which began broadcasting on ABC radio in 1975 thanks to an IWY grant specifically fulfilled this role. The group behind the show (the Australian Women's Broadcasting Cooperative) saw itself as promoting women professionally within the boundaries of the media industry, and at the same time presenting a programme that would help to counter the negative stereotypes of what feminism was actually about presented in the mainstream media.[51] To some extent this agenda was a success. The experience of my own mother, regularly tuning in on Saturday afternoons in the Adelaide suburbs in the 1970s, is a case in point. She recalled that 'just dealing with household things and kids can be a bit numbing', and that the program 'was genuinely interesting and aired issues

---

47 To some extent this process had already commenced prior to IWY, but gained momentum afterwards. The first meeting of the Media Women's Action Group, was in June 1972. Early members were Suzanne Baker, Lois Miles, Carolyn Jones and Julie Rigg. The initial issues the group sought to discuss were sexism in the AJA, childcare and maternity leave, and censorship of Germaine Greer's public talk on abortion, which was filmed by the ABC's current affairs flagship Four Corners but not put to air: Media Women's Action Group, 1972.

48 Fell, 1975.

49 Women Media Workers, 1976; Media Women's Action Group, 1979; Media Women's Action Group, 1975.

50 Activists such as Ann Summers who began working as a professional journalist by joining the *National Times* in 1976, were important in this process, raising rape or sexual abuse, albeit in Summers' case in a left wing publication, from a perspective that came from the women's movement, and was about exposing such issues as specific harms experienced by women. For a discussion of the nature of the journalism produced by Summers and also Adele Horin during this period, see Pearce, 1998, pp 183–255.

51 Topics covered by the show were wide ranging. The November 1978 program covered sexual abuse, the life of Louisa Lawson, and the conditions of black women both in Australia and the US: AWBC, 1978. See also AWBC, 1975.

which were sometimes outside my experience and the experience of my acquaintances and therefore had not been thought about or discussed'.[52] For her, and for many others,[53] listening was both a way to become involved, and as part of an audience, to give community currency to feminist issues.

These multiple fronts for feminist engagement with the media, which consciously worked at unravelling the image of feminism as whore, and defused attention on internal feminist squabbles, were also important as they involved a cross-fertilisation of feminists from different professional realms. From the late 1970s, women working in media and law began to co-operate to promote feminist concerns in a way that appealed to masculinist public sympathy, as opposed to erotic fear.

The engagement of feminists with the law *per se* began slightly after a feminist engagement with the media.[54] For example, at the Women and Politics Conference in 1975, the 'Women and Law' session ran more like a question-and-answer on credit and custody, as opposed to the kind of theorised debate being staged in the 'Women and the Media' forums.[55] Despite this, speaker Helen Coonan argued that law was a crucial topic for feminist thought, and in regard to scrutiny by women she was:

> [A]maze[ed] to think that of all society's institutions ... law is perhaps the least explored ... It's interesting to wonder why this happens. I don't know whether it's something to do with law itself ... but I certainly welcome ... an investigation into how everybody is affected by law because believe me, until women get some sort of legal equality ... most of the other reforms that people are aspiring for, are just a pipedream.[56]

Part of the problem Coonan identified may have been that until the 1970s there were very few women lawyers to approach these issues in a specialised kind of way.[57] Many that were in a position to do so, like Coonan, were heavily involved in the practical business of giving legal advice on company structure, tax, and property to emerging health centres, and other grassroots feminist agencies, and may not have had the time to theorise how to either use or challenge the law to address particular gendered harms.[58] The growth of the number of women in law schools in the 1970s began to change the idea of law for feminists. Not all women at

---

52 Personal communication, Mary Genovese, 7 April 2000.

53 A woman from rural Victoria wrote to the show, in 1979: 'I feel I must congratulate you all on the excellent production you have – it is the only contact we women have with what can only be regarded as "women's issues"': AWBC, 1979.

54 Kathleen Lahey has noted of North American thinking about the law in the 1970s that it was 'an uncatalogued item, a yet to be theorised experience', making it similar to the Australian experience: Lahey, 1985, p 519.

55 Coonan and Armstrong, 1977, pp 66–75.

56 *Ibid*, p 68.

57 Thornton, 1996a; Elliot, 1975, pp 139–54; O'Connor, 1975.

58 See, for example, Women's Health and Resource Foundation Ltd, 1975.

law school in the 1970s of course identified as feminists, but for many, the ideas and experiences they were encountering in other aspects of their lives, mingled with their experiences in law school, meant that 'law and feminisms', by the late 1970s, began to have a loosely defined profile within the community.[59] Legal feminist activist groups, (like the Feminist Lawyers, which began at Monash University in 1977, or FLAG – Feminist Legal Action Group – in Sydney in 1978)[60] began to identify key issues in dire need of reform. Even though many in these groups were *au fait* with the principles of Marxism and the Left, they recognised that law was inextricably wedded to liberalism, and as a result reform, although problematic, was an essential part of the road that legal feminists needed to follow to bring about change.[61] What this entailed, however, was a need to develop strategies for connecting private experience to the public, and then to use the mechanisms of the public sphere, usually so antithetical to women, to achieve change.[62]

It was this recognition that resulted in important alliances between feminists working in the law and the media. Although the ideological tensions that managed to disrupt IWY 1975 were still present, and the idea of a collective voice had always been arguably an aspirational myth, the approach to using the media to publicise 'legal' issues was remarkably coherent. When it came to issues on these agendas, the approach was very much one of casting the harmed subject in a sympathetic light, as a wronged madonna, garnering goodwill from 'the ordinary' listeners and readers who had been open to the ideas of those feminist journalists who were managing to be heard, then preying upon the good graces of 'the civilised state' to do something about it.

I do not mean to suggest that this approach was the same in every campaign. In some circumstances, the subject of the campaign for reform (like pornography) was the media itself, which then managed to diffuse debate about censorship by casting both feminist and public positions into

---

59 The Women and Law Conference held at Sydney University in 1978 was significant in this respect, as it brought together a wide range of women from the Movement, as well as from different disciplinary backgrounds, to discuss for the first time legal issues relating to women in a theorised way. See generally Lynch, 1979, pp 35–36.

60 Thornton, 1996a, pp 213–15; Ross, 1979, p 36.

61 O'Connor, 1975; Thornton, 1991, p 453. Part of this process entailed lobbying the state through writing submissions. Legislation was seen as the crucial way to achieve change as opposed to using precedent. This reflects a long tradition in Australian feminism/state relations, as Marian Sawer notes: '[b]oth social liberals and the women's movement frequently expressed the belief that while men had their unions, women had the state.' Sawer, 1993, p 3.

62 Thornton, 1991.

particularly constrained dichotomies.[63] Other issues, however, like domestic violence, rape, or reform to the law of homicide, were generated by legal feminist activists from a variety of persuasions, and yet managed to escape the media's tendency to seek out internal feminist disorder. Groups like the libertarian prison reform group Women Behind Bars (WBB), or the left legal FLAG, or the grassroots WLM refuge movement, despite their diverse attitudes, co-operated to use the media to create support for causes commonly identified as important and in need of reform. In the case of criminal law reform for battered women who kill, for example, the appeal to the press was unapologetically manipulated to gain public sympathy. Women in these groups approached mainstream media avenues with which they had personal contacts, like the television program *60 Minutes* on which Wendy Bacon, a WBB stalwart, had also worked, or the *Sydney Morning Herald*, presenting the human face and tragedy of specific cases.[64] They were aware of their audience and the need to appeal, to shore up public support for petitions, for letters to the editor, for the community to voice opinion.

This relationship of feminism with the media was, therefore, above all strategic. In the homicide reform campaign, staged in Sydney in 1980–81 an individual woman, Violet Roberts, who had been convicted for life for killing a violent spouse, became the embodiment of the whole problem with the Crimes Act NSW (1900), the inability of the state to understand domestic violence as a crime, and the difficulty of liberal law to understand female experience.[65] Confronting the spectre of the whore that had haunted feminism's public image, Roberts (and domestic violence as an issue) was portrayed as a madonna, enduring 'the private suffering of the brutalised wife'.[66] Libertarians and left feminists alike, from the media and the law and the refuge movement, as well as from other groups like Christian Women Concerned, promoted this image. They had learned to control the message they got out. Jennifer Neale (of WBB) spoke to *Women's Day*: 'Fighting back tears, Jennifer ... who visits Vi regularly, said: "Attitudes toward women

---

63 Catharine Lumby argues that feminism's approach to censoring representations of women, and their attitude to pornography, was anti-libertarian, and ultimately non-reflective of women's desires, playing into the hands of the moral majority and the Right. She follows through Catharine MacKinnon's intellectual trajectory which led to equating pornography as sexual harassment, which has resulted in the nexus between feminism and law reform/public policy being out of touch with the majority of women, tied into an outmoded notion of radical feminism. I would argue that Lumby has a point, but it is more applicable to the US situation where these debates had wider currency. I would also argue that pornography presents a unique kind of law/state/media relationship: the battle lines are different because it involved the critique of the media as a subject of the public, and it could not therefore be played out in the public in the same kinds of ways. See Lumby, 1997, pp 26–52.

64 See for example: *Daily Mirror*, 18 March 1980; *Sydney Morning Herald*, 4 September 1980; *Woman's Day*, September 1980; *Sixty Minutes* (television program), March 1980.

65 Genovese, 1998, pp 198–244.

66 *Women Behind Bars*, 1980. (Note that Violet Roberts was jointly accused with her son Bruce, a minor at the time of the killing.)

who have suffered the brutality of a husband as Vi did have changed so much in four years that we're convinced that if she had a retrial she'd get off"'.[67]

This line of attack was aimed, ultimately, at dealing with the paradox of liberalism within law: finding a way of negotiating women's invisibility within the public sphere, then using the public sphere to improve the situation.[68] It was a position that was also used by femocrats, and in many ways the agendas could not be separated, as they both appealed to the *noblesse oblige* of a masculinist public sphere to achieve change. They both recognised the condition of the 'incurable paradoxical condition'[69] of feminism's relationship to liberalism. As femocrat Helen L'Orange has reflected: 'I think it was easier to get progress on areas where male politicians felt chivalrous. Domestic violence, sexual assault ...'[70] The extent to which legal/reformist feminist ideas and campaigns succeeded as discourse in the 1970s and 1980s had a lot to do, then, with not just accepting the 'good graces of a masculinist public',[71] but doing so knowingly. The result was that the eroticised and reduced reaction to feminism as a movement by the public sphere, as witnessed in 1975 at least, had by the end of that decade been responded to by feminists working in different arms of the public sphere, who had concentrated attention instead on feminist reforms strategies instead of feminism *per se*, and had packaged those reforms in such way that was hard to ignore.

A NON-COLLECTIVE COLLECTIVE?

I think the kinds of concerns and approaches taken to the reform/media/feminism relationship in the recent past were very conscious, and strategic. To some extent feminism then was constitutionally post-structuralist without ever knowing what that meant. Despite the very real aspiration to collectivity, feminism was diversified, and responses to the media, state and law were diversified. Early on, there was even some debate and recognition of what effect the price of an engagement with the public sphere – in all its guises – would have on feminism even as it tried to change, both from within and outside, those arms of public masculinist civil

---

67 *Woman's Day*, 1980, p 8.
68 In the Roberts' case this was a success, the campaign provoked such a strong community and then Government reaction that the Criminal Code in NSW was altered to remove mandatory sentencing as a penalty, and also played a part in reforming the provocation defence, although the impact of those changes can be argued to be Pyrrhic: Genovese, 1998.
69 Scott, 1997, p 698.
70 Quoted in Sawer and Groves, 1994, p 12.
71 Thornton, 1995, p 7.

ordering. Feminism itself may have been painted as whore by the media in 1975, but that experience aided in producing a much more focussed attempt to harness debates, to find places in and control of agendas, to situate discourses in the public mind in a sympathetic, profeminist light.

The trouble is, I think, that the public debate about what feminism meant (as opposed to what it did) in 1995, as in 1975, returned to the eroticisation of bitching women and powerful disruptive bodies. (I do think the debate was, however, far more complicated, simply because epistemologies of media, law and feminism also now have the benefit of time to be thought about in more complex ways.) I would hesitate, however, to argue that we should return to 'madonna-ising' the things that traditionally matter to women concerned with law and state (how liberal law hinders women when it should help, how it fails to recognise women at all, how it can penalise and discriminate). I think such an approach, for its time, was contextually sophisticated. It used the public sphere to publicise.[72] But to revisit such an approach now comes very close to victimology, if enough attention isn't paid to the agency of those involved, and the need to hear their voices. It also comes very close to ushering women back to the private sphere, no matter that those very concepts have transmuted into something beyond a simple dichotomy.

I do not want to be a New Left conservative. I do not want to argue for some coherent intellectual or political position to re-invigorate the legal rights and access debate.[73] I also don't want to be a new free market libertarian, for though exhilarated by the opportunities that a conscious exploitation of diversity offers, I am still bothered that the insidious aspects of some issues won't get heard. US political philosopher William E Connolly has argued that when the Left is active, it enters into a series of 'connections with critical branches of the media, street activists, adventurous elements in organised labor and creative religious institutions.'[74] I think this is what was happening in terms of feminist struggles and campaigns in the 1970s and 1980s. Despite their differences, there was enough physical connectivity, enough faith in cross-professional strategy, enough rhizomatic aspiration for collectivity that certain issues could be promoted as feminist issues in the public consciousness. There was enough time to take dichotomies like madonna/whore and find ways to make them work.

---

72 Nancy Fraser has argued that feminist attention to publicity as a political weapon cannot be understood simply in terms of making public what was previously private: '... merely publicising some action or practice is not always sufficient to discredit it; that is only the case where the view that the practice is wrong is already widely held and uncontroversial ... where in contrast the practice is widely approved or contested, publicity means staging a discursive struggle over its interpretation.' Fraser, 1995, pp 190–91.

73 For a discussion of this 'Left malaise', see Robbins, 1999, p 33.

74 Connolly, 1999, p 48.

Such dichotomies and how to disrupt or re-invent them is now a far more nuanced and fraught proposition for feminisms. One apparent difficulty is that feminists who work 'in the state' and those who work 'in the academy' don't have that much in common anymore.[75] But there are practical, economic reasons for this as well as linguistic and theoretical ones. To maintain a place, no matter what field or sphere women are inhabiting, they have to work damned hard to stay there, or be heard individually. The old aphorism 'the personal is political' could be rethought as 'the political is the personal'. The fact that women, through their professions, managed to create small, but interconnected fields of influence in the public, has also, paradoxically, meant that they have increasingly had to work hard just to maintain a representative presence.[76] There seems to be no time to form a collective of interested parties committed to brokering new representative images, or maintaining existing agendas in a public, publicised way, especially when the ideology of economic rationalism casts a shadow over the public itself. There are specialised languages, and specialised spheres. Conversations about how the incurable paradox of liberalism can be managed are being held all the time, but in different rooms.

Connolly sees a particular role for academics in restoring connections with those of similar but different political beliefs and expectations, particularly in the current political climate, which also happens to coincide with an intellectual climate where diversity and identity matter more than ever. He argues that:

> The need today is for ... construction of a series of alliances across multiple lines of difference in assumption, priority, ethical source, and modes of politics. As we establish relations of agnostic respect across differences, we can also hope to strengthen our hand in the academy and improve communications with sympathetic parties in [for example] the media ...[77]

I agree. But two questions remain, which I find difficult to answer in a practical way. As feminists, how and where do the alliances begin, if in fact they ever really ended? And should we promote or rethink the political imperatives of forming non-collective collectives when the concept of 'we' has come to mean something very different than it did in 1975?

---

75 Lumby, 1997, pp 166–67.
76 This is part of what Thornton calls the 'Sisyphus syndrome', Thornton, 1996a, p 274.
77 Connolly, 1999, p 54.

CHAPTER 9

'THE BARMAID', 'THE LANDLADY' AND 'THE PUB[LICAN]'S WIFE': HISTORY, LAW AND THE POPULAR CULTURE OF WOMEN'S WORK IN PUBS[1]

Diane Kirkby

INTRODUCTION

The Australian pub has been a significant site of popular culture. There, the nexus between law, history and popular culture can be seen in the construction and shaping of the pub as workplace and the occupation of 'barmaid'.

To some, the relationship between law and popular culture is one of regulating and reforming working class recreation.[2] Thus, Alan Hunt has argued that the legal regulation of popular culture in earlier historical periods was part of a 'moralization of popular culture' that derived from anxieties about labour discipline. Working class idleness was attacked through control and surveillance of their pleasures and the spaces, the alehouses and inns, in which they occurred.[3] Hunt's thesis that the poor were the targets of these reforms sees only the recreational dimensions of these spaces. Illuminating the role of law in creating the pub as workplace, and the people within that space as workers, presents a complex interrelationship in which a further dimension – sexual difference – is paramount.

Like Hunt, I am concerned to broaden the exploration of popular culture through historical analysis.[4] Questions about how law manifests itself in everyday life must also be balanced by questions about how 'everyday life' manifests in the institutions and practices of 'Law'. Sexual difference is made and remade in the everyday world of work and leisure. The pub is a site of recreation and leisure to its customers, but a workplace to those serving behind the bar. Thus the interplay of work and leisure, exclusions and inclusions, law and popular culture, worked simultaneously to create a pub space and culture which differentiated while it celebrated the sex of the women working there.

In Australia at the turn of the 20th century, law (legislation) enacted the expressed desire for a sex segregated (men only) drinking and working

1   My thanks to Hilary Golder, Lee-Ann Monk and Tanja Luckins for help with research.
2   Hunt, 1995.
3   *Ibid*, p 18; see also Hunt, 1996.
4   Hunt, 1995.

culture. This culture however was not dependent on law. The spatial arrangement of Australian drinking and working spaces was sex-segregated even in those jurisdictions where formal law did not demand it. Custom and prescription dictated gendered and class-specific behaviour (for example, 'no woman who valued her reputation would dare put her head inside a public bar').[5] As women's liberationists asked in the 1970s, what about the women working there? Why didn't arguments applied to women drinkers that excluded them from all-male drinking communities also apply to barmaids? 'Were they of a lower order or different category?'[6] The short answer is they were categorised differently – but there were also categories of difference between them.

In a 1969 celebration of the English pub, author Maureen Cleave wrote that 'The ladies whom today we find behind the bar are of seven sorts'. Cleave described these as 'the tenant's wife (tenants being people who rent the pubs from the breweries and who take the profits); ... the manager's wife (a manager being someone who is paid a salary by the brewers); ... the barmaid who gets a weekly wage'. These, she said, were 'usually Irish' and were to be distinguished from the part time barmaids. Then she listed 'the lady tenants and the lady managers, though,' she conceded, 'these are rare'. And lastly, 'one of the wonders of our time, the Australian barmaid ...'[7]

In the popular imagination of the 1960s the barmaid, was, then, a category apart – 'the other of the other'[8] – the Australian barmaid most of all. Her body was an important focus: '... jokes about her centring on her bosoms, popularly required to be large enough to rest on the counter.'[9] Cleave said Australian barmaids 'are beautiful, clear-eyed, healthy, athletic girls, with long bare, brown legs beneath their mini-skirts'. She also said, 'They make excellent barmaids'.[10] Cleave's point was that this barmaid was not the tenant's wife, not the manager's wife, not the landlady, nor the woman who ran the pub on her own. She was an employee, exploiting her personality and physical appearance, whose presence was part and parcel of pub culture. 'A pub wouldn't be a pub without her. Give thanks, Gentlemen, to your friend and my friend, the greater British Barmaid.'[11] She could become the wife – 'Very often barmaids marry into the trade,' Cleave had claimed, yet she also quickly pointed out that hotelkeepers 'have one of the highest divorce rates in the country – as high as actors though not quite as

---

5   Caddie, 1953.
6   Anon, 1971, p 4.
7   Cleave, 1969, p 135.
8   Bell, 1994, p 2.
9   Cleave, 1969, p 132.
10 *Ibid*, p 135.
11 McGill, 1969, p 131.

high as dukes',[12] thus ensuring the categories of 'the barmaid' and 'the publican's wife' remained distinctive.

A journalist writing in an Australian brewing industry journal in the 1950s similarly differentiated categories of bar workers when he spoke of pub 'landladies', 'those who are rather younger than their barmaids and often form the chief glory of their own bar'.[13] Although in practice in the workplace such categories blurred into the single figure – 'Rubys and Lilys and Winnies and Pats', the women who 'brightened our pubs and sent the customers home in a better temper than they came in'[14] – the landlady was not 'the barmaid' because she was an independent businesswoman (maybe a wife or widow, maybe an unmarried daughter of the licensee), who served in the bar, 'her own bar', sustained the hotel trade and formed the backbone of her rural or suburban community. 'The Misses Bradley', for example, three sisters who together had kept hotels in rural Queensland for 36 years when they retired in 1963, were widely renowned for their 'gracious hospitality and good food'.[15] The barmaid, on the other hand, was a different figure, and in Australia, as in England, she had a long history. This history was important in constructing the workplace experience of women bar staff as continuities in the popular image and representation of 'the barmaid' were perpetuated in the late 20th century.

The occupation of barmaid emerged out of the changes in liquor consumption and trading which occurred in England in the early 19th century. These changes were subsequently transported to the Australian colonies along with the urban poor who made up the convict population, and in both the metropolitan centre and the antipodean outpost, 'the barmaid' became an important cultural figure, in Australia particularly, directly connected to the beer drinking culture of the men only public bar.[16] By the end of the 19th century images of barmaids were everywhere – in song, cartoons, plays, major metropolitan dailies and the popular press. They were the subject of farce – performed at the Tivoli Theatre in Sydney – of political debate, and serious medical discourse.[17]

This was not the tanned leggy Australian barmaid of 1960s London. She was, in the 1890s, bustled and breasted, a 'sexual lure' to those who opposed the work of women in pubs, a necessary servant to those who employed them. A contest arose between those who sought to ban women from public drinking places and those who saw their value to the industry. The 1960s

---

12 Cleave, 1969, p 143.

13 'The Old-Fashioned Barmaid?', 1951, pp 6–7.

14 *Ibid.*

15 AHA, 1963, p 60.

16 Kirkby, 1997; Bailey, 1990.

17 *Sydney Morning Herald*, 21 November 1908, p 2; 23 November 1908, p 3; see evidence given by doctors to the Royal Commission on Employees in Shops, Victoria, 1884.

profile of the barmaid however came closer than might be expected to the 1890s model, when campaigners wrote poems parodying male customers' desire for sexually attractive bar staff, 'Wanted, a beautiful barmaid ...', and cartoonists drew glamorous young women serving a sophisticated urban clientele.

The Boomerang, 13 December, 1890, reprinted courtesy of La Trobe Collection, State Library of Victoria.

'The barmaid' as a category apart was partly an outcome of this turn of the century conflict, which resulted in legislation in many jurisdictions requiring barmaids to be registered or disemployed. This legislation shaped the subsequent labour market because it imposed age limits on the occupation which made young women unavailable for the work, allowed only those already employed to keep working and therefore to grow old in the job, or it restricted the work to the wives and daughters of the licensee. It thus converted the occupation of 'barmaid' from the employment opportunity for young single women leaving domestic service into 'the publican's wife' as pub work became the preserve only of family members. Earlier laws had required that a liquor licence could only be granted when it accompanied hospitality: Australian pubs from then on had always to provide accommodation and housekeeping, thus creating an important space for women's employment in an otherwise limited labour market. It was therefore particularly attractive to older women, married or widowed, and women with children.

Labour market realities were however only part of the story. A contradictory image of the barmaid subsequently developed in Australian popular culture, a paradoxical mix of the simultaneously glamorised youthful sexual attraction of the younger working girl, and the older maternal housemaid figure, the 'licenced premises wife. Ministering angel, Pal'.[18] who promised sympathy, wisdom and understanding, and without whom the pub could not be run as a home away from home. 'Tall and stately and rarely unbending',[19] this was a powerful figure who dominated the male clientele. She was somebody a customer could rely on to know his routine likes and dislikes and someone who could be trusted with his secrets and confidences. 'The good barmaid always has time to listen to your troubles, and always has the right word of comfort, correction or advice ... [She] has preserved more marriages, saved more careers, averted more suicides, restored more damaged egos ... If you have troubles – go to your barmaid.'[20] She could be and often was addressed as 'Mother'[21] by drinkers at the bar. This figure is present in the character of 'Ma' in the 1970s film *Sunday Too Far Away*, a story about a shearers' strike in 1950s rural Australia. An early scene in the film has the hero (played by Jack Thompson) confiding in 'Ma', the licensee of the town's solitary pub, that he is reforming: saving his money, giving up fighting and drinking and planning to go to Sydney. 'Ma' nods wisely and makes little comment: no doubt she's heard it all before. She knows him well. As he has entered the pub, she has automatically reached for his usual drink.

This wife/mother barmaid as a cultural figure was probably at her height in the 1950s in Australia but she was not a new face on the block. Women had been licensees since the first liquor licences were granted in the colonies in the 1790s. As a woman of maturity and authority she ran the public bar from her position of deference and difference. Her housekeeping talents combined with her business acumen made her a woman of economic stature, authority and local respect. For example, when Eliza Murphy, proprietor of the Mount Pleasant Hotel at Alexandra in country Victoria,

18 Hindle and Hepworth, 1980, p 11.
19 'The Old-Fashioned Barmaid?', 1951, pp 6–7.
20 Hindle and Hepworth, 1980, p 12.
21 See, eg, Cleave, 1969, p 147.

died suddenly of influenza in 1899 the local paper reported the circumstances of her last hours in some detail and then said: 'The late Mrs Murphy will be missed by many. Although possessing strong likes and dislikes, which she made no pretence of hiding ... [She] was held in the highest esteem by all who knew her; and a more straightforward person in business was not known.' The township had lost 'one of its oldest identities, whose keen wit, good humour and large heartedness, combined with the strictest integrity, will be remembered by hundreds for many years to come'.[22]

Eliza Murphy was clearly a prominent figure in her community: she had been a resident in the Alexandra district for nearly 40 years and had run the same pub for most of that time as a partnership with her husband(s). (Her second husband was beside her in the bed when she died.) This was not the tanned leggy working girl of London pubs nor the sexual lure of 1890s popular imagination, but a powerful, prominent person in the town, a respected older woman, who ran her business her way, and possibly, as many women did, independently of her husband.[23]

Similarly, Maureen Cleave described 'Clara', the tenant/licensee of the Waggoners, a pub in Hertfordshire, England. Clara was 'a small square woman in her fifties, with kind brown eyes and a warmth of manner that combines with a certain dignity to make her remarkable'.[24] Clara was born into pub life, in the bedroom over the public bar of the Waggoners, which her family had run since 1904. Clearly intelligent, she had been educated at a convent school and had taken a secretarial course – 'thinks she might have gone into the world of commerce' – but had, since she was 18, instead devoted herself to running the pub. Clara was an expert on knowing and pulling beer but in doing so she was more than the barmaid: she was an excellent cook, produced all the food for the pub lunches, made her own pickles, spiced her own vinegar and grew all her own herbs as well as cleaning and maintaining the pub.

Clara's work was hard but rewarding, 'never lonely, never dull' because it was based on a strong sense of community and continuity with the past. The pub was full of objects from her father's and grandfather's day, there were no concessions to modernity in the decor ('no plastic flowers, no television sets, no rubber plants') but, most importantly, it was built around her relationship with her customers 'the nicest bunch you could meet', all regulars, some of them the grandchildren of people she had always known. She was therefore at the centre of a tight familial community but it was also one in which she, as the only woman, was also the matriarch. The

---

22 Obituaries, 1899.

23 Wright, 2001, has argued for greater historical recognition of women publicans in Australia.

24 Cleave, 1969, p 137.

atmosphere she created was 'geared to men', deliberately, as 'a refuge'. 'You can't really appreciate the atmosphere unless you're a man,' she said. Knowingly she kept their past alive for them – 'they've known this place as children' – and here they could escape responsibilities as husbands and fathers into memory, 'away from the television and their families'. Clara's work was her relationship with her customers, based on her knowledge of them and their expectations of her. Like good sons, occasionally they helped her out. 'Quite often they take over the bar; they fetch things from the cellar' and on one occasion they mended a table that broke in the bar, then and there, rather than be without it.[25]

The authority of such a maternal figure was crucial to keeping the public bar under control as liquor loosened tongues and unleashed tempers. The final scene in *Sunday Too Far Away* is a brawl between the striking shearers and the 'scabs' brought in to do their jobs and undercut their strike. On this occasion it is not an unexpected eruption but a fight that only proceeds when 'Ma' has given her approval. The barmaid was, in this maternal role, also 'the wife' to every man in the bar. 'Any good barmaid is in fact a sort of wife to a great number of men,' two Australian journalists joked on one occasion, the connection between customer and barmaid being 'a deep and intimate relationship ... to last a lifetime'.[26] In *Confessions of an Innkeeper*, written in 1938, John Fothergill put it more in terms that a barmaid 'must be a lover of all men; in a philosophic sense, that is, all women to all men, whether or not she cares, in closing hours, to be one woman to one man'.[27] Her promiscuity in the culture of the bar ('the polyandry of the pub'[28]) was akin to the common prostitute, not because she took money but because she kept company with more than one man. But in that role, she must at the same time be faithful to each and every one. As Cleave said in 1969, a barmaid was 'loyal'.[29] As a 'Mother' she not only looked after but also stood up for her boys. 'Ma's' approval of the brawl in *Sunday Too Far Away* is because in the end she supports the cause of her boys, the shearers who are her regulars, over the scabs from out of town, even though it means her premises will be destroyed in the ensuing violence.

In the culture of both the English and the Australian pub, the customers returned that loyalty. It was the way a clientele was built up: 'You would go to one pub rather than another because of the barmaids.'[30] It could also be exploited as a way to attract new custom – 'Chaps will follow a favourite barmaid for miles to a new pub'[31] – but could then also lead to exploitation,

---

25 *Ibid*, pp 137–41.
26 Hindle and Hepworth, 1980, pp 11–12.
27 Quoted in Cleave, 1969, p 148.
28 Hindle and Hepworth, 1980, p 12.
29 Cleave, 1969, p 148.
30 'The Old-Fashioned Barmaid?', 1951, p 7.
31 Hindle and Hepworth, 1980, p 12.

as the men 'tend to get nervous and grumpy if the girl is missing from her accustomed place'.[32]

This was because the sexual economics and fantasy of the pub space merged into a power relationship built around the public performance of sexual difference. Equating the barmaid with paid employee/servant rather than economically independent career or businesswoman shaped the relationship between bar staff and customer and had consequences for the women workers. While the differentiation between women owners, managers and employees working behind the bar was also a fiction, the distinction between barmaids and owners could be very real in the workplace and the labour market. While licensees, managers and landladies accrued respect and often financial success, barmaids working for wages did not have the same status or control over their workplace. Paid better than other women working in service or manufacturing industries they also had difficult and often personally confronting working conditions. In the words of Sydney barmaid Caddie at the very least you had to 'be nice to the boss ... [and] be nice to the drunks ... you get a bigger tip that way'.[33] More recent research correlates a high level of violence directed towards bar staff as a consequence of declining control over their working conditions.[34]

Here is where the barmaid of the 1890s begins to have much in common with that of the 1960s–70s. Physical attributes were an important characteristic of bar employees when the occupation first came into being in the early mid-19th century, but it was not until towards the end of the century that physical appearance became sexualised to such an extent, as it was again in the 1960s. Dress was crucial.[35] In the days when the miniskirt reigned, one popular book on Australian pubs claimed 'there's no more delectable a sight than the barmaid's bloomers. A man strides into the bar ... and the pastel panorama of a pair of panties signals a warm welcome, like a neon light outside a roadside café at night'. These 'floral frillies' were 'a proud professional symbol'.[36] Other barmaids were celebrated for their fashion sense or 'snug-fitting black dresses which set off their blonde hair'.[37] Sometimes advertisements said, 'No experience necessary: mini-skirts only'.[38]

Categorising female bar staff in this way was part of the fantasy that went with the pub as a place of masculine recreation, that like the theatre, was a paradoxical mix of the real and the imagined. One barmaid claimed

32 *Ibid.*
33 *Caddie* (the film).
34 Mayhew and Quinlan, 1996.
35 Barnes and Eicher, 1992.
36 Larkins and Howard, 1973, p 101.
37 *Telegraph* (Brisbane), 20 May 1967.
38 Cleave, 1969, p 131.

bar work was in fact the next best thing to being on the stage.[39] However, it was not just fantasy that created the archetypal barmaid of popular culture, it was significantly also the reality of workplace relations and the work of law, specifically licensing laws with clauses which stipulated 'no female shall be employed in any capacity in or about the bar-room of any licenced premises at any time while the bar room is open for the sale of liquor ... unless she be the wife sister or daughter of the licensee, the licensee being a woman, or [she be] registered as a barmaid under this Act'.[40] Only 'barmaids' – identified and registered as such – could work as employees behind the bar. Other women, 'respectable' women, must look for other work.

By the early years of the 20th century these licensing laws were actively controlling women's participation in paid labour in the liquor trade when they thus stipulated the ages and marital status of those women who could be employed behind the bar. In South Australia and Victoria, specific provisions required that all those currently working as barmaids should be registered, and made it a punishable offence for any woman found not to be registered. Specifically no new barmaids were to be employed. Other states imposed age restrictions on women seeking paid employment behind the bar, (usually 'no woman under the age of 21') or they limited the age at which a woman could hold a publican's licence. By this means young women were removed from the occupation. The number of barmaid employees (as opposed to the family of the publican) dramatically declined, and women outside the publican's family were prevented from acquiring the skills and knowledge needed to become licensees in their own right in the future (unless they married a publican and literally became the publican's wife). On the other hand publicans' families' dominance in the trade were enhanced and the skills needed for the industry were learnt while growing up in the family.

These were workplace considerations, which affected leisure activities. These licensing laws set boundaries of inclusion and exclusion as they declared pub spaces out of bounds to women workers who were not under the protective mantle of a husband or father publican. They also made it impossible for 'respectable' women then to be seen in the public bar as drinkers where they were in the company only of many men. Some jurisdictions actually made it a specific offence for women to drink alcohol in those pubs. Section 71 of the Liquor Act of Queensland 1912 prohibited anyone from selling liquor 'to any female in any bar or in any room adjacent to a bar which is especially set aside for drinking purposes'. The provision was repeated in 1926 when the clause 'of a licenced victualler's premises'

---

39 *Ibid*.
40 Licensing Act (Vic) 1928, s 207, repeated in the Licensing Act 1958, s 200 and quoted in *Vigilante*, 4 February 1971, p 3.

was added, and it remained in force through to the 1960s when women started challenging their right to be present in bars and to drink alongside men. Queensland never legally prevented women working behind the bar yet in 1963 many people believed women were not even allowed to attend an art show being held in a pub because they could not be served alcohol.[41]

Sex-segregated drinking and fantasising about the barmaid's body was not therefore restricted to those jurisdictions with restrictive labour laws. In New South Wales publicans were prominent members of the 20th century parliament, which did not ban barmaids but only restricted the age at which women could work in pubs. Nevertheless the drinking culture of NSW, described as 'most uncivilised' developed along the same sex-segregated lines. In 1959 a survey undertaken in NSW found that 71% of people surveyed believed women should be excluded from hotel bars. This was true of both men and women respondents. Only a minority (less than one quarter) expressed a preference for drinking in male only company, and more than half either wanted mixed company or didn't care. So most people actually preferred to drink in the hotel lounge or beer garden rather than the public bar.[42] However, it was still popular opinion that those public bars ought to be male only spaces. It was therefore not only licensing laws, which constructed this profile of women in pubs. Unwritten laws – custom and tradition – about appropriate feminine and masculine behaviour also worked powerfully to create the working and leisure environment of the pub as these ideas were written into formal laws and formal laws created and perpetuated boundaries.

The 1890s image of the barmaid in popular culture as 'sexual lure' thus resurfaced in the 1960s–70s. By then the laws restricting women's work as barmaids had been overturned and once again the market was opened up to a new youthful group of workers which from then on was becoming an increasingly casual workforce. Explicitly sexual dressing for barmaids became more pronounced in the 1960s as employers used the sexuality of these young barmaids to attract custom. The skill of their work was subsumed in an exploitation of their sexual commodification. The press reported that barmaids in some Sydney and Brisbane pubs were being asked by their employers to wear matador pants or hipster slacks, 'frilly aqua blouses ... teamed with high-heeled scuffs' on the understanding 'men like to see girls wearing something a bit different'. The barmaids reported 'occasionally we get a rude remark'. Employers reported 'business has never been better'.[43]

By the 1970s, some barmaids were being paid to go topless. This created immense pressure on the other barmaids: they too were expected to remove

41 Told in Kirkby, 1997.
42 Reported in AHA, 1959, p 34.
43 *Telegraph* (Brisbane), 30 January 1963; 1 February 1963.

much of their clothing, or the level of sexual innuendo and jeers from male customers in the bar was raised to new heights making their work that much harder to carry out. Constantly keeping a friendly, cheerful demeanour, and smiling at customers was the most important characteristic bar employees had. 'The customer's always right and always be polite no matter what they say,' was how one barmaid described it.[44] Another pointed out 'it's the continual smiling at customers that takes it toll more than anything else'.[45] Bar staff were instructed: 'Make it a point of concern and pride that no customer ever walks out of your bar disgruntled or dissatisfied, if it is humanly possible to avoid it. Treat them as guests, with proper respect ...'[46] In an atmosphere of harassment and derision, as the popular culture of the pub, and the cultural figure of the barmaid blurred into a greater sexualisation of the employed bar staff this important work skill became harder to maintain. As one barmaid working alongside topless waitresses said: 'I found it really embarrassing, really embarrassing ... I felt like everybody was looking at me and trying to see through my clothes because these girls had their clothes off ...' Another spoke of the risks that came from a new kind of customer now being attracted to the bar. 'They think we're not going to get offended because ... we put ourselves in that position' one barmaid claimed.[47] Perhaps it was this harassment and danger, which meant 'Very rarely will you find a local girl working in the pub of her home town'.[48] In the far outback of rural Australia in the prosperous 1960s–70s, barmaids were 'an anonymous, itinerant race, known only as Faye, and Dawn, and Pat, staying a few months then moving on, always moving on. Packing their panties and disappearing in search of goodness knows what'.[49] For women wage workers labour turnover has always been high and historically the explanation has been poor working conditions and low pay. Barmaids in Australia have been paid well, but the expectations imposed on them as the only women in a male only space has obscured the difficulties of the work (the long hours serving beer that ruins their shoes and stiffens their dresses) and the demeaning stature of them as not workers but as objects of unwanted ribaldry, dirty jokes and innuendo, however 'affectionate'.

Who drank in pubs, and where, was one question. Who ran the pubs was another. By the mid-20th century, the Victorian hoteliers' association was boasting it had more women hotelkeepers than anywhere else 'in the

---

44 Bastalich, 1991, p 54.
45 *Telegraph* (Brisbane), 20 May 1967, p 14.
46 Coombs, 1965, p 162.
47 Bastalich, 1991, pp 54–55.
48 Larkins and Howard, 1973, p 102.
49 *Ibid.*

world'.[50] This, too, was the outcome of law and popular culture in different jurisdictions. Although in the 19th century the common law doctrine of coverture made it almost impossible for a married woman to hold a licence in her own name if her husband was cohabiting with her (although colonial conditions made this sometimes difficult to maintain) the passage of Married Women's Property Acts at the end of the 19th century supposedly brought an end to these disabilities. However new laws and regulations in various industries circumscribed and redefined women's occupations. Hotel keeping was one of these.

In New South Wales, the Liquor Acts, which followed the Married Women's Property Act, constituted the married female licensee as an exceptional case (and interestingly also banned single women from holding a licence). In short in NSW the restrictions on married women were unaffected by the Married Women's Property Act in 1893. Western Australia in 1872 explicitly disqualified women licensees on the grounds of their sex though not their marital status; an 1886 amendment enabled single women to hold a licence if they were over 21 years of age and 1893 legislation provided that no female 'who is a widow of 30 years or more shall be disqualified to hold a publican's general licence ... by reason only of her sex'. This was the colony which only a few years later (1899) gave women the vote but first it ensured (1898) that the restrictions on women licensees were reiterated: 'A woman cannot hold a licence if her husband has one' and no concessions were made to the fact that they might be separated. Married women's property legislation apparently brought in fears of fraud and dummying.

These laws were helping to construct the maternal barmaid who was also the publican's wife. In 1884, a Victorian woman, Catherine Minogue, sought to acquire a second licence out of earnings she had made from her first pub held jointly with her husband. He was away a lot and she ran the pub on her own and kept the earnings. However, when she brought this to the attention of the lawkeepers by applying for a second licence, the licensing magistrate held it was against s 50 of the Victorian Licensing Act 1876 for a married woman to hold a licence. She was, he said, the publican's wife, not the publican. Catherine Minogue appealed his decision but the Supreme Court upheld his view. Although Justice Higinbotham argued that the Married Women's Property legislation should take precedence, his two fellow judges outvoted him.

This decision reportedly left 'hundreds' of married women licensees stranded and an Act was hastily passed to ensure that they could carry on trading. The 1885 Licensing Act allowed 'any person' to apply for a licence and s 3 provided that 'person' included a *'feme covert'*. Section 81 improved

---

50   *Vigilante*, 30 October 1958, p 10.

the situation of a female licensee who married by providing that her licence no longer automatically transferred to her husband and the decision to apply for a transfer was left to the bride. Although it seems fairly clear that the whole assumption of the Licensing Acts was that most licensees would be male, Victoria did not bother to legislate special conditions for separated, deserted etc wives, which further suggests that wives as a whole were allowed to keep hotels. The consequence then of Catherine Minogue's action in challenging the licensing magistrate was that new legislation was passed and the number of women licensees in Victoria subsequently increased.

Licensing courts in the mid-20th century were also active in constructing 'the pub[lican]'s wife' when they asked both husbands and their wives questions about the provisions and accommodations that were going to be provided before the court granted a licence. The licence was often then given 'on behalf of self and wife'. 'Many a case appears to have been determined in the applicant's favor because he was able to prove that his wife or manageress or housekeeper was capable of filling the role assigned to her,' an editorial in the hotelkeepers' journal, *Vigilante,* claimed in 1950. The expectation that a woman, notably the publican's wife, would provide this labour was almost as old as the first licensing laws in NSW and was aptly summed up in 1897 by the NSW parliamentarian who said: 'Anyone who lives in a hotel must know that no licenced house can be properly conducted unless there is a good woman in it.'[51]

In short there was a woman behind many a bar, and although licensing courts frequently favoured a married couple, it was often her house.[52] Law was therefore active in the creation of Australian pub culture. By stipulating hours of opening and imposing taxes, governments regulated the trade in alcohol and lined the Treasury's vaults. But from early colonial times licensing laws also required the provision of accommodation and dining facilities in hotels rather than just the provision of liquor, a requirement which drew women into the trade in substantial numbers as they took advantage of the legal provisions to provide for their own economic wellbeing.

Pubs were important to married women as their workplaces, as well as their domestic residences where they could raise their children and work alongside or in the absence of their husbands (colonial husbands were frequently absent). Running a pub was frequently a family concern, a partnership between husbands and wives, with sons and daughters learning the trade and subsequently continuing in their own house. And once the registration of barmaids was introduced in Victoria (1919) it was claimed within the trade that many licensees immediately registered their female

---

51 *NSW Parliamentary Debates,* 1897, p 2984.
52 *Vigilante,* 1958, p 10.

children so that in years to come they might be able to work outside the family's establishment, in someone else's premises, thus also perpetuating the tradition of hotel keeping as a family business.[53] Wartime Australian Labour Prime Minister John Curtin's mother was one such daughter of a publican who subsequently became the publican's wife when Curtin's father took out the licence for a hotel in inner Melbourne in the Depression years of the 1890s.[54] This was not a happy financial venture for the Curtin family. The 1890s were tough years for the hotel trade and many women publicans went bust. Wives' work in families was also being discounted in the 1890s census statistics.[55]

Law and popular culture thus worked together for women's economic activities. In Australia women's access to economic independence was frequently curtailed even as married women's property reform promised new possibilities of freedom: sometimes, as in regulations of the liquor trade and even the public service, it was through other legislation. Sometimes it was through popular or communal understandings of law, which sustained or obstructed women's ability to support themselves economically as 'the landlady' or the licensee.

Take the case of Elizabeth Fregon and Christina McDougall, whose story illustrates the way formal law worked at the local level and was informed by, and enforced, community attitudes. Elizabeth Fregon in partnership with her husband, John, was a storekeeper in a small rural town in Victoria in the 1880s, owning several properties including quite a large acreage of grazing land, and two pubs, the 'Tongio Inn' at nearby Tongio and the 'Golden Age' in Omeo, the town where she lived. Elizabeth Fregon was a 'landlady' in Omeo in the popular categorisation of women behind the bar, in Tongio 'the publican's wife' who, on her husband's death, continued to be a prominent businesswoman in the Omeo district who had access to that profit and power that came from hotel keeping. She was never the barmaid. But she was in the anomalous position of being the owner not the licensee of the 'Golden Age', and, when the building burnt to the ground, the licensee, Christina McDougall, continued trading in opposition to her landlady's wishes, in premises across the street. This pitted two women from one small community against each other in a contest for the profits from liquor trading. Mrs Fregon the landlady tried to stop Mrs McDougall the former publican's wife (now widow) from trading, by transferring the licence to someone else but the Licensing Court allowed McDougall (soon remarried) to continue trading in her new separate premises until the 'Golden Age' was rebuilt. By this means Mrs McDougall became the licensee in her own right,

---

53 Reported in the *Vigilante*, 1971, p 3.
54 Day, 1999.
55 Deacon, 1985, pp 27–47.

not the landlady, not the publican's wife, not simply the barmaid but now 'of her own bar'.[56]

Elizabeth Fregon's attempts to acquire the licence in her own name were always unsuccessful. Each time she tried, the Licensing Court (a local bench) granted the licence to Christina McDougall. Finally the local council's action under a Public Health ordinance of declaring the land behind the burnt-out hotel to be a public safety risk brought the matter to an end.[57] Like so many other women in the 1890s depression years, Elizabeth Fregon was subsequently declared insolvent and the Bailiff forcibly sold her properties.[58]

The stories of women like Eliza Murphy, Catherine Minogue, Christina McDougall and Elizabeth Fregon, 19th century economically active and often very successful business women, are visible to the historian today only through the lens of legal cases/documents. Their stories are the product of legal narratives through which we can see they depended on informal customs and popular understandings as much as formal rules to maintain their economic viability. It was they who became in the 20th century those powerful wife/mother figures portrayed in popular culture.

A century later licensing laws had been significantly overhauled and, as the old Australian pub culture disappeared, the barmaid, the landlady and the publican's wife were conflating into the single fantasy of the sexualised barmaid. Representative of the power of the woman licensee and symbolic of her maternal authority this figure had especially large breasts: 'There is one outstanding physical attribute of the barmaid,' according to one popular text. 'It is ... that she has what can only be called, not to put too fine a point on it, tits.' This attribute came with the job: 'It is in the nature of the barmaid species to lean forward over the bar when bending a sympathetic ear. This calls for a generous bosom ...'[59] This Australian pub culture has been described by Playboy features writer Michael Thomas as wallowing in nostalgia and wanting 'adolescence until death'.[60]

Yet a barmaid was also a vehicle for popularising feminist political goals when the film *Caddie* was released in 1976. Based on the autobiographical account of a Sydney barmaid which was a hugely popular story of the Depression published in the 1950s, *Caddie* became the expression of 1970s feminist concerns about work, wages, equal pay, childcare and sexual harassment.[61] Its nostalgic portrayal of Australian working class culture, the

---

56 Fregon in fact was held to be acting illegally because the Probate Commissioner now held the power to allocate the licence, given Mr McDougall's intestacy, and the town businessmen took sides in support of Mrs McDougall (possibly as a way of forcing Mrs Fregon out of business).

57 Omeo Licensing Court, *Omeo Telegraph*, 31 March 1893, p 3.

58 *Omeo Telegraph*, 13 February 1894, p 3.

59 Hindle and Hepworth, 1980, pp 12–13.

60 Thomas, 1987, p 50.

61 Curthoys, 1988; Kirkby, 1992, pp 235–45.

mateship and community of inner city living and pub camaraderie during the Depression years of the 1930s, was far removed from the cosmopolitan high-rise and consumerist Australia of the 1960s–70s when barmaids wore miniskirts and frilly panties and work was for pleasure not economic need. When Caddie's lover, Peter, a 'new Australian' who owned a clothing factory employing women on very low wages, challenged that old pub culture by asking Caddie to give up work when they married, it sparked an outburst from Caddie about a whole array of concerns Australian women had about their economic security. Caddie's defence of her own right to continue working became a speech for equal pay, for the needs of working mothers, and a denunciation of the sexual harassment of the pub workplace. These issues were firmly on the agenda of the Liquor Trades Union in the 1980s when popular culture celebrating the 'sonsy bird who pushes the foaming glass across before you have even called for it'[62] was at its height.

The gender dynamics of this workplace culture were now the subject of trade union and feminist politics much as they had been at the turn of the century when temperance campaigners and labour unions battled publicans and breweries for regulation of the workplace and the workforce. In neither period was it simply an attack on the recreation of the poor or working class. The targets for the greater surveillance which occurred were indeed the workers but it was as workers not as pursuers of unsupervised leisure. Sexual differentiation was at its core. The pub culture of the 19th and 20th centuries was itself both a result and a cause of restrictive legislation, and was now an outcome of the interaction of past legal regulation and customary practice in local communities. Importantly the pub was for women primarily a workplace, often also their home where they raised their children, or domestic residence when employees were required to live in. Law differentiated 'the barmaid' from 'the publican's wife', when legislation and licensing courts confined the work to married women as wives of the licensee not independent, single waged workers. Yet it simultaneously defined 'barmaid' as 'any woman who works for two hours or more per day serving in the bar', thus blurring the boundaries between the two and leaving space for popular imagination to create 'the barmaid' as 'licenced premises wife' and mother to the pub clientele.

Barmaids in 1969, in Cleave's words 'more than anyone else, work[ed] for the fun of it ...'.[63] Customers also enjoyed the fun, and the popular culture that celebrated pub life made much of the barmaid's body in sexual innuendo which was often at the expense of the barmaid. The popular culture which grew up around 'the barmaid' transcended legal prescription. Historicising the connection between popular culture and the role of law is a window on to the complexity of legality in everyday life.

---

62 Hindle and Hepworth, 1980.
63 Cleave, 1969, p 148.

PART FIVE

HETEROSEXING CYBERCULTURE

Small Judgements

The white pigeon
has not heard of the dove.

~•~

Jumping on sunshine
your child lands on flies.

~•~

The shadow left from the lovemaking
fits us all.

~•~

Astride my past
I imagine soon.

~•~

The future feels us deeply –
thus to become!

~•~

Any tragedy is in the moment
and our failure to fill it.

~•~

These tears
are my new eye.

~•~

Kill what pretends –
        what we pretend.

~•~

The boats have come in
with the news that still belongs to the world.

MTC Cronin

THE LEGAL REGULATION OF CYBERPORNOGRAPHY: LAW'S QUEST FOR BORDERS IN A BORDERLESS WORLD

Paula Baron

INTRODUCTION

Cyberculture[1] is complex and ambiguous. In many ways, the internet offers utopian possibilities. Its architecture is highly decentralised. It is multipurpose. It is 'interactive'. It offers near real time communication and is available at relatively low cost. It facilitates the sharing of all types of information. It promises a virtual community in which differences of age, gender, ability and race are irrelevant.[1a] Yet the internet also serves in many ways to reinforce, rather than overcome, existing social power relations. Like other media, it can operate to exclude and silence.[2] Rather than creating community, it can foster a growing isolation and alienation of individuals.[3] In many areas, capital has hijacked the democratic ideals of the internet, directing the internet's power to the reinforcement and expansion of markets.[4] Today one of the notable characteristics of the internet is its global consumer culture[5] and increasing homogenisation.[6]

Cyberculture is also characterised by a remarkable interest in sex and sexually explicit material. Sex is the number one searched topic on the internet[7] and some estimates have claimed that pornography accounts for as much as 40% of all internet traffic.[8] Alarmed at the proliferation of, and ease of access to, undesirable content, including the wide variety of available

---

1   In this paper, I use the term 'cyberculture' to refer to a way of life now common in Western developed nations in which day to day life and interaction are mediated by the computer and the internet. Increasing amounts of both work and leisure time are spent 'on line' interacting in virtual space. I use the term 'cybercommunity' to refer to members of the cyberculture.

1a Witheford, 1997, p 227.

2   Alshejni, 1999, p 216. Morahan-Martin, 1998a, p 1, notes that the internet is unrepresentative demographically and that internet users are more likely to be male, wealthier, better educated and younger than the general population.

3   Adams, 2000, p 32.

4   Witheford, 1997, p 230, argues that capital has attempted to 'recolonise' the unruliness of cyberspace through such endeavours as video on demand, tele-gambling, pay-per computer games and infomercials.

5   Alshejni, 1999, p 216.

6   ABA, 1997, p 20.

7   Cooper *et al*, 1999, p 2.

8   Arasaratnam, 2000, p 205.

cyberpornography, the Australian Government introduced the Broadcasting Amendment (Online Services) Act 1999 (Cth) (hereafter the Online Services Act). This legislation has met with considerable opposition from some sections of the cybercommunity who argue that pornography on the internet is no different to pornography in other media. They suggest that alarm at cyberpornography is merely a form of 'moral panic' commonly experienced with the introduction of any new technology. Censorship of the internet, they claim, is both unworkable and undesirable.

By considering the specific instance of cyberpornography, I want to make two claims about the relationship of popular culture and the law. The first claim relates generally to the dynamic between cyberculture and the law. This claim is that cyberculture poses a profound challenge to the authority of the law in its disruption of established boundaries. With specific reference to pornography, the internet's disruption of borders facilitates the creation, distribution and consumption of pornography, and simultaneously renders pornography highly resistant to legal regulation. The second claim relates more specifically to the impact of this dynamic upon the pornographic presence on the internet. This claim is that, despite the opportunity for change to our reading and regulation of pornography that the clash between cyberculture and law might offer, the status quo is likely to be maintained. These two cultures share common understandings, assumptions and goals such that the opportunity to reconsider the impact of internet pornography from a feminist perspective is unlikely to be realised.

The paper is in four parts: the first part considers the incidence of pornography on the internet; the second outlines the provisions of the Online Services Act; and the third and main part of the paper explores the claim that cyberculture poses a profound challenge to the authority of the law in its disruption of established boundaries. The final section explores the claim that, although this clash of cultures offers the potential for a reassessment of pornography, this potential is unlikely to be realised.

Before proceeding, it is necessary to acknowledge that there is no agreed definition of 'pornography'. One's definition of 'pornography' will depend upon whether one takes a moral stance (pornography is material that offends the reasonable person); an equality stance (pornography is material that violates, objectifies and/or denigrates the subject); or a free speech stance (pornography is merely a means of free expression). Definitions may also vary with the individual's geographic and cultural situation.

In a thoughtful attempt to define pornography, Nagel argues that pornography is material that objectifies sexuality.[9] On this reading, the remarkable routine sameness of much pornographic material allows pornography to function as a consumer product, 'a taken-for-granted, ready-

---

9   Nagel, 2002.

made object with a specific purpose'. I have used pornography in a wide sense in this paper to refer to sexually explicit and/or violent material that is intended to sexually arouse,[10] while acknowledging Nagel's point that pornography and the consumer culture are inextricably intertwined.

THE INCIDENCE OF CYBERPORNOGRAPHY

The adoption of new technologies, particularly new information and communication technologies, has traditionally been strongly gendered.[11] Much of the cyberculture, despite increasing usage by women, remains a masculine culture.[12] Studies have found that males make up two-thirds of internet users and account for 77% of online time. They go online on a daily basis more frequently than females and feel more competent and comfortable using the internet than women.[13] They use the internet for a wider variety of reasons and are more likely to use the internet for recreational purposes.[14] One such 'recreational purpose' is consumption of pornography.[15] This, too, remains a strongly gendered activity.[16] Studies continue to show that the majority of pornography consumers are male.[17] Despite the fact that the gender gap of internet users changed rapidly over the period 1994–98, from 20:1 to 2:1, studies continue to show that men are overwhelmingly the largest consumers of sexually explicit internet material. Where women do access sexually explicit sites on the internet, their pattern of usage tends to be quite different. They prefer more interaction and

---

10   Voon, 2001, p 10.

11   Silverstone and Hirsch, 1992, p 8; Cockburn, 1992, p 41. Originally, the internet was the domain of 'male scientists, mathematicians and technologically sophisticated computer hackers': Morahan-Martin, 1998a, p 4.

12   Morahan-Martin, 1998a; Morahan-Martin, 1998b; see also Witheford, 1997, p 229 who describes the internet as a domain of 'techno-puerility'.

13   Morahan-Martin, 1998a, p 6, also notes that men dominate discussion groups and where women try to have equal footing on male dominated lists, they are ignored, trivialised or criticised by men.

14   Cooper et al, 1999, p 6. A recent study of Australian families and internet usage confirms these trends. Males were more likely to use a range of internet services than females: 80% of males surfed the net compared with 69% of females; 23% of males traded goods as compared to 14% of females; 58% of males accessed news compared to 38% of females; 25% of men used the internet for looking at sexual content compared to 6% of women; and 36% of men used the internet for transaction processing, compared to 25% of women. Similarly, male children in the surveyed households were more likely to download music or games than female children: ABA, 2000.

15   Moore, 1998, p 101, links the rise of pornography generally to the rise of a techno-rational culture in which sensuality is ignored.

16   This would appear to reflect a more general tend noted by Altman, 2002, that, although the growth of the consumer society has tended to create the possibility of recreational sex for women as well as men, the overall imbalance remains.

17   Morahan-Martin, 1998a, observes that the imbalance starts in childhood: two-thirds of computer games sold in the US are sold to and for boys.

development of relationships and are less interested in visual stimuli alone.[18]

Pornography on the internet is clearly big business.[19] In 1999, the revenue from pornography and live sex shows on the internet was estimated at $US1bn. It comprised 69% of internet content sales. Pornographers in the United States harvested a majority of the money.[20] By the year 2003, it is expected that these sales will triple and generate half the revenue of online content sales.[21]

Consumers can find explicit material on the internet in a variety of forms: from pictures and short animated movies, to sound files and stories. Internet users can discuss sex, see live sex acts, arrange sexual activities from individual computer terminals and join sex-related discussion groups on the Internet Relay Chat and exchange messages and files.[22] Most pornographic content is available through World Wide Web ('WWW') pages. Figures from the NEC Research Institute show that approximately 600 million WWW pages are open to the public and 1.5% is focused on pornography. At least nine million pornographic pages are said to exist, much of the material at the hard core end of the spectrum.[23] As Catherine MacKinnon has observed, '[p]ornography takes up much of the Internet's collective brain'.[24]

Access to pornography on the internet is easy. Pornographic WWW sites and newsgroups are generally accessible through the internet by any online user. While usenet discussion groups are free to access, many of the commercial WWW sites with pornographic content require proof of age and payment by credit card before access is granted.

THE ONLINE SERVICES ACT

Alarmed at the growth of undesirable discourse, including pornography, on the internet, the Australian Government introduced the Online Services Act. The legislation takes a moral conservative approach.[25] In essence, the Act

---

18 Cooper *et al*, 1999, p 9. Note also the gender gap in viewing sexual content in the figures in fn 14 above.

19 There is also a strong link between pornography and organised crime. Pornography is believed to be organised crime's biggest source of revenue after drugs and gambling: Akdeniz, 1997, p 17.

20 More than 60% of all materials generally on the internet come from the US: Akdeniz, 1997, p 12.

21 Hughes, 2001.

22 Akdeniz, 1997, p 2.

23 See further http://www.neci.nj.nec.com/neci-website/lab-tour/lab-tour.html.

24 MacKinnon, 1995, pp 1963–64.

25 Voon, 2001, 170. The Act is intended to censor not only pornography but other 'inappropriate' content such as drug use and language.

applies the government's censorship classification scheme used in other media to the internet. The Act empowers the Australian Broadcasting Authority (ABA) to investigate complaints made about online material or to investigate material of its own volition (ss 26 and 27). Regulation is directed to 'prohibited' or 'potential prohibited' internet content.[26] Because of the absence of national borders on the internet (a characteristic discussed below), once the ABA identifies prohibited or potentially prohibited content, its response depends upon where the material is hosted and whether or not the material has been classified.

If the material is hosted in Australia and is unclassified, the ABA may issue interim takedown notices to the hosting Australian sites[27] and refer the material to the Office of Film and Literature Classification (OFLC) for classification (s 30(2)(a)). Depending on the ultimate classification of the material, the ABA may revoke its notices (ss 32–35) or issue final takedown orders (s 30(4)(b)).[28] However, less than 1% of illegal or offensive internet material is hosted in Australia.[29] Where material is hosted outside Australia and the material is classified X or RC, the ABA's response depends on whether or not there is an industry code in place. If there is not, the ABA can issue an access prevention notice requiring Internet Service Providers (ISPs) to take all reasonable steps to prevent end users from accessing the content (s 40(1)(c)). If there is a registered industry code of practice,[30] ISPs must comply with it (s 40(1)(b)).

In addition to registering Codes and monitoring compliance with them, the ABA is empowered to play a community education role, research related issues and gather information on industry trends, and liaise with relevant industry bodies. It was the Commonwealth's intention that a second tier of uniform State and Territory legislation regulating content providers support the initiative of the Online Services Act. Accordingly, NSW and SA have

---

26 'Prohibited content' is defined to include Australian hosted R-rated material that is not subject to a restricted access scheme, and all material rated X or RC (s 10). 'Potential prohibited content' is unclassified content that, if classified, would be substantially likely to be prohibited content (s 11).

27 Unless the material is believed to be R-rated, in which case it will not be subject to takedown orders as it is considered to be less serious (s 30(2)(b)).

28 The ABA can also issue notices for removal of material that is 'substantially similar' to content that is the subject of the notice (s 36).

29 Garnett, 2000, p 239.

30 Currently, if ISPs are notified of overseas hosted prohibited content under the Designated Notification Scheme they must provide an approved filter to subscribers. Where its subscribers are commercial, the ISPs must provide appropriate software or arrange access to a consultancy service with the relevant technology. These measures are unnecessary if subscribers already have prevention systems in place. ISPs and Internet Content Hosts (ICHs) must also take reasonable steps to make certain internet access accounts are not provided to people under 18 without responsible adult consent.

subsequently introduced internet censorship Bills[31] to complement the Online Services Act.

CYBERCULTURE, LAW AND THE ISSUE OF BOUNDARIES

Despite its 'light touch' approach, the response to the Online Services Act from some sections of the cybercommunity has been vociferous.[32] Critics have accused the legislation of stifling the development of the internet, introducing anti-information politics to the internet, obstructing the exploitation of commerce on the internet, introducing political censorship by means of politicised filtering software, potentially over censoring the internet and putting Australia out of step with the global information community.[33] Some critics have labelled concern about internet pornography 'moral panic' on the part of government, law enforcement bodies, the media in general and internet users and non-users alike.[34]

Commentators have observed a tendency for new technologies, such as the internet, to give rise to such 'moral panic'. Although individuals who live in developed western democracies are great consumers of technology, we also evidence a neurosis about technology's capacity to consume us.[35] This is particularly the case for information and communication technologies, which problematise the project of creating ontological security.[36]

Is concern about internet pornography mere 'moral panic'? Is it the case that censorship of the internet is both undesirable and unworkable? I want to suggest that the debate over internet censorship is, at least in part, the clash of traditional legal culture and the emerging cyberculture over the

---

31 Alston, 2000, p 197. The Classification (Publications, Films and Computer Games) Enforcement Amendment Bill 2001 (NSW) and Classification (Publications, Films and Computer Games) (Miscellaneous) Amendment Bill (No 2) 2001 (SA) are currently under consideration. Victoria, Western Australia and the Northern Territory enacted internet censorship legislation prior to the Commonwealth legislation (respectively, Classification (Publications, Films and Computer Games) (Enforcement) Act 1995 (Vic); Censorship Act 1996 (WA); and Classification of Publications, Films and Computer Games Act, 1996 (NT). This pre-existing legislation tends to be less restrictive than the Commonwealth legislation.

32 The response to similar attempts to censor the internet by state governments has been the same. The proposed state legislation has been labelled 'ridiculous': McAulliffe, 2000.

33 Links to a number of articles criticising the Online Services Act can be found at Libertus.net, 'The Net Censorship Dilemma: Opinion Articles and media reports', http://libertus.net/liberty/artic9910.html.

34 Akdeniz, 1997, p 1. One study by the ABA suggested such 'moral panic' in its finding that parents without internet access at home were more concerned about the risk to children from access to pornography or predatory conduct than parents with internet home access: ABA, 2001.

35 Silverstone and Hirsch, 1992, p 2.

36 Silverstone, Hirsch and Morley, 1992, p 20.

issue of boundaries. In particular, cyberculture disrupts at least five boundaries, which I shall explore in turn: the boundaries between private and public space; the boundaries between production and consumption; the boundaries between reality and virtuality; the boundaries between nation states and the boundaries between entertainment and information. This disruption of boundaries at once facilitates the pornographic presence on the internet and renders it difficult to regulate.

Private and public space

The internet's restructuring of private and public space is in some ways an extension of the restructuring of private and public space that started with the adoption of the home computer. The computer in the bedroom and technologies such as the television and telephone transformed spaces within the home from those that served a common need for family members to those that supported the separate existence of individuals all day.[37] Similarly, the multifunctional nature of the computer as games machine, educator and work facilitator created an extension and transformation of the boundaries in and around the home.[38]

Despite the public nature of cyberspace, the internet gives an individual the ability to access publicly available information from the relative physical privacy of their living room, bedroom or office.[39] This blurring of public and private space gives rise to a somewhat naïve sense of security. A US commentator highlighted these altered boundaries of private and public space recently. In the course of expressing the view that the Online Services Act was doomed to failure, he said: 'Vice is part of human existence. You wouldn't dump your kids on the sidewalk of a big city and tell them to fend for themselves, and you shouldn't do that on the internet either.'[40] Yet most of us would not think of the internet as being equivalent to the 'sidewalk of a big city', simply because our net surfing generally takes place in the comfort, perceived security and relative privacy of home or office (or even school or net café).

This restructuring of public and private space has a number of implications for the pornographic presence on the internet. Firstly, the blurred divide between public space and private space creates opportunities

---

37   Strathern, 1992, p ix.
38   Haddon, 1992, p 48.
39   In Australia, the study or office (42%) is the most common location for the internet-connected computer, followed by the family room/lounge room (32%); the 'spare' room (7%); and the adult bedroom (5%). Only 4% of homes had the internet connection in the child's bedroom. Children with internet connections in their rooms were generally older: ABA, 2000.
40   Bill McCarthy, editor of Broadwatch Magazine, interviewed by Garry Barker, 'Internet Regulation Doomed: US expert' (2000) *The Age*, 16 August.

for sexually predatory behaviour. One aspect of such behaviour is paedophiliac activity on the internet. Children unsupervised on the internet are not necessarily safe, even if their computer is in their own room. Although there has been a fair degree of 'moral panic' on the issue of predatory exploitation of children,[41] it is true to say that this is an occurrence that has happened frequently enough to be of concern.[42]

A second implication of the blurring of private and public space is that a greater number of people have the opportunity to access pornography. These are people who would not otherwise have access to pornography in other media, either because they are under age, or because they might be embarrassed to go into a sex shop, or even because they would not have the time to go out and buy pornographic products. For those who are already pornography consumers, the internet facilitates easy access to materials. In addition, it facilitates 'efficient' consumption, in the sense that the consumer can download those images that they want, rather than having to buy a book or magazine to obtain one or two particular images. It is also easier to hone in on particular images or practices and to contact other users with similar interests.[43]

A third implication of the blurring of public and private space is that, despite the fact that cyber footprints can be traced, many people can enjoy pornography in relative physical privacy, concealing their consumption from colleagues, friends, partners and family. New technologies allow this secrecy to be sustained more easily than in the case of traditional media, such as magazines or videos. Two recent examples illustrate the way in which secrecy plays a role in the consumption of internet pornography. A study of users of explicit internet material, most of whom were in full time relationships, revealed that almost three out of four concealed from their partners the amount of time they spent online for sexual pursuits.[44] The second illustration is provided by a recent WA case. A collector of child pornography concealed from friends and family his carefully catalogued collection of over 162,000 images of child pornography, kept on three hard drives and 11 CDs.[45] In sum, the breakdown of the public/private divide dramatically increases the potential for private pornography consumption.

At the same time, the disruption of the public/private divide increases the difficulty of effective regulation. Conventional forms of pornography regulation rely on tangible borders for their success. In the case of

41 See fn 34 above.

42 See further, Akdeniz, 1997.

43 Newsgroups (which can be used to post and receive images as well as text) in particular cater to a variety of 'specialised tastes': 'high heel', 'bondage', 'plumpers and large', 'female anal', 'fetish latex', 'bestiality', 'child erotica' and so on: http://www.sexynewsgroups.com.

44 Cooper *et al*, 1999, p 10.

45 *R v Jones* [1999] WASCA 24 (24 May 1999).

conventional media, legal prohibitions are maintained by blocking production within particular physical jurisdictions and empowering customs to block the importation of prohibited materials at the physical point of entry. Restricting access to certain materials also depends on the ability to create boundaries in physical space, for instance, by restricting access to theatres or shops to adult individuals.

The internet's breakdown of the borders between private and public space, however, make the adoption of such a scheme in cyberspace problematic. Prohibition is difficult because there are no physical borders to police and producers targeted within a jurisdiction can simply move offshore and send the same material back into the jurisdiction through cyberspace. Similarly, rules restricting access to particular individuals do not work easily in a realm that has no physical boundaries. Although access can be restricted to some extent by, for instance, requiring credit card details,[46] cyberspace identity, as we all know from the fascinating stories that circulate, is a fluid and uncertain concept.[47] A computer does not know whether the individual who taps in those credit card details is really who they say they are or whether they are really of age.

The successful operation of legislation such as the Online Services Act, at least in its stated intention of protecting children from internet content, cannot depend upon law alone. Because of the fluid and uncertain borders between private and public space, regulation must depend largely upon technological measures, such as software filters and successful parental supervision to supplement law's authority.[48]

Production and consumption

The second border disruption I wish to highlight is between production and consumption. Digitisation, which allows for rapid, cheap and exact duplication of material, has greatly facilitated the production of pornography, while the internet has facilitated the distribution of

---

46   In 1999, the ABA tabled in Parliament its declaration for restricted access systems. Such access is achieved by the use of a PIN or password. Users must supply age and identity verification information in their applications for a PIN.

47   Misrepresentation is something of a characteristic on the internet. The survey by Cooper *et al*, which involved adults (and for the most part, adults in the professions) revealed that 61% represented themselves online as being a different age; 5% as being a different gender and 14% as misrepresenting themselves on other unspecified factors (1999, p 10).

48   However, parental supervision is not always a reality. Recent figures from the US show that despite attempts to lower child care costs and expand choices, increasingly children are left alone after school ends and before their parents come home from work. A survey of 44,000 households of working parents found that one in five children aged between six and 12 were regularly left without adult supervision. http://www.usatoday.com/life/health/lhd1.htm (accessed 14 September 2000). And children often speak to each other about ways to sidestep filter systems. See Wilson, 2000.

pornography. Together, these technologies have increased both the volume and the diversity of commercial pornographic material in cyberspace. These technologies also allow any consumer of pornography to become a producer with relative ease.[49] The ABA notes that, '[o]f all the functions being performed in the online environment the distinction between "users" and "content providers" may be the most complex'.[50] It goes on to observe that drawing a distinction between providing and accessing content is in reality a theoretical construct: '[I]t is important to acknowledge that in reality these are often performed by the same participant in the online environment.'[51]

Thus, not only is there a significant commercial market in internet pornography, there is also a strong non-commercial presence. This was a more limited phenomenon in traditional media. Amateur pornographic videos and magazines devoted to amateur pornography did and still do exist. The amateur pornographer alone, however, did not have the ready distribution outlet that is offered by the internet. Today, worldwide publication is within the reach of anyone with a computer and internet access. Some web sites are devoted to amateur pornographers while individuals maintain their own pornographic home pages (and links pages, of course, to other pornographic sites).[52] Even the categories of commercial and non-commercial pornography have become blurred as amateurs swap, exchange and sell pornographic products over the internet.[53]

The blurring of lines between production and consumption is also evidenced by the way in which the internet can facilitate the development of market share for pornographers. Every time consumers log on, their transactions can assist pornographers to compile databases of information about their buying habits and sexual tastes. In turn, this can assist pornography producers to identify images and materials that that they should try to market more aggressively. These technologies allow pornographers to move from a market saturation policy to a market segmentation or targeted individual marketing strategy.[54]

This border disruption between production and consumption not only increases the amount and variety of pornographic materials on the Web, it makes regulation more difficult. The law's approach to pornography regulation is 'designed for oligopoly media models', rather than 'a

---

49 For instance, the study by Cooper *et al*, 1999, showed that sexually oriented Usenet newsgroups are frequently used to both post and download sexually explicit materials.

50 ABA, 1997, p 12.

51 *Ibid*.

52 Around 1997, the economics of free porn sites changed dramatically with the development of banner ads. Running a free porn site actually became lucrative. One estimate at that time suggested that a free, advertising-supported Web sites containing pornographic images could net $US19,150 per month. See Barrett, 1997.

53 Barcan, 2002.

54 Rimm, 1995, p 25.

pluralistic communications medium'.[55] Regulating access is difficult: although many commercial sites may restrict access to content by requiring credit card details as proof of identity, most non-commercial sites will not. Prohibiting access is difficult when non-commercial producers, in particular, are free to move their web sites around at will, evading regulation. The large numbers of non-commercial pornographers also means that the argument that pornography is merely a form of personal expression is much stronger than in other media where the commercial presence dominates.

Reality and virtuality

The third type of border disruption that I want to highlight is that between reality and virtuality. As Phillip Adams has commented, '[T]he internet offers sex without touching, eroticism without bodily fluids. The solitary orgasm of masturbation is now a mass-marketing exercise. Orgasm is online'.[56]

This border disruption is an extension, in many ways, of a phenomenon that began with television: we have become accustomed to consuming second hand 'experiences' on a screen in the same way we do other consumer goods.[57] The internet provides a 'safe' and viable alternative to 'real' sex in a time where AIDS and other sexually transmitted diseases are prevalent. Unlike other media, pornography on the internet is capable of a relatively high degree of interactivity. The consumer can now take part in the pornographic scenario. In addition to the interactivity between real people made possible by, for instance, chat rooms, the internet offers interactivity between the individual and pornographic images. For instance, some programs allow the consumer to command a human image to perform a variety of sexual acts.[58] The image, without personality or substance, readily obeys. Alternatively, the user can 'plug in' his penis to a peripheral device for virtual sex while viewing pornography online.[59] And there are proposals for virtual reality suits that will allow users to have virtual sex over the internet.[60]

Digital technologies blur the boundaries between reality and virtuality not only for pornography consumption, but for production as well. Pornographers can create graphic pornographic images simply by altering

---

55   Chen, 2000, p 221.

56   Adams, 2000, p 32.

57   Berns, 1989, p 33.

58   A review of such products is detailed (graphically) at:
      http://www.adultgamereviews.com/vsexjenna.shtml.

59   http://www.vrinnovations.com/news/ABCNews.html.

60   Fox, 2001.

non-pornographic images. In *R v Pecchiarich*,[61] for example, Pecchiarich created his own child pornography collection by altering the characteristics of pictures of children modelling underwear and swimsuits he had scanned from store catalogues. The pornographer, then, does not necessarily need a 'live' model. The pornographic subject can be constructed from any photograph. On this basis, anyone at all (who has had a photograph taken) is potentially the object of pornography.

In terms of regulation, the blurring of boundaries between reality and virtuality is a development the law has yet to come to terms with. It certainly undermines one of the traditional justifications for legal regulation: that is, that regulation is justified on the basis that people are harmed by the production of pornography. For instance, Akdeniz argues that 'while pornography may benefit from freedom of speech arguments and less severe laws, the line should be drawn with child pornography at least where physical harm to real children is involved as it almost inevitably will be with the production and use of child pornography'.[62] In the case of pseudo-photographs, justification for rendering them illegal must rest on the idea that 'the picture itself may be associated with a danger that is distinct from the harms related to the original making of the picture'.[63]

Nation states

The fourth aspect of boundary disruption caused by the internet, and the one most widely acknowledged, is the breakdown of national borders. National governments are still bound by territorial limits. But the internet is specifically designed so as to have no centre. If one route to a particular page is blocked, another route can be followed.[64]

This poses a profound challenge for legal regulation, based traditionally on physical borders. Regulation of pornography has always been difficult.[65] The problem is, however, exacerbated by the lack of jurisdictional borders. It is difficult to enforce national laws relating to content, because of the vast amount of content, the decentralised nature of the internet and the inconsistencies in the laws of different countries. Material prohibited in Australia may be stored and accessed from countries where the material is legal.[66] Sites are often 'mirrored' in different jurisdictions around the world to facilitate ease of access for users. If a site contains objectionable content, it

---

61   (1995) 22 OR (3d) 748–66.

62   Akdeniz, 1997, p 4.

63   *Ibid*, p 5.

64   This is the result of the internet's original design as a communications system that would survive nuclear war. See further Witheford, 1997, p 227.

65   Berns, 1989, p 36, observed that the laws in place at that time in Australia which sought to control pornographic video content were either unenforced or unenforceable or both.

66   Argy, 2000, p 265.

is difficult to prevent access not only to that site but to its mirror sites around the world. Material may be transmitted through a number of countries, each with its own laws.[67] The ability to communicate anonymously means that detection of content providers and consumers may be extremely difficult. Anonymous remailing services can exacerbate this difficulty, as can encryption of content.[68]

On the other hand, although nation states are relatively powerless to control the internet, decisions they make may reach far beyond their territorial borders. This is particularly the case where powerful first world nations make those decisions. The US Supreme Court acknowledged this in *Reno v American Civil Liberties Union*,[69] where it held that the Communications Decency Act 1996 violated the First Amendment. The Court was aware that its decision had a number of implications internationally: content posted in the US could enter any community; and the implications of its stand on free speech reached out to any country that has internet users, setting a precedent for other countries which might be considering internet regulation.[70]

Because the internet is highly resistant to national regulatory regimes, it is likely that, increasingly, international regulatory regimes to govern internet transactions will be introduced. Justice Kirby has suggested that the apparent 'lawlessness' of the internet is, in reality, a 'gap' between the demise of national law and the emergence of international law initiatives.[71] Commentators have, however, suggested that an international consensus is unlikely in relation to pornography. Conventional regulatory regimes determine what is liable to censorship by reference to 'community standards'. Community standards on the issue of pornography vary considerably. The irrelevance of physical geography in cyberspace makes it very hard to know whose community standards should apply.

Information and entertainment

The final border disruption is that between information and entertainment. Because the internet is multipurpose, providing us with entertainment, library resources, communications and education,[72] it seems likely that pornographic representations will exert an increasing influence over other aspects of popular culture because of the ready interplay of images and ideas.

---

67   ABA, 1997, p 18.
68   *Ibid*.
69   521 US 844 (1997).
70   Kirby, 1998, p 4.
71   *Ibid*, p 6.
72   For an overview of the internet as a multifunctional resource, see ABA, 1997, pp 15–16.

The implications for regulation relate to the free speech opposition to censorship.[73] Consumers and producers of pornography have traditionally relied upon the notion of free speech to justify the presence of pornography and to resist censorship. In some ways, this is a simplistic argument. The right to free speech may also be used to deny others rights, to subordinate and to oppress them.[74] Free speech is not the only public good, nor is pornography to be necessarily equated with free speech. However, the way in which the internet disrupts the borders between information and entertainment can lend credence to the free speech argument. If the law seeks to censor the internet in the same way it censors other media, it may well suppress sources of sex and sexuality information, suppress images of alternative sexualities that do not conform to the heterosexual paradigm, and suppress artistic expression.[75] These dangers have always been a problem of censorship in traditional media. The problem is, however, more acute in the case of the internet.[76] The internet's value lies in the coincidence of two features: firstly, the internet is an extraordinary public information resource; and secondly, this information may be accessed privately without embarrassment or shame:[77]

> The Internet is already being used to address a host of sexual issues in our society. Disenfranchised minorities (eg, the disabled, survivors of sexual trauma, transsexuals) are meeting, forming virtual communities, and exploring sexuality and relationships online. Teens are taking their sexual questions from the locker room to their terminals. Lonely people are bringing their romantic hopes to online matchmaking services. Each groups has unique questions, anxieties and fears. Sending simplistic messages that online sexuality is not for them (especially to teens) only heightens curiosity and intensifies shame. It causes them to go underground with their sexual concerns, perhaps compounding their difficulties. If this happens, we have little hope of intervening and facilitating positive outcomes.[78]

---

73 See further, Voon, 2001.

74 Jones, 2000.

75 Increasingly, people are viewing art on the internet, rather than in a traditional gallery environment. See Gilchrist, 2000, p 268.

76 Recognised by the Supreme Court in *ACLU et al v Janet Reno*, 929 F Supp 824 (1996):

> As the most participatory form of mass speech yet developed, the internet deserves that highest protection from government intrusion. Just as the strength of the internet is chaos, so the strength of our liberty depends upon the chaos and cacophony of the unfettered speech the First Amendment provides.

77 Arasaratnam, 2000, p 209, notes that in the USA, filter software resulted in breast cancer sufferers being unable to access government sponsored web sites.

78 Cooper *et al*, 1999, p 18.

THE CLASH OF CULTURES OR BUSINESS AS USUAL?

I have claimed that cyberculture poses a profound challenge to the authority of the law in its disruption of established boundaries. With specific reference to pornography, the internet's disruption of borders facilitates the creation, distribution and consumption of pornography and simultaneously renders pornography highly resistant to legal regulation.

For many feminists who take an anti-pornography stance, these developments will be of significant concern. To anti-pornography feminists,[79] pornography is at once the clearest example and the source of sexualised, systemic gender inequality.[80] It constitutes a serious and pervasive form of sex discrimination, normalising female subordination,[81] and eroticising male dominance:[82]

> Pornography on the Internet is particularly harmful. Although the new technologies imagine alternative futures, their shadow stares directly at us: in the case of pornography, new technologies not only help to immortalize a distorted view of sexuality within patriarchal societies, but help create a community of the predatory and the violent. Rapists and paedophiles can create a virtual world in which taboo behaviour becomes normalized and those 'on the edge' are led to proceed with behaviours they may previously have problematized.[83]

Despite concerns about internet pornography, many feminists have joined the anti-censorship cyberculture critics in their condemnation of the Online Services Act. Chris Kendall, for instance, accuses the Act of being misdirected, focusing upon pornography as an issue of immorality and thus failing to provide recourse and protection for those who need it. He also claims that the Act risks imposing unjustified limits on legitimate forms of sexual expression.[84]

The apparent alliance of the anti-censorship cyberculture critics of the Online Services Act and feminist critics of the Act, brings me to my second claim, which relates to the impact of the dynamic between cyberculture and law upon internet pornography. This claim is that, despite the opportunity for change the clash of cultures might offer, the status quo is likely to be maintained. These two cultures share common understandings, assumptions and goals such that the opportunity to reconsider the impact of internet pornography from an alternative perspective is unlikely to be realised.

---

79 The best known anti-pornography feminists are Dworkin and MacKinnon. See, for example, Dworkin and MacKinnon, 1988; Dworkin, 1985; MacKinnon, 1984.

80 Kendall, 1999, paras 21, 67.

81 *Ibid*, paras 6, 48.

82 *Ibid*, para 72.

83 Inayatullah and Milojevic, 1999, p 81.

84 Kendall, 1999.

On an initial reading, the clash between cyberculture and the law appears to hold considerable promise for feminists. If the law cannot control the internet in traditional ways, that is, ways based upon tangible borders and boundaries, then it must assert its authority by adapting and transforming, assimilating cyberculture into legal culture. It must abandon its reliance upon tangible boundaries and work in ways that respect the values of cyberculture: co-operation, community, fluidity, flexibility and diversity. The criticisms of the Online Services Act and its apparent lack of impact on internet pornography[85] should open up space for dialogue about internet pornography, our relationship to it and the law's role in its regulation. On a closer reading, however, the clash suggests that, for those concerned about internet pornography from an equality perspective, what will emerge from this transformation is not so much a new way of being, but rather business as usual. Two aspects of the internet pornography debate lend credence to this view.

First, although there is agreement that child pornography should be prohibited, both sides of the internet pornography debate start from a general consensus that all forms of internet pornography other than child pornography should be freely available to adults.[86] Despite the considerable debate about internet censorship, there has been very little mainstream consideration of the wider social ramifications of large quantities of accessible internet pornography.[87] Rather, the place of heterosexist pornography in our culture seems to be taken for granted. A recent study into the attitudes of 10–15 year olds to content filters is reported as observing that accessing pornographic material on the internet was considered a 'rite of passage' for children.[88] Male children were sold downloaded, readily marketable, pornographic images at school.[89] Children's interest in such sites signaled a change in status from child to adult as they approached puberty.[90] The underlying assumptions about the normalisation of pornography and the commodification of women's bodies in these observations are at once breathtaking and profoundly disturbing.

Secondly, a careful reading of the internet pornography debate suggests that the primary concerns for both sides, the vocal representatives of a

---

85 Penfold, 2001, p 14.

86 See, for instance, Akdeniz, 1997, p 16.

87 Although there has been much debate about the validity of studies which show that pornography can be directly linked to violent acts against women, reported studies clearly show the pervasive and damaging effects of stereotyping (a characteristic feature of much pornography) upon women. See, for example, Adler, 2000; Motluk, 1999.

88 Lebihan, 2000, reporting on Nightingale, Dickenson and Griff, 2000.

89 Girls, on the other hand, while relatively unperturbed by this, were offended if they stumbled across pornography while surfing the net: *ibid.*

90 Many children were introduced to pornography after stumbling across their parents' access records. *Ibid.*

censorship-free cyberculture and the conservative representatives of law, is to ensure that the internet is safe for commerce and that Australia remains globally competitive. Trade, rather than social wellbeing is the primary concern. As one commentator has pointed out, the central promise to governments of the internet is the net's potential to facilitate domestic and international commerce.[91] In an increasingly global, service-based and competitive market, 'one of the main price differentiators will not be geography, but rather the efficiency of the communications medium and the delivery or carriage costs of the provision of these services'.[92] It is hardly surprising, then, that one of the main objections to the Online Services Act is that Australian ISPs and ICHs will be governed by a more restrictive content than their overseas counterparts, thus placing them at a competitive disadvantage.[93] From the government's view, child pornography and the ready availability of offensive material to minors are bad for business because it might dissuade families from engaging in e-commerce.

CONCLUSION

An examination of the debate over internet pornography reveals on the one hand, the tension between cyberculture and the law and, on the other, some of the understandings and assumptions that they share. I have argued that, although the clash of cultures may promise the potential for transformation of the law, the commonalities between cyberculture and the law seem likely to reinforce the status quo, rather than open a space for change, in relation to pornography.

For those concerned about internet pornography and its effects from an equality perspective, this leaves few options. Some commentators have long argued that a creative anti-censorship stance is the best way to overcome pornography's deleterious effects.[94] Ultimately, this may be the only available avenue. Yet, even here, the increasing commercialisation of the internet brings with it homogeneity, banality, control and commodification, a

---

91 Chen, 2000, p 221.

92 Scott, 2000, p 215.

93 Arasatnam, 2000, p 208. Chen, 2001, identifies three, relatively stable, competing coalitions in the debate, each lobbying for different levels of action and intervention (from no regulation, to a strong regulatory model). 'While conflict within the subsystem varied, overall the framework's analysis shows the dominance of a coalition consisting largely of professional and business interests favouring a light, co-regulatory approach to online content.'

94 Nadine Strossen has been an outspoken campaigner for an anti-censorship approach. See, for example, Strossen, 1995, 1993a and 1993b. Other feminists have pursued this line. Blair, 1998, for example, argues that the anonymity of the internet offers the potential for women to discover their own sexuality. See also Rodgerson and Wilson, 1991.

culture that is likely to reinforce the heterosexist pornographic presence and resist attempts to undermine it.[95] As Nagel notes,[96] although the pornographic experience is potentially ambiguous and open to interpretation, the pornographic experience guided strictly by convention closes off these potential interpretations. It habituates viewers to see sexuality in terms of a homogenised consumer culture. As the internet becomes increasingly the conduit for e-commerce and consumerism the potential for a 'constant and creative dialogue'[97] about pornography seems likely to be lost.

---

95 A number of commentators have the internet's apparent diversity, opportunity, agency community and multiculturalism as a mere sham which covers the relentless commercial colonisation of cyberspace. See, for example, Kroker and Weinstein, 1994, p 4; Belausteguigoitia Rius, 1999, 24–25.

96 Nagel, 2002.

97 Moore, 1998, p 110: 'We should not expect a complete solution or a perfect balance to the problem of erotic imagery and pornography. The best we can hope for is a constant and creative dialogue so that the pornographic does not become debilitating and the erotic is not lost amid our fears of the pornographic.'

CHAPTER 11

JAIL BABES: TURNING THE SEX OF WOMEN'S IMPRISONMENT INSIDE OUT

Susanne Davies and Sandy Cook

JAIL BABES: THE STORY

Welcome to the world of *Jail Babes*.[1] The barred door of a prison cell, behind which lays a large red heart, is your entry point. Click on that door and you can enter the lives of America's imprisoned women. For the cost of $7 – American of course – and a small handling fee, you can buy the full name, address and Department of Corrections issued prison number of any one of the hundreds of women prisoners whose profiles adorn this site. And, if you buy 10, you get two free. There are, after all, 'hundreds of beautiful ladies sitting in prison, just waiting for someone to love and care about them'.[2]

If you think this is a joke, it isn't. This is *Jail Babes*, an online pen pal and singles introduction service that bears the motto, 'Introducing you to women in jail'.[3] The site was first posted on the web on 1 April 1998 and is the brainchild of American Ken Kleine, a 60-something year old bachelor retiree, who with his 'white beard and smiling eyes' has been described by one commentator as looking 'like a trim Santa Claus'.[4] And it is within the spirit of giving that Klein explains the origins of *Jail Babes*: 'I read an article one day saying that the most common ingredient in American life is loneliness … And who are the loneliest people? Inmates. I wanted to somehow open some door and help these people.'[5]

As fate or fortune would have it, Kleine subsequently 'ran into' a female friend from Florida, who was on parole, but kept an address book of friends who were still in prison.[6] He borrowed the book, mass-mailed women who were in prison, and a short time later had 100 responses. These were his

---

1   Since beginning research into this subject, the fundamental nature of the *Jail Babes* website has remained consistent, however, its layout together with the specific entries that are listed in it, have varied. For this reason, dates of specific visits to the site are provided in the footnotes. Similarly, commentaries published on the internet concerning *Jail Babes* have appeared, sometimes only to disappear. The specific dates when these were accessed are therefore supplied in the references.

2   *Jail Babes*, website, accessed 25 April 2000.

3   Crescent, 3–9 September 1998.

4   *Ibid*.

5   Chandler, 7 September 1998.

6   Gornstein, 30 August 1998.

initial enlistees when he launched the site on April Fool's Day. According to Kleine, scores of requests from incarcerated women soon followed. Some, he says, requested as many as 50 or 100 applications at a time.[7] By November 1998, more than 700 women from 13 different states featured as *Jail Babes*,[8] and by mid-1999, 250 women were signing up each month.[9] By March 2000, the site had featured more than 3,000 inmates from correctional facilities in 28 different states scattered from one side of the United States to the other.[10]

Of course, it was not merely women inmates who were signing up to *Jail Babes*. So too were customers, predominantly, if not exclusively, men. According to Klein, within two years of being posted, the site was attracting between 60,000 and 70,000 hits per day.[11] By mid-1999, between 300 and 350 new customers were being signed up each month[12] and letters and emails were pouring in from across the United States and from more far-flung places such as Australia, England, Belgium and Japan. They came from 'lawyers, doctors, skilled tradespeople and retirees'.[13] Some customers, such as the 'shy Tokyo businessman' who placed an order for '24 girls', preferred to buy in bulk.[14]

One of the men who heard about *Jail Babes* was Mark Cromer, a former crime reporter. Not long after the launch of the site, Cromer raised the lucrative possibilities of *Jail Babes* with Larry Flynt, the self-styled entrepreneur who founded the *Hustler* Empire and who is well known for his much publicised anti-censorship stance. According to Cromer, 'America is obsessed with sex and fascinated with crime'.[15] The mix of criminality and sex embodied in *Jail Babes* was all too alluring and was seen to present a distinct business opportunity; a chance to fill an all-important gap in *Hustler*'s range of R-rated magazines and X-rated videos. As Cromer later recounted: 'There are 50 titles of just about every genre you can imagine, boobs, butts, age, weight, hair color, barely legal, way legal, elderly, whatever. It's a freak show out there but no one has ever blended sex and crime.'[16]

So compelling, it seems, was Cromer's social commentary that Flynt not only bought the idea that sex and crime could be marketable, he also took over copyright of the *Jail Babes* website. The introductory page was

---

7   *Ibid.*
8   Anon, November/December 1998.
9   Malisow, 14 July 1999.
10   Goldman, 17 March 2000.
11   *Ibid.*
12   Malisow, 14 July 1999.
13   Anon, November/December 1998.
14   Crescent, 3–9 September 1998.
15   Phillips, 14 May 1999.
16   *Ibid.*

revamped. Although this page has since reverted to the more demure image of a red heart behind a cell door, had you visited the site in mid-April 1999 soon after Flynt's takeover, you would have been faced with a far more confronting welcome. At that time, a photograph of an amply endowed blonde-headed woman, dressed in a black see-through negligee, and leaning against a wire fence bearing the sign 'no trespass', invited visitors to venture into the forbidden territory of sex and crime. To either side were images of what perhaps might follow should one be so brave. A photograph of a woman's bare buttocks, with her hands cuffed behind her, appeared to the left, and to the right, was a photograph of another woman sitting on a bed with a bottle poised to the lips of her mouth and the straps of her diminutive dress falling from her shoulders. Beneath these images was an ad for the *Jail Babes* videos, volumes one, two and three.[17] A short time later, a flashing sign was added to the page. It read: 'RIGHT deprived BABES finally getting some COCK.'[18]

Under Flynt's regime, the idea of *Jail Babes* was extended to the production of pornographic magazines and videos. In regard to the women who featured in the *Jail Babes* videos, *Hustler* claimed to have 'taken these girls from the slammer to the stage'.[19] Today, copyright of the website appears to have again changed hands, and *Hustler*'s endeavours seem to have become largely confined to video production. It is a business that has flourished, however. There are now 21 X-rated *Jail Babes* videos and these are available over the counter, mail order or on-line. Like the website and the magazines, their claim to fame is that they feature 'real' women criminals, although the boundary does occasionally get a little blurred. The sixth volume of the video series, for example, featured 'Vivi Anne', who was described as a 'Nasty 19-year-old AUSSIE SLUT'. The promotional material proudly announced: 'We got her before she goes to jail'.[20]

REALITY AND REPRESENTATION

Jail Babes is only one of a number of on-line introduction services featuring prison inmates to have sprung up in recent years. Other notable sites include *Meet-An-Inmate.com*, *Prisonbabes* and *Jail Dudes* which is linked to the *Jail Babes* site. Of these however, it is *Jail Babes* that is the most developed and which, by virtue of *Hustler*'s involvement, has gone well beyond mere introductions.

---

17 *Jail Babes*, website, accessed 13 April 1999.
18 *Jail Babes*, website, accessed 20 April 1999.
19 *Jail Babes*, magazine, June 1999, p 64.
20 *Jail Babes*, magazine, October 1999, p 83.

The growth in the number of these sites is particularly interesting given that over the past few decades, prisons, prisoners and the everyday realities of prison life have become increasingly hidden from public view. The closure of inner city prisons and their replacement with larger, newer penal institutions that are located near or well beyond city limits is just one example of this gradual disappearance. So too is the limiting of publicly available information about prisons and their operation that has accompanied privatisation.[21] This is also arguably part of a broader shift in penal management, one that is characterised by increased bureaucratisation, economic rationalism and secretiveness. At the same time, however, sensationalistic and fanciful depictions of prisons, prisoners and prison life have proliferated via the internet and various media and entertainment mediums.

No representations – whether they be verbal, literary or visual – can ever of course capture reality. As Susanne Kappeler has noted, 'representations are not just a matter of mirrors, reflections, key-holes. Somebody is making them, and somebody is looking at them, through a complex array of means and conventions'.[22] When it comes to women in prison, dominant conventions concerning sex, gender, sexuality, age, race, criminality and imprisonment constitute just some of the aspects of the cultural prism through which women are often represented by others, and indeed, through which they often represent themselves.

It is notable, for example, that the women who feature on the *Jail Babes* website are presented in a manner that echoes the classification system that is a staple feature of prisons across the world. There is an individual entry on each woman and each entry follows a set form. It features a photograph of the woman alongside a list of basic information that includes her age, height, weight, hair and eye colour, body measurements, marital status, whether or not she has children, her educational and occupational background and release date. Offence is not included, although some commentators have noted with humor and sometimes more than a little concern, that a large number of *Jail Babes* describe themselves as widows. Accompanying this information, which is provided by the women themselves, are details of the sex, race and age of the pen-pals being sought, and in nearly all cases, a more personalised self-description. These range from the sedate to the seductive.

There is, for example, Daisy, who describes herself as an 'outgoing and loving woman who loves exercising, jogging, cooking and fishing and is looking for a good guy who wants a gentle, caring Christian girl'.[23] Her photograph is a simple portrait. There is also Tonya. She is photographed in

21   George and Lazarus, 1995, pp 162–63; Grimwade, 1999, pp 304–06.

22   Kappeler, 1986, p 3.

23   *Jail Babes*, website, accessed 25 April 2000.

a raunchy pose wearing a backless swimsuit and a matching garter. The style of her photograph is matched by her message: 'I am a caring, color-blinded, sincere sexy kitten. I enjoy dancing, reading, traveling, and communicating with others. I'm a beautiful chocolate bunny with full sensual lips and curves to die for and legs made for stiletto heels.'[24] And then there is Diana. She is classified in the 'other women' category and has not provided a photograph. Instead, her entry is adorned with a sketch that appears in the entries of some of the other 'othered' women. It is of a large-mouthed woman of indistinguishable age and race, whose hands point to below her waist and whose shoulders are draped by a large black hand.[25] The image suggests she is available but not necessarily desirable to all of those who might browse the site.

Despite their individual differences, the representations that are offered of women on the *Jail Babes* website fit within a broader pattern. They reflect a cultural system of stereotyping that easily distinguishes the 'good' woman from the 'bad' and which is clearly bound by dominant notions of sex and gender, sexuality, race and age. Before browsing the entries of individual women, visitors are in fact invited to narrow down their selection according to a small number of preselected criteria. Early visitors could elect to survey only those who fell within a particular age range or who were imprisoned in a particular state. There were also three other specified categories to choose from, namely 'black girls', 'white girls' and 'other girls'.[26] Despite their differences, the infantilisation and sexualisation of all of these women is made obvious in their designation as 'girls'. Visitors to the site in more recent times have been given an opportunity to select with more precision, or less, if they so desire. They can disregard ethnicity entirely, or select from the categories of African American, Asian/Pacific Islander, Caucasian, Hispanic, Native American or 'other'.[27]

Much of the commentary that has been written on the internet as a system of communication has contended that this technology has provided individuals with the possibility of representing themselves in ways that leave behind the materiality of their bodies and their lives. In other words, it is suggested that characteristics such as sex, race and age may be divorced from one's cyberspace identity. According to Marj Kibby, however, 'the myth that on-line personas, even those unaccompanied by images of self, can ... transcend gendered sexuality is just that, a myth'.[28]

In her examination of women's home pages on the web, Kibby ponders why it is that despite the 'possibility of presenting an identity that

24 *Jail Babes*, website, accessed 13 April 1999.
25 *Jail Babes*, website, accessed 13 April 1999.
26 *Jail Babes*, website, accessed 13 April 1999.
27 *Jail Babes*, website, accessed 17 November 1999.
28 Kibby, 1997, p 42.

transcends stereotypical indicators of sex and gender'; women still tend not to do so.[29] Her explanation of this is twofold. On the one hand, she points to the way in which language, and hence forms of self-representation, are dependent on existing genres and are determined by a social and material context of which gender, sexuality, race and numerous other elements are a part. Thus whether it is intended or not, the traces of one's lived identity can never entirely be eradicated. On the other hand, Kibby also suggests that women find it difficult to separate their sexuality from their identity and that they indeed find such a separation undesirable. She concludes that this refusal to separate mind from body is an acknowledgment on the part of a woman that 'her (sexual) body is her social reality; her identity a product of her embodied knowledge and experience'.[30] It is important to note, however, that the linking of sexuality and identity in women's representations of themselves may not always be an indication of their agency or necessarily a positive assertion of self. Women's opportunities for self-representation as Jail Babes, for example, are clearly limited and shaped by the context in which these representations are produced and transmitted, as well as by long held and pervasive social stereotypes of women, particularly those who are lawbreakers and prisoners.

While the representations of women that feature on the *Jail Babes* website may appear to some to be contrived as a consequence of their conformity to dominant stereotypes, the fact that 'real' women are featured on it lends a degree of authenticity to the site that is not shared by others that are expressly devoted to fantasy or role-play. It is similarly the participation of women who have been in prison that is touted by *Hustler* as distinguishing its *Jail Babes* magazine from all others. According to Mark Cromer, who ensconced himself as editor: '[It is] the first magazine, as far as I can tell, to ever feature women who are, for the lack of a better description, criminals. Ex-cons. Bad girls. In some cases, really bad girls.'[31] The same claim is made in respect to the videos. Volume one was advertised in this way: 'Just when you thought you've seen everything porno has to offer, here comes Larry Flynt with his new video series, *JAIL BABES* – a skin flick that breaks the rules by featuring women who have really broken the rules.'[32]

It is promised that in the *Jail Babes* videos and magazines, 'real' women criminals will tell their 'real' stories about crime, imprisonment, and most importantly, sex. Consider, for example, this description of a *Jail Babes* video: 'Watch in the safety of your own home as these prison sluts reveal for the first time the seedy sex that goes on behind bars. Listen to them confess their

---

29 *Ibid*, p 41.

30 *Ibid*, p 44.

31 *Jail Babes*, magazine, June 1999, p 7.

32 *Ibid*, p 62.

actual crimes and gleefully testify about their bizarre sexual fantasies.'[33] The use of words such as 'confess' and 'testify' is particularly noteworthy, for both in religion and law, they are bound to the notion of truthfulness. Their use in this context not only lends a sense of legitimacy to what is said, but also places the listener or viewer in the position of judge or juror. It is up to the observer to pass judgment on these women and their stories. But of course, the verdict has already been made. The badness of these women is already there and is captured in photographs and videos for everyone to see.

A promotional piece for the *Jail Babes* video series that appeared in the June edition of the magazine illustrates this process. It was headed 'OUT of the SLAMMER ... but STILL GETTING SLAMMED!!!' and featured a photograph of a young somewhat innocent looking woman, clad in a white negligee, leaning on a pillow on a bed. Seated in a chair at the side of the bed is a man who has the lens of his video camera firmly focussed upon her. In this instance, the constructedness of the scene is made obvious, yet it is visually and textually overwhelmed by allusions to truth. A heading at the bottom of the page promises 'An Insider's Scoop on the Making of [the] *Jail Babes* Video', whilst the accompanying text alerts potential customers to what they can expect: 'In each volume, the women relate their sordid stories of crime, their lives behind bars and their passions in prisons. Then, of course, comes the sex, which is as real as the interviews. No bullshit setups. We give you the stripped-down truth – nothing held back and nothing fake.'[34] As if to illustrate this, another photograph of the same woman, this time topless, dominates the bottom of the page. Pictured from the waist up and with all sign of her surroundings removed, her figure looms large. She gestures an 'up yours' at the reader. It is as if the now invisible camera has laid bare this woman's fundamental and defiant 'badness'.

Hustler's Jail Babes magazine uses various other devices in order to claim authenticity, and beyond this, to establish itself as the arbiter of truth in all matters to do with women, crime, sex and imprisonment. Through fact-based articles, the occasional book review, and accounts of 'true crime', the magazine claims to tell the 'real' facts about such well-known figures as the female members of the Manson family, Myra Hindley, and the 'Christchurch schoolgirl murderers'. Features on less well-known women such as Ashley Kennedy, a former policewoman who is now on death row for murder, and Darlene Gillespie, a childhood Mouseketeer whose shoplifting later in life landed her in jail, suggest that even the most law-abiding and innocent of women are liable to fall from grace. An article about Barbara Graham, who was convicted and executed in 1955 for the murder of an elderly woman, is particularly interesting, for it seeks to distinguish the real character and life of Barbara Graham from its representation in the movie *I Want to Live*. For all

---

33 *Jail Babes*, magazine, October 1999, p 83.
34 *Jail Babes*, magazine, June 1999, p 62.

of the film's grittiness, *Jail Babes* warns against accepting the movie as a truthful depiction of Graham's character or life. As it puts it: '… the problem with the movie is that the liberties it takes with her life get mixed up with reality.'[35] The bottom line, according to *Jail Babes*, is that 'the movie got it wrong'.[36] Despite the murkiness of the case, which also involved four men, *Jail Babes* is seemingly untroubled in its assertion that Graham was not 'an innocent woman in the wrong place at the wrong time', but rather a vicious and unrepentant killer. By denouncing other representations as partial, distorted or flawed, the *Jail Babes* magazine lends weight to its own authority. That *Jail Babes* might itself offer partial, distorted or flawed representations of its subjects is of course beyond contemplation.

The assertiveness with which *Jail Babes* expresses itself, like the manner in which it represents its subjects, may be understood as indicative of the general 'thrust' of Larry Flynt's media mission. Laura Kipnis describes *Hustler*, Flynt's flagship men's magazine, as 'the most reviled instance of mass circulation porn' available, and as a magazine that 'devotes itself to what tends to be called "grossness"'.[37] 'According to Kipnis, *Hustler*'s aim is to offend middle class sensibilities through the display of the unromanticised body; a body that amongst other things may be overweight, middle-aged, pregnant, mutilated, incomplete or leaky.[38] She goes on to suggest that this unapologetic display constitutes a powerful articulation of working class resentment. Whether this resentment and its expression is transgressive, however, is a matter for some conjecture.

As Kipnis notes, the models that feature in *Hustler* generally depict working class women, rather than those who are rich or famous or even moderately well-to-do. The fact that it is working class women who are the targets or vehicles of working class men's resentment is hardly new however. Nor is it new for women prisoners and their bodies to be objectified as they are in *Jail Babes*. More than a century ago, the so called 'father of criminology', Cesare Lombroso, argued that criminal women could be distinguished from others of their sex by virtue of their temperament and distinctive bodily characteristics, including their genitalia.[39] *Jail Babes*, in emphasising the abject body of the 'criminal woman' is thus following a well established line of masculinist thought; one which is arguably intensified by the claim that those who appear in *Jail Babes* are not merely models, but 'real' criminal women. The race of women featured in *Jail Babes* is also noteworthy. While African American, Hispanic and Native American women are disproportionately over-represented in

---

35 *Ibid*, p 74.

36 *Ibid*, p 75.

37 Kipnis, 1992, p 375.

38 *Ibid*.

39 Lombroso and Ferrero, 1898; Davies and Cook, 1999, pp 55–59.

United States prisons, the women who feature in the *Jail Babes* magazines are overwhelmingly, indeed almost exclusively, Caucasian. This exclusion perhaps reflects the 'whiteness' of the *Jail Babes* readership, the limits of its desire, and the contours of its resentments.

In the various *Jail Babes* productions, the space between reality and representation is filled through reference to familiar stereotypes and stories. It is these stereotypes and stories that inform the construction of representations, and which moreover, serve to make these representations meaningful to those who view them. Their significance becomes even clearer when they are considered in relation to the notions of reform that are articulated in respect to Jail Babes. For women prisoners and ex-prisoners, it seems there are only two reform options available. The first involves romance and rescue and finds expression in the *Jail Babes* website. The second involves reform through further abuse and exploitation and is articulated in *Hustler's Jail Babes* magazines and videos.

REFORM NARRATIVE ONE: ROMANCE AND RESCUE

According to Kleine, the *Jail Babes* online introduction service 'does a good deed' for women in prison,[40] for 'one of the biggest problems in [prisons] is [that] the girls have lost contact with family and friends and the outside world'.[41] It is the women's loneliness, their needs and their right to dignity that Kleine uses to justify his entrepreneurial endeavours. As he puts it: 'They are people, too, and they have rights and feelings and thoughts and emotions. Just because they are confined doesn't mean they have lost all privileges of life. They are still humans.'[42]

Kleine it should be pointed out is very familiar with the needs of women, including those who are imprisoned. He has an impressive list of priors. He was once a legal specialist, later a private eye and, immediately before conceiving *Jail Babes*, a Russian wife broker for American men. The latter had not been an easy affair. Indeed none of the relationships he organised through his agency International Singles Introductions had worked out because of what he called 'cultural differences'. As he describes it: 'American girls, they know what hot dogs, apple pies, Chevrolets and baseball are … Russian ladies don't have a clue.'[43]

---

40 Gornstein, 30 August 1998.
41 Anon, November/December 1998.
42 Gornstein, 30 August 1998.
43 Crescent, 3–9 September 1998.

Kleine, who reportedly now refers to himself as 'the Warden',[44] has experienced far greater success, both professionally and personally, introducing would-be suitors to women prisoners. Some of the couples who have been introduced through *Jail Babes* have become engaged, and Kleine reports that he too has found true love with an inmate; one who interestingly enough never enlisted as a Jail Babe. He visits her twice a week in prison, they talk of marriage and he looks forward to conjugal visits. In his words: 'You get a little house out back, like a little Motel 6 room. It's just like going to jail, too.'[45]

Romancing women in prison does take some effort though. The *Jail Babes* website offers careful instructions to assist would-be suitors, but is also quick to point to the virtues and future prospects of forming a lasting relationship with the right woman:

> Even though these ladies are in prison, it doesn't mean that they are bad women. The majority of these ladies are fun, loving, clever, reliable, sexy and very passionate lovers. They enjoy sports, music, arts and bond well in a family environment. These qualities, along with the fact that they are incarcerated, means that you will find a woman who is dedicated to spending the rest of her life crime free and drug free, while looking forward to a much better future.[46]

Would-be suitors are advised to personalise their letters, to type them if their handwriting is poor, and to include at least two photographs with their first letter; the first featuring a close up view of face and upper body, and the second, a full body pose. Posing, it is advised, should involve making 'a friendly and pleasant smile' and apparently it's good to pose with a pet or with children if any live with you. *Jail Babes* further advises clients not to be too bashful in their quest to find the right woman:

> Don't hesitate to choose 20 or 30 or more women to write to. The more you write to the greater the chances you will have in finding that very special one that you could very easily end up spending the rest of your life with. It is sometimes very difficult to choose between women because they are all so very beautiful and have such great personalities ... Keep in mind that all of these women have already taken their first step to find a man by putting their ad on our home page. If they didn't seriously want a man they would not have come forward and joined *Jail Babes*.[47]

Various explanations have been offered as to why men use *Jail Babes* and other similar services to make contact with women prisoners. It has been suggested, for example, that men who had emotionally unavailable mothers

---

44 Cromer, 4 August 1998.
45 Crescent, 3–9 September 1998.
46 *Jail Babes*, website, accessed 13 April 1999.
47 *Ibid.*

when they were children are driven in later life to seek out women who are similarly unavailable. It's also been suggested that some men are motivated by a desire to 'break social taboos', or to avoid the anxiety, and one suspects the possible disappointments, that may be involved in entering a club or bar in the hope of meeting a woman. The desire to feel very manly, and indeed hyperpotent, by being able to save a fallen woman and restore her to respectability, has also been noted. So too, have the motivating forces of desperation and fantasy.[48]

Greg Lewis, a salesman from Buffalo Grove, Illinois, describes his involvement with *Jail Babes* as a 'transaction born of years of frustration'. Like Kleine, he is a failed veteran of the international marriage market:

> With international dating services, some of them are not very informative as to how old an address is ... And the language barrier can be impossible. It is difficult to really find someone who is attractive but doesn't think she is unapproachable, so I am taking an unorthodox approach. I work in a male-dominated industry, so I find it particularly difficult. I am good-looking and make decent money, but it is difficult.[49]

Peter, a 50 year old resident of San Jose, had been writing to women in prison for several years before discovering *Jail Babes* in 1998. He writes about three letters a week, all for a good cause: 'My fantasy is to get two or three of them to come live with me at once so I can get my harem. But no one's showed up yet.'[50]

Despite Peter's lack of success, *Jail Babes* promises that love can be found within and later beyond prison walls. Romancing women prisoners – like all romance involving women though – is not without its dangers. Prison authorities warn that romancing and rescuing women prisoners is a risky business, and that 'customers should be wary of the "Babes"'.[51] This is a theme that emerges consistently in discussions of *Jail Babes*. On the website, a lengthy disclaimer absolves the site's owner from any responsibility for damages that might arise to users of the service. While this disclaimer also extends to the harm that might be suffered by any of the women prisoners whose profiles adorn the site, they are not commonly recognised as being at risk of harm. Indeed it is they, and only they, who are designated as dangerous. 'Criminals', to use the words of one commentator, 'are not known for their honesty'.[52] While there are no rules to prevent inmates from receiving personal correspondence, Kati Corsaut, a spokeswoman for the California Department of Corrections, urges prospective correspondents to use common sense, and not to give out personal information such as their home addresses or telephone numbers to the women. As she puts it: 'You

---

48 Goldman, 17 March 2000.
49 Gornstein, 30 August 1998.
50 Anon, November/December 1998.
51 Crescent, 3–9 September 1998.
52 *Ibid.*

should keep in mind that these people are convicted felons. Until you know the person, know a lot about them, I think you need to be cautious.'[53]

But caution alone, it is suggested, may not be sufficient to distinguish the innocent from the conniving. Tony Howard, a Texas prison investigator, warns that 'some female inmates are pros at luring men into their webs'.[54] Indeed it is experience, he claims, which makes them so adept: 'Living the life on the streets or the hustle. They are some of the best psychologists and psychiatrist[s] in terms of profiling other people and knowing what their weak spots are'.[55] A journalist expounds on the theme:

> The inmates play on [the] sympathetic emotions of widowers by writing sob stories which tell of hard labour and abusive guards. Just like direct marketers, they craft successful fundraising appeals. They often send out the same letters to different pen pals ... the relationship stops when the money stops flowing.[56]

Although prisoners have no access to the internet, it is reported that application forms to join *Jail Babes* circulate widely within America's women's prisons. And according to Investigator Howard and other prison officials, so too does information on how to scam prospective correspondents. Attempting to solicit money is a breach of prison rules, but according to Howard 'many of these women know how to write a letter that shrewdly does not directly ask for money'.[57] It is a gradual process of seduction, the finer points of which are supposedly taught to younger inmates by those who are more experienced. A journalist thus recounts an interview with inmate Yen Nguyen about what she learnt in prison:

> They gave me introduction letters. And they said look write it like this you will get an answer.
>
> Nguyen says the first letter tells the lonely heart that they're looking for someone special like him.
>
> The second letter says after sweating and working in the fields all day I'm lying here thinking of you.
>
> The third letter which we call the hook which would be consisting of I stayed up all night long and washed out somebody's socks or undergarments or stuff like this in order to get a stamp to mail it to you.[58]

Depending upon the success of the seduction, money, sometimes visits, and sometimes proposals of marriage, may follow.

---

53 Anon, November/December 1998.
54 Riggs, 8 July 1999.
55 *Ibid.*
56 *Ibid.*
57 *Ibid.*
58 *Ibid.*

According to investigator Howard, it is Caucasian men aged between 45 and 65, usually widowers, who are commonly the targets of the women in this 'lonely hearts scam'.[59] Referred to as 'sugar daddies' or 'tricks' by the women with whom they correspond, these men are apparently so besotted that they are often unable to recognise their pen pal's duplicity. Thus Howard recalls how $15,000 from the Bank of England came to Gatesville Prison for one inmate and how 'this gentleman wouldn't believe anything we had to tell him because he was in love ... He was hooked'.[60] So convincing are the women that, according to prison warden, Nancy Botkin: 'We have a lot of elderly men that send nearly their entire income to support these females. We have family members that call and beg us to make us stop writing them.'[61]

Stories of 'hooked' men, unrequited love and lost fortunes abound in commentaries on *Jail Babes* and attest to the women's seductive criminality. It is as if Otto Pollack's 1950 claim that women can disguise their crimes due to their ability to fake orgasm has found new life.[62] There is, for example the instance of the Japanese man from Osaka, 'who showed up at [a] prison with a box full of love letters from the inmate to whom he had sent $3,000'.[63] There is also the story of the man who came from Russia and who 'claimed that his sweetheart was being mistreated worse than the conditions in the Soviet Union's infamous Gulag [would allow]'.[64] And then there are the experiences of Jay, a 72 year old Dallas widower, with no living family and few surviving friends. When asked why he had looked for 'companionship and friendship in a prison of all places', Jay responded: 'I've asked myself that. At 72 how many people are interested in you? Finding someone who is interested. This is the avenue I went where people were interested.'[65] In his dealings with *Jail Babes*, Jay received more interest than he had probably expected or perhaps wanted. He had been sent 'stacks of letters from female inmates. They c[a]me stamped with lipstick kisses, promises of marriage, and not so subtle hints for money'.[66] He had married one inmate by proxy, and had sent her $US150 a month, but she had divorced him after he had refused to send her any more. Then letters had begun to arrive from other inmates. Jay subsequently ceased his letter writing. As he put it, 'It's one thing to be lonely and it's another thing to be a fool'.[67]

---

59 *Ibid.*
60 Riggs, 9 July 1999.
61 Riggs, 8 July 1999.
62 Pollack, 1950, p 10.
63 Riggs, 9 July 1999.
64 *Ibid.*
65 Riggs, 10 July 1999.
66 *Ibid.*
67 *Ibid.*

While Jay's story can be read as a sad reflection on ageing and loneliness in modern America, its inclusion in an expose on *Jail Babes* is clearly intended to be cautionary. Jay's experiences are presented as attesting to the fact that *Jail Babes* are without mercy and that even the most vulnerable will not be saved from their treachery. His concluding explanation as to why he no longer writes to women inmates, reinforces this view but, at the same time, also oddly unsettles it. Contained within this explanation is an underlying acknowledgment that it takes 'two to tango' and that those who choose to initiate contact with women inmates are not without responsibility for their actions. Indeed, it is not unreasonable to suggest that it is those outside of the prison walls who have the greater power. It is they who choose whether or not to initiate contact, and who determine who they have contact with, what form that contact takes, how long it lasts and, finally, what they choose to disclose or invent about themselves and their intentions. An exchange between interviewer Robert Riggs and prisoner Mardie Swartz suggests that the possibilities for deceiving, misleading and exploiting, like the possibilities for being deceived, misled and exploited, are shared. The exchange concerns a man in England, one of 200 men who have written to Swartz. Whether he has sent one of the 30 marriage proposals she has received is left unstated:

> He's a doctor. He's a heart cardiovascular surgeon. thirty-five. Never been married. He's a very nice guy.
>
> How do you know he's telling you the truth?
>
> How does he know I'm telling him the truth?[68]

REFORM NARRATIVE TWO: ABUSE, DEGRADATION AND EXPLOITATION

The notion that women prisoners are conniving, manipulative and irretrievably wicked perpetually threatens to unsettle the achievement of reform based on romance and rescue, however, it is this very negative stereotype that underpins a second model of reform which is articulated in *Jail Babes* magazines and videos. It involves the further abuse, degradation and exploitation of women during and after imprisonment. In the premier edition of *Hustler's Jail Babes* magazine, there is a blurb directed at would-be *Jail Babes*. It reads: 'If you are an aspiring Jail Babe who needs to start repaying her debt to society by getting naked (hell, it's legal work), call our 24-hour ex-con hotline.'[69] The type of women who this might appeal to, and who might appeal to timid readers, is also described:

---

68 Riggs, 8 July 1999.

69 *Jail Babes*, magazine, June 1999, p 3.

Hard-luck women

You know the type. Smoke dangling precariously off her lips, scotch on her breath, only one or two tattoos showing. She's been around the block – and through some bedroom windows too. A little worn from all the wear, perhaps, but there's a certain majesty in her decline. You'd like to pick her up, but you're afraid of black widows. Understandably so.

That's where we come in.

Hustler's Jail Babes:

We're here to help.[70]

Allegations that women who feature in *Jail Babes* magazines and videos are exploited are sharply derided by Cromer. His response to them is simple: 'Of course, *Hustler's Jail Babes* is, in fact, exploiting these women. Absolutely. Just as surely as they are exploiting our never-ending need for new and different female bodies to look at. We're exploiting people who understand that we are exploiting them'.[71] And if you follow *Jail Babes'* line, then it becomes clear that these women are particularly well trained in being exploited and abused. The first article in *Jail Babes* premier edition, for example, focussed upon 'Women in Prison'. It informed readers that while women constitute only 6% of America's prisoners, the incarceration rate for women was more than double that of men. It pointed out that in California alone, the women prisoner population had increased by 305% in 12 years and that most of these women had been convicted of non-violent offences, primarily drug-related. A fuller profile of the women was then offered:

> Who are these women? The typical inmate in a California prison is a black or white woman in her 30s. Odds are good she has at least one child; odds are better that the father is long gone. She is probably a drug addict or alcoholic, and more than likely she was physically abused at least once before she turned 18. Chances are 50/50 she's been raped at least once. In other words, life has prepared her well for her time behind bars.[72]

And it is to life behind bars that the article then turns, detailing at some length, well publicised instances of sexual abuse perpetrated by male prison guards upon women inmates in Michigan and Washington prisons. Such cases of course rarely make it into the pages of the daily press, but for *Hustler's Jail Babes* they have a particular salience. They certainly aren't unusual; indeed they are a way of life. The women's prisons in Michigan, *Jail Babes* tells readers, 'aren't the only ones where incarcerated women are viewed as the pleasure toys of their jailers'.[73] 'According to Human Rights

---

70 *Ibid.*

71 *Ibid*, p 79.

72 *Ibid*, p 6.

73 *Ibid*, p 81.

Watch,' it notes, 'Sexual harassment and abuse are as much a part of the daily regimen of female inmates in the United States as breakfast and dinner'.[74] Although pointing to the fact that state authorities have been sued for violating prisoner's rights as a consequence of such abuse, that it seems is where *Hustler*'s concern stops. Whose side it is on is made glaringly clear:

> Though women face a far more sexualised atmosphere in our nation's prisons, it would be misleading to say that they are treated worse than men by the justice system. Correctional experts agree that despite ever-stricter mandatory sentencing guidelines, judges and juries still tend to take a more compassionate view of women defendants, especially mothers with small children.[75]

Shorter sentences, the lower execution rate for women convicted of murder, together with the furore that prevented an Alabama prison commissioner from putting women prisoners in leg irons, are all offered as evidence of the merciful treatment women receive.[76]

Within the pages of *Jail Babes*, 'bad girls' abound – or should we say – are bound. If women in prison can't be put in leg irons, then *Jail Babes*, it seems, is prepared to give them what they deserve once they get out. A multipage pictorial of a woman bound to a chair with battery clamps attached to her labia in some shots, and in others, to her nipples, was one of the more extreme features in the July 1999 edition. In that edition too, was a spread on 'Daddy's Girl'; a young woman photographed in various poses and states of undress with a washed up middle-aged rock star who once regularly appeared on stage in drag. The final photograph shows 'Daddy's Girl' bare-breasted, smiling naughtily as he squeezes her nipples. According to the accompanying caption:

> Stella couldn't believe that a man who once looked like her mommy could help fill the gap left by her daddy. But fill the gap is exactly what this jet boy did. No more personality crisis for Killer Kane, and as for Stella, she was just looking for a kiss. She got more than she bargained for.[77]

In *Jail Babes*, representations of women's lives before and during imprisonment are intertwined into an amalgam that presents pleasure and danger, abuse and sex, as indivisible. Perhaps then, it should not come as a surprise, that life after imprisonment should also be presented and expected to follow the same path. As *Jail Babes* explains: 'These tough girls have done some hard crimes. But they've done their time and they're ready to continue their rehabilitation by letting us exploit them.'[78]

---

74 *Ibid*, p 6.
75 *Ibid*, p 81.
76 *Ibid*.
77 *Jail Babes*, magazine, July 1999, p 67.
78 *Jail Babes*, magazine, June 1999, p 62.

WHERE REPRESENTATION AND REALITY MEET

In discussing *Jail Babes*, it is difficult not to fall headlong into a debate over who is exploiting whom. In early 1999, this question took on an added dimension with speculation in the United States that Larry Flynt was under investigation for breaching Son of Sam Laws.[79] These laws are intended to prohibit convicted felons from profiting from their crimes, but as such, it is likely that it is the women who feature as Jail Babes, rather than Flynt himself, who are most liable to bear the consequences of any legal action. Such an outcome would indeed be consistent with the commonly held view that these women, like women prisoners generally, are dangerous and that society, or to be more specific its men folk, need to be protected from them.

While *Jail Babes* have been commonly accused of scamming hapless men, the managers and clients of the *Jail Babes* enterprise appear to have been largely forgotten. No one has asked if their pursuit of profit and/or pleasure might result in harm, especially to those women prisoners whom they court. Some feminists might therefore consider the redistribution of guilt and blame to be a crucial first step in addressing the *Jail Babes* phenomenon. One strategy for shifting the balance of blame might be to adopt the well established feminist stance that equates pornography with harm and which, in direct opposition to individuals such as Flynt, staunchly advocates censorship and prohibition.[80] At first glance, seeking to censor or prohibit the *Jail Babes* website, magazines and videos may appear to have some merit, however, it is not without its dangers for it is a strategy that tends to replicate dominant notions concerning women and sexuality. Within it, sexuality is constructed as inherently dangerous to women, women's sexuality is envisaged as passive rather than active, and those women who transgress norms of acceptable sexual behaviour are liable to be cast as guilty or gullible.[81] Historically, such ideas have contributed to the policing of women, not merely by the state but also by feminists and others who have sought to 'save' them. It has also contributed to their imprisonment.

In vilifying and attempting to eradicate *Jail Babes* through legal means, there is also an added danger of treating it as though it can easily be divorced from the cultural and political terrain that has produced it. Numerous commentators have noted that women's imprisonment, like women's experiences of imprisonment, can only be understood through historical and social contextualisation.[82] If we pursue this line of thinking,

---

79 Ricker, 17 May 1999.

80 Influential examples of this perspective are provided by Dworkin, 1981 and MacKinnon, 1987. For an introduction to different feminist perspectives on pornography, see Segal and McIntosh, 1992.

81 Vance, 1984, pp 6–7; DuBois and Gordon, 1984, pp 33–34.

82 Carlen, 1983; Rafter, 1985; Davies and Cook, 1999.

then the origins of *Jail Babes* might usefully be traced to the inequitable power relations that limit women's life opportunities and choices, and which powerfully contribute to their offending, criminalisation and imprisonment. Similarly, the representations and practices that are promulgated and eroticised in *Jail Babes* can be seen as inextricably related to the gendered disciplinary practices that are at work everyday everywhere,[83] but which often find their most obvious and cruellest expression within the secretive confines of prisons.

In representational terms, there is it seems little space for women prisoners to manoeuvre. As *Jail Babes* amply illustrates, within dominant conventions, women prisoners are depicted almost without exception as being either bad women who deserve to be abused, degraded and exploited, or as women who have some possibility of being reformed, that is, if they are willing to be romanced and rescued. Either option depends upon their relationship with men. There is no space here for independent women, who are able to decide for themselves what paths they will follow, who they will associate with and how.

But are these representations and the pathways they depict very far removed from the realities that confront women prisoners and ex-prisoners everyday? Historically, women's prisons have sought to train women for marriage and domestic life, and there is much to suggest, that this continues today. What is certainly beyond doubt is that the abuse, degradation and exploitation of women within prisons persist. The *Jail Babes* magazines and videos may be full of women's flesh, but how far removed is that from the prison strip search or from the practice of making women prisoners supply a urine sample on demand and in full view? Are the pictures in *Jail Babes* of women who are nude except for handcuffs any less intolerable than the circumstances of women prisoners who are expected to undergo gynaecological examinations in the presence of male officers whilst shackled? And are the men with the hard drives and the cameras any more objectionable than the pimps and pushers who routinely meet women as they leave prison? These questions are not posed in order to legitimate or excuse such representations.[84] Rather they are intended to illustrate the fact that focussing attention solely upon *Jail Babes* may simply not be enough. One day, the *Jail Babes* enterprise may meet its demise, but it is unlikely to do so, until the will to imprison, control and punish women is itself laid to rest.

---

83 Howe, 1994, p 216.

84 For an overview of current issues relating to women's imprisonment, see Cook and Davies, 1999.

PART SIX

FICTIONS OF THE REAL

Death Ache

Because we are women
there are acres of light

There is yellow in the zoos even
and all the right kind of drama in our love

We lie on top of our paintings
like red butterflies who have lost all their vowels

Over the other side of the sun
is the food of our uncast punctuation

Shaving the stars' points
are the marks in our books

Whirling Whirling
we shake the questions from our wombs

We turn in the life-burn
the turn of life

Filled with the death ache
the ache of death

MTC Cronin

THE MORAL OF THE STORY: GENDER AND MURDER IN CANADIAN TRUE CRIME MAGAZINES OF THE 1940s

Carolyn Strange and Tina Loo

INTRODUCTION

Thanks to the recent retro revival of 1940s pulp magazine images, which adorn everything from fridge magnets to glossy art books, this genre is typically remembered for its covers, not its content.[1] Beyond their glossy covers, most magazines published in North America during the pulps' heyday, from the 1920s to the 1940s, offered thrills and frights. Crime fiction monthlies like *The Black Mask* and *Dime Detective*, along with romance, science fiction, and adventure magazines, were the staple products in pulp publishers' warehouses. Rather than offering classic mystery stories set in parlours and solved by aristocratic sleuths, these magazines featured short, fast-paced fictional narratives in which low life evildoers tried (unsuccessfully) to outwit crafty detectives.[2] Many Hollywood screenwriters and novelists, including Dashiell Hammett and Raymond Chandler, made their start in pulp magazines where they honed their trademark hard-boiled style.

Because several pulp fiction writers became famous, and because crime fiction has gained literary legitimacy, scholars of popular crime writing have paid comparatively little attention to the non-fiction pulps that advertised themselves as 'true crime' magazines. Like their better known counterparts, they attracted readers with splashy cover images of women either brandishing guns and knives or screaming in fright at rapacious and murderous men. Stark primary colours and bold mastheads advertising CRIME added luridness to true crime's allure. For 15 or 25 cents, readers bought the promise of red-hot entertainment.

They also got the truth in the bargain. True crime magazines proudly proclaimed that they offered 'true facts from official files' and traded profitably on their authenticity. By relating the lived experience of crime – real victims, real criminals, and real lawmen – true crime could claim the status of actuality, if not literary finesse.[3] Although the Canadian stories in

---

1   Lesser, 1997; Server, 1993.
2   Biressi, 2001, pp 112–12.
3   Haste, 1997, p 16; Cameron and Fraser, 1987, p 47.

true crime magazines were indeed based on official accounts and newspaper trial coverage, the facts of each case required a particular packaging style. Publishers favoured stories written as engaging police procedurals in which writers retraced heroic lawmen's efforts to hunt for criminals and bring them to justice.[4] But the re-articulation of actual crimes and individuals into entertaining narratives and colourful characters was far more artful than that, both in the evocation of classic concepts of good and evil, and in the blending of narrative genres.[5] Drawing inspiration from pulp fiction's snappy dialogue and hard-edged male heroes, adventure stories' thrilling hunts, film noir's exploration of dark desires, and romance's fixation on heterosexuality and betrayal, writers of the 1940s commodified real crimes into true crime pulp.[6]

The moral of the story in true crime pulps never wavered: crime did not pay. While images of violence and nearly naked women on the covers of true crime magazines defied the tenets of mid-20th century propriety, the stories tucked within propped up the pillars of law and order. As theorists of true crime have noted, retribution is the penal philosophy in popular accounts of crime that show how criminals are caught, explain how they went wrong and justify why they deserve to be punished.[7] True crime asserts that people who commit murderous deeds and imagine that they can get away with crime are wrong, not because murder will out somehow, but because criminal justice agents always catch criminals. By the last paragraph of every true crime story the killer is held to account, usually after the slow process of trial and legal punishment, but sometimes swiftly, as a result of shootouts or suicides. For every fear-inducing real criminal there were reassuringly real heroes, whom readers could count on to bring bad people to justice.

The conservatism of true crime was especially marked in Canada, a place famous not for its criminals but for its national police force, whose officers 'always got their man'. The mythic Mountie, a stock character in early 20th century adventure stories and the lead character in dime novels, 'northern' magazines, and later Hollywood feature films, made frequent appearances in 1940s Canadian true crime stories, chasing miscreants across the vast open spaces of the north and far west and helping frontier city police forces to solve local murders.[8] In Canada's biggest cities, Toronto, Montreal, and Vancouver, less glamorous detectives proved themselves equally committed to ferreting out urban criminals, who used the anonymity of city life to cover their tracks. The stakes were high: each of the pulp stories in 1940s

---

4   Vicarel, 1995.

5   Newman, 1990.

6   Knox, 1998.

7   Biressi, 2001, p 111; Cameron and Fraser, 1987, p 46; Mandel, 1984.

8   Dawson, 1997; Hutchinson, 1998.

magazines was a tale of murder, crimes that had actually occurred in Canada, especially during the 1920s and 30s. While writers might have chosen any of the hundreds of Canadian capital cases over this period, they invariably selected ones in which brave or brainy police work had led to criminals' capture. There were no unsolved or bungled cases, and nor were there corrupt cops in these stories. Unlike true crime writing today, which often explores the tragic consequences of bad policing and incompetent lawyering,[9] Canadian true crime of the 1940s related stories of crime and policing to a popular audience, emphasising lawmen's good judgment and crime-solving capabilities.

True crime's conservatism extended beyond its embrace of law and order, however, and was further expressed in its characterisations of race, class, and especially gender. While Canadian readers would rarely have heard of local cases published in nationally distributed true crime magazines, the moral truths woven into true crime stories affirmed dominant notions of identity and hierarchy in Anglo-Canadian society. True crime writers spared little typewriter ribbon to describe individual criminals' motivations because magazines like *Scoop Detective* and *True Police Stories* published formulaic narratives, which relied on and reiterated commonly held understandings that native people and 'foreigners' were driven by 'primitive' passions; that illegitimate desires for love or money drove desperate people to kill; that normal heterosexual desire could erupt into violence; and that crimes involving women always turned on sex. Retelling tales of murder thus provided fertile ground for writers to explore the consequences of breaching social and economic boundaries, or violating relationships, both intimate and contractual.

Although most of the stories published in Canadian magazines of the 1940s described men's crimes against men (fur trappers who killed rivals for their spoils, bandits who shot bank tellers during hold-ups and the like) we turn here to real cases of intergender crime that were published as true crime stories in the 1940s. Four stories, two featuring women as violent criminals, and two in which men killed women, serve to illustrate the gender conventions and conventionality of true crime. A close analysis of the narrative devices and characterisations in these stories reveals that true crime writers' renderings of male and female criminality and victimhood owed as much to romantic literature and the dialogic style of pulp fiction and film noir as it did to the 'true facts'. These stories of villainy, doused with sexual imagery, provided voyeuristic pleasures for male and female readers, and thereby opened up possibilities for interpretations that strayed beyond the didactic frame. As Deborah Cameron argues of the genre, true crime provides 'a balance of licit and illicit pleasures, the one defusing the

---

9   Knox, 1998, p 10; Biressi, 2001, p 125.

anxiety of the other'.[10] Even in its salaciousness, however, Canadian true crime writers managed to moralise about gender and crime by turning to the tropes of the designing woman, the thrill-seeking bad girl, the oversexed man, and the hardworking innocent daughter. Before moving to the stories that commodified real murder cases into mythic constructions, we begin by charting the rise of the Canadian true crime industry, and the publishers, writers, and audiences that it brought together in the 1940s.

TRUE CRIME CANADIAN-STYLE

Canadian true crime might never have found a pulp magazine audience had the Second World War not spawned a publishing industry north of the US border. The federal government, in an effort to conserve Canada's balance of trade with the USA, imposed an importation ban at the war's outset on non-essential goods, including pulp magazines. The War Exchange Conservation Act specifically prohibited periodicals that featured 'detective, sex, western, and alleged true or confession stories'.[11] Suddenly deprived of cheap entertaining reading, English Canadian readers were a market waiting to be tapped by opportunists who scrambled to supply Canadian versions of American magazines. In Toronto, Vancouver, and Montreal, operations like Super Publications and Daring Productions flourished, and churned out comic books, romance titles, men's humour magazines, and true crime pulps. While local content began to appear in Canadian true crime magazines, publishers stuck to the American industry's marketing practices, imitating the bold, sexy covers and salacious advertisements, and specialising in dramatic murder cases. With the war's end and a shift toward a consumer-driven economy, importation restrictions were lifted and American products once again appeared on newsstands. Canadian true crime magazines began to fold in the face of stiff competition, but they also declined because of the pulp novel's growing popularity. By the 1950s, Canadians turned to paperbacks and later television journalism for true crime accounts. Thus the consumption of Canadian crime in magazine form was short lived but commercially successful during the 1940s.

Because the pulps were cheap and cheaply produced (the low-quality paper stock gave them their name) very few have survived beyond the hands of private collectors. As a result it is impossible to provide a definitive account of the true crime magazine industry in Canada. The country's largest publicly accessible pulp collection at the National Library of Canada nonetheless provides a solid base from which to observe patterns in the sorts

---

10 Cameron, 1990, p 137.
11 War Exchange Conservation Act 1940 (Can) para X.

of cases featured in Canadian magazines.[12] True crime did not attract the cream of the literary crop. Unless famous writers used aliases it seems that all of the stories were written by people who were known only to publishers and to the secretaries who wrote out cheques for any amount from 10 to 20 dollars – the price range for features in a Canadian pulp in the 1940s. As long as authors had access to the facts and could write according to true crime's formulas, publishers were not fussy when it came to finding writers. Three men dominated the Canadian ranks, however. One, CV Tench, was based in Vancouver and might have been a court reporter or a police officer, since he appears to have had access to internal justice files.[13] Another was Philip H Godsell, a former employee of the Hudson Bay Company and a specialist in 'Northerns' – stories, usually featuring Mounties, set in the remote west or the Arctic. The third, WW Bride, was a Toronto-based writer and possibly a reporter. Each of them dabbled in fiction as well as true crime and Godsell, especially, had literary pretensions. The 1940s explosion of the true crime market in Canada sent these and other writers to work, searching for the sorts of cases in Canadian history that would make good copy.

But to whom was that copy meant to appeal? Given the masculinist conservatism of the stories and the lasciviously posed women on the covers, true crime magazines would seem to have been meant for male readers. Unfortunately the pulp industry, a business known for its fly-by-night operators and shady business practices, did not conduct readership surveys or keep subscriber or distributor lists. Publishers' hunches about what sold and where to sell their products determined marketing practices. Certainly confession magazines and those for movie star fans were marketed to female readers, but publishers evidently assumed that women comprised a significant sector of the true crime market as well. Interspersed among stories about Mountie manhunts were advertisements for birth control manuals and 'date blouses'. Household items, including the ubiquitous steak knives, were also advertised alongside books with exotic titles like *Chinese Love Tales* ('copiously illustrated'). True crime magazines were not only sold in cigar stores and barbershops but also in train stations and

---

12 The collection, acquired in 1997, is catalogued in its manuscript holdings as the 'Pulp Art Collection'. There is no way to ascertain the total number of pulp publications nor the definitive number of Canadian stories published because the business was volatile (eg, editorial offices moved addresses frequently); because publishers did not maintain systematic records; because of the ephemeral nature of the product and the poor quality of the paper; because the business declined by the 1950s; and because very few Canadian pulps have been collected systematically. The National Library's collection is acknowledged as the most comprehensive to date. Interview with George Flie (professional collector and donor), August 2001.

13 *True Police Cases* (Vol 1, 1943) expressly solicited journalists on the police beat: 'You, the police reporters and court reporters especially, are in the best position to supply the market.'

drugstores,[14] places where women and men passed as they went to work or shopped.

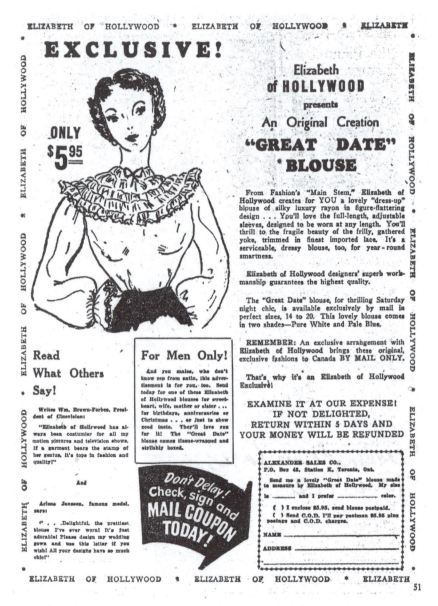

Date Blouse: Scoop Detective Cases, from the Rare Book Collection of the National Library of Canada, November–December 1943, Pulp Art Collection, Box 10

14   Interview with George Flie, Toronto, August 2001.

Aside from ads for products pitched at women, true crime magazines had plenty to offer female readers. As Cameron and Fraser have argued, women have consistently been avid consumers of true crime literature, from the 19th century's penny dreadfuls to today's accounts of serial killers, like *The Stranger Beside Me*.[15] Women might have read features such as 'The Bloody Knife Points to Death' (a story of a young Winnipeg woman stabbed to death on her way home from the movies) as a cautionary tale about unescorted women's vulnerability but they could also have felt reassured by the swift and competent police work that brought a killer to justice. In every true crime story, male Euro-Canadian police officers and detectives had starring roles. Thanks to Nelson Eddy ('The Singing Mountie' of Hollywood fame) and a host of playwrights and novelists, true crime magazines tapped into a tradition of portraying the mounted policeman as a romantic figure, whose bravery could appeal to women as well as men. Stories that featured women as perpetrators or instigators of violence permitted upstanding readers to share in writers' condemnation of immoral women, while accounts of women who lived fast and hard allowed other female readers to indulge fantasies of exacting revenge or walking on the wild side. And finally, in a period well before sexually charged female imagery was produced for a lesbian market, true crime covers of curvaceous women in states of semi-undress made these magazines well worth their price. Thus while the morals of stories were delivered with didactic certainty, what female and male readers sought and derived from Canadian true crime magazines was less assured.

VIXENS AND VICTIMS: WOMEN IN CANADIAN TRUE CRIME

True crime magazines could well have been accused of false advertising. Almost every pulp featured a cover image of a woman as a victim or perpetrator of a crime, yet only a quarter (23 of the 84 cases in surviving Canadian magazines) of the stories involved women. In keeping with the genre's reliance upon stereotypical characterisations of all sorts, true crime stories traced women's involvement in crime to the fatal corruption of normal heterosexual relationships. Women's seductive power, their attraction to ruthless men, and their vulnerability to brutes were themes that arose repeatedly in true crime magazines. In this respect the cover art fit the feature articles (although artistic licence routinely trumped realistic portraiture).

---

15 Cameron and Fraser, 1987, pp 47, 50.

Stories starring women interwove sex and death, enduring obsessions of both high literature and popular culture.[16] Trials of female murderers were rare in Canada, and most involved straightforward cases of lethal marital breakdowns or tragic infanticides. Rather than choose these, true crime writers selected the sexier cases in which women's taste for violent men and fast times had led to murder. Since the prime criterion for selection was an exciting police hunt publishers favoured stories about female murderers who had tested the skills of Canada's lawmen. In these stories women challenged detectives' power but masculine legal authority, dressed up nattily in uniform, ultimately triumphed. As a close reading of the stories about convicted murderers Dolores Brooks and Doris McDonald illustrates, normative concepts of heterosexuality and intergender relations, reinforced by racial and class hierarchies, triumphed as well.

Nothing but a modern Delilah

The discovery of the body, a common device in crime fiction as well as true crime, provided the typical opening in pulp stories. What followed from that point was the breathless search for the killer based on clues and tips gathered expertly by the police. Often the cops knew the killer's identity, and the object was to track him down, either through the wilderness or, in urban cases, through the dark corners of the city.[17] When writers opened without revealing the culprit's identity they borrowed from detective fiction by allowing readers to share the thrill of solving a crime. The involvement of a woman always added a touch of mystery to a true crime story because lawmen used to trailing male killers and tracing masculine motivations found the female killer inscrutable.[18] Moreover female suspects had charms that worked as potently on police officers as they did on the men whom they manipulated to do their violent bidding.

The case of Dolores Brooks, convicted for her part in the 1939 murder of a restaurant owner, showed how feminine wiles could obscure a female killer's trail, making her difficult to track down even when she was under the authorities' noses. CV Tench's account of Brooks and her partners in crime appeared in *Scoop Detective* under the title, 'Torrid Love Drove Him to Murder'.[19] The action begins with police racing over to Vancouver's Savoy Hotel, where a clerk had found a dead 'Chinaman': 'Why it looks like he's been murdered! Geeze! I'm calling the cops!' Members of Vancouver's homicide squad, all of them white, drive to the city's extensive Chinatown, an area visited more often in this era by the city's vice squad. For true crime

---

16 Biressi, 2001, p 119; Bloom, 1996.

17 Ingebretsen, 1998.

18 Hutchings, 2001, p 87.

19 All subsequent quotes from 'Torrid Love Drove Him to Murder', taken from Tench, 1949.

readers, the first few paragraphs of the story would have sufficed to link this case to other popular portrayals of Chinatown as the quintessential urban cesspool, where only the lowest Euro-Canadians congregated. When the police scratched their heads and pondered who might have killed Woo Dack, their first guess was that it had been another Chinese man. But Woo had been killed in his bed and the bloodstains on his sheets indicated that the killer had likely kneeled there. Turning to the murdered man's brother, Inspector Petit asks: 'Did your brother have a white mistress?'

Illicit relationships between white women and Chinese men had been a keen concern for Canadians ever since federal immigration laws had specifically targeted Chinese immigrants, restricting their entry first through head taxes and, in 1923, by excluding Chinese nationals outright. Woo's brother explained this to the Inspector, introducing a sexually and racially transgressive subtext to the murder: '... we are not allowed to bring our own women to Canada ... so perhaps my brother at times associated with white women.' Racist characterisations of Chinese men as inordinately drawn to white women and willing to use opium and exotic seduction techniques to induce compliance had led numerous Canadian jurisdictions to pass legislation restricting the employment of white women by Chinese men. If Woo had been such a man, a possibility that Anglo readers would readily have assumed, perhaps a white woman had fought back? The Chinese business community of Vancouver thought otherwise, guessing that Woo had been killed in a botched robbery attempt. When business leaders (in their 'Oriental wisdom') put up a $2,000 reward for help in finding their compatriot's killer, the police and Vancouver's Chinese community combined their efforts in a rare instance of solidarity.

Who was the murderer? When a waitress, calling herself Linda Wilson, came to the police to identify the culprits, the case appeared to be solved. The young woman reported that two young men, whom she had met at one of the city's dance halls, had boasted that they had 'killed the Chinaman', and vowed that they would 'knock her off' if she dared squeal to the police. She commented that the killers were swell dancers but they were 'as bad as can be'. Tipped by 'the girl', officers picked up the men: 'hard-eyed' Harry McMillan denied involvement but the younger Arthur Rennie, 'his eyes the eyes of a tortured animal', confessed. Under interrogation the men revived the detectives' earlier theory of a woman's involvement. Rennie claimed that Dolores Brooks, a waitress whom Woo Dack had fired, had put him up to the crime, tempting him with information about the large amounts of money Woo kept in his hotel room. Rennie, not the first man to kill at a woman's command, came across as a hapless dupe and victim in Tench's estimation: 'Dolores Brooks had led him on with all the feminine wiles at her command until he became her virtual slave.' Thus the story shifted from racist tropes about lusty Chinamen and seduced white women to archetypal gender scripts of designing women using men to do their bidding. The hunt was on for Dolores Brooks.

Inspector Petit and his fellow homicide cops began to scour Chinatown for the illusive waitress but the crafty Inspector Petit began to suspect that the killer would come to him. Sure enough, the woman who called herself Linda Wilson returned; ready to take the reward money and run. Threatened with a visit from Chinese employees from Woo's chop suey restaurant, the duplicitous Dolores revealed her true identity. But she continued to deny her role in the murder, pinning the blame squarely on her young male hanger-on. The story ended with a brief account of the trio's trial and closed, typically, with a moral. Quoting from the judge in Rennie's trial, Tench quoted his biblical condemnation: 'Dolores Brooks brazenly betrayed both McMillan and Rennie to the police ... I maintain that Brooks is nothing but a modern Delilah.' As Tench told it, while the 'girl with the flashing black eyes' had proven to be more than a couple of unemployed petty criminals could handle, she was no match for the no-nonsense homicide cops who cracked the case. Far from being an innocent girl led astray by murderous men, Tench concluded that Brooks was 'the real instigator of this heinous crime'.

Wronged Girl: Daring Crime Cases, Vol 9(1), March 194? (date illegible), from the Rare Book Collection of the National Library of Canada, Pulp Art Collection, Box 6

True crime magazine covers (not to mention Hollywood movies) routinely featured brazen women who used their sexual appeal to tip the balance of power between the sexes. Whether they were employers or dates, men called the shots for working class women, but not the female criminals in true crime. Tench's story of Dolores Brooks likely appealed to *Scoop Detective*'s women readers who might have fantasised about dating two 'swell dancers', robbing the boss, and getting a man to do their dirty work. True crime stories provided vicarious thrills but it also explored the lethal consequences of failing to accept one's proper place. Whether or not perpetrators were men or women, writers traced criminals' downfall most often to greed or envy – the craving to have what they had not earned or been owed. Advertisements published alongside true crime stories catered to working class readers' desire for popularity and class mobility ('It's easy to learn how to dance!'; 'How to write correctly') but aspirants had to send two or three dollars, post paid, to learn the secrets. Stories such as 'Torrid Love Drove Him to Murder' showed what happened to people who were unwilling to pay and unwilling to wait for their shot at a better life.

The primrose path to perdition

In true crime magazines chivalrous readings of women's involvement of murder were rare. For instance, a story about notorious rumrunner 'Emperor Piccarello', convicted for shooting a Royal Canadian Mounted Police officer, tarred the bootlegger's daughter-in-law with the same brush of lawlessness. Florence Lassandro, who had been in the 'Emperor's' car when the officer was killed, was executed in 1923 for her part in the crime and the family business.[20] During the 1920s and 30s, Canadian parliamentarians, who had not ordered a woman's execution since 1899, regained their resolve that women ought not to be spared the death penalty. Over this two-decade period, five women were executed in Canada, all but Lassandro having been convicted of murdering their husbands. True crime writers were not squeamish about the death penalty (stories almost always ended with a brief account of an execution) but because they followed the police procedural formula, a cracking good police hunt and detective case offered more publishing appeal than the easily solved cases of wives who had killed their husbands. Thus the typical homicide involving a female culprit in interwar Canada did not fire true crime writers' imaginations: extraordinarily daring and sexually adventurous female killers who sidestepped the gallows did.

Canada had its own prohibition era Bonnie and Clyde, only the pair did not die in a hail of bullets. In 1928, George McDonald died more quietly on

---

20 *Factual Detective Cases*, August 1942.

the gallows, while his wife, Doris, was sent to prison for life for her part in the robbery and murder of a French Canadian cab driver. Phillip Godsell's version of the case recounted how the couple's trail of unpaid hotel bills, phony identities, bad cheques, bullet-pierced cars, and boozy parties had ultimately led police in Canada and the USA to capture them. Although the case also involved a male accomplice as well as George McDonald, Godsell devoted far more attention to the woman, the 'beautiful blonde murderess' who had vowed to her captors, 'I shall not hang'.[21]

Godsell's story, 'Montreal's Honeymoon Slayers', opened with the chance discovery of a man's body lying in a ditch near the Quebec-New York border. A bullet wound in the head confirmed that the man had been murdered but other articles discovered at the scene – a fancy pair of shoes, silk hosiery, 'lace-trimmed under things and a light silk summer dress, all stained with blood' – raised the possibility that a woman had been wounded and abducted. And not just any woman. The delicate material and dressy shoes denoted a stylish woman of means, who took pride in her appearance. While rural police searched the countryside for the woman, Montreal police found an abandoned Packard marked by bullet holes and bloodstained seats. Tracing the car to its owner, detectives found that it belonged to a cab driver, which had been hired to drive a honeymooning couple from Montreal to New York. Both the newlyweds and the victim's 300 dollars in expense money were missing. Police officers called off their search for an injured lady and switched to a man and woman hunt. Godsell put the words of a Hollywood movie detective into the French-speaking Police Chief Durocher's mouth: 'There's a girl in the picture – probably a good-looker, and snappily dressed from the clothes we've picked up. That may be a lead.'

A frenzied round of sleuthing allowed police to reconstruct the crime and to put the 'girl' into the centre of the murder picture. Bellhops at Montreal's luxurious Mount Royal Hotel confirmed that a young 'smartly dressed' couple by the name of Palmer had stayed in an expensive suite and left a few days earlier in a Packard. They returned shortly afterwards and ordered bottle after bottle of champagne. Their high living had attracted hotel management's attention, as had the fact that they had left behind empty suitcases and an unpaid bill. More damning information came from an American immigration officer who had refused the couple entry on the night of the murder. When they were stopped at the border, the 'extraordinarily beautiful blonde' was 'plastered' and naked from the waist down, covered only by a rug. Cursing 'like a trooper' the 'tough and cocky' woman created a unforgettable impression. If ever there was a wanted criminal who could have modelled for a sexy magazine cover woman, Doris McDonald, 'the lovely gun girl', was her.

---

21 All subsequent quotes from 'Montreal's Honeymoon Killers' taken from Godsell, 1943.

The honeymooners' taste for the high life and their disinclination to earn their money through honest work ensured that they would eventually be caught. Their trail of worthless cheques eventually stopped in Butte, Montana, where lawmen nabbed the couple and their male accomplice. Doris's good looks and bad mouthing jogged US police officers' memories of the bulletin about the Montreal murder and it also prompted them to dig deeper into the couple's background. George McDonald was a Maritimer from a poor mining town who had drifted into fraud and petty crime; Doris's history, in contrast, was worthy of a Hollywood melodrama. Doris's mother was a working class woman who had had given up her girl after her husband had deserted her and left her penniless. A wealthy childless couple in New York had adopted the girl and tried to raise her respectably but, as Godsell explained, 'her headstrong nature and avid desire for excitement' prompted her to run away with George McDonald when she was still a teenager. Together they had travelled the States in stolen cars, turning to robberies, stick-ups, fraud, 'and whatever means happened to present themselves of acquiring easy money.' Becoming a Hollywood movie star was Doris' dream, but the aspiring starlet failed to make it in the talkies. Back on the east coast, the couple maintained a flashy lifestyle through Doris's gigs at nightclubs and cabarets and George's conman talents. In her young life she had gone from poor castoff, to pampered daughter, to fast-living swindler – all the while dressed in the latest fashions.

Doris McDonald's life of crime confirmed the judgment, emblazoned on true crime covers, that female beauty was a dangerous asset, particularly if unconstrained by the institutions of family and marriage to a respectable man. Doris's foster parents had proven unable to eradicate their adopted daughter's true nature (and class origins), and nor could they compete with the temptations of modern life. According to Godsell, Doris was a tragic product of a postwar cultural shift in femininity: 'Doris had confessed to being just another of the those thrill-crazy girls who emerged from the dislocation of the last war. She had, she admitted, taken up with McDonald for the sheer thrill and love of excitement until the wild life of the underworld and the night clubs had gotten into her blood.' While modern city life offered up new ways for young women to get mixed up in crime, there was nothing novel about the moral of this story. Doris had been given the chance for a settled respectable life but she had strayed from a virtuous course and danced the devil's tune along 'the primrose path to perdition'. As Godsell concluded, the 'dazzling blonde', who had yearned to see her name up in lights, faced a fate worse than death: her lover executed and her 'life behind the grilled bars of the prison cell with a number for a name'.

One love too many

The McDonald pair, young, attractive, and in love, provided the stuff of romance as well as true crime.[22] While the romanticisation of crime and the aestheticisation of violent death in popular culture have troubled feminist critics of popular retellings of rape and murder,[23] other analysts have pointed to the overlapping genres of romance and crime, and the attraction of female readers to both kinds of literature.[24] In falling victim to male killers, women in true crime stories were not merely objects of violence but the embodiment of the feminine succumbing to superior masculine force.[25] True crime's male murderers of women were not unlike the darkly attractive and vaguely villainous men of 19th century romance novels and their cheap modern counterparts in magazines such as *True Confessions*. In Canadian true crime magazines of the 1940s, men killed women not as a product of psychological abnormalities (expert psychological evaluations rarely appeared in Canadian stories in this period); rather, men murdered because they were inordinately passionate or enraged when heterosexual love went wrong. Although their crimes transgressed legal norms the perpetrators were simply extreme examples of normal men, driven to the ultimate form of mastery – murder. Thus, men who killed women out of jealousy or desire were ambiguous figures, simultaneously criminals and romantic anti-heroes, for whom the threat of the death penalty could not stop the primitive force of love and lust.

Albert Westgate was such a man, as his female victims discovered too late. His story, published in a 1946 issue of *Daring Crime Cases*, was told by Phillip Godsell (writing as Phil Blackstone) as that of a dashing World War One veteran who had killed the objects of his desire. The first was Lottie Adams, a married woman of 30, who was found axed to death in the winter of 1928. Describing the discovery of her body, Blackstone painted a macabre fairy tale picture: protruding from a snow bank her 'lovely hand and bare arm [were] almost as white as snow', while her 'pitifully small' figure and beautiful face presented 'the picture of a sleeping beauty'.[26] Once the police identified the woman they began to suspect that she might not have been the happy housewife of her husband's description. Ten years her senior, Mr Adams was an unassuming department store employee who claimed that he and his wife never quarrelled. He did, however, mention that Lottie had received mysterious boxes of chocolates and that a man had been seen running from their house. And then she went missing. 'It sounds screwy to

22 Haste, 1997; Bloom, 1996.
23 Ward Jouve, 1986; Cameron and Fraser, 1987.
24 Knox, 1998, p 97; Radway, 1984.
25 Caputi, 1987.
26 All subsequent quotes from 'Marriage and Murder', Blackstone, 1946.

me, chief,' one of the detectives asserted: 'Women don't just walk away from a happy home …!'

What followed in 'Marriage and Murder' was Blackstone's account of typically meticulous detective work. In this case police had managed to connect Albert Westgate, one of Mrs Adams' 'masculine friends,' to the dead woman's disappearance. Westgate was a married man who had suffered a shrapnel wound which required frequent treatment at Winnipeg's veterans' hospital. Under an alias he had rented a car on the day of Mrs Adams' disappearance, and he had asked the garage man to keep mum, lest he get into trouble with his wife. The charmer had also managed to induce a hospital orderly to provide him with an alibi, to establish that he had been hospitalised over the period when Mrs Adams went missing. Nevertheless, Winnipeg detectives managed to press witnesses to identify Westgate, which 'figuratively put the noose around his neck', Blackstone foreshadowed. At his trial a string of evidence and testimony established that Westgate had been seeing Mrs Adams for some time, and that the pair had argued frequently. The evidence was compelling and Westgate was convicted and sentenced to death. But an attractive wounded veteran who had served in the Great War made a good candidate for mercy. With the help of veterans' associations Westgate earned himself a commuted sentence of life in prison.

Extramarital sex was a recipe for trouble in true crime, and in spite of the femme fatale's frequent appearance on magazine covers, stories of women and crime showed that they were more likely than men to pay with their lives when love soured. Mrs Adams, like Anna Karenina, Madame Bovary, and a host of tragic romantic heroines before her, had played with fire: she had deceived her own husband and consorted with another woman's partner in a sordid adulterous relationship. But Lottie Adams was no countess: she was the wife of a sales clerk in a provincial department store. She might have imagined that she had found her Prince Charming in the passionate ex-soldier but his brand of love, spicier than her husband's, was deadly. And no less deadly with age. Westgate's apparent ability to woo women remained intact after he was released in 1942, as a young waitress was to learn at her peril. Unlike the hard-bitten Dolores of dance hall fame, Grace Cook's encounter with a violent man left the 16 year old the victim. Found strangled in her hotel room, witnesses testified that she had been the object of the ageing parolee's infatuation. On trial again for killing a woman who had failed in some way to satisfy his romantic desires, Westgate was convicted and sentenced to death a second time. The unusual story, published just prior to the homme fatal's execution, closed in a typically moralistic fashion: 'He has murdered one love to[o] many'.

The reference to love, rather than hatred, signalled true crime's disinclination to challenge romantic heterosexual norms. Stories of femicidal men in 1940s pulps were not platforms for moralising about gender inequality or misogyny; rather they confirmed that heterosexual desire, unleashed from its proper marital and domestic restraints, was a dangerous force that could leave women dead and men executed. In true crime pulps, sex and crime went together like glycerol and nitrogen: explosively. In the 1940s writers did not yet refer to expert psychiatric knowledge about deviance in their explorations of criminal motivation, preferring to stick to folk wisdom about the potentially deadly consequences of straying from the normative path of heterosexual virtue.[27] More significantly the detailed accounting of police cases in stories such as 'Marriage and Murder' affirmed that no killer could escape justice, thanks not to professionals' expertise but to police officers' horse sense about human nature (happy wives don't just leave home). Thus if Westgate's deadly 'love' showed that some women found dangerous cads irresistible, his execution proved that Canadian lawmen would never give up until they ensured that criminals got what they deserved. What bad men destroyed, good men restored.

A sex-fiend of the worst type

Canadian true crime magazines of the 1940s were produced at the dawn of what Jane Caputi called 'the age of sex crime'.[28] Although most of the stories in surviving magazines concerned murders committed by men who had known their victims, several stories of stranger danger, the staple subject of today's reportage and crime fiction, were published in this decade. When writers submitted stories about men killing male strangers, they focused on robberies and heists of various sorts, in which the main object had been easy money; when they trawled Canadian newspapers for crimes involving female strangers they dredged up heterosexual attacks on young attractive innocents. Only one story, a case of a boy sexually assaulted and killed while skiing on Mount Royal in Montreal, involved a homosexual offence (described obliquely as the crime of a 'degenerate').[29] In the 1940s, Canadian publishers stuck to more conventional but nevertheless sensational cases in which normal heterosexual desire had been inordinately amplified, not perverted. In the judgmental framework of true crime stories, these men were bad, not sick. Only an exceptionally irrational killer, such as a Métis youth who freely confessed that he had knifed a woman who had refused his advances, was a credible candidate for detention in a psychiatric facility.[30] More commonly, true crime writers of the 1940s preferred cases in which sexually violent men had paid for their murderous desires with their lives.

---

27 Surette, 1998.
28 Caputi, 1987; Soothill and Walby, 1991.
29 Bride, 1948. On themes of non-normative sexuality in paperbacks, see Striker, 2001.
30 Bride, 1947.

Ruth Taylor, a young woman brutally killed on her way home from work in 1935, was a quintessential innocent victim.[31] The Depression had made jobs precious, and women like Taylor, employed as a clerk in a Toronto insurance firm, could ill afford to turn down late shifts. One chilly rainy night in November she left work at 11 pm and never made it home to her parents. The author of 'Toronto's Love Slayer' WW Bride, was at pains to distinguish Taylor from 'the type to allow herself to be picked up by strangers'.[32] In fact, as the police discovered, 'she was very reserved and quite dignified. A serious minded girl, her friends said. Her employers had nothing but praise for her.' Taylor's unblemished character did not prevent Bride from detailing the horribly undignified way in which her body was left in a ravine and discovered by a group of 'curious urchins'.

The fiend had attacked the girl on the street, then carried her into the darkened gulley.

(Specially Posed)

Toronto's Love Slayer: Daring Crime Cases, April 1946, from the Rare Book Collection of the National Library of Canada, Pulp Art Collection, Box 16.

---

31 For another example, see Davis, 1942.
32 All subsequent quotes from 'Trailing Toronto's Love Slayer' taken from Bride, 1946.

The story of Taylor's murder, the hunt for her killer, and his just punishment was based, as *Daring Crime Cases* advertised on every cover, on 'true facts from official files'. But Bride's account was as much a gothic tale as a police procedural.[33] The opening, for instance, recast a Toronto gully into a sinister place: 'The soggy leaves of the ravine glistened in the drizzle of the rain. The bare trunks of the trees shone. The leafless branches pointed their long fingers over the bundle of rags that lay on the deep mold ...' Children from the working class Anglo neighbourhood nearby were playing in the muck when they come upon Taylor. Like Mrs Adams, the frozen sleeping beauty, Taylor was 'a pretty girl, even in death', according to the first police inspector on the scene. Bride then describes how three men – the inspector, his sergeant, and the city coroner – proceeded to peel back what little clothing remained on the woman's body. True crime's pornographic predilection for graphic, sexually lurid depictions of death is well in evidence in the description of the inspector's assessment: 'He turned back the tweed coat. Her clothes had been ripped from her. The sweater hung in shreds, her underwear lay damp, torn and soggy against the cold flesh. Over to one side lay a torn black skirt. One shoe was missing.' The capacity of criminal events to supply graphic material for true crime was well appreciated by Canadian publishers, who could not otherwise have sold explicit sexual material in drug stores and train stations.[34] Stories such as 'Toronto's Love Slayer' allowed readers to share in male police officers' violation of the body, thereby implicating them in the criminal act. But lawmen, like medical doctors, gazed with the eyes of authority: it was their duty to do so. Accordingly, the account of the ensuing investigation and the capture of the culprit allowed readers, who might never have considered purchasing explicit pornography, to rationalise the prurient pleasures of reading about sexual violence.

Switching to a police procedural approach, Bride moved on to explain how Toronto lawmen's 'careful painstaking work' turned an apparently 'dead-end trail' into clues. True crime authors sometimes gave the police a little boost along the way, as Bride did in this story. News accounts of the gruesome discovery led to Taylor's identification; her fellow employees confirmed when she had left work and how she had travelled home; people who lived near the ravine reported that they had heard a struggle, but nobody could identify the person who had killed the young woman. Using a variation on the police chase line ('round up the usual suspects') from the 1942 hit *Casablanca*, Bride recounts how the less glamorous Toronto police used the same tactic. When the inspector asks his officers for names of

---

33 Halttunen, 1998, p 240.

34 According to pulp collector George Flie, pulp publishers, such as Toronto's Al Valentine, learned how to push the limits of tolerance for sexual imagery without facing prosecution. Valentine informed Flie that he did face an obscenity charge in the 1940s in regard to one of his covers, but the specifics of the case are unknown: Strange, 2001.

known troublemakers he adds: 'I don't mean anyone with a record, but anyone with a reputation for living pretty fast, you know the stuff.'

Had Bride actually used official police files (or indeed, if he had merely read the contemporary news coverage faithfully) he would have known that Harry O'Donnell, the man whom local police officers identified as a prime suspect, did have a criminal record.[35] Perhaps the non-disclosure of O'Donnell's extensive record for sexual violence, criminal mischief, and trespass (peeping into windows) was an attempt to make the police appear brilliantly intuitive, rather than failures at monitoring the behaviour of a known sex offender.[36] Or perhaps the publisher deprived readers of knowledge about O'Donnell's apparently compulsive acts of sexual violence toward women in order to fit the story with its romantic title: 'Toronto's Love Slayer'. The 'specially posed' picture that accompanied the story, an image of a man with matinee idol looks, carrying a swooning woman, her plunging neckline exposing her chest, further associated O'Donnell with the anti-heroes of melodrama – men who stopped at nothing to get what they wanted.[37] Here was a passionate monster, who had killed a woman in the course of forcing himself upon her. An unfortunate crime, a tragedy, but consistent with the gendered codes of romance and crime fiction as well as true crime.

Cardboard characterisations of criminals and victims, standard elements of plot-driven stories that spat out the details of crime, hunt, capture and punishment in fewer than 2,000 words, left women such as Ruth Taylor free of blame for their awful fates. The stranger danger features in Canadian true crime of the 1940s were non-judgmental about women's vulnerability to dangerous men. Taking the streetcar alone at night, or stopping off for a hotdog on the way home after the movies was an unremarkable activity for young single victims in these stories. The wartime context during which these stories were published may have inclined writers to take women's participation in public life for granted. It was certainly a period unlike our own, when police advisors and women's safety officers 'responsibilise' women into avoiding all possible risks of victimisation. If a woman became a strange man's prey in the 1940s, it was because she was unlucky, not asking for it. More significantly, Canadian true crime stories of female victimhood affirmed that good men in uniform could be counted on, perhaps not to prevent crime but to catch crooks and to ensure that bad men, like O'Donnell and Westgate, would expiate their crimes on Canadian gallows.

---

35 This was determined by comparing Bride's account to the official records in O'Donnell's capital case file: National Archives of Canada, 1936. There were no other stories in which the facts were omitted or altered so significantly.

36 O'Donnell served a federal sentence for indecent assault and was released from prison under the provisions of the Ticket of Leave Act. The specific details of his release agreement are unknown, but convicted criminals were typically required to make regular visits to local police until their sentences expired.

37 Hays and Nikolopoulou, 1996.

CONCLUSION

As the four exemplary cases discussed above suggest, the ideological work of Canadian true crime magazines of the 1940s was staunchly conservative. These popular cultural forms not only took a pro-law and order stance, but because they were written as police procedurals they also drew the reader toward the point of view of lawmen who pursued and prosecuted wrongdoers. Moreover, through the writers' and publishers' selection of murders that they deemed worthy of becoming stories and the morals with which they invested those stories, Canadian true crime affirmed conventional understandings of gender, class and racial hierarchies. By providing illicit pleasures within a moralising framework, true crime's transgressive appeal served surprisingly conformist ends. Whether writers probed the relationship between seduction and manipulation (as in the Dolores Brooks case), or traced the trajectory from thrill-seeking to law-breaking (in the story of Doris McDonald), or explored the boundaries between love, lust, and obsession (in the cases of Albert Westgate and Harry O'Donnell), the consequences for those who crossed normative lines was predictably grim: violent death, life-long incarceration, or execution.

Although sexually explicit covers offended the tenets of good taste,[38] their Canadian content provided an unauthoritative but commercially successful forum for the exploration of law and justice in Canada. Crime did pay during the 1940s when Canadian publishers pumped out pulps under the protection of importation bans. Writers based in Canada quickly learned the true crime formula and found crimes that fit. That meant that every case was solved, every victim vindicated, every criminal caught and punished – perfectly consistent with authoritative images of Canadian criminal justice. But true crime magazines were not published with a market of legal officials in mind. As their low price and garishness flagged, they were produced and distributed for anyone on the lookout for cheap thrills. Their lowbrow appeal, reinforced by risible and ribald sidebar advertisements (for bachelors' joke books and 'tales from the boudoir') undercut didactic narratives and amplified the excitement of violence, particularly when stories mixed murder with sex. Cases involving women as victims or perpetrators of violence provided ideal raw material for true crime's blend of romantic, melodramatic, and gothic moralising.[39] Like the eye-catching magazine covers, stories of women's victimisation and capacity for violence were the definitive vehicles for true crime's ambiguously pornographic vernacular of law and order.

---

38 Adams, 1995.
39 Cameron and Fraser, 1987, pp 122–23.

CHAPTER 13

'THE MYSTERY OF THE MISSING DISCOURSE': CRIME FICTION READERSHIPS AND QUESTIONS OF TASTE[1]

Sue Turnbull

INTRODUCTION

I've long been fascinated by what people read. While others might confess to a penchant for peeking in the bathroom cupboard, I've always been the one sidling along the bookshelves sizing up my hosts as I scrutinise their reading matter. Indeed, I've just had one of those holidays in a beach house owned by people I don't know which left me with some delightful speculations about their taste in books. On the same shelf as a copy of Franz Kafka's *The Trial* (in its pristine unopened condition) was a biography of Richard Nixon (used) and a well thumbed suntan-oily Judith Krantz, not to mention a collected Agatha Christie. I warmed to these people in their eclecticism and instinctively felt I understood the Kafka, the kind of book one always intends to read, though probably not on holiday.

In other words, I know I've always been guilty of making judgments about people on the basis of what they read. As a student of English Literature at London University in the late sixties, I used to be a literary snob, conspicuously reading Dostoevsky on the bus as an aesthetic style statement. As a consequence of this snobbery, I had some miserable transatlantic flights in my youth because I chose to travel with the kind of reading matter I'd like to be seen reading rather than with what I actually wanted to read. But I'm over that now.

Now, as a student of popular culture, I'm much more interested in the politics of taste, who gets to define what is 'good' taste and why, in everything from our choice of reading matter to what we watch on the television. And I'm interested in the moral dimension implicit in such judgments of good taste and bad, and the ways in which such judgments become part of our assessment of others. But most of all I'm interested in what can be said about taste, especially when people are called on to justify a love of soap opera, science fiction, the horror film or, in this particular instance, crime fiction. In other words, I'm interested in the discourses of value which are in circulation about crime fiction as a popular form.

---

1 An earlier version of this paper was presented as the keynote address to the 'Where we R @: Media 99', Ninth Biennial Media Education Conference, University of Auckland, New Zealand, 14–17 January 1999.

It would seem that what people can say about their taste depends to a large extent on their understanding of how their preference articulates with broader questions of cultural value, and their ability to justify that preference with regard to such perceived values. Let me try and make this issue of discourse and value explicit with reference to my own study of taste conducted in 1997 on the Australian readership network, *Sisters in Crime*, of which I have been a member and convenor for the last eight years. As I hope to demonstrate, this study reveals that asking people why they read crime fiction may leave us with more questions than answers about how readers' tastes relate to real world issues of crime, law and order.

SETTING THE SCENE

The American *Sisters in Crime* was formed in 1986 by crime writer Sara Paretsky with the express purpose of lobbying publishers and reviewers to pay more attention to women's crime writing. The Australian *Sisters in Crime*, inspired by Paretsky's move, was launched in September 1991 during the Australian Feminist Book Fortnight, and shares a similar charter, printed on every membership leaflet, press release and letterhead.[2] This states that *Sisters in Crime* exists in order: 'To promote a forum for discussion of women's crime fiction and mystery fiction, to further the careers of women in the mystery/crime field, to correct imbalances in the treatment of women writers, and to promote recognition of their contribution to the field.'

There are about 400 members of *Sisters in Crime* Australia-wide with 'chapters' in each State, which come in and out of focus as people take responsibility for organising events in their own area. Of these chapters, the Sydney Sisters have maintained the strongest presence, even putting out their own local newsletter to complement the national newsletter emanating from Melbourne. The Sisters in Melbourne are, however, at the centre of the hub, holding up to six events a year attended by numbers varying from about 20 (for a business meeting) to over 300 or so for one of the more well known authors such as Minette Walters, Lynda La Plante or Lisa Scottoline, an American ex-trial lawyer blurbed as the 'female John Grisham', whose visit to Melbourne I shall discuss later.

And I'm usually the one up the front, dressed in my best Melbourne black, reading the raffle ticket numbers into a badly tuned mike before interviewing the guest or chairing the discussion. It's a role I've grown into, somehow becoming the public face of *Sisters in Crime* while secretly wondering if I've taken the notion of participant observation a little too far.

---

2   The first issue of the *Sisters in Crime Newsletter* (No 1, Summer 1991) describes the origins of the group and also contains an interview with Sarah Paretsky.

Of course, I didn't know I was going to end up researching the organisation of which I have become a part, it just sort of dawned on me like a ton of bricks that I was in a privileged spot to do a bit of audience research, inspired by the realisation that at our meetings the Sisters so often end up disagreeing about the literary or cultural value of the books they are promoting.

In this regard, I have to confess to being a very active participant in these debates. That's the way I started out and it's too late now for me to disappear into the wallpaper. My literary tastes and cultural values are on the table along with everyone else's. However, any anxiety that I might have had about my own influence in these matters was completely allayed after administering a survey of the *Sisters in Crime* membership in 1997, when it became apparent that even though the majority of the 131 respondents were in the same age bracket as myself and most had had access to post secondary education, there were very few whose taste in crime fiction seemed to accord with my own. What we did seem to share, however, was a knowledge and implementation of the same discourses of cultural value when called upon to justify our taste for crime.

These discourses I have identified as:

- a discourse about the literary value of crime fiction;

- a discourse about cultural value of the 'real' in fiction;

- a discourse about the political value of crime fiction;

- a discourse about the compensatory value of reading crime;

and were particularly apparent in the open ended answers to Question 22 on the initial survey questionnaire, which asked simply: 'Why do you like reading crime fiction?' This question was answered both briefly, 'Because it has a STORY' (Respondent 5, hereafter R5) or at great length – one single spaced side of A4 (R131). It is upon these answers that I shall be basing much of the following analysis, acknowledging that these written responses may well have been conditioned by each respondent's knowledge that this was a study being conducted by an academic who was also a crime reader and one of them, with whatever implications that might have for the ways in which they might frame their responses. There is, of course, much more to be said about the chosen methodology and its limitations but this would merit a whole chapter in itself on the politics of audience research, which I will reserve for another time and place. For the moment, let me try and frame some of the issues arising from this study, which I hope will illuminate the complexity of the value systems in circulation about crime fiction.

THE DISCOURSE OF LITERARY VALUE

Whatever cultural value the respondents wanted to attribute to crime fiction, there was a sense in which many of their responses were framed in such a way as to take account of a discourse of literary value in which crime fiction is something other than what is identified as literature: 'I read them as fluff, when I'm too tired/exhausted mentally to read something else' (R15). Or: 'It's like watching an OK movie – you don't have to think. It's sort of like junk food for the brain' (R34).

The discourse of literary value from which these two comments arise has an exceedingly long history, one it would seem almost as long as the history of crime fiction itself. If we take Edgar Allen Poe's short story *The Murders in the Rue Morgue*, published in 1841, as an arguable starting point, then it can be argued that the growth of crime fiction as a genre develops in tandem with such social factors as the emergence of a reading public with access to cheap mass produced magazines and books, available at the chain stores, lending libraries and railway station book stalls which were a product of the industrial revolution in Britain.

The consequences of technological change and modernisation in the 19th century are only too familiar to students of media who are well acquainted with a version of mass media history, which locates the emergence of a discourse of anxiety about the mass media to this time. This discourse derives from anxiety about a notional vast mass of consumers with too much money, too much time and not enough taste or moral fibre to distinguish the purely sensational from the asethetically good. Mathew Arnold described this hypothetical mass as the 'barbarians at the gate' in his influential critical study, *Culture and Anarchy* published in 1869, while Gustave Le Bon imagined the mass as a mindless mob in his seminal study, *The Crowd*, with its ominous sub-title 'A Study of the *Popular* Mind' (my italics), published in 1896. Such anxiety found vivid expression in subsequent criticism of the mass culture enabled by new media technologies (such as the photograph, the radio and the cinema) voiced by both cultural conservatives and left wing intellectuals. It should, however, be remembered that these anxieties were initially expressed about what people were reading, from broadsheet newspapers to penny dreadfuls, dime novels and magazines.

Hence in 1927, the former British Minister of Education, Lord Eustace Percy, addressed the Joint Session of the Associated Booksellers and National Book Council to this effect:

> Our purpose is not to create or stimulate the reading habit. Nearly everyone in this country already has the habit and has it very badly. It has been discovered that the greatest 'mind opiate' in the world is carrying the eye along a certain number of printed lines in succession ... The habit of reading is one of the most

interesting psychological features of the present day. Discomfort and exhaustion seem only to increase the need for the printed word. A friend, in describing the advance of one of the columns in East Africa during the war, has remarked how his men, sitting drenched and almost without food round the camp fire, would pass from hand to hand a scrap of a magazine cover, in order that each man might rest his eyes for a moment on the printed word. One of the great evils of present day reading is that it discourages thought.[3]

As a teacher of media, I find these sentiments oddly comforting. Substitute any more recent media technology for the dreaded magazine cover mentioned above, and you have the dystopian argument, which has been voiced ever since about the corrupting and mind-numbing effects of the media.

Percy's speech is quoted at length in QD Leavis' 1932 study entitled *Fiction and the Reading Public* in which she suggests the four primary functions of reading fiction to be:

- to pass time not unpleasantly;

- to obtain vicarious satisfaction or compensation for life;

- to obtain assistance in the business of living;

- to enrich the quality of living by extending, deepening, refining, co-ordinating experience.[4]

Of these functions, it is clear in the ensuing commentary, that only the fourth function, in QD's opinion, is of any real cultural or social value and that reading without any 'artistic, moral, or informative purpose' is nothing less than a form of 'dissipation'.[5] What QD Leavis thinks people should be reading is therefore exactly what her husband Frank was teaching at Cambridge University in the thirties and at London University in the sixties, and what I was taught to value as the great tradition of English literature, which included such writers as Henry James, DH Lawrence, Virginia Woolf, and James Joyce. Reading novels by these authors is perceived to be a morally improving form of labour; reading detective novels for mental relaxation is not.

It is, therefore, interesting to note how a contemporary crime writer saw the function of crime fiction in relation to the kind of modern novel championed by the Leavises. Writing only four years earlier in 1928, Dorothy L Sayers made a virtue of the detective story's refusal to confront the reader with too many home truths:

---

3 Quoted in Leavis, 1932, p 56.

4 *Ibid*, p 48.

5 *Ibid*, pp 49–50.

... make no mistake about it, the detective story is part of the literature of escape, and not of expression. We read tales of domestic unhappiness because that is the kind of thing which happens to us; but when these things gall too close to the sore, we fly to mystery and adventure because they do not as a rule happen to us.[6]

Writing in *The Atlantic Monthly* one year later, American academic, Marjorie Nicolson, proposed a rather different kind of escapism suggesting: 'Yes, the detective story does constitute escape; but it is escape not from life, but from literature'.[7]

The literature from which Nicolson is escaping she identifies as the literature of emotion, subjectivity and formlessness, in other words, what had come to be called, the modern psychological novel – and there were clearly echoes of this discourse apparent in the *Sisters in Crime* responses:

> I also like to read crime as a break from reading 'serious' literature, the day or two spent reading a good crime novel are a real escape and very good for my mental health (R21).

> [I like reading crime as a] break from concentration of work, research, good literature – which can't be said for much modern writing (R23).

Sometimes, the respondents revealed themselves to be in a state of conflict as a result of these still virulent discourses of literary value, overwhelmed by the moral implications of a perceived distinction between reading for pleasure and reading as intellectual work:

> As a child/adolescent, I read for escape – anything. As an adult I read for entertainment (fiction) and to make sense of my/the world (non-fiction). The best read is a book that makes me think. Crime Fiction is largely escapism, 'entertainment' (reading about murder is hardly entertainment hence the quotes!) but it rarely makes me think. I am therefore unable to shake off the feeling that it's 'lightweight' not really 'literature' (R60).

As a long term reader of crime fiction, I find myself genuinely puzzled by the suggestion that reading crime fiction rarely makes one think, since I find the opposite to be true, and am therefore at a loss to understand how a respondent who cites her favourite authors as Sara Paretsky, Sue Grafton and Minette Walters, all of whom write complex and often politically challenging books, can make this claim. Other respondents who cite the same authors argue the opposite case, that one of the pleasures they derive from reading crime novels is that they are 'thought provoking' (R8); or 'intellectually stimulating' (R35), etc. Clearly something is going on here for Respondent 60 in terms of the cultural value attached to notions of literature as opposed to crime fiction that is overriding other considerations. Is it

---

6   Sayers, 1947, p 109.
7   Nicolson, 1947, p 114.

because she knows she is addressing an academic who she thinks will value reading literature over reading for entertainment? Note also how worried she is about the suggestion that reading murder mysteries might be entertaining, another, and frequently recurring moral conflict experienced by the *Sisters in Crime* readers.

There are, of course, many different ways of committing murder in crime fiction and Raymond Chandler was totally disparaging of the kinds of murder committed in the genteel English detective novel of what is frequently referred to as the Golden Age of crime fiction between the two World Wars. Making a claim for more 'realism' in crime fiction, in his much quoted essay 'The Simple Art of Murder', Chandler characterised the readers of what has come to be called the 'cosy' crime novel, in which the murder is frequently bloodless and usually occurs off stage, as: '... flustered old ladies – of both sexes (or no sex) and almost all ages – who like their murders scented with magnolia blossoms and do not care to be reminded that murder is an act of infinite cruelty'.[8]

Note the gendering of the gutless reader with no stomach for the real thing. This feminisation of the reader of popular fiction has a long history. In his essay 'Mass Culture as Woman: Modernism's Other', Andreas Huyssens discusses Gustave Flaubert's *Madame Bovary* as a case in point: '... woman (Madame Bovary) is positioned as a reader of inferior literature – subjective, emotional and passive – while man (Flaubert) emerges as a writer of genuine, authentic literature – objective, ironic and in control of his aesthetic means.'[9]

Chandler's comment therefore reveals the persistent gendering of a discourse about the cultural and moral value of 'realism' (the genuine and authentic voice of the objective and ironic male narrator), as opposed to something that might be identified as 'escapism' as preferred by the flustered lily-livered *female* reader. This is a discourse which extends to the valuation of news, current affairs and documentary as well as something called 'realism' in the representation of crime on screen or on the page: the valuation (in what passes for television criticism in the press) of such series as *Prime Suspect* over *Murder, She Wrote*, *The Practice* over *Ally McBeal*, and it is to this discourse I shall now turn.

THE DISCOURSE OF THE 'REAL'

Discourses of the real are as confused and confusing in relation to crime fiction as they are in relation to any other representational form. At one level

---

8   Chandler, 1947, p 237.
9   Huyssens, 1986, pp 189–90.

we have the rather basic, though misleading distinction, between something called crime fiction and something that is labelled true crime. I suggest that this distinction is misleading because true crime covers a broad spectrum of story telling which ranges from the novelistic endeavours of Truman Capote's *In Cold Blood*[10] or John Berendt's *Midnight in the Garden of Good and Evil*[11] to the banal descriptions of murder and mayhem recounted by the notorious Australian former criminal, Chopper Read. And in each case we know that these accounts are storied representations of something that is supposed to have happened. What complicates this matter is that from Poe's *The Mystery of Marie Roget* (first published in 1842) onwards, crime fiction has often been based on events that have taken place in the real world. While the distinction between the real and the fictional may be quite hard to sustain at a philosophical level, publishers and book shop owners all seem to agree on the need to distinguish between true crime and crime fiction in order to market and sell them to readers who know what they prefer.

It might be noted here that when I asked the male owner of one large London crime bookstore who bought true crime, he informed me that it was mainly middle-aged ladies with rape fantasies; the female owner of an American crime book store told me it was largely dirty old men in raincoats, and the owner of an Australian store suggested it was consumed principally by nurses on night duty. Whatever the truth of the matter (and I'm working on it) true crime seems to be read most avidly by the crime fiction writers I have interviewed as an important aspect of their research, rather than their readers who prefer what one *Sisters in Crime* reader described as the 'safety barrier' of fiction (R7).

Indeed, true crime proved to be far and away the least popular sub-genre of crime amongst the *Sisters in Crime* readers with one respondent clearly identifying the intellectual challenge of crime fiction as part of its pleasures, but not the crime itself:

> 'I like reading crime because it makes me think. I enjoy the challenge of trying to solve the "who dunnit" factor. Also if there is a technical perspective, that is, gadgets, gizmos, etc it keeps me interested. I don't particularly like true crime as I'd prefer to keep the "victim" faceless' (R8).

Keeping the victim faceless would seem to be one way of avoiding precisely the confronting aspect of crime fiction which Chandler perceives as one of its moral imperatives, and indeed there did seem to be considerable anxiety about the 'violence' of crime as expressed in crime fiction.

In an open ended question which asked respondents to identify what they 'did not' enjoy in crime fiction, the violence they didn't like was variously described as unnecessary, gratuitous, excessive, graphic, and sexual. Also objected to were sadism, cruelty, and gore. As if to contradict this finding, the favourite authors of the group appeared to be Minette

---

10 Capote, 1965.
11 Berendt, 1994.

Walters and Patricia Cornwell, who frequently deal with violence, which might be described in any of these ways. How then to account for this apparent contradiction?

Clearly, the problem presented by crime fiction is the need to justify the pleasure that derives from reading stories in which murder figures largely with the need to distance oneself from any suspicion that such pleasure might depend upon the obscenity of murder itself. The writers of the Golden Age had this one sewn up; they weren't after the real thing at all. Here's EM Wrong writing in 1926:

> What we want in our detective fiction is not a semblance of real life, where murder is infrequent and petty larceny common, but deep mystery and conflicting clues ... Moreover, murder involves an intenser motive than any other peacetime activity: the drama is keyed from the start for the murderer is playing for the highest stake he has.[12]

In this analysis, murder is seen simply as a narrative ploy, a way to make the story more intense and exciting, it's a requirement of the genre, a necessary element in the formal structure of the detective/crime story. At one level, many of the *Sisters in Crime* readers know this and are exquisitely aware of the requirements of the genre. However, there is also genuine anxiety about murder as a social fact and an uncomfortable suspicion of any pleasure they might derive, or be thought to derive, from reading about it.

Hence the conflict in a deployment of the discourse of the real between the perceived need to distance oneself from the violence of crime by describing the genre as unrealistic, at the same time as there is a contradictory desire to draw upon the moral value of the real in order to justify one's reading of crime. To this end, some *Sisters in Crime* readers applauded crime fiction for its 'gritty realism' (R10), its 'social commentary' (R25), the insights it can provide into character and motivation (R106) and the ways in which it tries to 'explain the dark elements/undercurrents of society' (R28). In this analysis, crime fiction approaches the status of social documentary and reading it becomes a form of sociological and anthropological investigation: a worthy endeavour indeed.

One aspect of the commitment of crime fiction to this level of documentary truth is the careful delineation of place. I have written elsewhere about the role of the map in crime fiction, in particular the mapback series produced by the Dell publishing company from 1942–51 and the continuing popularity of the map in the works of crime writers such as Minette Walters.[13] What was clear in the responses of many *Sisters in Crime* was that a 'strong sense of place', often involving a form of armchair cultural tourism, was definitely one of the pleasures of reading crime: 'I have

---

12 Wrong, 1947, p 25.
13 Turnbull, 1999.

experienced Paris with Maigret, Amsterdam with Van der Valk, New York with Nero Wolf and Archie Goodwin, Oxford with Harriet Vane, the California Coast with Kinsey, etc, etc' (R44). *Sisters in Crime* readers therefore wanted their fiction to be realistic, in terms of place, character, motive, and procedures, but it must not be 'too real' in terms of the representation of the violence associated with the enactment of murder.

I would argue that there is gendered aspect to this anxiety about the representation of violence, an anxiety that at one level has to do with the frequency with which women are represented as the victims of violent crime, in crime fiction as well as in other forms of media. Such representations are in direct contradiction to the frequently cited police statistics (in Australia, the US and Britain), which suggest that it is babies and young men who are the most likely victims of violent assault. While crime fiction may therefore distort the reality of women as victims, it may also distort the role of women as heroes, though this latter distortion was one of the many justifications given by the *Sisters in Crime* respondents for their pleasure in reading crime, which brings us to the discourse of political value.

THE DISCOURSE OF POLITICAL VALUE

Given the feminist principles outlined in the *Sisters in Crime* charter, it is hardly surprising that many of the respondents in this self-selecting group explicitly referred to their preference for feminist crime fiction emerging since the late seventies featuring idealised strong female heroes: 'Feminist crime fiction seems to be the one place where one reliably finds strong, funny, clever, female characters. Within the imaginary world of crime fiction, women can do things that are often denied them in real life and thus in more realistic fiction' (R88).

A number of readers specifically mentioned the political value of lesbian crime fiction even relating them to their own political career, and I quote a length from the following response because it demonstrates the overlap between the discourse of the real and the discourse of political value:

> I started reading these books in the early 80s. I started teaching them also. For reasons unbeknownst to me school support centres (that is, that supported curriculum initiatives of their group of schools run by the ministry of educ) were full of dykes. They stocked a lot of these books, that is, Women's Press, Seal Press, Virago. This was a time when there was govt support for equal opp issues, gender equity stuff, racism stuff, etc. All schools had an e/o co-ordinator (I was one) that used the schools support centres. I started borrowing books from there. I had not read very much previous to that. I'm from a working class background and felt that reading really had nothing to do with me! Didn't speak to me. Prior to them I'd read a bit of lesbian fiction, short

stories, or feminist theory or what I absolutely had to for my degree. One of the earliest ones that got me in was *Murder in the Collective* by Barbara Wilson: If you've ever been involved in a feminist org and seen how collective, co-operative, inclusive and accommodating they are you may well understand how someone could be murdered. Particularly if there are lesbians involved and everyone's sleeping with everyone (I'm not speaking from experience on that point). Anyway, I found that book exciting, funny and relevant. I went in search of others. Some years later B Wilson wrote a sequel called *Sisters on the Road*. To my horror, the hero was brutally raped and in great lengthy detail. I was pissed off by this treatment of the character and quickly axed B Wilson from my interest list. It brought to my attention the expectations I had of these books and to be the loser was not one of them. I think it was unforgivable really (R74).

In the discourse of political value, crime fiction is therefore judged primarily in terms of its perceived politics. Thus, Sally Munt's *Murder by the Book* works through the history of the crime novel written by women assessing the novels of every female crime writer from the mid-18th century onwards on the strength of her feminist agenda.[14] It's a worthy and somewhat depressing scenario, which concludes, with praise for the postmodernist crime novel of Sarah Schulman who deploys:

> ... the metafictional framing devices and parodic forms of postmodernism to problematise further modern, urban, sexual, racial, and gender identities, deconstructing the binaries such as self/other, and truth/fiction. She replaces the linear teleological form of the detective story, rejects the male narrative of transcendance, and regenders/resexualises the hard-boiled novel as female and lesbian ...[15]

In other words, if to transcend is to succeed as a man, then such transcendence renders conventional crime fiction (which depends on a linear narrative and the triumph of the hero) an unsuitable genre for a feminist.

This is, of course, a real problem for those readers who like their feminised 'masculine' heroes, and the gender reversals implicit in feminist appropriations of the genre, particularly the hard-boiled private eye novel:

> The books I like feature a strong, independent female character, who is also aware of her foibles. She gets those – I wish I'd said that – lines and to beat the tough guys, but she's also dealing with unpaid bills or a clapped out car – things we can identify with. They also give a sense of problem solving in a pro-active way and therefore a sense of control over the confusing and difficult realities of life (R105).

---

14 Munt, 1994.

15 *Ibid*, p 206.

Munt's comments, and those of the Sisters cited above, point to another contradiction in the discourse of political value. While Munt values crime fiction which sacrifices the generic form of the novel to its politics, the respondent above finds the form itself to be of political value through its commitment to problem solving and the move towards narrative resolution. In other words, many readers valued crime fiction precisely because it offered a vision of a better world in which problems are solved, and a definite conclusion arrived at. Another rewarding aspect of such a conclusion was the acknowledgment that this frequently involved retributive justice: 'I believe in fair play, justice (not necessarily legal justice), and wrongdoers being made to pay in appropriate fashion for their misdeeds. Also I believe in equality and opportunity for women. Crime fiction written by women with a woman protagonist usually feature these ideals' (R17).

The idealism of the feminist crime novel and the better, fairer world it offered was but one of many criteria which the *Sisters in Crime* respondents used as a justification for their pleasure in the genre, but it serves to introduce the fourth category of discourse with which I want to deal with here, the discourse of compensation.

THE DISCOURSE OF COMPENSATION

A number of respondents justified their reading of crime as a compensation for the pressure they experienced in their daily lives: 'How do I read crime fiction? In batches, at those times in my world of work when "chaos" is unbearable and the ability to pursue problems/issues to suitable resolutions seems impossible. There is a standing query among my small circle of friends/colleagues: "Is it a three or four who-done-it-week?"' (R22). References to the chaos of stressful reality and the need to escape by reading about a focussed world in which one problem is addressed and pursued to a logical conclusion were frequent. The sense of an ending in crime fiction was therefore much appreciated: 'One of the things that appeals is a definite conclusion. So much in life just drags on and on that it's nice, when reading, to get to an ending that is satisfying' (R15). That one reader was aware of this particular compensatory discourse, but not sure if she bought into it, was also apparent:

> I've heard it [pleasure in reading crime] explained as a response to a modern 'chaotic' lifestyle. Previously women 'escaped' into romance novels. The 'knight in shining armour' is less realistic as a solution to day to day pressures and the shape of the crime novel ... problem, investigation, solution meets a need to feel that life can be controlled. Seems a bit 'deep' as an explanation when I'd always thought it was simple enjoyment but, at the same time, it has a logical ring about it (R95).

This last comment I want to dwell on because it seems to me to be doing a number of things. Firstly, the author is very careful to contextualise her comments in terms of already existing notions of cultural value ('I've heard it explained as ...'). In so doing, Respondent 95 demonstrates a clear understanding of the conventions of formulaic fiction from romance to crime, what literary theorist Frank Kermode in the aptly named *The Sense of an Ending* described as 'the consoling plot'.[16] In the end, however, while she would like to assert that crime fiction is about 'simple enjoyment', she acknowledges that a 'deep' explanation of its pleasures may have some validity. In other words, this respondent is aware of the discourses of cultural value attached to crime reading which depend upon a denigration of the compensatory pleasures of formulaic fiction accused of offering little in the way of political engagement with chaotic reality. Crime fiction is finally assessed in terms of its relationship to a notion of the real and found wanting – but is this fair? What is missing from these discourses of value about crime fiction?

THE MISSING DISCOURSE

In his study of the intersections between law and popular culture, Richard Sherwin identifies three kinds of truth in what he describes as 'legal storytelling', factual truth, higher or legal truth and symbolic truth.[17] While Sherwin is specifically talking about the kinds of narratives that are employed in the legal process of the courts, I want to take his notion of symbolic truth and argue for its potential role in explaining why and how people read crime fiction. If, according to Sherwin, *factual truth* is about historical accuracy and empirical evidence, while *higher or legal truth* refers to the abstract concepts and principles of law, *symbolic truth* transcends both because it speaks to our deepest cultural beliefs, values and aspirations.[18]

In other words, there is a truth in stories (let's say in crime fiction), which we recognise not because these stories are 'real', but because they are 'true' in so far as they address our conscious and unconscious desires. Setting aside for the moment the vexed question of whether or not it is a 'good thing' to have such desires addressed, the key issue for the success of a crime novel is how well it can balance our commitment to the 'real' world problem of crime with our desire for stories which are 'true' to our desires, for as Sherwin puts it although 'we crave enchantment', yet we 'fear deceit'.[19]

---

16   Kermode, 1970, p 31.
17   Sherwin, 2000, p 49.
18   *Ibid*, p 50.
19   *Ibid*, p 205.

Listening to legal thriller writer, Lisa Scottoline, talk about her work at a *Sisters in Crime* event in Melbourne provided a valuable insight into the way in which she endeavours to acknowledge her readers' need for enchantment while being keen to disabuse them of any desire to deceive. Indeed, the first detail you encounter about Scottoline in the publicity material sent out by her publishers or on her website (scottoline.com), is the fact that her claim to authenticity as a writer of legal thrillers depends on her seven years' experience as a trial lawyer. Furthermore, when addressed directly about whether the central plot mechanism of her crime series, an all woman legal firm set in Philadelphia, could really exist, Scottoline was immediately prepared with the 'factual truth':

> Absolutely! There's five women only law firms in Philadelphia now. They started out getting a lot of work from the government and they were called Women Only Law Firm and their acronym was WOLF. It was like they got government work because they were women owned, like minority owned. I have some good friends who started one and if you go into their offices they have pictures of wolves everywhere, you know they are 'women who run with the wolves'.[20]

While Scottoline was eager to defend her crime novels in terms of their 'factual truth', she was also keen to make it clear that she was aware of her reader's investment in her fictions, particularly in the character of Bennie Rosato, the head of her women only legal firm:

> I met a woman in a library who started telling me about Bennie Rosato and all the things that Bennie does and at one point she mentioned the perfume that Bennie wears. And I thought, I never specify a perfume, in fact I don't think she wears a perfume, she's not the perfume type. When I questioned her, the woman in the library told me all these other things I hadn't written about this character. At first I thought 'Gee this is weird'; and then I understood how people bring their own stuff to a novel.[21]

Perhaps we will never know what symbolic truth Scottoline's woman in the library recognised in Bennie Rosato; all we have is an indication of an intense investment in a fictional character, an investment which is not unusual in popular culture where fictional characters, especially women hero figures such as TV heroes *Xena: Warrior Princess* or *Buffy the Vampire Slayer*, can inspire enormous quantities of fan generated fiction on the web.[22] While these characters are superhuman and therefore 'unreal', they are clearly venerated because of their mythic power, the fact that they speak to symbolic desires which fans articulate in their own (often erotic) stories, or slash fiction, as it is known.[23]

20 Scottoline, 2001, p 31.
21 *Ibid*, pp 30–31.
22 Gwenllian-Jones, 2000.
23 Jenkins, 1992.

Clearly, the discourse which was missing in the above study of crime fiction readers was a discourse which would have enabled the participants to speak about crime fiction in relation to some notion of symbolic truth – in other words, how the narrative form and content of a crime novel articulated with their own deepest desires about crime, law, order and social justice. The only traces of such a discourse to be found were in the frequent allusions to the importance of a female protagonist in the feminist crime novel as a wish fulfilling dream – or to the compensations of formula and the ways in which crime fiction may satisfy a need for order and rationality in a chaotic postmodern world. But then the respondents always ran up against their anxieties about justifying a taste for the fanciful and the escapist: the perception that crime fiction must be of lesser value precisely because it does not always deal with the world as it is – but rather the world as it is imagined.

Readers of crime fiction can't win in terms of current cultural discourses of value. While notions of order and rationality are most definitely out, postmodern uncertainty and openness are definitely in, everywhere from legal theory to literary taste. And yet crime fiction continues to rate, and the membership of *Sisters in Crime* continues to swell, largely I would argue because crime fiction continues to concern itself with stories which satisfy our need for symbolic truth, not only in terms of their content, but also in terms of their form. As Dorothy L Sayers wrote: 'There is one respect, at least, in which the detective story has an advantage over every kind of novel. It possesses an Aristotelian perfection of beginning, middle and end. A definite and single problem is set, worked out, and solved; its conclusion is not arbitrarily conditioned by marriage or death.'[24]

With reference to this last comment, let me include here Sayers' footnote directed to a producer of a different kind of novel: 'This should appeal to Mr EM Forster, who is troubled by the irrational structure of the novel from this point of view. Unhappily, he has openly avowed himself "too priggish" to enjoy detective stories. This is bad luck indeed.'[25] The critique of the detective story implicit in the anecdote about Forster brings us back to the discourse of literary value, a discourse clearly present in the responses of the readers in this study, women whose formal education in English was undoubtedly as Leavis-driven as my own. It is apparent that the legacy of this discourse is still with us, with *Sisters in Crime* members still bogged down in accounting for their taste in crime fiction in terms of its status as a literary genre, its authentic 'realism', its perceived political value, or even its formulaic structure.

The answer to the question why people like reading crime fiction and how this relates to their experience of crime, law and justice in the 'real' world, will continue to remain a mystery – at least until the value of the

24 Sayers, 1947, p 101.
25 *Ibid*, p 101.

symbolic truth to be found crime fiction becomes both expressible and accountable. Such a conclusion begs a sequel, and the elaboration of a discourse of symbolic value, which can articulate the repressed desires addressed by popular culture, desires which may eventually be productive of cultural transformation. Whether those transformations are to the benefit or not of a more democratic and fairer society depends on such desires and symbolic truths at least being spoken and debated. In order to change the world, one first has to imagine it differently. Crime fiction, like popular culture in general, offers readers both utopian and dystopian fantasies with which to plot the transformation.

CHAPTER 14

THE ILLUSION OF THE 'REAL' IN IAN CALLINAN'S *THE LAWYER AND THE LIBERTINE*[1]

Margaret Thornton

Fiction will never again be a mirror held toward the future, but a desperate rehallucination of the past.[2]

INTRODUCTION

This chapter explores the nexus between the 'real' and the fictional through a consideration of *The Lawyer and the Libertine*, a novel by Australian High Court Judge, Ian Callinan. It addresses the homologous relationship between masculinity, law and public life, out of which conventional images of 'the lawyer' emerge. It shows how popular culture, popular fiction, in particular, plays a role in affirming such images.

While we are persistently warned against extrapolating from the fictional to the real, it can be argued, drawing on a strand of the work of Jean Baudrillard, that simulacra are 'true'. That is, in many aspects of life, particularly where change has been dramatic, some sectors of society prefer to cleave to fictionalised representations rather than accept the nature of change that has occurred. The lingering antipathy towards the entry of women into the legal profession, which has disturbed a time honoured masculinist monopoly, illustrates this proposition.

Masculinity can be imagined as a permanent *trompe l'oeil* to legal practice and public life. Its graphic presence, supported by key symbols of fraternity, including boys' schools, sport, militarism, and club life, cause it to become the hyperreal, that is, more real than the real. In contrast, the feminised hyperreal is one that is eroticised and corporealised. Just as women appear to be making inroads into the legal profession in 'real life', a recuperation of a phallocentric past is effected through the creation of a hyperreal.

---

1 Callinan, 1997. This chapter is an elaboration of my review of *The Lawyer and the Libertine*. See Thornton, 1998b. I thank the Sydney Law Review for permission to use some of the ideas developed in the review.

2 Baudrillard, 1994b, p 122.

FICTION AS THE HYPERREAL

The relationship between law and the image is a tantalising one. Where do the shared symbols and meanings come from that produce the commonly understood perceptions of 'the lawyer' or 'the judge' of the legal culture? While lawyers appear frequently in the news media, their roles tend to be confined to the disembodied voices behind the visages of more newsworthy figures, reifying the facilitative role of law, or lawyer as hired gun. The most compelling media images are fictionalised – such as *Rumpole of the Bailey*, *LA Law* and *Ally McBeal* of television fame, and the figures that populate the genres of legal and crime fiction. These are the images that are most likely to have shaped law students' understanding of the legal culture and the *dramatis personae* of the legal profession. So pervasive are these images of the legal culture and its primary players that they have become the hyperreal.

The master theorist of the reality of illusion in contemporary culture is Jean Baudrillard. His theory is that images, or simulacra, have to be invoked in order to make an unknowable world 'real' because 'the reality of the world is a total illusion'.[3] The mimetic act of turning the illusory into the 'real' is effected insidiously, not by violence, but by seduction, as the viewer/reader is bombarded with images, which cause the line between representation and reality to implode. Baudrillard builds upon Marshall McLuhan's idea that the content of any medium is always another medium, captured most famously by McLuhan's aphorism 'the medium is the message'.[4] According to Baudrillard, we, 'the masses' are rendered inert through fascination with the illusory world of the hyperreal. In the Baudrillardian world, there appears to be little space for individual human agency because the force that we are up against is so powerful as to be virtually irresistible. In any case, 'reality' is unattainable; it is a figment of the human imagination. It is artifice that is at the very heart of the real: 'The rationality that one has to invoke in order to make the world 'real' is really just a product of the power of thought itself, which is itself totally anti-rational and anti-materialist'.[5] Postmodern scholarship teaches us that we are all subjectively engaged in producing our own reality. Hence, the attempt by any theorist, including, ironically, Baudrillard himself, to make sense of the world is doomed as there is no such thing as objectivity, for the 'real' is just as evanescent as the image.

Baudrillard's critique of contemporary culture is threatening and extreme, so it is not surprising that he is dismissed as a crank and a crackpot

---

3   Baudrillard, 1987, p 44.
4   Baudrillard, 1990, p 88. See also, McLuhan, 1967, pp 15–16; Stearn, 1968; McLuhan and Fiore, 1967.
5   Baudrillard, 1987, p 44.

– 'a French gimmick-monger'.[6] What's more, he describes himself as a nihilist: 'He who strikes with meaning is killed by meaning.'[7] The implications of Baudrillard's ideas for law and legal theory, at least of the positivist kind, as elaborated upon in Chapter 1 above, would appear to be devastating. Certainty, stability and closure, all encompassed by liberal legalism, are threatened by the dangerousness of the image.

The idea that the simulacra of popular fiction can become the real, that is, the hyperreal, which is more real than the real, is tantalising. The suggestion is that because the real is no longer what it used to be, nostalgia can summon up a new meaning by revisioning the 'real'. I want to apply the simulacra as the hyperreal to a consideration of Ian Callinan's novel, *The Lawyer and the Libertine*, which is unlikely to gain fame as an elegant work of fiction, but *because* the author is a High Court judge. The novel purports to capture a slice of legal culture that is presented as real and is accorded the imprimatur of legitimacy because it is authored by a judge.

Indeed, most readers are bound to want to know what light the book sheds on the workings of a 'real' judicial mind, and the extent to which such a book might be useful in predicting the outcome of 'real' decisions. Before even commencing the novel, then, some readers will have been seduced into believing that they are about to enter a real world, which has been produced by a real judge. I initially toyed with the idea of exploring the linkages between Callinan's fiction and his judgments, as I thought that it would be worthwhile to contrast two types of legal imagining. I was particularly interested in the way that the 'real' was constructed in the respective genres of creative fiction and judgment writing, or what some would consider to be another type of fiction, but abandoned the project. Prediction is always a fraught exercise, and I am reminded of the questionable pursuit of jurimetrics, with its tendentious belief that adjudication could have predictive value if only the art of predicting were to be made more scientific – that is, if closure could be effected in respect of human behaviour. A colleague who spent some years plotting judicial decisions on a graph finally decided that the entire exercise was futile, for there was no way that one could capture and measure the myriad human variables that an accurate predictive instrument would require. In any case, as we all know, human beings simply do not always act in ways that are predictable. The 'real' defies measurement or, if one accepts the Baudrillardian proposition, there is no such thing as the real to be measured anyway.

Callinan's novel is not about the adjudicative process, but it has a lot to say about the legal culture. It presents the reader with a picture of an extraordinary masculinist and homosocial world populated by lawyers, corporate tycoons and public figures. This picture mirrors what we

---

6   Goshorn, 1992.
7   Baudrillard, 1994b, p 161.

understand to be the real world of power, thereby suggesting an explanation as to why the legal profession has been so resistant to the acceptance of women and 'others' as authoritative members of the jurisprudential community. We see the bald ambition, greed, jealousy, and vindictiveness, as well as the narrowness, of professional men as they pursue money, power and 'success' to the virtual exclusion of all else. Having conducted a study of women in the legal profession in Australia,[8] I found that the book supported my thesis that the fraternal ties linking Anglocentricity, class, boys' schools, sport, militarism, heterosexuality and corporate wealth effectively combine to produce normative images of law that subtly relegate women and racialised 'others' to fringe dweller status. This theorisation challenges the liberal progressivist understanding that it is just a matter of time before substantive equality is effected through the admission of comparable numbers of women.

NARRATIVES OF MASCULINIST CONSERVATISM

'The Lawyer' of the title is Stephen Mentmore, whose life trajectory is traced from his early years to his appointment as Chief Justice of the Australian High Court, and then to his illness and premature death. 'The Libertine' is George Dice, Mentmore's lifelong rival, who became a politician and Attorney General. Between the two is their mutual friend, Edward Lester, a journalist, who is presented as occupying the 'neutral' role of observer and commentator.

The book spans half a century from the 1930s to the 1980s. It is set against the backdrop of 'real' historical events – the post-Depression era, World War II, the Cold War, and the election and downfall of the Whitlam Labor Government in Australia (1972–75). While the novel contains the usual disclaimer that 'no resemblance of any kind is intended to any living person', there is a more equivocal statement relating to 'real people now deceased'. There is no clear line of demarcation between the 'real' and the 'hyperreal' within the legal imaginary. 'Real' historical figures, such as HV Evatt, are clearly identifiable.[9] Evatt is depicted as a vainglorious character called Doc Neroty. I assumed that the moniker was intended to suggest 'neurotic', but a colleague thought the allusion was to 'Nero', with its even more damning megalomanic overtones. Perhaps, both allusions are intended.

---

8   Thornton, 1996a; Thornton, 1996b; Thornton, 1998a.

9   Dr HV Evatt was prominent as both a jurist and a Labor politician from the 1920s to the 1950s. Career highlights included a stint as a member of the High Court of Australia (1930–40), a position from which he resigned to return to politics. He was President of the General Assembly of the UN (1948–49), in which capacity he played a key role in the drafting of the UN Declaration of Human Rights.

Dice, the libertine of the title, is thoroughly reprehensible: 'traitor, blunderer, hypocrite ... wife beater',[10] a 'violent, deceitful lecher, a vile libertine, a voluptuary'.[11] His career as a lawyer-turned politician, together with some of the events in which he engages suggests that he is based on a pastiche of 'real' Labor men, including, most notably, the late Justice Lionel Murphy, who was Attorney General in the Whitlam Government before appointment to the High Court. What is clearly discernible through the lens of 'accuracy' claimed by the author for the 'real' historical background is that anyone associated with the Labor Party, or left wing politics, is utterly contemptible.

The uniformly negative depiction of characters associated with the Labor Party's historical 'canon' of influential figures illustrates the diabolical dimension of Baudrillardian simulacrum theory. That is, Callinan reproduces a string of historical events, such as those which occurred under Whitlam, including Murphy's raid on the ASIO office in Melbourne and the international 'loans affair',[12] so that we are in no doubt about the historical veracity of the allusions, and the understanding that they were perpetrated by amoral Labor Party politicians with questionable aims. The idea of hyperreality is clear enough in the novel – despite the cumbersome prose – but, no doubt, will be even more so when we see the film, for the images will be fixed in our minds and that of the next generation – so that the historical real, whatever that is, will fade away and be replaced by the imagined real.

In contradistinction to Dice, is Mentmore, 'the Lawyer' of the title. While he is a not a particularly likable character either, we are expected to admire and respect him. He is described as a 'narrow, fastidious man' and a 'social neuter',[13] whose lack of imagination induced some to say that 'his mind ran on railway lines'.[14] We are nevertheless informed on many occasions that he is 'brilliant', although the evidence in support of this claim is somewhat thin, as he seems to possess not an iota of insight, reflexivity or vision about either law or life. Readers are expected to accept that technical ability and skill in devising ways around regulation are equated with brilliance. Justice for Mentmore would seem to be incidental, but then we know that law and justice are not the same thing at all. What is of interest here is that Mentmore, the quintessential legal positivist, 'arch-conservative', and Barwick-like figure, is presented as an ideal lawyer and judge. There is

---

10 Callinan, 1997, p 315.

11 *Ibid*, p 322.

12 Hocking, 2000, pp 162–69, 230–31.

13 Callinan, 1997, p 293.

14 *Ibid*, p 3. Sir Garfield Barwick, like Lionel Murphy, had a career as a lawyer, politician and High Court Judge. In the Foreword to Jenny Hocking's biography of Murphy, Justice Kirby draws attention to the similarities in background between Barwick and Murphy and the profound differences that were to develop in their social philosophy. See Hocking, 2000, p iii.

nothing subtle about where Callinan's political sympathies lie: Labor leaders and creative lawyers are irredeemably bad, while political conservatives and 'black letter' lawyers are paragons of virtue.

Dice and Mentmore both prove their masculinity on the football field, in war, and in the bedroom, as well as in the courtroom. Militarism and/or sport produce cultural capital that is vital to 'success'. For example, Mentmore joins the Air Force during the World War II and participates in the bombing of Dresden – which is applauded. In contrast, Dice's decision to enlist at a very late stage, and his assignation to a lesser theatre of war – Intelligence in Borneo – is derided as tokenistic. Mentmore's 'good war service' is subsequently noted as a factor in his favour in the context of appointment to the Bench. Not only do we see here the ancient idea of rewarding military heroes with high public office, but the normalisation of masculinist violence. The underlying assumption would seem to be that militarism, including the perpetration of acts of destruction, is appropriate training for the adversarialism, masculinity and legitimation of violence associated with legal practice, adjudication and public office.

The protagonists both grew up in the Sydney working class suburb of Mascot during the Depression, where life was further divided along religious lines. The issue of class ostensibly disrupts the idealised middle class man of law. However, the suggestion is that any perceived disadvantage emanating from working class origins can be overcome by consciously positioning oneself close to sources of power and wealth in accordance with the liberal myth that anyone can succeed by dint of hard work and their own efforts. The distinction between the artificial and the real merge through the simulacra of the successful men of law. Dice, whose parents run a general store and become rich through Mick's SP betting shop, attended a prestigious boys' school run by the Jesuits – St Bartholomew's, or St Bart's, which appears to be based upon St Ignatius' School, Riverview, located on Sydney's affluent North Shore. At school, fraternal bonds are forged which underpin and sustain Dice's political and professional life: 'He made a number of friends among the boarders. Later those friendships came to provide him with a valuable network of supporters among some of the richest and most influential Catholics in the country'.[15]

In fact, Dice's first legal job was in a firm where the son of the senior partner had been a classmate at St Bart's. The suggestion is that the tribal and nepotistic aspects of Irish Catholicism are stronger than for Protestantism. Non-Christian religions are largely written out of this narrow world altogether; 'hyperreality has no recollection of reality'.[16] Similarly, racial or ethic diversity, a significant facet of Sydney culture during the

---

15   *Ibid*, p 59.
16   Borgmann, 1992, p 161.

relevant period, is totally erased from life in the law, which is represented as an entirely Anglo-Celtic preserve.[17]

Mentmore, whose father is a union official goes to Inner Street High School, which would seem to be based on Fort Street High School, an old, inner city selective school in Sydney.[18] We learn nothing of the experience, and it is inferred that the cultural capital acquired in a government public school, or even a public university, is unlikely to be of assistance in legal practice, compared with educational institutions designed to foster religious and class bonds. Thus, Mentmore is compelled to embark on a career at the Bar with 'no contacts, no influence, no money, not even legal friends, just his brilliant results and a will to succeed'.[19] Nevertheless, he is rescued by a fairy godfather – the salvation of many an ambitious young man – a leading 'silk',[20] who takes him under his wing. He marries, moves from his humble working class suburb to Sydney's affluent North Shore, has children (whom he sends to private schools), joins a prestigious club (nominated by his master) and specialises in equity and commercial work (the 'carriage trade'), thereby firmly aligning himself with the rich and conservative powerbrokers of the city. Like his model, Sir Garfield Barwick, Mentmore effects a political and class transmogrification.[21] Thus, the reader is presented with an idealised picture of the 'real' successful benchmark lawyer – an ambitious, conservative, heterosexual, well to do, married man.

Mentmore's fortunes come to be intimately intertwined with corporate capital, for he is retained by a powerful newspaper proprietor, Dinny O'Ryan (Warwick Fairfax).[22] As a result of this patronage, he is offered 'one of the safest seats in the country' if he agrees to stand for Parliament against 'the dishonesty and destructiveness of people like Dice'.[23] Mentmore is even assured of the position of federal Attorney General, although he has displayed no interest whatsoever in politics to date. In any case, he declines the offer. Instead, he becomes Chief Justice of the High Court – complete with automatic knighthood – at the behest of the newspaper proprietor, O'Ryan, who categorically informs the Liberal Prime Minister: 'I've decided Stephen Mentmore should be the next Chief Justice.'[24] Here, we see how conservatism, corporate power and benchmark masculinity are imbricated

---

17   The narrowness of this approach contrasts with Callinan's subsequent novel, *The Coroner's Conscience*, 1999. In this book, his central character, Sidney Marcus, is the son of a Holocaust survivor, of which the reader is informed on the very first page.

18   Sir Garfield Barwick, the Mentmore model, attended Fort Street Boys High. See Marr, 1992, pp 6–8.

19   Callinan, 1997, p 174.

20   A senior barrister, or Queen's Counsel (QC), now generally known as Senior Counsel.

21   Marr, 1992.

22   The Fairfax family has been associated with Sydney's leading daily newspaper, *The Sydney Morning Herald*, since 1842.

23   Callinan, 1997, p 280.

24   *Ibid*, p 289.

with each other in the constitution of merit. The fact that Mentmore is a good technical lawyer clinches his acceptance as the 'best person for the job'. The technocratic veneer effectively occludes the political partiality underpinning the decision, which is treated as unremarkable. The normativity of such decisions in high level appointments is accepted as evidence of fair decision making. Readers are assured that the masculinist, technocratic legal world is synonymous with the just world, a fictional conjunction that has long been projected as the hyperreal in legal texts.

THE FICTIVE FEMININE

If one factor is altered in the class/sex conjunction, particularly with regard to the masculine identity of the legal subject, vociferous cries of partiality are heard. The point is thrown into high relief in *The Lawyer and the Libertine* when a woman is appointed as Chief Justice, following Mentmore's resignation from the Bench. Shirley Leeme emerges from nowhere, even though she must have had a spectacular career somewhere, having been appointed as a Queen's Counsel at the age of 33. Despite the claimed attention to the 'real' historical background, there is no sign of the dramatically changed gender profile of the legal profession that began to occur in the 1960s and 1970s, apart from Leeme's disruptive appointment. It would seem that the erasure of the narratives of struggle and the increasing visibility of women represents an attempt to retain the appearance of masculinist homogeneity as the 'real'.

The values of Shirley Leeme, the new Chief Justice, are the antithesis of those of Mentmore. Instead of neutrality, order and deference to the rule of law, we have partiality and disorder (is her name meant to be an unsubtle anagram of melee?):

> She was an avowed centralist. If she had her way, the Constitution would be interpreted to hasten the accrual of power to the central government. She would be receptive to all the fashionable arguments to expand the rights of minorities. She would be a bold and fearless innovator according to her own confident opinions, and without regard, when it suited her, to precedent.[25]

This representation of Shirley Leeme as purposive in adjudication, but of questionable competence, contrasts with the ponderous style of the admirable Mentmore who, presumably, *always* deferred to the legislature. He merely interpreted the law – never made it – in accordance with the liberal myth of judge as conduit.[26] Furthermore, Leeme's is a 'blatantly political appointment with unimpeachable Labor credentials extending back

---

25 *Ibid*, p 307.

26 The representation of Shirley Leeme may be compared with the negative representation of women lawyers in Hollywood films who, in contrast to confident and competent men, appear to be inadequate and even incompetent. See Lucia, 1997.

to her great grandfather who had been a prominent Unionist and agitator ... in the 1890s'.[27] Leeme is a literal, as well as a metaphorical, 'balls breaker', as she was once imprisoned for kicking a policeman in the testicles during a demonstration. Like the Labor men referred to, she is stereotypically unscrupulous and ambitious, having 'clambered' over the bodies of others to succeed.[28] To drive home the point that the reader should feel no empathy for Shirley Leeme whatsoever, she is also depicted as physically unattractive: 'She wore no makeup and her hair was pulled tightly back in a bun. She was a tall, competent, hard-looking woman whose face was no stranger to experience.'[29]

Capping Leeme's catalogue of alleged physical, sexual, political and legal shortcomings is the fact that she is also made the victim of that grossest of gender stereotypes: she has slept her way to the top to compensate for her (obvious) lack of 'merit'. This sexualised fiction about 'successful' women has been repeated so many times that it has indeed assumed the status of the hyperreal within the social script. Drawing attention to Shirley Leeme's promiscuity and intemperate acts succeeds in raising doubts about her fitness to occupy the country's pre-eminent legal office and, by association, that of other women.[30] Nevertheless, while such representations may pander to the benchmark men of law, I do not think that one could say that the sexually undifferentiated 'masses' necessarily sink into inertia and do nothing when they encounter them. Feminist activists are inspired to critique, challenge and disrupt such representations, albeit pervasive within mass culture.

The other women, who appear in the novel as rather shadowy background figures, are also manifestations of the hyperreal, or what I have called the 'fictive feminine', that is, the fictionalised characteristics conventionally attributed to women within the social script.[31] Callinan's female characters are good women who tend the hearth and provide comfort for the important men, or are preyed upon sexually, or even beaten, by them. Unlike Shirley Leeme, they are all described as very attractive, even alluring, and invariably have large breasts – typical of the pulp fiction genre. Also, unlike Shirley Leeme, they accept their subordinate social roles. If they must venture into the workforce, it is not out of misplaced ambition, but necessity, as in the case of Mentmore's mother or his old flame, Hannah East; they then pose no threat to the main players, the powerful men of law and politics.

---

27 *Ibid*, p 14.
28 *Ibid*, p 16.
29 *Ibid*, p 13.
30 Lucia shows how similar anxieties are conveyed through the representation of women lawyers in Hollywood films. See Lucia, 1997, esp p 161.
31 Thornton, 1996a, esp pp 29–32.

A little sexual precocity on the part of these docile women is nevertheless highly acceptable, in marked contrast to the predatory and unappealing conduct in which Leeme is supposed to have engaged. In a rather crass and fanciful overture, Margaret, Dice's wife, says to Mentmore: 'Forgive me for asking, but would you like to fuck me? ... I'm very frustrated. I'm sorry if that sounds clumsy. I like you that's why I'd like you to fuck me, now, soon, please.'[32] We are told that the 'contradiction of her language and wholesome appearance' worked on Mentmore 'like an aphrodisiac'.

It nevertheless must be stressed that both the alluring Margaret Dice, as well as the unattractive Shirley Leeme, are constructed as 'others' to the important men of the public sphere. The corporealisation and sexualisation of the feminine 'other' is a classic means of ensuring the rational normativity of benchmark men in law and public life.[33] Callinan effects this 'othering', whether it be through the eroticisation of Margaret, or the defeminisation and demonisation of Shirley Leeme. As a woman who is already an ostensibly prominent member of the jurisprudential community, Callinan's depiction of Leeme gives voice to the fear that the entry of women into authoritative positions aroused among those nostalgic for the homosocial legal world of the past. Although Margaret is also 'othered' in respect of intellect and career, her sexualised 'comfort woman' role provides an idealised and nostalgic haven for men engaged in the dog-eat-dog world of public life.

CONCLUSION

The novel evokes a social and legal world that may be anachronistic, but culture is an amorphous concept; it defies clear lines and neat categories. The boundary between the 'real' legal world and Callinan's fictional world, with its 'real' markers, implodes in the way suggested by Baudrillard. In constructing a legal world of macho-men, in which women are professional aberrations but sexual certainties, Callinan, according to the Baudrillardian analysis, is pandering to the 'masses' by creating the fantasies after which they hanker. (I note in passing that 'the masses', the mindless blob of humanity to which Baudrillard seems to assign us all, does evince certain masculinist traits.) The seduction of the masses by the simulacra of an outdated masculinist world insidiously permits it to become the hyperreal so that resistance becomes more difficult. Indeed, the signs become simulacra for the real, and the two seamlessly converge.

Callinan presents a window onto the masculinist values underpinning the legal profession, which are entrenched through the intimate linkages

32 Callinan, 1997, p 225.
33 Thornton, 1998a.

forged between Anglocentricity, class, private boys' schools, militarism, sport, able-bodiedness, heterosexuality, corporate capital and political power – confirming what we think we already know about the legal professional culture. The novel also shows how benchmark masculinity is ethically corrosive, a phenomenon that may be less obvious. I am not talking about corruption on the overt scale attributed to Dice, but about the way that the granting of reciprocal favours has come to be accepted as a permanent subtext of fraternity. The ready acceptance of the exchange of favours as the basis of the homosociality of public and professional life suggests why women are still regarded as intrusive 'others' within the jurisprudential community. The value of the application of Baudrillard's theory of hyperreality is to challenge 'real' legal practice to 'defend itself and ... try to show how the real is not as corrupt, or as hollow, or as simulated'[34] as Callinan reveals it to be.

Another seemingly positive factor that emerges phoenix-like from the nihilism of Baudrillard is that once an idea is elevated to a universal, that is a prelude to it becoming transparent which, in turn, is a prelude to its disappearance. That is, universality contains the seeds of its own destruction:

> If there is no longer any possibility of a philosophy of transcendence, since thought has been exiled to the other side of the looking-glass, there is no longer any possibility of conquering power either, since the political has been exiled to the other side of representation. There are no longer any heights to storm, either in the political domain or anywhere else ...[35]

Baudrillard presents us with a paradox. While Ian Callinan depicts a simulacrum, that is, a copy without an original – at least in today's world – of the 'real' world of lawyers. The novel presents this simulacrum as the hyperreal, that is, a world that is more real than the real. However, the completeness of the representation, the degree of closure that is effected, and its patriarchal perfection, all suggest that it is on the point of dissolution. As Baudrillard observes, 'Every idea and culture becomes universalized before it disappears'.[36]

We can therefore take heart from this Baudrillardian-assisted reading of *The Lawyer and the Libertine*, for it suggests that the masculinist legal culture it describes is on the verge of collapse. But a word of caution – since Baudrillard espouses neither a progressivist nor a teleological thesis – anything that replaces Callinan's one-dimensional and masculinist vision of the hyperreal, including a feminised, diverse or ethically conscious legal world, must be similarly doomed.

---

34 Goshorn, 1992, p 225.
35 Baudrillard, 1994a, p 105.
36 *Ibid*, p 104.

EPILOGUE

The Law of Questions Unanswered

for Peter Boyle

These I ask
My friend the poet
And he smiles and tells me
How he writes poetry
With the help of children
From inside the sun
With words he is afraid will die
Too quickly adrift
In the nervous systems
Of others

These I ask
My lover at night
(When I have a lover)
And without turning
He places his hand on my back
Without turning
He is more solid and still
Than any answer
He whispers and I use that sound
For other purposes

These I ask
The I that hides from me
Or is it me
That hides from I?
Long-time traders who met
Sharing money in the womb
Coseismal in matters of love
My doors to the emptiest room
They are certain of my panic
And patient not to answer

These I ask
The world in the form of a day
But a day I choose
Still and in pain
In the tall distance
How many sounds in stone?
Who can afford this life?
Why are our bodies
Untrusted by our laws?
Are we afraid forever?

And my voice
Floods the world
With temptation
And settles here and there
Like a large fly
I am more than two people
Wandering
And lost by my own act
My names now are Angela
Oriana and Perpetua

I know all the things
Which laughter told me
I know that fire and night
Are unforgettable
I am the messenger-
Angel and dawneverlasting
And know the sigh
Within me
Is sighing toward
The sigh within me

Do you understand this?
Do you know why the feast
Is in the home
Of your living reflection?
The one who sees you?
Why your fear of the dark
Is too hard to explain?
What is it you have to do?
That if you understood
It would mean nothing to you?

These I ask
Of the sky I see
With my eyes closed tight
Of the love
Not good enough
Of the parts of me
Living for weeks and years
On nothing
Of the children whose questions
Are always flavoured 'Oh!'

And I am the author
Of these questions
Of the contradiction and gods
Little hates and recognition
That all questions find in me
And my language is whole
In those moments
When I have asked them all
When the answers lose their way
In silence

MTC Cronin

BIBLIOGRAPHY

ABA, 'Australian Families and Internet Usage', 2000
www.aba.gov.au/internet/research/families.htm, last accessed 6 July 2002.

ABA, 'Internet@home – What do Australian Users Want?', 2001
www.aba.gov.au/internet/research/home/index.htm, last accessed 6 July 2002.

ABA, 'The Internet and Some International Regulatory Issues Relating to Content: A Pilot Comparative Study commissioned by the United Nations Educational, Scientific and Cultural Organisation (UNESCO)', 1997, unpublished paper.

Abrams, Kathryn, 'The Narrative and the Normative in Legal Scholarship', in Heizelman, Susan Sage and Wiseman, Zipporah Batshaw (eds), *Representing Women: Law, Literature, and Feminism*, 1994, Durham NC and London: Duke UP, pp 44–56.

Adams, Mary Louise, 'Youth, Corruptibility, and English-Canadian Postwar Campaigns against Indecency' (1995) 6 J History Sexuality 89.

Adams, Phillip, 'Isolation Technology' (2000) *The Weekend Australian*, 30 September–1 October, p 32.

Adler, Robert, 'Pigeonholed' (2000) 167 New Scientist 38.

AHA Queensland Branch, ULVA Rev, May 1959; QHA Rev, November 1963.

Akdeniz, Yaman, 'The Regulation of Pornography and Child Pornography on the Internet' (1997) 1 Information, L & Tech
elj.warwick.ac.uk/jilt/internet/97_1akdz/default.htm, last accessed 6 July 2002.

Alshejni, Lamis, 'Unveiling the Arab Woman's Voice through the Net', in Harcourt, Wendy (ed), *Women @internet: Creating New Cultures in Cyberspace*, 1999, London: Zed Books, pp 214–18.

Alston, Richard, 'The Government's Regulatory Framework for Internet Content' (2000) 23 UNSWLJ 192.

Althusser, Louis, *Lenin and Philosophy and Other Essays*, 1971, London: New Left Books.

Altman, Dennis, 'Sex, Politics, and Political Economy' (2002) J Mundane Behaviour
mundanebehavior.org/issues/v3n1/altman.htm, last accessed 6 July 2002.

Anderson, Benedict, *Imagined Communities: Reflections on the Origin and Spread of Nationalism*, 1983, London: Verso.

Anderson, Gavin, 'Corporations, Democracy, and the Implied Freedom of Political Communication: Towards a Pluralistic Analysis of Constitutional Law' (1998) 22 MULR 1.

Anderson, Terence and Twining, William, *Analysis of Evidence: How to Do Things with Facts Based on Wigmore's Science of Judicial Proof*, 1991, Boston: Little, Brown.

Anon (1971) 1:1 Shrew: Women's Liberation Newsletter, January, p 4.

Anon, 'The great e-scape', Networker, vol 9 no 1, Nov/Dec 1998 www.usc.edu, accessed 6 July 2002.

Appadurai, Arjun, 'Disjuncture and Difference in the Global Cultural Economy', in Featherstone, Mike (ed), *Global Culture: Nationalism, Globalization and Modernity; Theory, Culture & Society* (Special Issue), 1990, London: Sage, pp 295–310.

Appadurai, Arjun, *Modernity at Large: Cultural Dimensions of Globalisation*, 1996, Minneapolis and London: U Minnesota Press.

Arasaratnam, Niranjan, 'Brave New (online) World' (2000) 23 UNSWLJ 205.

Argy, Philip N, 'Internet Content Regulation: An Australian Computer Society Perspective' (2000) 23 UNSWLJ 265.

Arnold, Mathew, *Culture and Anarchy*, 1960, Cambridge: Cambridge UP.

AWBC, 'International Women's Year 1975: Meeting For All Interested Women in the ABC', unpublished leaflet, 1975, First Ten Years Collection, Sydney.

AWBC, 'The Coming Out Show AWBC Newsletter', unpublished newsletter, 1978, First Ten Years Collection, Sydney.

AWBC, 'The Coming Out Show AWBC Newsletter', unpublished newsletter, 1979, First Ten Years Collection, Sydney.

Bailey, Frankie Y and Hale, Donna C (eds), *Popular Culture, Crime, and Justice*, 1998, London: Wadsworth.

Bailey, Peter, 'Parasexuality and Glamour: The Victorian Barmaid as Cultural Prototype' (1990) 2 Gender & History 148.

Bal, Mieke, *Double Exposures: The Subject of Cultural Analysis*, 1996, New York: Routledge.

Barcan, Ruth, 'In the Raw: "Home-Made" Porn and Reality Genres' (2002) J Mundane Behaviour mundanebehavior.org/issues/v3n1/barcan.htm, last accessed 6 July 2002.

Barnes, Ruth and Eicher, Joanne B, *Dress and Gender: Making and Meaning in Cultural Contexts*, 1992, New York and Oxford: Berg.

Barrett, Randy, 'Adult Web Sites: Virtual Sex, Real Profits' (1997) Inter@ctive Week, 3 March www.danni.com/press/interactive_week_030397.html, last accessed 6 July 2002.

Barthes, Roland, 'Writing Reading', in *The Rustle of Language*, 1986, Oxford: Basil Blackwell.

Bartlett, F, 'Public Stories of the Stolen Generations', 1999, unpublished PhD thesis, La Trobe University.

Bastalich, Wendy, 'Gender and Skill in Australia: A Case Study of Barmaids', 1991, unpublished MA thesis, Women's Studies, 1991, U Adelaide.

Baudrillard, Jean, *The Illusion of the End*, 1994a, trans Turner, Chris, Cambridge: Polity.

Baudrillard, Jean, *Simulacra and Simulation*, 1994b, trans Glaser, Sheila Faria, Ann Arbor: U Michigan Press.

Baudrillard, Jean, *Revenge of the Crystal: Selected Writings on the Modern Object and its Destiny, 1968–1983*, 1990, Sydney: Pluto Press in association with the Power Institute of Fine Arts, U of Sydney.

Baudrillard, Jean, *The Evil Demon of Images*, 1987, Mari Kuttna Memorial Lecture, Sydney: Power Institute Publications, U of Sydney.

Bauman, Zygmunt, *Postmodernity and its Discontents*, 1997, Cambridge: Polity.

Beecher, Mrs Henry Ward, *The Home: How to Make and Keep It*, 1883, Minneapolis: Buckeye Publishing.

Belausteguigoitia Rius, Marisa, 'Crossing Borders: From Crystal Slippers to Tennis Shoes', in Harcourt, Wendy (ed), *Women @internet: Creating New Cultures in Cyberspace*, 1999, London: Zed Books, pp 23–30.

Bell, Shannon, *Reading Writing and Rewriting the Prostitute Body*, 1994, Bloomington: Indiana UP.

Berendt, John, *Midnight in the Garden of Good and Evil*, 1994, London: Vintage.

Bergman, Paul and Asimow, Michael, *Reel Justice: The Courtroom goes to the Movies*, 1996, Kansas City: Andrews & McMeel.

Berns, Sandra Spelman, *To Speak as a Judge: Difference, Voice, and Power*, 1999, Aldershot UK and Brookfield Vt, USA: Dartmouth/Ashgate.

Berns, Sandra Spelman, 'Pornography, Women, Censorship and Morality' (1989) 7 Law in Context 30.

Beverley, John, 'The Margin at the Centre', in Smith, Sidonie and Watson, Julia (ed), *De-colonizing the Subject*, 1992, Minneapolis: U of Minnesota Press, pp 169–95.

Binder, Guyora and Weisberg, Robert, *Literary Criticisms of Law*, 2000, Princeton: Princeton UP.

Biressi, Anita, *Crime, Fear and the Law in True Crime Stories*, 2001, Basingstoke: Palgrave.

Blackstone, Phil, 'Marriage and Murder' (November 1946) 4 Daring Crime Cases, Toronto: Alval.

Blackstone, William, *Commentaries on the Laws of England, Volume II, Of the Rights of Things*, 1979 [1766], Chicago and London: U of Chicago Press.

Blair, Charlene, 'Netsex: Empowerment through Discourse', in Ebo, Bosah, *Cyberghetto or Cyberutopia: Race, Class and Gender on the Internet*, 1998, Westport, Conn: Praeger, pp 205–18.

Block, Suzette, 'Outrage over Jeans Rape Ruling' (1999) *Sydney Morning Herald*, 13 February.

Bloom, Clive, *Cult Fiction: Popular Reading and Pulp Theory*, 1996, London: Macmillan.

Boehringer, Gill H, 'Infamy at Macquarie: Economic Rationalism and the New McCarthyism' (1999) 24 Alt LJ 30.

Borgmann, Albert, 'The Artificial and the Real: Reflections on Baudrillard's America', in Stearns, William and Chaloupka, William (eds), *Jean Baudrillard: The Disappearance of Art and Politics*, 1992, London: Macmillan, pp 160–76.

Bottomley, Anne, 'Figures in a Landscape: Feminist Perspectives on Law, Land and Landscape', in Bottomley, Anne (ed), *Feminist Perspectives on the Foundational Subjects of Law*, 1996, London: Cavendish Publishing, pp 109–24.

Bottomley, Stephen and Parker, Stephen, *Law in Context*, 2nd edn, 1997, Sydney: Federation.

Bourdieu, Pierre, *Language and Symbolic Power*, 1991, Cambridge: Polity.

Bourdieu, Pierre, *The Logic of Practice*, 1990, Cambridge: Polity.

Bride WW, 'The Bloody Knife Points to Death' (February 1947) 5 Daring Crime Cases, Toronto: Alval.

Bride WW, 'The Body on the Mountain' (March 1948) 4 Startling Crime Cases, Toronto: Al White.

Bride WW, 'Trailing Toronto's Love Slayer' (April 1946) 4 Daring Crime Cases, Toronto: Alval.

Brodie, Joanna, '"All Youse Three Will Be Dead in the Morning": The *Kontinnen* Case', in Greenwood, Kerry (ed), *The Thing She Loves: Why Women Kill*, 1996, Sydney: Allen & Unwin, pp 123–34.

Brooks, Peter, 'The Law as Narrative and Rhetoric', in Brooks, Peter and Gerwitz, Paul (eds), *Law's Stories: Narrative and Rhetoric in the Law*, 1996, New Haven, Conn: Yale UP, pp 14–22.

Brown, Rita Mae, 'Leadership vs Stardom', Queensland Women's Liberation Newsletter, unpublished newsletter, 1978, First Ten Years Collection, Sydney.

Brown, Wendy, *States of Injury: Power and Freedom in Late Modernity*, 1995, Princeton, NJ: Princeton UP.

Browne, Angela, *When Battered Women Kill*, 1987, New York: Free Press.

Bulletin Morgan Poll, 'The Professions We Trust the Most' (1999) *The Bulletin*, 29 June.

Burke, Greg, 'Judged by Her Jeans' (1999) 153(8) *Time Magazine*, 1 March, p 41.

Burrows, JF, Finn, Jeremy and Todd, Stephen, *Cheshire and Fifoot's Law of Contract*, 8th edn, 1992, Wellington: Butterworths.

Busch, Ruth and Robertson, Neville, '"What's Love Got to Do With It?" An Analysis of an Intervention Approach to Domestic Violence' (1993) 1 Waikato LR 109.

Busch, Ruth, Robertson, Neville and Lapsley, Hilary, 'Protection From Family Violence: A Study of Protection Orders Under the Domestic Protection Act', 1992, unpublished report, Hamilton, NZ: U Waikato.

Buti, T (ed), *After the Removal*, 1996, Perth: WA Aboriginal Legal Service.

Butler, Gerald, *Love and Reading: An Essay in Applied Psychoanalysis*, 1989, New York: P Lang.

Butler, Judith, 'Performativity's Social Magic', in Shusterman, Richard (ed), *Bourdieu: A Critical Reader*, 1999, Oxford: Blackwell, pp 113–28.

Butler, Judith, *Excitable Speech: A Politics of the Performative*, 1997, New York: Routledge.

Butler, Judith, *Gender Trouble: Feminism and the Subversion of Identity*, 1990, New York: Routledge.

Caddie, *Caddie: The Autobiography of a Sydney Barmaid, Written by Herself*, 1953, London: Constable.

Cain, Maureen, 'The Symbol Traders', in Cain, Maureen and Harrington, Christine B (eds), *Lawyers in a Postmodern World: Translation and Transgression*, 1994, Buckingham, UK: Open UP, pp 15–48.

Callahan, A Renee, 'Will the "Real" Battered Woman Please Stand Up? In Search of a Realistic Legal Definition of Battered Woman Syndrome' (1994) 3 Am U J Gender & L 117.

Callinan, Ian, *The Coroner's Conscience: A Murder Mystery*, 1999, Rockhampton, Qld: Central Queensland UP.

Callinan, Ian, *The Lawyer and the Libertine*, 1997, Rockhampton, Qld: Central Queensland UP.

Cameron, Deborah, 'Pleasure and Danger, Sex and Death: Reading True Crime Monthlies', in Day, George (ed), *Readings in Popular Culture*, 1990, London: Macmillan, pp 131–38.

Cameron, Deborah and Fraser, Elizabeth, *The Lust to Kill: A Feminist Investigation of Sexual Murder*, 1987, New York: New York UP.

Capote, Truman, *In Cold Blood*, 1965, New York: Random House.

Caputi, Jane, '*Sleeping with the Enemy* as *Pretty Woman, Part II*? Or, What Happened after the Princess Woke Up' (1991) 19 J Popular Film and Television 2.

Caputi, Jane, *The Age of Sex Crime*, 1987, Bowling Green, Ohio: Bowling Green UP.

Carlen, Pat, *Women's Imprisonment: A Study in Social Control*, 1983, London: Routledge & Kegan Paul.

Carlson, James M, *Prime Time Law Enforcement: Crime Show Viewing and Attitudes towards the Criminal Justice System*, 1985, NY: Praeger.

Carrington, Kerry, *Who Killed Leigh Leigh? A Story of Shame and Mateship in an Australian Town*, 1998, Sydney: Random House.

Carty, Anthony, 'Introduction: Post-Modern Law', in *Post-Modern Law: Enlightenment, Revolution and the Death of Man*, 1990, Edinburgh: Edinburgh UP, pp 1–39.

Chandler, Raymond, 'The Simple Art of Murder' in Haycraft, Howard (ed), *The Art of the Mystery Story*, 1947, New York: Grosset and Dunlap.

Chandler, Rick, 'She's Young, Hot, Available and Incarcerated', Impression, 7 September 1998, www.ironminds.com/impression/index.shtml, accessed 6 July 2002.

Channel Nine, 'Justifiable Homicide?', 60 Minutes, unpublished transcript, 1980, Wendy Bacon, private papers.

Chase, Anthony, 'Lawyers and Popular Culture: A Review of Mass Media Portrayals of American Attorneys' [1986a] American Bar Foundation Research J 281.

Chase, Anthony, 'Towards a Legal Theory of Popular Culture' [1986b] Wisconsin LR 527.

Chen, Peter, 'Pornography, Protection, Prevarication: The Politics of Internet Censorship' (2000) 23 UNSWLJ 221.

Chen, Peter, Australia's Online Censorship Regime, 2001, unpublished PhD thesis www.webprophets.net.au/websites/chen/thesis/contents2.html, last accessed 6 July 2002.

Christie, Suzanne, '"Judge Judy" The Courtroom as Classroom' (2000) 13 Aust Fem LJ 86.

Cixous, Helene, 'The Laugh of the Medusa' (1976), in Marks, Elaine and de Courtivron, Isabelle (eds), New French Feminisms, 1980, NY: Schocken, pp 245–64.

Clark, Elizabeth, 'Religion and Rights Consciousness', in Fineman, Martha and Thomadsen, Nancy (eds), At The Boundaries of Law: Feminism and Legal Theory, 1991, New York: Routledge, pp 188–208.

Clawson, Mark A, 'Telling Stories: Romance and Dissonance in Progressive Legal Narratives' (1998) 22 Legal Studies Forum 353.

Cleave, Maureen, 'The Greater British Barmaid', in McGill, Angus, Pub: A Celebration, 1969, London: Longmans.

Clover, Carol, 'Law and the Order of Popular Culture', in Kearns, Thomas R and Sarat, Austin (eds), Law in the Domains of Culture, 1998, Ann Arbor: U Michigan Press, pp 97–119.

Cockburn, Cynthia, 'The Circuit of Technology: Gender, Identity and Power', in Silverstone, Roger and Hirsch, Eric (eds), Consuming Technologies, 1992, London: Routledge, pp 32–47.

Collier, Richard, 'Masculinism, Law and Law Teaching' (1991) 19 Internat J Sociology Law 427.

Connolly, William E, 'Assembling the Left' (1999) 26 Boundary 2: Internat J Literature & Culture 47.

Cook, Sandy and Davies, Susanne (eds), Harsh Punishment: International Experiences of Women's Imprisonment, 1999, Boston: Northeastern UP.

Cooks, Leda M, Orbe, Mark P and Bruess, Carol S, 'The Fairy Tale Theme in Popular Culture: A Semiotic Analysis of *Pretty Woman*' (1993) 16 Women's Studies in Communication 86.

Coombs, James H, *Bar Service*, 1965, London: Hutchinson.

Coonan, Helen and Armstrong, Susan 'Women and the Law', in Department of Prime Minister and Cabinet, Women and Politics Conference 1975, Vol 2, 1977, Canberra, AGPS, pp 66–75.

Cooper, Alvin, Scherer, Coralie R, Boies, Sylvain C and Gordon, Barry L, 'Sexuality on the Internet: From Sexual Exploration to Pathological Expression' (1999) 30 Professional Psychology: Research and Practice 154.

Corner, John, *Television Form and Public Address*, 1995, London: Edward Arnold.

Crawford, Ben, 'Saturday Morning Fever', in Cholodenko, Alan (ed), *The Illusion of Life* (1991) Sydney: Power Publications, pp 113–30.

Crenshaw, Kimberle, 'Mapping the Margins: Intersectionality, Identity Politics, and Violence Against Women of Color' (1991) 43 Stan LR 1241.

Crescent, Samantha, 'Jail Bait', New Times Los Angeles, Web Extra, 3–9 September 1998
www.newtimesla.com, accessed 6 July 2002.

Cromer, Mark, 'Jail-Order Brides', Wirednews, 4 August 1998
www.wirednews.com, accessed 6 July 2002.

Cunneen, Chris, *Conflict, Politics and Crime*, 2001, Sydney: Allen & Unwin.

Curthoys, Ann, 'Where is Feminism Now?', in Mead, Jenna (ed), *Bodyjamming: Sexual Harassment, Feminism and Public Life*, 1997, Sydney: Vintage, pp 189–212.

Curthoys, Ann, 'Feminism, Citizenship and National Identity' (1993) 44 Feminist Review 19.

Curthoys, Ann, *For and Against Feminism*, 1988, Sydney: Allen & Unwin.

Cvetkovich, Anne, *Mixed Feelings: Feminism, Mass Culture, and Victorian Sensationalism*, 1992, New Brunswick, NJ: Rutgers UP.

Dalton, Clare, 'Domestic Violence, Domestic Torts and Divorce: Constraints and Possibilities' (1997) 31 New Eng LR 319.

Davies, Margaret, *Delimiting the Law: 'Postmodernism' and the Politics of Law*, 1996, London: Pluto.

Davies, Margaret, *Asking the Law Question*, 1994, Sydney: Lawbook Co; London: Sweet & Maxwell.

Davies, Susanne and Cook, Sandy, 'The Sex of Crime and Punishment', in Cook, Sandy and Davies, Susanne (eds), *Harsh Punishment: International Experiences of Women's Imprisonment*, 1999, Boston: Northeastern UP, pp 53–78.

Davis, Angela, 'Race and Criminalization: Black Americans in the Punishment Industry', in James, Joy (ed), *The Angela Y Davis Reader*, 1998a, Oxford: Blackwell, pp 61–73.

Davis, Angela, 'Racialized Punishment and Prison Abolition', in James, Joy (ed), *The Angela Y Davis Reader*, 1998b, Oxford: Blackwell, pp 96–107.

Davis, Angela, 'The Prison Industrial Complex', Speech, Sydney Town Hall, May 1998c.

Davis, E, 'Edmonton's Maniacal Killer and the Innocent Girl' (May 1942) 1 Factual Detective Cases, Toronto: Norman Book.

Davis, Mark, *Gangland: Cultural Elites and the New Generationalism*, 2nd edn, 1999, Sydney: Allen & Unwin.

Dawson, Michael, '"That Nice Red Coat goes to my Head like Champagne": Gender, Antimodernism and the Mountie Image, 1885–1960' (1997) 32 Canadian Studies 119.

Day, David, *John Curtin: A Life*, 1999, Sydney: HarperCollins.

Day, George (ed), *Readings in Popular Culture: Trivial Pursuits?*, 1990, London: Macmillan.

Deacon, Desley, 'Political Arithmetic: The Nineteenth-century Australian Census and the Construction of the Dependent Wife' (1985) 11 Signs 27.

Deane, Karen, 'Public Eyes Censorship Plans' (2002) Australian IT, 13 March www.australianit.com.au.

Denver, John (ed), *Legal Reelism: Movies as Legal Texts*, 1996, Urbana & Chicago: U Illinois Press.

Dobash, R Emerson and Dobash, Russell, *Women, Violence and Social Change*, 1992, London: Routledge.

Douzinas, Costas, 'Prosopon and Antiprosopon: Prolegomena for a Legal Iconology', in Douzinas, Costas and Nead, Linda (eds), *Law and the Image: The Authority of Art and the Aesthetics of Law*, 1999, Chicago and London: U of Chicago Press, pp 36–67.

Douzinas, Costas, Goodrich, Peter and Hachamovitch, Yifat, *Politics, Postmodernity and Critical Legal Studies: The Legality of the Contingent*, 1994, London: Routledge.

Dowse, Sara, 'The Women's Movement's Fandango with the State: The Movement's Role in Public Policy since 1972', in Baldock, Cora and Cass, Bettina (eds), *Women, Social Welfare and the State in Australia*, 1983, Sydney: Allen & Unwin, pp 205–26.

DuBois, Ellen Carol and Gordon, Linda, 'Seeking Ecstasy on the Battlefield: Danger and Pleasure in Nineteenth-century Feminist Thought', in Vance, C (ed), *Pleasure and Danger*, 1984, Boston: Routledge & Kegan Paul, pp 31–49.

Duncanson, Ian and Tomlins, Christopher, 'Law, History, Australia: Three Characters in Search of a Play', in Duncanson, Ian and Tomlins, Christopher (eds), *Law and History in Australia*, 1982, Bundoora: La Trobe Uni, pp 1–28.

Duncanson, Ian, 'Scripting Empire: The "Englishman" and Playing for Safety in Law and History' (2000) 24 MULR 952.

Dworkin, Andrea and MacKinnon, Catherine, *Pornography and Civil Rights: A New Day for Women's Equality*, 1988, Minneapolis: Organizing Against Pornography.

Dworkin, Andrea, 'Against the Male Flood: Censorship, Pornography and Equality' (1985) 8 Harvard Women's LJ 1.

Dworkin, Andrea, *Pornography: Men Possessing Women*, 1981, London: Women's Press.

Eisenstein, Hester, *Inside Agitators: Australian Femocrats and The State*, 1996, Sydney: Allen & Unwin.

Elliot, Lorraine, 'Inequalities in the Australian Education System: Part 2: Women in the Professions', in Mercer, Jan (ed), *The Other Half: Women in Australian Society*, 1975, Melbourne: Penguin, pp 139–54.

Elsie Women's Refuge Collective, 'Report on Activities Being Carried Out and the Services Being Provided with Commonwealth Funds by Elsie Women's Refuge, to the Health Commission of New South Wales, Inner Region', unpublished report, 1975, First Ten Years Collection, Sydney.

Elsie Women's Refuge Collective, 'Statement: Funding Cuts', unpublished pamphlet, 1978, First Ten Years Collection, Sydney.

Farber, Daniel A and Sherry, Suzanne, 'Legal Storytelling and Constitutional Law: The Medium and the Message', in Brooks, Peter and Gewirtz, Paul (eds), *Law's Stories: Narrative and Rhetoric in the Law*, 1996, New Haven and London: Yale UP, pp 37–53.

Favret, Mary A, *Romantic Correspondence: Women, Politics, and the Fiction of Letters*, 1993, Cambridge and New York: Cambridge UP.

Fell, Liz, 'Women and the Media: Women and Politics Conference 1975', unpublished report, 1975, First Ten Years Collection, Sydney.

Findlay, Isobel M, 'Just Expression: Interdisciplining the Law and Literature', 1998 www.usask.ca/english/colloqu/ifindlay.htm.

Fineman, Martha, 'Images of Mothers in Poverty Discourses', in Fineman, Martha and Karpin, Isabel (eds), *Mothers in Law: Feminist Theory and the Legal Regulation of Motherhood*, 1995, New York: Columbia UP, pp 205–23.

Fineman, Martha A and McCluskey, Martha T (eds), *Feminism, Media and the Law*, 1997, New York and Oxford: OUP.

Foucault, Michel, *History of Sexuality, Vol 1: An Introduction*, 1997, New York: Vintage.

Foucault, Michel (ed), *I, Pierre Rivière, Having Slaughtered my Mother, my Sister and my Brother ... : A Case of Parricide in the 19th Century*, 1975, Lincoln and London: U Nebraska Press.

Foucault, Michel, *Discipline and Punish: The Birth of the Prison*, 1977, trans Sheridan, Alan, London: Penguin.

Foucault, Michel, *The Order of Things: An Archaeology of the Human Sciences*, 1970, London: Tavistock.

Fox, Barry, 'Take your Partners' (2001) 169 New Scientist 7.

Fraser, Nancy, 'Sex, Lies and the Public Sphere' in Leonard, Jerry D (ed), *Legal Studies as Cultural Studies*, 1995, New York: State U of New York Press, pp 175–95.

Friedman, Lawrence M, 'Law, Lawyers, and Popular Culture' (1989) 98 Yale LJ 1579.

Gajowski, Evelyn, 'The Female Perspective in *Othello*', in Vaughan, Virginia and Cartwright, Kent (eds), *Othello: New Perspectives*, 1991, Rutherford: Fairleigh Dickinson UP, pp 97–113.

Gajowski, Evelyn, *The Art of Loving: Female Subjectivity and Male Discursive Traditions in Shakespeare's Tragedies*, 1992, Newark: U of Delaware Press.

Garnett, Richard, 'Regulating Foreign-based Internet Content: A Jurisdictional Perspective' (2000) 23 UNSWLJ 238.

Genovese, Ann, 'The Battered Body: A Feminist Legal History', unpublished PhD thesis, 1998, UTS.

George, Amanda and Lazarus, Sabra, 'Private Prison: the Punished, the Profiteers, and the Grand Prix of State Approval' (1995) 4 Aust Fem LJ 153.

George, Stephen and Bache, Ian, *Politics in the European Union*, 2001, Oxford: OUP.

Gerbner, George and Gross, Larry, 'Living with Television: The Violence Profile' (1976) 26 J Comm 178.

Gewirtz, Paul, 'Victims and Voyeurs', in Brooks, Peter and Gerwitz, Paul (eds), *Law's Stories: Narrative and Rhetoric in the Law*, 1996, New Haven, Conn: Yale UP, pp 135–61.

Gilchrist, Kate, 'Millenium Multiplex: Art, the Internet and Censorship' (2000) 23 UNSWLJ 268.

Giles, Judy, '"You Meet 'Em and That's It": Working Class Women's Refusal of Romance Between the Wars in Britain', in Pearce, Lynne and Stacey, Jackie (eds), *Romance Revisited*, 1995, London: Lawrence & Wishart, pp 279–92.

Gillers, Stephen, 'Taking *LA Law* More Seriously' (1989) 98 Yale LJ 1607.

Gillespie, Cynthia, *Justifiable Homicide: Battered Women, Self-Defence and the Law*, 1989, Columbus: Ohio State U.

Ginibi, Ruby Langford, *Haunted by the Past*, 1999, Sydney: Allen & Unwin.

Ginibi, Ruby Langford, *Don't Take Your Love to Town*, 1988, Ringwood, Vic: Penguin.

Ginzburg, Carlo, *Myths, Emblems, Clues*, 1990, London: Hutchinson Radius.

Glebe, The, 15 October 1975 (a Sydney suburban newspaper).

Godsell, Philip H, 'Montreal's Honeymoon Slayers' (September–October 1943) 3 Factual Detective Cases, Toronto: Norman Book.

Goldman, Michael, 'Dating Services Match Men with Women Behind Bars', Columbia News Service, 17 March 2000.

Goldner, Virginia *et al*, 'Love and Violence: Gender Paradoxes in Volatile Attachments' (1990) 29 Family Process 343.

Goodrich, Peter, 'Epistolary Justice: The Love Letter as Law' (1997) 9 Yale JL & Humanities 245.

Goodrich, Peter, 'Law in the Courts of Love: Andreas Capellanus and the Judgments of Love' (1996a) 48 Stan LR 633.

Goodrich, Peter, *Law in the Courts of Love*, 1996b, London: Routledge.

Goodrich, Peter, *Reading the Law: A Critical Introduction to Legal Methods and Techniques*, 1986, Oxford: Blackwell.

Goodrich, Peter and Hachamovitch, Yifat, 'Time out of Mind: An Introduction to the Semiotics of the Common Law', in Fitzpatrick, Peter (ed), *Dangerous Supplements: Resistance and Renewal in Jurisprudence*, 1991, Durham: Duke UP, pp 159–81.

Gordon, Avery F, 'Globalism and the Prison Industrial Complex: An Interview with Angela Davis' (1998–99) 40 Race & Class 145.

Gordon, Avery, *Ghostly Matters: Haunting and the Sociological Imagination*, 1997, Minneapolis: U Minnesota Press.

Gornstein, Leslie, 'Jail Babes Use Net to Seek Love', Lexington Herald-Leader, 30 August 1998 www.kentucky.com/mld/kentucky, accessed 6 July 2002.

Goshorn, A Keith, 'Jean Baudrillard's Radical Enigma: "The Object's Fulfillment Without Regard for the Subject"', in Stearns, William and Chaloupka, William (eds), *Jean Baudrillard: The Disappearance of Art and Politics*, 1992, London: Macmillan, pp 209–29.

Grattan, Scott, and McNamara, Luke, 'The Common Law Construct of Native Title: A Re"feudalisation" of Australian Land Law' (1999) 8 Griffith Law Rev 50.

Gray, Kevin and Gray, Susan F, 'The Idea of Property in Law', in Bright, Susan and Dewar, John (eds), *Land Law: Theme and Perspectives*, 1998, Oxford: OUP, pp 15–51.

Graycar, Regina, 'The Gender of Judgments: An Introduction', in Thornton, Margaret (ed), *Public and Private: Feminist Legal Debates*, 1995, Melbourne: OUP.

Graycar, Regina and Morgan, Jenny, *The Hidden Gender of Law*, 1990, Sydney: Federation Press.

Grbich, Judith, 'The Scent of Colonialism: Mabo, Eucalyptus and Excursions within Legal Racism' (2001) 15 Aust Fem LJ 121.

Grbich, Judith, 'Reading the Phantom: Taxation Law, Psychoanalysis and Apparitions' (1997) 8 Aust Fem LJ 81.

Grbich, Judith, 'Writing Histories of Revenue Law: The New Productivity Research' (1993) 11 Law in Context 57.

Grimwade, Cherry, 'Diminishing Opportunities: Researching Women's Imprisonment', in Cook, Sandy and Davies, Susanne (eds), *Harsh Punishment: International Experiences of Women's Imprisonment*, 1999, Boston: Northeastern UP, 291–313.

Grosz, Elizabeth, *Space, Time and Perversion: The Politics of Bodies*, 1995, Sydney: Allen & Unwin.

Gwenllian-Jones, Sara, 'Starring Lucy Lawless?' (2000) 14 Continuum 9.

Habermas, Jürgen, *The Structural Transformation of the Public Sphere: An Inquiry into a Category of Bourgeois Society*, 1989, Cambridge: Polity.

Haddon, Leslie, 'Explaining ICT Consumption: The Case of the Home Computer', in Silverstone, Roger and Hirsch, Eric (eds), *Consuming Technologies*, 1992, London: Routledge, pp 82–96.

Hall, Stuart, 'Encoding, Decoding', in During, Simon (ed), *The Cultural Studies Reader*, 1999, London and New York: Routledge, pp 507–17.

Hall, Stuart, 'Cultural Studies and its Theoretical Legacies', in Morley, David and Chen, Kuan Hsing (eds), *Critical Dialogues in Cultural Studies*, 1996, London and New York: Routledge, pp 262–75.

Halttunen, Karen, *Murder Most Foul: The Killer and the American Gothic Imagination*, 1998, Cambridge, Mass: Harvard UP.

Hanigsberg, Julia E, 'Glamour Law: Feminism through the Looking Glass of Popular Women's Magazines', in Fineman, Martha A and McCluskey, Martha T (eds), *Feminism, Media and the Law*, 1997, New York and Oxford: OUP, pp 72–83.

Haraway, Donna, *Modest-Witness, Second-Millennium: Femaleman Meets Oncomouse: Feminism and Technoscience*, 1997, New York: Routledge.

Hart, HLA, *The Concept of Law*, 1961, Oxford: Clarendon.

Hartley, John, *Popular Reality: Journalism, Modernity, Popular Culture*, 1996, New York: St Martin's.

Hartley, John, *The Politics of Pictures: The Creation of the Public in the Age of Popular Media*, 1992, London and New York: Routledge.

Haste, Steve, *Criminal Sentences: True Crime in Fiction and Drama*, 1997, London: Signus Arts.

Haycraft, Howard (ed), *The Art of the Mystery Story*, 1947, New York: Grosset and Dunlap.

Hays, Michael and Nikolopoulou, Anastasia (eds), *Melodrama: The Emergence of a Genre*, 1996, New York: St Martin's.

Heilbrun, Carolyn and Resnik, Judith, 'Convergences: Law, Literature, and Feminism' (1990) 99 Yale LJ 1913.

Heitman, Kimberley, 'Vapours and Mirrors' (2000) 23 UNSWLJ 246.

Herman, Judith Lewis, *Trauma and Recovery*, 1992, London: Pandora.

Heydon, John D (ed), *Cross on Evidence*, 5th Aust edn, 1996, Sydney: Butterworths.

Hindle, John and Hepworth, John, *Boozing Out in Melbourne Pubs*, 1980, Sydney: Angus & Robertson.

Hocking, Jenny, *Lionel Murphy: A Political Biography*, 2000, Cambridge: Cambridge UP.

Hoff, Lee Ann, *Battered Women As Survivors*, 1990, London: Routledge.

Honigmann, EAJ (ed), *Othello*, 1997, Surrey: Thomas Nelson.

Howe, Adrian (ed), *Sexed Crime in the News*, 1998, Sydney: Federation.

Howe, Adrian, *Punish and Critique: Towards a Feminist Analysis of Penality*, 1994, London: Routledge.

Hughes, Donna, 'Men Create the Demand, Women are the Supply' (2001) 4 Feminista www.feminista.com/v4n3/hughes.html, last accessed 6 July 2002.

HREOC, *Bringing Them Home: Report of the National Inquiry into the Separation of Aboriginal and Torres Strait Islander Children and their Families*, 1997, Sydney: HREOC.

Hunt, Alan, *Governance of the Consuming Passions: A History of Sumptuary Regulation*, 1996, London: Macmillan.

Hunt, Alan, 'The Role of Law in the Civilizing Process and the Reform of Popular Culture' (1995) 10 Can JLS/RCDS 5.

Hutchings, Peter, *The Criminal Spectre in Law, Literature and Aesthetics*, 2001, London: Routledge.

Hutchinson, Don (ed), *Scarlet Riders: Pulp Fiction Tales of the Mounties*, 1998, Oakville, Ont: Mosaic Press.

Huyssens, Andreas, 'Mass Culture as Woman: Modernism's Other', in Modleski, Tania (ed), *Studies in Entertainment: Critical Approaches to Mass Culture*, 1986, Bloomington, Indiana: Indiana UP.

'Imprison and Detain: Racialised Punishment in Australia Today', 2001 www.transforming.cultures.uts.edu.au/imprisonforum.

Inayatullah, Sohail and Milojevic, Ivana, 'Exclusion and Communication in the Information Era', in Harcourt, Wendy (ed), *Women @internet: Creating New Cultures in Cyberspace*, 1999, London: Zed Books, pp 76–88.

Ingebretsen, Edward J, 'The Monster in the Home: True Crime and the Traffic in Body Parts' (1998) 21 J American Culture 27.

Jail Babes, Lary Flynt Productions, June, July, October 1999, www.jailbabes.com.

Jamal, Mumia Abú, *Live from Death Row*, 1996, New York: Avon.

Jenkins, Henry, *Textual Poachers: Television Fans and Participatory Culture*, 1992, New York and London: Routledge.

Jesse, F Tennyson (ed), *Trial of Madeleine Smith*, 1927, Notable British Trials, Edinburgh: William Hodge.

Jones, Melinda, 'Free Speech and the Village Idiot' (2000) 23 UNSWLJ 274.

Justinian, *Institutes*, 1913, Book II, trans Moyle, JB, Oxford: Clarendon.

Kahn, Paul W, *Law and Love: The Trials of King Lear*, 2000, New Haven and London: Yale UP.

Kahn, Paul W, *The Cultural Study of Law: Reconstructing Legal Scholarship*, 1999, Chicago and London: U Chicago Press.

Kalman, Laura, *The Strange Career of Liberal Legalism*, 1996, New Haven: Yale UP.

Kalman, Laura, *Legal Realism at Yale 1927–1960*, 1986, Chapel Hill: U North Carolina Press.

Kant, Immanuel (trans Meredith, James Creed), *The Critique of Judgement*, 1952, Oxford: Clarendon.

Kappeler, Susanne, *The Pornography of Representation*, 1986, Cambridge: Polity.

Karpin, Isabel, 'Pop Justice: TV, Motherhood, and the Law', in Fineman, Martha A and McCluskey, Martha T (eds), *Feminism, Media and the Law*, 1997, NY & Oxford: OUP, pp 12–35.

Kendall, Christopher, 'Australia's New Internet Censorship Regime: Is This Progress?' (1999) 1 Digital Technology LJ wwwlaw.murdoch.edu.au/dtlj/1999/vol1_3/kendall.htm, last accessed 6 July 2002.

Kennedy, Flo, 'Women and the Media' (1975), in Department of Prime Minister and Cabinet Women and Politics Conference 1975, Vol 2, 1977, Canberra: AGPS, pp 228–35.

Kermode, Frank, *The Sense of an Ending: Studies in the Theory of Fiction*, 1970, London: OUP.

Kerruish, Valerie, 'Barefoot in the Kitchen: A Response to Jack Goldring' (1989) 18 UWA L Rev 167.

Kibby, Marj, 'Babes on the Web: Sex, Identity and the Home Page' (1997) 84 Media International Australia 39.

Kipnis, Laura, '(Male) Desire and (Female) Disgust: Reading *Hustler*', in Grossberg, Lawrence, Nelson, Carly and Treichler, Paula A (eds), *Cultural Studies*, 1992, New York: Routledge, pp 373–91.

Kirby, Michael, 'Privacy in Cyberspace' (1998) 21 UNSWLJ 323.

Kirby, Vicki, *Telling Flesh: The Substance of the Corporeal*, 1997, New York and London: Routledge.

Kirkby, Diane, *Barmaids: A History of Women's Work in Pubs*, 1997, Cambridge: Cambridge UP.

Kirkby, Diane, 'The Politics of Paradox', in Campbell, Marion, Fincher, Ruth and Grimshaw, Patricia (eds), *Studies in Gender*, 1992, Melbourne: Melbourne U Committee for Gender Studies, pp 235–45.

Kleiner, Kurt, 'Free Speech, Liberty, Pornography' (2001) 169 New Scientist 32.

Knox, Sara L, *Murder: A Tale of Modern American Life*, 1998, Durham NC: Duke UP.

Koh, Adele, 'The Press and the Supergirl' (1975), in Department of Prime Minister and Cabinet Women and Politics Conference 1975 Vol 2, 1977, Canberra: AGPS, pp 220–24.

Kroker, Arthur and Weinstein, Michael A, *Data Trash: The Theory of the Virtual Class*, 1994, New York: St Martin's.

Lahey, Kathleen, 'Until Women Themselves Have Told All That They Have to Tell ...' (1985) 23 Osgoode Hall LJ 519.

Lake, Marilyn, *Getting Equal: The History of Australian Feminism*, 1999, Sydney: Allen & Unwin.

Lapsley, Robert and Westlake, Michael, 'From *Casablanca* to *Pretty Woman*: The Politics of Romance' (1992) 33 Screen 27.

Larkins, John and Howard, Bruce, *Australian Pubs*, 1973, Adelaide: Rigby.

Larson, Jane, 'Women Understand So Little, They Call My Good Nature "Deceit": A Feminist Rethinking of the Seduction' (1993) 93 Col LR 374.

Laster, Kathy, *Law as Culture*, 2nd edn, 2001, Sydney: Federation.

Le Bon, Gustave, *The Crowd: A Study of the Popular Mind*, 1986, London: E Benn.

Leavis, QD, *Fiction and the Reading Public*, 1932, London: Chatto & Windus.

Lebihan, Rachel, 'Kids Selling Porn in Playground' (2000) ZD Net Australia, 13 November
www.zdnet.com.au/newstech/news/story/0,2000025345,20107304-1,00.htm.

Lenoir, Remi, 'A Living Reproach', in Bourdieu, Pierre, *et al*, *The Weight of the World: Social Suffering in Contemporary Society*, 1999, Cambridge: Polity, pp 239–54.

Leslie, John, *A Defence of the Honour of the Right Highe, Mightye and Noble Princesses Marie Queene of Scotlande and Dowager of France, Lond Eusebius Dicaeohile*, 1569, Liege: Walter Morbers.

Lesser, Robert, *Pulp Art: Original Cover Paintings for the Great American Pulp Magazines*, 1997, New York: Grammercy Books.

Levi-Strauss, Claude, *The Elementary Structures of Kinship*, 1969 [1949], trans Bell, JH, von Sturmer, JR and Needham, R, London: Eyre & Spottiswoode.

Lombroso, Cesare and Ferrero, William, *The Female Offender*, 1898, New York: Appleton.

Lowe, L, 'Work, Immigration, Gender: New Subjects of Cultural Politics', in Lowe, L and Lloyd, D (ed), *The Politics of Culture in the Shadow of Capital*, 1997, Durham: Duke UP, pp 354–74.

Lucia, Cynthia, 'Women on Trial: The Female Lawyer in the Hollywood Courtroom', in Fineman, Martha A and McCluskey, Martha T (eds), *Feminism, Media and the Law*, 1997, New York and Oxford: OUP, pp 146–67.

Lumby, Catharine, *Bad Girls: The Media, Sex and Feminism in the 90s*, 1997, Sydney: Allen & Unwin.

Lynch, Lesley, 'Women and Law Conference' (1979) Refractory Girl, March, 35.

Macaulay, Stewart, 'Popular Legal Culture: An Introduction' (1989) 98 Yale LJ 1545.

MacKinnon, Catharine, 'Vindication and Resistance: A Response to the Carnegie Mellon Study of Pornography in Cyberspace' (1995) 83 Georgetown LJ 1959.

MacKinnon, Catharine, *Feminism Unmodified: Discourses on Life and Law*, 1987, Cambridge MA: Harvard UP.

MacKinnon, Catharine, *Toward a Feminist Theory of the State*, 1989, Cambridge, Mass: Harvard UP.

MacKinnon, Catharine, *Only Words*, 1993, Cambridge: Harvard UP.

MacKinnon, Catharine, 'Not a Moral Issue' (1984) 2 Yale Law & Policy Rev 321.

Mahoney, Martha 'Legal Images of Battered Women: Redefining the Issue of Separation' (1991) 90 Mich LR 1.

Mahoney, Martha, 'Exit: Power and the Idea of Leaving in Love, Work and the Confirmation Hearings' (1992) 65 Southern Calif LR 1283.

Maine, Sir Henry, *Ancient Law*, 10th edn, 1909, London: John Murray.

Malisow, Ben, 'Jailbabes, Anyone?' Las Vegas Weekly, 14 July 1999 www.lasvegasweekly.com, accessed 6 July 2002.

Mandel, Ernest, *Delightful Murder: A Social History of the Crime Story*, 1984, London: Pluto.

Marr, David, *Barwick: The Classic Biography of a Man of Power*, 2nd edn, 1992, Sydney: Allen & Unwin.

Mayhew, Clare and Quinlan, Michael, 'Occupational Violence: An Epidemic in the Hospitality Industry?' (1996) 67 Australian Safety News 30.

McAulliffe, Megan, 'South Australian Government Censors Net' (2000) ZNet Australia, 9 November www.zdnet.com.au/newstech/news/story/0,2000025345,20106865,00.htm, last accessed 6 July 2002.

McGill, Angus, *Pub: A Celebration*, 1969, London: Longmans.

McLuhan, Marshall and Fiore, Quentin, *The Medium is the Massage: An Inventory of Effects*, 1967, Harmondsworth: Penguin.

McLuhan, Marshall, *Understanding Media: The Extensions of Man*, 1967, London: Sphere.

McRobbie, Angela, *In the Culture Society: Art, Fashion and Popular Music*, 1999, London and New York: Routledge.

Mead, Jenna, 'Introduction: Tell It Like It Is', in Mead, Jenna (ed), *Bodyjamming: Sexual Harassment, Feminism and Public Life*, 1997, Sydney: Vintage, pp 1–41.

Media Women's Action Group, 'Guidelines for the Media – For the Avoidance of Sex Bias', unpublished report, 1975, First Ten Years Collection, Sydney.

Media Women's Action Group, 'Media Women's Action Group Bulletin', unpublished newsletter, 1972, First Ten Years Collection, Sydney.

Media Women's Action Group, 'Sexism and the Media: What Can an Angry Woman Do About It?', unpublished leaflet, 1979, First Ten Years Collection, Sydney.

Menkel-Meadow, Carrie, 'The Sense and Sensibilities of Lawyers: Lawyering in Literature, Narratives, Film and Television, and Ethical Choices Regarding Career and Craft' (1999) 31 McGeorge Law Rev 1
www.lexis.com.

Mercer, Colin, 'Regular Imaginings: The Newspaper and the Nation', in Bennett, Tony, Buckridge, Pat, Carter, David and Mercer, Colin (eds), *Celebrating the Nation: A Critical Study of Australia's Bicentenary*, 1992, Sydney: Allen & Unwin.

Mercer, Jan, 'The Women's Electoral Lobby and the Women's Liberation Movement: The History of WEL', in Mercer, Jan (ed), *The Other Half: Women in Australian Society*, 1975, Melbourne: Penguin, pp 395–404.

Miller, DA, *The Novel and the Police*, 1988, Berkeley, U California Press.

Miller, David, Kitzinger, Jenny, Williams, Kevin and Beharrell, Peter, *The Circuit of Mass Communication: Media Strategies, Representation and Audience Reception in the Aids Crisis*, 1998, London: Sage.

Minow, Martha, 'Stories in Law', in Brooks, Peter and Gewirtz, Paul (eds), *Law's Stories: Narrative and Rhetoric in the Law*, 1996, New Haven and London: Yale UP, pp 2–13.

Minow, Martha, *Making All the Difference: Inclusion, Exclusion, and American Law*, 1990, Ithaca, NY: Cornell UP.

Mitchell, WJT, *Picture Theory: Essays on Visual and Verbal Representation*, 1994, Chicago: U Chicago Press.

Mohanty, Chandra, 'Cartographies of Struggle: Third World Women and the Politics of Feminism', in Mohanty, Chandra, Russo, Ann and Torres, Lourdes (eds), *Third World Women and the Politics of Feminism*, 1991, Bloomington: Indiana UP, pp 1–47.

Moore, Thomas, *The Soul of Sex*, 1998, New York: HarperCollins.

Morahan-Martin, Janet, 'The Gap in Internet Use: Why Men use the Internet more than Women – A Literature Review' (1998b) 1 CyberPsychology & Behaviour 3.

Morahan-Martin, Janet, 'Women and Girls Last: Females and the Internet', 1998a, paper presented at IRISS Conference, March 1998
www.sosig.ac.uk/iriss/papers/paper55.htm, last accessed 6 July 2002.

Morgan, Jenny (1997) 'Sexual Harassment: Where Did It Go in 1995?', in Mead, Jenna (ed), *Bodyjamming: Sexual Harassment, Feminism and Public Life*, 1997, Sydney: Vintage, pp 101–15.

Morgan, Sally, *My Place*, 1987, Fremantle: Fremantle Arts Centre Press.

Morley, David, 'Changing Paradigms in Audience Studies', in Seiter, Ellen, Borchers, Hans, Kreutzner, Gabriele and Warth, Eva-Maria (eds), *Remote Control: Television, Audiences and Cultural Power*, 1991, London and New York: Routledge, pp 16–43.

Morris, Allison, *Women's Safety Survey 1996*, 1996, Wellington: Victimisation Survey Committee.

Morrissey, Philip, 'Writing from Behind Bars' ABR, February/March 2000, p 20.

Motluk, Alison, 'Sexism takes its Toll' (1999) 163 New Scientist 6.

Muller, Eddie, *Dark City: The Lost World of Film Noir*, 1998, New York: St Martin's.

Munt, Sally, *Murder by the Book*, 1994, London: Routledge.

Naffine, Ngaire 'Possession: Erotic Love in the Law of Rape' (1994) 57 MLR 10.

Naffine, Ngaire, *Feminism and Criminology*, 1997, Philadelphia, Temple UP.

Nagel, Chris, 'Pornographic Experience' (2002) J Mundane Behaviour
mundanebehavior.org/issues/v3n1/nagel3-1.htm, last accessed 6 July 2002.

National Archives of Canada, 1936, RG 13, Vol 1601 (O'Donnell).

National Collective of Independent Women's Refuges (NCIWR), *Fresh Start: A Self Help Book for New Zealand Women in Abusive Relationships*, 1993, Wellington: NCIWR.

National Library of Canada, 'Pulp Art and Fiction Collection'.

Newman, Graeme, 'Popular Culture and Criminal Justice: A Preliminary Inquiry' (1990) 18 Criminal Justice 261.

Nicolson, Marjorie, 'The Professor and the Detective', in Haycraft, Howard (ed), *The Art of the Mystery Story*, 1947, New York: Grosset & Dunlap, pp 110–27.

Nietzsche, Friedrich, *On the Genealogy of Morals*, 1969, trans Kaufmann, Walter and Hollingdale, RJ, NY: Vintage Books.

Nightingale, Virginia, Dickenson, Diane and Griff, Catherine, *Children's Views About Media Harm*, 2000, Sydney, ABA, Monograph 10.

Norris, Rebecca, 'Children's Death Most Tragic in Violent Year', 7 January 1995, The Dominion, Wellington.

NSWLRC, *Report on De Facto Relationships* (LRC 36), 1983, Sydney: NSWLRC.

NSW Parliamentary Debates, 1897, Series 1, Vol 89.

Obituaries, 'Sudden Death of Mrs Murphy. A Victim to Influenza', *Alexandra and Yea Standard*, 3 November 1899.

O'Connor, Deirdre, 'Should the Women's Movement Rely on Law Reform as a Major Weapon In Their Struggle?', unpublished paper, 1975, First Ten Years Collection, Sydney.

Olsen, Frances, 'Feminism and Critical Legal Theory: An American Perspective' (1990) 18 Internat J Sociology Law 199.

Olsen, Frances, 'The Myth of State Intervention in the Family' (1986) 18 U Mich J L Reform 835.

Omeo Telegraph, 31 March 1893; 13 February 1894.

Ong, Aihwa, *Flexible Citizenship: The Cultural Logics of Transnationality*, 1999, Durham and London: Duke UP.

Padgham, Hugh and The Police (Producers), 'Every Breath You Take', 1983, A & M Records.

Paglia, Camille, *Sexual Personae: Art and Decadence from Nefertiti to Emily Dickinson*, 1990, New Haven: Yale UP.

Panjabi, Kavita, 'Probing "Morality" and State Violence: Feminist Values and Communicative Interaction in Prison Testimonios in India and Argentina', in Alexander, Jacqui and Mohanty, Chandra (eds), *Feminist Genealogies, Colonial Legacies, Democratic Futures*, 1997, New York: Routledge, pp 151–69.

Pateman, Carole, *The Sexual Contract*, 1988, Cambridge: Polity.

Pearce, Dennis, Campbell, Enid and Harding, Don, *Australian Law Schools: A Discipline Assessment for the Commonwealth Tertiary Education Commission*, 1987, Canberra: AGPS.

Pearce, Sharon, *Shameless Scribblers: Australian Women's Journalism 1880–1995*, 1998, Rockhampton: U Central Queensland Press.

Pence, Ellen and Paymar, Michael, *Power and Control: Tactics of Men Who Batter*, 1986, Duluth: Duluth Abuse Intervention Pilot Project.

Penfold, Carolyn, 'Nazis, Porn and Politics: Asserting Control over Internet Content' (2001) J Information, Law and Technology elj.warwick.ac.uk/jilt/01-2/penfold.html, last accessed 6 July 2002.

Perera, Suvendrini, 'What is a Camp?' Borderlands, 2002 (forthcoming).

Perera, Suvendrini, 'Racialised Punishment and Mandatory Sentencing in Australia' (2000) 42 Race & Class 73.

Perera, Suvendrini, '"You were Born to tell these Stories": The Edu-ma-cations of Doctor Ruby' (1998) 17 Meridian 15.

Perry, Gail S and Melton, Gary B, 'Precedential Value of Judicial Notice of Social Facts: Parham as an Example' (1983–84) 22 J Family Law 633.

Pether, Penny and Threadgold, Terry, 'Feminist Methodologies in Discourse Analysis: Sex, Property, Equity', in Lee, Alison and Poynton, Cate (eds), *Culture and Text: Discourse and Methodology in Social Research and Cultural Studies*, 2000, Sydney: Allen & Unwin, pp 132–51.

Phillips, Kyra, 'Jailbabes.com', A CBS 2 News Special Assignment, 14 May 1999.

Plato, *The Republic*, 1955, trans HDP Lee, Harmondsworth, UK: Penguin.

Pollack, Otto, *The Criminality of Women*, 1950, Philadelphia: U Pennsylvania Press.

Pollock, Frederick and Maitland, Frederic W, *History of English Law before the Time of Edward I*, 1968, Cambridge: Cambridge UP.

Pollock, Frederick, 'Note C – Villenage, Villein Tenure and Copyholds', in Pollock, Frederick, *The Land Laws*, 1887, London: Macmillan, pp 202–14.

Pollock, Frederick, 'Notes on Early English Land Law', extracted in Maine, Henry S, *Dissertations on Early Law and Custom*, 1901, London: John Murray.

Posner, Richard A, *Law and Literature*, revised edn, 1998, Cambridge, Mass and London: Harvard UP.

Post, Dianne, 'Why Marriage Should be Abolished' (1997) 18 Women's Rights L Reporter 283.

'President Plans Anti-Violence Meeting' (1999) *New York Times*, 30 April.

Propp, Vladimir, *Morphology of the Folktale*, 2nd edn, 1968, trans Scott, Laurence, Austin: U Texas Press.

Propp, Vladimir, *Theory and History of Folklore*, 1984, trans Martin, Ariadna Y and Martin, Richard P, Manchester: Manchester UP.

Radford, Gail, 'Reform and Revolution' (1975), in Department of Prime Minister and Cabinet Women and Politics Conference 1975, Vol 2, 1977, Canberra: AGPS, pp 158–61.

Radway, Janice A, *Reading the Romance: Women, Patriarchy and Popular Literature*, 1984, Chapel Hill NC: U North Carolina P.

Rafter, Nicole Hahn, *Partial Justice: Women in State Prisons, 1800–1935*, 1985, Boston: Northeastern UP.

Ramsay, Iain, *Advertising Culture and the Law: Beyond Lies, Ignorance and Manipulation*, 1996, London: Sweet & Maxwell.

Rapoport, Nancy B, 'Dressed for Excess: How Hollywood affects the Professional Behavior of Lawyers' (2000) 14 Notre Dame J Law Ethics & Public Policy 49 www.lexis.com.

Rehnquist, William, 'Chief Justice's 1991 Year-End Report on the Federal Judiciary' (Jan 1992) The Third Branch: Newsletter of the Federal Court 1.

Rhode, Deborah L, 'Media Images/Feminist Issues', in Fineman, Martha A and McCluskey, Martha T (eds), *Feminism, Media and the Law*, 1997, New York and Oxford: OUP, pp 8–21.

Richter, Juliet, 'Reflections on WEL's Third National Conference: Women in Politics' (Winter 1975) Refractory Girl 39.

Ricker, Di Mari, 'Son of Ol' Blue Eyes Sings a "Son of Sam" Tune', The Recorder/Cal Law, 17 May 1999.

Ricketson, Matthew, 'Helen Garner's *The First Stone*: Hitchhiking on the Credibility of Other Writers', in Mead, Jenna (ed), *Bodyjamming: Sexual Harassment, Feminism and Public Life*, 1997, Sydney: Vintage, pp 79–100.

Riggs, Robert, '*Jail Babes* on the Web: Part One', Dallas/Fort Worth Channel.

Riggs, Robert, '*Jail Babes* on the Web: Part Two', Dallas/Fort Worth Channel.

Riggs, Robert, '*Jail Babes* on the Web: Part Three, Dallas/Fort Worth Channel.

Rimm, Marty, 'Marketing Pornography on the Information Superhighway: A Survey of 917,410 Images, Descriptions, Short Stories, and Animations downloaded 8.5 million times by Consumers in over 2,000 Cities in Forty Countries, Provinces and Territories' (1995) 83 Georgetown LJ 1849.

Robbins, Bruce, 'Disjoining the Left: Cultural Contradictions of Anti-Capitalism' (1999) 26 Boundary 2: International J Literature and Culture 29.

Rodgerson, Gillian and Wilson, Elizabeth (eds), *Pornography and Feminism: The Case against Censorship*, 1991, London: Lawrence & Wishart.

Rosenberg, Charles B, 'An LA Lawyer Replies' (1989) 98 Yale LJ 1625.

Rosenberg, Gerald N and Williams, John M, 'Do not go Gently into that Good Right: The First Amendment in the High Court of Australia' (1997) 11 Supreme Court Rev 439.

Ross, Kim, 'FLAG' (1979) 4 Legal Services Bulletin 36.

Rozanski, Stella, 'Obscenity: Common law and the Abuse of Women' (1991) 13 Adelaide Law Rev 163.

Rubin, Gretchen Craft and Heller, Jamie, 'Restatement of Love: Tentative Draft' (1994) 104 Yale LJ 707.

Rush, Peter, 'An Altered Jurisdiction: Corporeal Traces of Law' (1997) 6 Griffith Law Rev 144.

Russell, Margaret M, 'Rewriting History with Lightning: Race, Myth, and Hollywood in the Legal Pantheon', in Denver, John (ed), *Legal Reelism: Movies as Legal Texts*, 1996, Urbana and Chicago: U Illinois Press, pp 172–98.

Sachs, Albie and Wilson, Joan, *Sexism and the Law: A Study of Male Beliefs and Legal Bias in Britain and the United States*, 1978, Oxford: M Robertson.

Sanger, Carol, 'Less than Pornography: The Power of Popular Fiction', in Heizelman, Susan Sage and Wiseman, Zipporah Batshaw (eds), *Representing Women: Law, Literature, and Feminism*, 1994, Durham and London: Duke UP, pp 75–100.

Sarat, Austin D, 'Redirecting Legal Scholarship in Law Schools' (2000) 12 Yale JL & Humanities 129.

Sawer, Marian, 'Reclaiming Social Liberalism: the Women's Movement and the State', in Howe, Renate (ed), *Women and the State: Australian Perspectives*, Special Edn J Australian Studies, 1993, Bundoora Victoria: La Trobe UP, in Association with the Centre for Australian Studies Deakin University, and the Ideas for Australia Program, pp 1–21.

Sawer, Marian and Groves, Abigail, *Working From Inside: Twenty Years of the Office of the Status of Women*, 1994, Canberra: AGPS.

Sawyer, Philippa, 'Fictions of White Australia Identity: Land and Community in Contemporary Australian Women's Life Narratives', 1996, unpublished MA thesis, Melbourne: La Trobe University.

Sayers, Dorothy, 'The Omnibus of Crime', in Haycraft, Howard (ed), *The Art of the Mystery Story*, 1947, New York: Grosset & Dunlap, pp 71–109.

Schneider, Elizabeth, 'Particularity and Generality: Challenges of Feminist Theory and Practice in Work on Woman-Abuse' (1992) 67 NYULR 520.

Schroeder, Jeanne L, *The Vestal and the Fasces: Hegal, Lacan, Property and the Feminine*, 1998, Berkeley: U California Press.

Scott, Brendan, 'Silver Bullets and Golden-egged Geese: A Cold Look at Internet Censorship' (2000) 23 UNSWLJ 215.

Scott, Joan W, 'Comment on Hawkesworth's "Confounding Gender"' (1997) 22 Signs 697.

Scottoline, Lisa, 'Guilty as Charged' (2001) 22 Stiletto: Sisters in Crime Newsletter 28.

Seelye, Katherine, 'A Clinton Conference on Youth Violence' (1999) *New York Times*, 11 May.

Segal, Lynne and McIntosh, Mary (eds), *Sex Exposed: Sexuality and the Pornography Debate*, 1992, London: Virago.

Server, Lee, *Danger is my Business: An Illustrated History of the Fabulous Pulp Magazines, 1896–1953*, 1993, San Francisco: Chronicle Books.

Seuffert, Nan, 'Locating Lawyering: Power, Dialogue and Narrative' (1996a) 18 Syd LR 523.

Seuffert, Nan, 'Lawyering for Women Survivors of Domestic Violence' (1996b) 4 Waikato LR 1.

Shapiro, Barbara J, 'Beyond Reasonable Doubt' and 'Probable Cause', in *Historical Perspectives on the Anglo-American Law of Evidence*, 1991, Berkeley: U California Press.

Sherwin, Richard K, *When Law Goes Pop: The Vanishing Line Between Law and Popular Culture*, 2000, Chicago and London: U Chicago Press.

Shrum, Larry, 'Crime and Popular Culture: Effects of Television Portrayals of Crime and Violence on Viewers' Perceptions of Reality: A Psychological Process Perspective' (1998) 22 Legal Studies Forum 257.

Siegel, Reva, '"The Rule of Love": Wife Beating as Prerogative and Privacy' (1996) 105 Yale LJ 2117.

Silverstone, Roger and Hirsch, Eric, 'Introduction', in Silverstone, Roger and Hirsch, Eric (eds), *Consuming Technologies*, 1992, London: Routledge, pp 1–14.

Silverstone, Roger, Hirsch, Eric and Morley, David, 'Information and Communication Technologies and the Moral Economy of the Household', in Silverstone, Roger and Hirsch, Eric (eds), *Consuming Technologies*, 1992, London: Routledge, pp 15–31.

Silverstone, Roger, *Television and Everyday Life*, 1994, London and New York: Routledge.

Smith, Clarissa, '"They're Ordinary People, not Aliens from the Planet Sex!": The Mundane Excitements of Pornography for Women' (2002) J Mundane Behaviour http://mundanebehavior.org/issues/v3n1/csmith.htm, last accessed 6 July 2002.

Smith, Claude J, 'Bodies and Minds for Sale: Prostitution in *Pretty Woman* and *Indecent Proposal*' (1997) 19 Studies in Popular Culture 91.

Soothill, Keith and Walby, Sylvia, *Sex Crime in the News*, 1991, London: Routledge.

Special Issue on Legal Education (1988–89) 5 Aust JLS.

Spelman, Elizabeth V and Minow, Martha, 'Outlaw Women: *Thelma and Louise*', in Denver, John (ed), *Legal Reelism: Movies as Legal Texts*, 1996, Urbana and Chicago: U Illinois Press, pp 261–79.

Stacey, Jackie and Pearce, Lynne, 'The Heart of the Matter: Feminists Revisit Romance', in Pearce, Lynne and Stacey, Jackie (eds), *Romance Revisited*, 1995, London: Lawrence and Wishart, pp 11–48.

Stearn, Gerald Emanuel (ed), *McLuhan: Hot and Cool*, 1968, Penguin: Harmondsworth.

Stevens, Richard, 'Two Cheers for 1870: The American Law School', in Fleming, Donald and Bailyn, Bernard (eds), *Law in American History*, 1971, Boston: Little Brown.

Stewart, Susan, *On Longing*, 1993, Durham and London: Duke UP.

Strange, Carolyn, Interview with George Flie, August 2001, Toronto.

Strathern, Marilyn, 'Forward', in Silverstone, Roger and Hirsch, Eric (eds), *Consuming Technologies*, 1992, London: Routledge, pp viii–xiii.

Striker, Susan, *Queer Pulp: Perverted Passions from the Golden Age of the Paperback*, 2001, San Francisco: Chronicle Books.

Strossen, Nadine, 'A Feminist Critique of "the" Feminist Critique of Pornography' (1993b) 79 Virginia LR 1099.

Strossen, Nadine, 'Fighting Big Sister for Liberty and Equality' (1993a) NYLSLR 1.

Strossen, Nadine, *Defending Pornography: Free Speech, Sex and the Fight for Women's Rights*, 1995, New York: Scribner.

Sun Herald, 1 April 1995.

Surette, Ray, *Media, Crime and Criminal Justice: Images and Realities*, 1998, Belmont, Cal: Wadsworth.

Sydney Morning Herald, 21, 23 November 1908; 4 September 1980; 4 April, 13 May, 12 August 1995.

Tagliabue, John, 'Where Jeans are a Rape Defence' (1999) *New York Times*, 14 February, p 2.

Tasmanian Women's Liberation Group, 'Liberaction', unpublished newsletter, 1975, First Ten Years Collection, Sydney.

Telegraph (Brisbane) 30 January 1963; 1 February 1963; 20 May 1967.

Tench, CV, 'Torrid Love Drove him to Murder' (April 1949) 7 Scoop Detective: Toronto, Pastime Publications.

'The Old-Fashioned Barmaid?', What's Brewing? December 1951, pp 6–7.

Thomas, Michael, 'The Decline and Fall of Ocker Chic', *Australian Playboy*, April 1987, 50.

Thompson, EP, *Whigs and Hunters: The Origin of the Black Act*, 1975, London: Allen Lane.

Thornton, Margaret, 'Among the Ruins: Law in the Neo-Liberal Academy' (2001) 20 Windsor Yearbook of Access to Justice 3.

Thornton, Margaret 'Authority and Corporeality: The Conundrum for Women in Law' (1998a) 6 Feminist Legal Studies 147.

Thornton, Margaret, 'Review of Ian Callinan, *The Lawyer and the Libertine*' (1998b) 20 Syd LR 652.

Thornton, Margaret, 'Technocentrism in the Law School: Why the Gender and Colour of Law Remain the Same' (1998c) 36 Osgoode Hall LJ 369.

Thornton, Margaret, 'The Judicial Gendering of Citizenship: A Look at Property Interests During Marriage' (1997) 24 JLS 486.

Thornton, Margaret, *Dissonance and Distrust: Women in the Legal Profession*, 1996a, Melbourne: OUP.

Thornton, Margaret, '"Liberty, Equality And?": Endowing Fraternity with Voice' (1996b) 18 Sydney Law Review 553.

Thornton, Margaret (ed), *Public and Private: Feminist Legal Debates*, 1995, Melbourne: OUP.

Thornton, Margaret, 'The Cartography of Public and Private', in Thornton, Margaret (ed), *Public and Private: Feminist Legal Debates*, 1995, Melbourne: OUP, pp 2–16.

Thornton, Margaret, 'Feminism and the Contradictions of Law Reform' (1991) 19 International J Sociology of Law 453.

Threadgold, Terry, 'Law as/of Property, Judgment as Dissension: Feminist and Postcolonial Inverventions in the Networks' (1999a) 12 Internat J Semiotics of Law 369.

Threadgold, Terry, 'Review of Posner, Richard A, *Law and Literature*, Revised and Enlarged edition, 1998, Cambridge, Massachusetts and London: Harvard UP' (1999b) 23 MULR 3.

Threadgold, Terry, 'Performativity, Regulative Fictions, Huge Stabilities: Framing Battered Woman's Syndrome' (1997a) 3 LTC 210.

Threadgold, Terry, 'Narrative and Legal Texts: Telling Stories About Women Who Kill' (1997b) 3(1) UTS L Rev.

Threadgold, Terry, *Feminist Poetics: Poiesis, Performance, Histories*, 1997c, London: Routledge.

Trent, Judy Scales, 'Commonalities: On being Black and White, Different and the Same', in Heizelman, Susan Sage and Wiseman, Zipporah Batshaw (eds), *Representing Women: Law, Literature, and Feminism*, 1994, Durham and London: Duke UP, pp 57–74.

Turnbull, Sue, 'The Scene of Murder: Mapping the Moral Logic of Space in Crime Fiction' (1999) 2 Beyond the Divide 6.

Twining, William, *Rethinking Evidence: Exploratory Essays*, 1990, Oxford: Basil Blackwell.

Vance, Carole, 'The Pleasures of Looking: The Attorney General's Commission on Pornography versus Visual Images', in Squires, Carol (ed), *The Critical Image*, 1990, Seattle: Bay Press, pp 38–58.

Vance, Carol, 'Pleasure and Danger: Towards a Politics of Sexuality' in Vance, C (ed), *Pleasure and Danger*, 1984, Boston: Routledge & Kegan Paul, pp 1–27.

Vicarel, Jo Ann, *A Reader's Guide to the Police Procedural*, 1995, New York, GK Hall.

Victorian Royal Commission on Employees in Shops, Parliamentary Papers, Vol 2, 1884.

Vigilante, 30 October 1958; 4 February 1971.

Voon, Tania, 'Online Pornography in Australia: Lessons from the First Amendment' (2001) 24 UNSWLJ 142.

Walsh, PG (trans), *Andreas Capellanus on Love*, 1982, London: Duckworth.

Ward, Biff, 'The Politics of Feminism' (1975), in Department of Prime Minister and Cabinet Women and Politics Conference 1975, Vol 2, 1977, Canberra: AGPS, pp 149–58.

Ward Jouve, Nicole, *'The Streetcleaner': The Yorkshire Ripper Case on Trial*, 1986, New York, M Boyars.

Watson, Irene, 'Kaldowinyeri-Munaintya in the Beginning' (2000) 4 Flinders J Law Reform 3.

Watt, Ian, *The Rise of the Novel*, 1957, Berkeley: U California Press.

Weisberg, Richard H, *The Failure of the Word*, 1984, New Haven: Yale UP.

Weisberg, Richard, *Poethics and other Strategies of Law and Literature*, 1992, NY: Columbia UP.

Weisbrot, David, *Lawyers*, 1990, Melbourne: Longman Cheshire.

Welsh, Alexander, *Strong Representations: Narrative and Circumstantial Evidence in England*, 1992, Baltimore: Johns Hopkins UP.

White, Constance, 'Review/Fashion Visions Brazen and Conventional' (1999) *New York Times*, 18 February, Sec B, p 11, column 1.

White, Hayden, *The Content of the Form: Narrative Discourse and Historical Representation*, 1987, Baltimore: Johns Hopkins UP.

White, Hayden, *Tropics of Discourse: Essays in Cultural Criticism*, 1978, Baltimore: Johns Hopkins UP.

White, James Boyd, *Justice as Translation: An Essay in Cultural and Legal Criticism*, 1990, Chicago and London: U Chicago Press.

White, James Boyd, *The Legal Imagination: Studies in the Nature of Legal Thought and Expression*, 1973, Boston: Little, Brown.

Wideman, John Edgar, 'Introduction', in Jamal, Mumia Abú, *Live from Death Row*, 1996, New York: Avon.

Wigmore, John Henry, *A Treatise on the Anglo-American System of Evidence*, 1970, Boston: Little, Brown.

Wigmore, John Henry, *The Principles of Judicial Proof*, 1988, Littleton, Colorado: Fred B Rothman.

Williams, Evan (1975) 'Handling the Media', in Department of Prime Minister and Cabinet Women and Politics Conference 1975, Vol 2, 1977, Canberra: AGPS, pp 224–28.

Williams, Glanville, 'The Problem of Domestic Rape' (1991) 141 NLJ 205.

Williams, Glanville, *Textbook of Criminal Law*, 2nd edn, 1983, London: Stevens & Sons, Sweet & Maxwell.

Williams, Patricia J, 'Hate Radio: Why We Need to Tune in to Limbaugh and Stern', in Fineman, Martha A and McCluskey, Martha T (eds), *Feminism, Media and the Law*, 1997, New York and Oxford: OUP, pp 22–26.

Williams, Patricia J, *The Alchemy of Race and Rights*, 1993, London: Virago.

Wilson, Ashleigh, 'We don't need Porn Filters, say Young' (2000) *The Australian*, 5 December, p 3.

Witheford, Nick, 'Cycles and Circuits of Struggle in High-Technology Capitalism', in Davis, Jim, Hirschl, Thomas and Stack, Michael (eds), *Cutting Edge: Technology, Information, Capitalism and Social Revolution*, 1997, London: Verso, pp 195–242.

Woman's Day, September 1980.

'Women Behind Bars, Release Bruce and Violet Roberts Campaign', unpublished leaflet, First Ten Years Collection, Sydney.

Women Media Workers, 'New Journalist', unpublished newsletter, 1976, First Ten Years Collection, Sydney.

Women's Health and Resource Foundation Ltd, 'Submission to NSW Community Health Program: Application for Grant from Women's Health and Resources Foundation: Project Women's Legal Aid and Community Service', unpublished report, 1975, First Ten Years Collection, Sydney.

Wood, Thomas, *An Institute of the Laws of England*, 1720, London: R Sare.

Woolf, Virginia, *A Room of One's Own*, 1981 [1929] London: Penguin.

Wright, Clare, 'Of Public Houses and Private Lives: Female Hotelkeepers as Domestic Entrepreneurs' (2001) 32 Australian Historical Studies 57.

Wrong, EM, 'Crime and Detection', in Haycraft, Howard (ed), *The Art of the Mystery Story*, 1947, New York: Grosset & Dunlap, pp 18–32.

Young, Alison, 'The Wasteland of the Law, the Wordless Song of the Rape Victim' (1998) 22 MULR 442.

Young, Alison, 'In the Eyes of the Law: The Look of Violence' (1997) 8 Aust Fem LJ 9.

Young, Alison, *Imagining Crime: Textual Outlaws and Criminal Conversations*, 1996, London: Sage.

Zizek, Slavoj, *The Metastases of Enjoyment: Six Essays on Woman and Causality*, 1994, London, New York: Verso.

INDEX

Index